GW00480791

PEN(
MY LIFE

RABINDRANATH TAGORE was born in 1861. His family house at Jorasanko was a hive of cultural and intellectual activity and Tagore started writing at an early age. He was involved in the Swadeshi campaign against the British in the early 1900s. In 1913 he won the Nobel Prize for Literature. Tagore was knighted in 1915, an honour he repudiated in 1919 after the Jallianwala Bagh massacre. In the 1920s and 1930s he lectured extensively in America, Europe, the Far East and Middle East. Proceeds from these went to Visva-Bharati, his school and university at Santiniketan. A prolific writer, Tagore's works include poems, novels, plays, short stories, essays and songs. Late in his life he took up painting. He died in 1941.

UMA DAS GUPTA did her postdoctoral research on Rabindranath Tagore and the history of the institutions he founded at Santiniketan and Sriniketan, 1940–41. Das Gupta was head of the United States Educational Foundation in India for the Eastern Region. Her recent publications include *The Oxford India Tagore: Selected Writings on Education and Nationalism* and *Rabindranath Tagore: A Biography*. Her forthcoming publications include a collection of Tagore's writings on India's history and culture.

Praise for the Book

'It is a totally new idea to bring together Rabindranath's autobiographical writings in chronological order. I wondered whether it works, Tagore being so poetically inexact about his own life. Now I am convinced. It has been a huge task to bring the mass of letters, autobiographical essays and poems into a sensitive order. Indeed a work of love'—Martin Kämpchen

'Uma Das Gupta breaks new ground in Tagore studies'—*The Statesman*

'A seamless interweaving of reminiscence, memoirs, letters and public lectures . . . A reliable and honest guide to Rabindranath's life in his own words as could ever be attempted'—*The Hindu*

'Uma Das Gupta's intuitively selected and arranged collage from Tagore's English writings shapes an unforgettable portrait'—*Tehelka*

'What Uma Das Gupta does best is to show us a glimpse of the other Tagore—the family man, the husband and father, the visionary educationist who struggled to set up and then devoted a considerable part of his life to Shantiniketan, and the patriot who stood up to the British when honour demanded and who was not afraid to go against popular trends of his time, as was obvious in his displeasure over the Swadeshi agitators. She does a marvellous job bringing Tagore alive to those who know him only from his numerous creative works'—*Time Out*

RABINDRANATH TAGORE

my life
in my words

selected and edited
with an introduction by

Uma Das Gupta

PENGUIN BOOKS

PENGUIN BOOKS

Published by the Penguin Group

Penguin Books India Pvt. Ltd, 11 Community Centre, Panchsheel Park,
New Delhi 110 017, India

Penguin Group (USA) Inc., 375 Hudson Street, New York, New York 10014,
USA

Penguin Group (Canada), 90 Eglinton Avenue East, Suite 700, Toronto, Ontario,
M4P 2Y3, Canada (a division of Pearson Penguin Canada Inc.)

Penguin Books Ltd, 80 Strand, London WC2R 0RL, England

Penguin Ireland, 25 St Stephen's Green, Dublin 2, Ireland (a division of Penguin
Books Ltd)

Penguin Group (Australia), 707 Collins Street, Melbourne, Victoria 3008, Australia
(a division of Pearson Australia Group Pty Ltd)

Penguin Group (NZ), 67 Apollo Drive, Rosedale, Auckland 0632, New Zealand
(a division of Pearson New Zealand Ltd)

Penguin Group (South Africa) (Pty) Ltd, 24 Sturdee Avenue, Rosebank, Johannesburg
2196, South Africa

Penguin Books Ltd, Registered Offices: 80 Strand, London WC2R 0RL, England

First published in Viking by Penguin Books India 2006
Published in Penguin Books 2010

Copyright © Penguin Books India 2006

Photographs courtesy of Rabindra Bhavana, Visva-Bharati, Santiniketan

Rabindranath Tagore's paintings on pages 266 and 272 courtesy of Lalit Kala
Akademi

ISBN 9780143415350

Typeset in Minion by Eleven Arts, New Delhi
Printed at Yash Printographics, Noida

ALWAYS LEARNING   **PEARSON**

To Mil and Jenny
my young and kind family

CONTENTS

PART TWO: MY THOUGHTS

ACKNOWLEDGEMENTS

M y research for this work is based mainly on the material in the
Rabindra Bhavana Archives and its specialized library at
Santiniketan. At the archives I would like to thank Shri Dilip Kumar
Hazra, Shri Tushar Kumar Singha and Shri Utpal Mitra for all the help
they readily provided. I would also like to thank the Rabindra Bhavana's
librarians, its photo archives and its reprography section for their valuable
assistance. I have used other archival holdings of Rabindranath's letters
and papers in the course of my research over several years now, and would
like to express my gratitude especially to the Department of Western
Manuscripts of the Bodleian Library, University of Oxford, for their
holdings of the Edward Thompson Papers, the Robert Bridges Collection,
and the Gilbert Murray Papers. I am grateful also to the Senate House
Library of the University of London for the use of the Thomas Sturge
Moore Papers and their beautifully quiet reading room.

It is also my pleasure to thank Shri Subimal Lahiri and Shri Anath
Nath Das, both formerly of Visva-Bharati University, whose competence
as bibliographers of Tagore's life and work is widely acknowledged and
appreciated. I would like to record my appreciation to Rabindranath's
biographer Prasanta Kumar Paul for the benefit we derive from his
invaluable contribution to Tagore Studies. I would like to thank my young
friend Manisha Banerjee in Santiniketan who allowed me to store some
of the material for this volume in her computer when my laptop was giving
trouble. Professor Swapan Majumdar of Jadavpur University's Department
of Comparative Literature kindly gave me a reference to an important
biographical essay by Rabindranath. I thank Shri Saktidas Ray for his

generous help from the Ananda Bazar Patrika Library which is a fine
resource for published source material on Rabindranath. I am grateful to
my friend Peter Marshall, formerly Rhodes Professor of Imperial History
at the University of London, for his help in tracing the biographies of
some of the Englishmen Rabindranath mentioned in the letters he wrote
from his first visit to England in 1878-79. I thank William Radice for his
carefully considered suggestions. I am grateful to Professor Abhijit Ghosh
of Jadavpur University's Department of Sanskrit for transliterating and
translating the slokas given in Rabindranath's letters on pages 48 and
134 of this text. I thank Gopalkrishna Gandhi for identifying an
incomplete reference in one of Rabindranath's letters to the nationalist
leader R.P. Paranjpye.

In all my scholarly efforts, my deepest debt is to my husband Ashin
Das Gupta who showed the way by his love of historical research and his
honesty to it. I also feel greatly in debt to my parents Sudhindra Chandra
Ray and Sati Ray who valued education more than all material things.

July 2006   Uma Das Gupta
Santiniketan

INTRODUCTION

When Penguin Books invited me to do an 'autobiography' of Rabindranath Tagore—a Rabindranath in his own words—my editor's idea, as she put it, was for me to 'write' his autobiography as it were. I am very thankful for the idea as the reading for this work has been so enjoyable and inspiring. How wonderfully and untiringly Rabindranath Tagore wrote, with feeling and frankness, at times hard-hitting and repetitive but not without a sense of balance and tolerance. But even with this advantage, 'writing' another's autobiography was a daunting task, made even more difficult by the great author's indifference to dates. He admitted to it. He wrote, for example, to his youngest daughter:

> Like you, we too are having poetry sessions here. Teachers come after their afternoon meals to hear interpretations of my poetry and its associations with the story of my life. I see them earnestly taking notes. Ajit[1] is going to read something about my work on my birthday. He is driving me mad with questions about the dates and years of my poems—but I just can't remember dates. You know well how the dates on my letters are at variance with those in the almanac. I never won any accolades in my history class at school. I am afraid my biography will have to be published without taking the trouble to verify dates . . .[2]

[1] Ajit Kumar Chakravarty (1886–1918), early teacher at Santiniketan and author of two classics on Tagore, *Rabindranath* (1911) and *Kavyaparikrama* (1915).

[2] Rabindranath to Mira Devi, *Chaitra* 1317 (March 1910), *Chitthi Patra*, Volume IV, Calcutta: Visva-Bharati, 1943, pp. 19–21. Translated by UDG. (Hereafter, *Chitthi Patra* IV.)

Rabindranath believed that 'life history' was realistically only a collection of 'pictures' of 'life's memories' rather than a chronicle of dates and events. He was very conscious of the fleeting and fluid nature of what one can retain about what *actually* happened. In his view, the past was a matter of resurrection and the future a world full of mystery. He wrote explaining how those 'pictures' of 'life's memories' came to life when writing his autobiographies, and how he valued them for their literary worth more than anything else.

> Some years ago, when questioned about the events of my past life, I had occasion to pry into this picture-chamber. I expected to be content with selecting a few materials from my life's memories for my life's story, but discovered as I opened the door, that life's memories are not life's history. Memories are the original work of an unseen artist. The variegated colours are not reflections of outside lights, but belong to the painter himself, and come passion-tinged from his heart, thereby disqualifying the canvas as evidence in a court of law.

> But though the attempt to gather precise history from memory's storehouse may be fruitless, there is a fascination in looking over the pictures. This fascination cast its spell on me.

> The road and wayside shelter are not pictures while we travel; they are too necessary, too obvious. When, however, before turning into the evening rest house, we look back upon the cities, fields, rivers and hills where we have travelled in the morning of our life, they are pictures indeed. Thus, when my opportunity came, I looked back, and was engrossed.

> Was this interest only a natural affection for my own past? There must have been some personal feeling, of course, but the pictures also had an artistic value of their own. No event in my reminiscences is worthy of being preserved for all time, but the quality of the subject is not the only justification for a record. What one has truly felt if only it can be made sensible to others, is always of importance to one's fellowmen. If pictures which have taken shape in memory can be brought out in words, they are worth a place in literature.

> It is as literary material that I offer my memory pictures, to take
> them as autobiography would be a mistake. In such a view these
> reminiscences would appear useless as well as incomplete.[3]

The autobiographies Rabindranath wrote were *Jibansmriti*, published in
1912, when he was fifty years old, and *Chhelebela*, published in 1940, a
few months before his death. *Jibansmriti* and *Chhelebela* were translated
into English in his lifetime as *My Reminiscences* and *My Boyhood Days*,
respectively. Besides these, there is *Atmaparichay* (Knowing Oneself), a
collection of six of his inward-looking essays, published posthumously
in 1943. *Atmaparichay* has not been translated into English as a whole
book but some of the contents of those essays can be traced in his English
writings elsewhere. In the fourth essay of that collection, he writes about
how difficult it is to know oneself—his favourite autobiographical theme.

> It is not easy to know oneself. It is difficult to organize life's various
> experiences into a unified whole. Had God not given me long life,
> had He not permitted me to reach seventy years of age, I could hardly
> have got a clear picture of myself. I have tried to make sense of my
> life at different times through its various activities and experiences.
> The only thing I have been able to conclude about myself is that I
> am a poet, nothing else, no matter all the other things I may have
> done with my life.[4]

I find this verdict about himself worthy of consideration, particularly after
going over a large amount of material on his life, so much of which is
about his social activities and his serious involvements in that sphere. He
was the first ever to start work on rural and educational reform, and it
remained a lifelong commitment with him. He could never keep himself
from worrying over what was needed for his country. His prose reflects

---

[3]Rabindranath Tagore, *My Reminiscences*, London: Macmillan, 1933, pp. 2-3. (Hereafter, *Reminiscences*.)

[4]Rabindranath Tagore, *Atmaparichay*, Reprint, Calcutta: Visva-Bharati, Bengali Year 1400 (1993), p. 73. Translated by UDG. (Hereafter, *Atmaparichay*.)

that inward and outward struggle in his life. He wrote every word with reasoned passion. On reading him again and again, I realized that his prose is repetitive mainly because he was anxious to convey the problems that bothered him. One gets the strong sense that he was hammering out those words because they were critical to the changes he wanted to bring about. That is not so in his poetry. Except very occasionally, his poetry was never didactic. It may be said, perhaps, that his life was a fusion of ideas and artistic creativity.

In selecting and presenting the material about his life from 'his words', I have largely relied on his prose consisting of his autobiographies, essays, speeches, lectures and letters, and included only a little of his poetry. The reason for giving poetry less space is from my personal reluctance to link his poetry to anything specific in his life. Given his views about writing poetry, I think he would have approved of my restraint in deducing all manner of hidden meaning in his poetry. He wrote, for instance:

> But does one write poetry to explain something? Something felt within the heart tries to find outside shape as a poem. So when, after listening to a poem, anyone says he has not understood, I am nonplussed. If someone smells a flower and says he does not understand, the reply to him is: there is nothing to understand, it is only a scent. If he persists, saying: '*that* I know, but what does it all *mean*?' Then one either has to change the subject, or make it more abstruse by telling him that the scent is the shape which the universal joy takes in the flower . . .
>
> That words have meanings is just the difficulty. That is why the poet has to turn and twist them in metre and verse, so that the meaning may be held somewhat in check, and the feeling allowed a chance to express itself.
>
> This utterance of feeling is not the statement of a fundamental truth, or a scientific fact, or a useful moral precept. Like a tear or a smile a poem is but a picture of what is taking place within. If Science or Philosophy may gain anything from it they are welcome, but that is not the reason of its being.[5]

---

[5]*Reminiscences*, pp. 222-23.

Even so, I have reproduced some of his poetry contextually, where I found it meaningful to my presentation, or if the context was directly taken from particular moments of his life. There is that kind of hard data for a few of his poems. And rather than translating his poetry, I have offered it in his own English writing or in his translation. Fortunately, there is as considerable a body of his poetry and prose in English also. The majority of his English writings have been compiled by Sisir Kumar Das and published in three volumes by the Sahitya Akademi, New Delhi. Titled *The English Writings of Rabindranath Tagore*, each volume comes with a scholarly introduction. The first volume contains only poems and the other two volumes his various prose.

In this volume, *My Life in My Words*, I have used Rabindranath's writings in English wherever possible, using the original publications in English from his lifetime without any alterations to the language. The exact references to the texts will be found in the footnotes and the editions cited are listed in the Select Bibliography at the end which also gives the names of the translators of his works. Almost forty per cent of his writing is in English. This is quite substantial considering that he was a poet and writer primarily in Bengali. He remarkably turned himself into a bilingual writer in his advanced years. When he did not directly write in English, or translate his work into English himself, he at least oversaw the translations that were done by others.

My own translations in this volume are in each case from his original Bengali works. These have been done *mainly* from his letters, and the sources are provided in the footnotes. His letters are a very helpful resource in a presentation of his life. Rabindranath wrote and received a very large number of letters. His correspondence was international. He once explained in a letter to his fellow-poet W.B. Yeats that his letters 'act like a footpath' in his 'life history', 'unconsciously laid by the treading of his thoughts'.[6]

He put far greater reliance on thoughts than on the happenings of life. He admitted to being bemused over life's day-to-day business because

---

[6]Rabindranath to W.B. Yeats, 17 June 1918, *Selected Letters of Rabindranath Tagore*, edited by Krishna Dutta and Andrew Robinson, Cambridge: Cambridge University Press, 1997, p. 209. (Hereafter, *Selected Letters*.)

he was convinced it all amounted to little or nothing at the end of the day. He wrote a funny letter to that effect by putting himself in the picture.

> We have to tread every single moment of the way as we go on living our life, but when taken as a whole it is such a very small thing, two hours' uninterrupted thought can hold all of it.
>
> After thirty years of strenuous living Shelley could only supply material for two volumes of biography, of which, moreover, a considerable space is taken up by Dowden's chatter. The thirty years of my life would not fill even one volume.
>
> What a to-do there is over this tiny bit of life! To think of the quantity of land and trade and commerce which go to furnish its commissariat alone, the amount of space occupied by each individual throughout the world, though one little chair is large enough to hold the whole of him! Yet, after all is over and done, there remains only material for two hours' thought, some pages of writing!
>
> What a negligible fraction of my few pages would this one lazy day of mine occupy! But then, will not this peaceful day, on the desolate sands by the placid river, leave nevertheless a distinct little gold mark even upon the scroll of my eternal past and eternal future?[7]

I have divided this collection of Rabindranath's autobiographical writings into two parts: 'My Life' and 'My Thoughts'. The first part, 'My Life', is chronologically arranged and is based on the major events of his life. I have introduced each of the twenty-five chapters which make the first part with a very short passage highlighting usually one or two of the contexts from the concerned chapter. I hope this will help the reader understand the flow of Rabindranath's life. Apart from these introductory passages written by me for chapters 1 to 25, the rest of the writing is all Rabindranath's. In the second section, called 'My Thoughts', there are seven chapters in all. There are no introductory passages for these chapters. Here I assume that the reader will not require chronological guidance to

---

[7]Rabindranath Tagore, 16 *Phalgun* (27 February) 1895, *Glimpses of Bengal: The Letters of Sir Rabindranath Tagore 1885–1895*, London: Macmillan, 1921, pp. 155–57. (Hereafter, *Glimpses of Bengal*.)

his thoughts. My selection of the themes for his thoughts is based upon issues that were very close to his heart.

It is good to remember that Rabindranath was an exceptionally prolific writer and that there is no end to the material he has left us from his unusually active life. There is a household saying in Bengal that it is impossible to finish reading in a lifetime all that Rabindranath wrote in one life. I should make the point that this collection of his autobiographical material is only a *selection* and not anything complete. However, as Penguin Books have been generous with space, this volume is a substantially representative selection.

I should add a word of caution about Rabindranath's writing in English. His style may seem old-fashioned today given that most of it was written close to a century ago. He used to write in a free style and his sentences tend to be long-winded. He was not always mindful of his prepositions and his punctuations. He admitted repeatedly to being untutored in and diffident about English. To take an example, here is what he wrote to his English biographer Edward Thompson:[8]

> You know I began to pay court to your language when I was fifty. It was pretty late for me ever to hope to win her heart. Occasional gifts of favour do not delude me with false hopes. Not being a degree holder of any of our universities I know my limitations—and I fear to rush into the field reserved for angels to tread.[9]

What was of the utmost importance to him was that he wanted to communicate with the world and reach out to a larger humanity. With that wonderful ideal he heroically turned himself into a dynamic bilingual writer in his middle age. But his writing is not suitable for fast reading; it is rich in thought and feeling, broad-minded and far-sighted, large-hearted

---

[8]Edward John Thompson (1886–1946), poet, missionary, and historian, author of *Rabindranath Tagore: His Life and Work* (1921) and *Rabindranath Tagore: Poet and Dramatist* (1926).

[9]Rabindranath to Edward Thompson, 2 February 1921, *A Difficult Friendship: Letters of Edward Thompson and Rabindranath Tagore 1913–1940*, edited by Uma Das Gupta, New Delhi: Oxford University Press, 2003, p. 128. (Hereafter, *Difficult Friendship*.)

and universal. What he wrote a century ago is still believed to be significant among those who know his writings, and there is a continuing interest in him globally.

The University of Toronto has just held an international seminar on him, which they named 'Claiming a Cultural Icon: Interpretations and Misrepresentations of Rabindranath Tagore'. There are continuing translation projects of his works in France, Germany, Hungary, Russia and Japan, as well as in India both in English and in the regional languages. A German scholar has very recently completed a volume of almost 700 pages of direct translation from a varied selection of Rabindranath's poetry, songs, plays, short stories, a novel, essays, letters and conversations. The book was launched in Berlin in 2005.[10] A student from Slovenia is currently working for a PhD on Rabindranath at London's School of Oriental and African Studies with a grant from the Slovenian government. Rabindranath is included in Hungarian literature, with reprints of *Gitanjali* and *Lover's Gift and Crossing* published in 1991 and 1995, respectively. Oxford University Press, India, is currently running a project of translating a wide spectrum of Rabindranath's writing into English. There is a very strong interest in him in Bangladesh. Activists there are trying to capture in celluloid his life and times in East Bengal, what is now Bangladesh, from the 1890s to the 1920s. Besides these larger projects, one occasionally chances upon individuals whose lives are touched by his words irrespective of their nationality. I have just learnt of an American professor at the University of Illinois in Urbana who regularly reads Rabindranath's poetry in English ever since he chanced upon a book of his poetry. Several years later, when his teenage son died, he found solace in a poem from Rabindranath's *Sisu* (1903), written when the poet himself was grieving. He has two lines from that poem inscribed on his son's gravestone at Urbana.

Some years ago I was approached by an elderly British lady in an Oxford cafe who asked me if I was from India. She then went on to tell me that she reads Rabindranath for her morning prayers. Many know of

---

[10]*Rabindranath Tagore: Das Goldene Boot. Lyrik, Prosa, Dramen*, edited by Martin Kämpchen, Verlag Artemis & Winkler, Düsseldorf 2005.

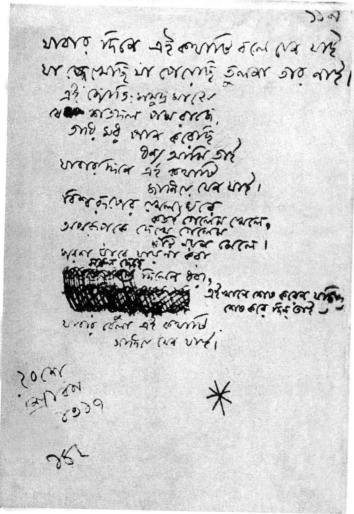

This is a facsimile in Rabindranath's handwriting of the Bengali original of the poem Wilfred Owen read in its English translation. The Bengali original is in *Gitanjali*, poem no. 142. A title is given for the same poem in the collection *Sanchaita* as 'Jabar Diney' (On the Day of My Departure).

the young English poet Wilfred Owen[11] who died in the First World War. A diary was recovered from his pocket which had the following lines from the English *Gitanjali* scribbled in it:

> When I go from hence let this be my parting word,
> that what I have seen is unsurpassable.

It is also on record that Prime Minister Clemenceau[12] was reading out aloud from the *Gitanjali* when the War broke out in France. The influence of great literary figures is never very overt. But they live in people's consciousness in an intangible form as something good and precious. That can be said of the way Rabindranath abides in all of us who know something of what he wrote and thought, irrespective of where we live and what our nationality is.

---

[11]Wilfred Owen (1893–1918), poet, served in the Artists' Rifles during the First World War and was killed in France one week before the Armistice.

[12]Georges Clemenceau (1841–1921), prime minister of France twice, 1907–10 and 1917–20.

PART ONE

MY LIFE

MY FAMILY AND THE CHANGING TIMES

Rabindranath Tagore (1861–1941) was born in the city of Calcutta, the capital of British India, in a Brahmin family. But an early contact with Muslims sent them down to the caste of 'Pirali' Brahmins. Professionally, they were revenue collectors for the English East India Company. There was a split in the family in the 1760s from which one member of the family moved to north Calcutta and built a house in Jorasanko. This was Nilmoni, Rabindranath's great-great grandfather. In Nilmoni's time, the family owned two zamindaris in East Bengal and Orissa. Their wealth was greatly enhanced when Rabindranath's grandfather, Dwarkanath (1794–1846), established a new agency house called Carr, Tagore and Company with his British trading partners. The success of this business enabled Dwarkanath to purchase two more zamindaris. His wealth and his large-hearted philanthropy earned him the title of 'Prince' among his countrymen. His eldest son Debendranath (1817–1905) was Rabindranath's father. Debendranath abandoned his father's lifestyle and became a spiritual leader. He adopted Ram Mohan Roy's Brahmo Dharma in 1843 and broke with the Hindu tradition of idol worship. But he did not break with Hinduism, arguing forcefully that Brahmo Dharma was an integral part of Hinduism. He wrote learned essays on the ancient scriptures and their scientific interpretation in the *Tattwabodhini Patrika*.[1] The family thus found themselves drawn into the heated debates of those times on religion and politics. This was the air young Rabindranath breathed in his Jorasanko family house.

---

[1] *Tattwabodhini Patrika* (1843), journal of the Adi Brahmo Samaj. The Adi Brahmo Samaj was formed under the leadership of Debendranath Tagore and was the first of the three Brahmo Samaj establishments.

There was something remarkable about our family. It was as if we lived close to the age of pre-Puranic India through our commitment to the Upanishads. As a boy, I grew up reciting slokas from the Upanishads with a clear enunciation. We had no experience of the emotional excesses prevalent in Bengal's religious life. My father's spiritual life was quiet, and controlled.

Along with that there was a genuinely deep love of English literature among my elders. Shakespeare and Sir Walter Scott had a strong influence over our family. There was not much patriotism in the air at the time. Poems like Rangalal's 'Swadhinata-hinatay key bachitey chay' (Who wants to live without freedom) and, then, Hemchandra's 'Bingshoti koti manusher bas' (A nation of over twenty crore men) were no more heard than the call of the morning birds. Our family was at the centre of plans for establishing the patriotic Hindu Mela, a National Fair, whose principal organizer was Nabagopal Mitra. My second brother wrote the hymn 'Jai Bharater Jai' (Victory to India, victory), Ganadada wrote 'Lajjay Bharat-jash gaibo ki korey' (How can we sing India's praise in shame), and Barodada wrote 'Molin mukhochandrama Bharat tomari' (Sad is your graceful face, India)—all for the Hindu Mela.[2]

I was born in 1861: that is not an important date of history, but it belongs to a great period of our history of Bengal. You do not know perhaps that we have our places of pilgrimage in those spots where the rivers meet in confluence, the rivers which to us are the symbols of the spirit of life in nature, and which in their meeting present emblems of the meeting of spirits, the meeting of ideals. Just about the time I was born the currents of three movements had met in the life of our country.

One of these movements was religious, introduced by a very great-

---

[2]*Atmaparichay*, pp. 78-79. Translated by UDG. The Hindu Mela or Fair became an annual event from 1867 for the display of national talent and the indigenous arts. Nabagopal Mitra (1840–94) was an early nationalist and founder editor of the *National Paper*. 'Second brother' was Satyendranath Tagore (1842–1923); 'Ganadada' was Rabindranath's cousin Ganendranath Tagore (1841–69); 'Barodada' was Dwijendranath Tagore (1840–1926), eldest of Rabindranath's brothers.

hearted man of gigantic intelligence, Raja Ram Mohan Roy.[3] It was revolutionary, for he tried to reopen the channel of spiritual life which had been obstructed for many years by the sands and debris of creeds that were formal and materialistic, fixed in external practices lacking spiritual significance.

A great fight ensued between him and the orthodox who suspected every living idea that was dynamic. People who cling to an ancient past have their pride in the antiquity of their accumulations, and in the sublimity of their high-walled surroundings. They grow nervous and angry when some lover of truth breaks open their enclosure and floods it with the sunshine of thought and life. Ideas cause movement, but they consider all forward movements to be a menace against their warehouse security.

This was happening about the time I was born. I am proud to say that my father was one of the great leaders of that movement, a movement for whose sake he suffered ostracism and braved social indignities. I was born in this atmosphere of the advent of new ideals, which at the same time were old, older than all the things of which that age was proud.

There was a second movement equally important. A certain great man, Bankim Chandra Chatterjee[4] who, though much older than myself, was my contemporary and lived long enough for me to see him, was the first pioneer in the literary revolution which happened in Bengal about that time.

Our self-expression must find its freedom not only in spiritual ideas but in literary manifestations. But our literature had allowed its creative life to vanish. It lacked movement and was fettered by a rhetoric as rigid as death. This man was brave enough to go against the orthodoxy which believed in the security of tombstones and in that perfection which can only belong to the lifeless. He lifted the deadweight of ponderous forms from our language and with a touch of his magic wand aroused our literature from her age-long sleep. What a vision of

---

[3]Ram Mohan Roy (1772?–1833), political and religious thinker, writer, founder of the Brahmo Samaj Movement for religious reform. His earliest work on religion is the *Tuhfat-al-muwahhidin* (1803-04), 'Gift to Monotheists'.

[4]Bankim Chandra Chatterjee (1838–94), Bengali novelist and founder of the Bengali literary journal *Bangadarshan* in 1872.

beauty she revealed to us when she awoke in the fullness of her strength and grace.

The third movement which started about this time in my country was national. It was not fully political, but began to express our people who were trying to assert their own personality. It was a voice of indignation at the humiliation heaped upon us by those who were not oriental, and who had, especially at that time, the habit of sharply dividing people into good and bad according to what was similar to their life and what was different.

This contemptuous spirit of separateness was perpetually hurting us and causing great damage to our own world of culture. It generated in the young men of our country distrust of all things that had come to them as an inheritance from their past. Our students, imitating the laughter of their European schoolmasters, laughed at the old Indian pictures and other works of art.

Though latterly our teachers themselves have changed their minds, their disciples have hardly yet fully regained confidence in the merit of our art traditions even where such merit is permanent. They have had a long period of encouragement in developing an appetite for third-rate copies of French pictures, for gaudy oleographs abjectly cheap, for the pictures that are products of mechanical accuracy of a stereotyped standard, and they still consider it to be a symptom of superior culture to be able disdainfully to refuse oriental works of creation.

The modern young men of India nodded their heads and said that true originality lay not in the discovery of the rhythm of the essential in the heart of reality but in the full lips, tinted cheeks and bare breasts of imported pictures. The same spirit of rejection, born of utter ignorance, was cultivated in other departments of our culture. It was the result of the hypnotism exercised upon the minds of the younger generation by people who were loud of voice and strong of arm.

The spirit of revolt had just awakened when I was born and some people were already trying to stem the tide. This movement had its leaders in my own family, in my brothers and cousins, and they stood up to save the people's mind from being insulted and ignored by the people themselves.

We had to find some basis that is universal, that is eternal, and we have to discover those things which have an everlasting value. The national movement was started to proclaim that we must not be indiscriminate in our rejection of the past. This was not a reactionary movement but a revolutionary one, because it set out with great courage to deny and to oppose all pride in mere borrowings.

These three movements were on foot and in all three the members of my own family took active part. We were ostracized because of our heterodox opinions about religion and therefore we enjoyed the freedom of the outcaste. We had to build our own world with our own thoughts and energy of mind. We had to build it from the foundation, and therefore had to seek the foundation that was firm.

We cannot create foundations, but we can build a superstructure. These two must go together, the giving of expression to new life and the seeking of foundations which must be in the heart of the people themselves. Those who believe that life consists of change because change implies movement should remember that there must be an underlying unity or the change, being unmeaning, will cause conflict and clash. This thread of unity must not be of the outside, but in our own soul.

As I say, I was born and brought up in an atmosphere of the confluence of three movements, all of which were revolutionary. I was born in a family which had to live its own life, which led me from my young days to seek guidance for my own self-expression in my own inner standard of judgement. The medium of expression doubtless was my mother tongue. But the language which belonged to the people had to be modulated according to the urging which I as an individual had.[5]

My family had broken from the mainstream well before I was born. There was little or no conventional custom and ritual in our home when I grew up. Similarly, the family's old wealth was gone. My grandfather had lighted

---

[5]Rabindranath Tagore, 'Autobiographical', *Talks in China*, Calcutta: Visva-Bharati, 1925, pp. 24–30. (Hereafter, *Talks.*)

lamps of wealth everywhere, but they went out with him. All that remained of that festival of wealth were the black marks of the burnt lamps, their ashes, and a single quivering and weak flame. There may still be some symbolic objects from that age laden with dust in their respective corners but they signify nothing. I was not born into wealth, nor even into memories of wealth.

Thanks to our seclusion, my family enjoyed a certain freedom, somewhat like the freedom that a secluded island gives to its plant and animal life. That characterized our language which Calcuttans called 'Thakurbari-r bhasha' or the Tagore family dialect. The same was true of the dress of the men and women of our family, and their way of living.[6]

When I was born, the family's special puja building was no longer in use. I had no knowledge about the rituals and practices of my ancestors. In my upbringing, there was not even a shadow of the recent aberrations in religious behaviour affecting our communities, nor of the conflict among peoples and races which has spread hatred and enmity throughout the world. I have no memory of such things from my years of growing up. The point of saying this is to assert that my childhood was not regulated by any ancient sacramental laws, that my young creativity was not subjected to the accusing finger of ancient norms.

In my mind, the world has always been full of wonder, full of the inexpressible. No ancient myth nor icon nor ritual has ever broken into my world of wonder. My instinctive response to this world was an intimate part of my childhood. That was my very own puja, for which I constructed my own mantra and composed my own hymn.[7]

The greatest man of modern India, Raja Ram Mohan Roy was born in Bengal and was the best friend of my grandfather. He had courage to

---

[6]*Atmaparichay*, pp. 77-78. Translated by UDG.

[7]Rabindranath Tagore Manuscript Collection, Ms. Accession no. 190, in Bengali, p. 7. Translated by UDG. Rabindra Bhavana Archives, Visva-Bharati, Santiniketan. (Hereafter, RBA.)

overcome the prohibition against sea-voyage, and came into touch with the great Western minds.

My father was fortunate in coming under the influence of Ram Mohan Roy from his early years which helped him to free himself from the sectarian barriers, from traditions of worldly and social ideas that were very rigid, in many aspects very narrow and not altogether beneficial. My father drew from our ancient scriptures, from the Upanishads, truths which had universal significance, and not anything that were exclusive to any particular age or any particular people. We were ostracized by society and this liberated us from the responsibility of conforming to all those conventions that had not the value of truth, that were mere irrational habits bred in the inertia of the racial mind. In my boyhood's dreams I claimed such freedom that we had tasted, for all humanity.[8]

I was born in what was then the metropolis of British India. My ancestors came floating to Calcutta upon the earliest tide of the fluctuating fortune of the East India Company. The conventional code of life for our family thereupon became a confluence of three cultures: the Hindu, the Mohammedan and the British. My grandfather belonged to that period when an amplitude of dress and courtesy and generous leisure were gradually being clipped and curtailed into Victorian manners, economical in time, in ceremonies and in the dignity of personal appearance. This will show that I came to a world in which the modern city-bred spirit of progress had just begun driving its triumphal car over the luscious green life of our ancient village community.[9]

Calcutta is an upstart town with no depth of sentiment in her face and in her manners. It may truly be said about her genesis: In the beginning

---

[8]Rabindranath Tagore, 'Ideals of Education', *The English Writings of Rabindranath Tagore*, edited by Sisir Kumar Das, Volume III, Reprint, New Delhi: Sahitya Akademi, 2002, p. 611. (Hereafter, *English Writings*.)

[9]Rabindranath Tagore, 'A Poet's School', *Santiniketan Vidyalaya 1901–2000*, Calcutta: Visva-Bharati, 2001, p. 18. (Hereafter, *Santiniketan Vidyalaya*.)

there was the spirit of the Shop, which uttered through its megaphone, 'Let there be the Office!' and there was Calcutta. She brought with her no dower of distinction, no majesty of noble or romantic origin; she never gathered around her any great historical associations, any annals of brave sufferings, or memory of mighty deeds. The only thing which gave her the sacred baptism of beauty was the river. I was fortunate to be born before the smoke-belching iron dragon had devoured the greater part of the life of its banks; when the landing-stairs descending into its waters, caressed by its tides, appeared to me like the loving arms of the villages clinging to it; when Calcutta, with her up-tilted nose and stony stare, had not completely disowned her foster-mother, rural Bengal, and had not surrendered body and soul to her wealthy paramour, the spirit of the ledger bound in dead leather.[10]

Though the trampling process was almost complete around me, yet the wailing cry of the past was still lingering over the wreckage.

Often I had listened to my eldest brother describing with the poignancy of a hopeless regret a society hospitable, sweet with the old-world aroma of natural kindliness, full of simple faith and the ceremonial poetry of life. But all this was a vanishing shadow behind me in the dusky golden haze of a twilight horizon—the all-pervading fact around my boyhood being the modern city newly built by a company of Western traders and the spirit of the modern time seeking its unaccustomed entrance into our life, stumbling against countless anomalies.[11]

I remember my childhood. How humble was the mode of life in those days and how simple its paraphernalia compared with modern ways, but there was not the least feeling of embarrassment in our minds on this

---

[10]Rabindranath Tagore, 'The Modern Age', *Creative Unity*, Reprint, London: Macmillan, 1962, p. 116. (Hereafter, *Creative Unity*.)

[11]Rabindranath Tagore, *The Religion of Man, Being The Hibbert Lectures For 1930*, London: George Allen and Unwin, 1931, p. 171. (Hereafter, *Religion of Man*.)

account; for at that time there was no sharp difference in the standard of life: it was roughly the same in every household. What difference there was lay in general culture, in the cultivation of art and music, in the difference of family traditions, in the distinction of speech, manners and customs.

The pride arising from the difference of wealth has come to our country from the West. When money began to flow into the houses of office-goers and businessmen, articles of foreign luxury became the measure of respectability.[12]

From an outside point of view, many a foreign custom would appear to have gained entry into our family, but at its heart flames a national pride which has never flickered. The genuine regard which my father had for his country never forsook him through all the revolutionary vicissitudes of his life, and this in his descendents has taken shape as a strong patriotic feeling. Love of country was, however, by no means a characteristic of the times of which I am writing. Our educated men then kept at arms' length both the language and thought of their native land. Nevertheless, my elder brothers had always cultivated Bengali literature. When on one occasion some new connection by marriage wrote my father an English letter it was promptly returned to the writer.

The Hindu Mela was an annual affair, which had been instituted with the assistance of our house. Babu Nabagopal Mitra was appointed its manager. This was perhaps the first attempt at a reverential realization of India as our motherland. My second brother's popular national anthem, 'Bharater Jaya', was composed then. The singing of songs glorifying the motherland, the recitation of poems of the love of country, the exhibition of indigenous arts and crafts and the encouragement of national talent and skill, were the features of this mela.

On the occasion of Lord Curzon's Delhi durbar,[13] I wrote a prose-

---

[12]Rabindranath Tagore, *Letters from Russia*, translated by Sasadhar Sinha (1934), Calcutta: Visva-Bharati, 1960, p. 8.

[13]Lord Curzon (1859–1925), Governor General and viceroy of India, 1899–1905, held the Delhi durbar for King Edward VII, Emperor of India, in 1903.

paper—at the time of Lord Lytton's,[14] it was a poem. The British Government of those days used to fear the Russians, it is true, but not the pen of a fourteen-year-old poet. So, though my poem lacked none of the fiery sentiments appropriate to my age, there were no signs of any consternation in the ranks of the authorities from Commander-in-Chief down to Commissioner of Police. Nor did any lachrymose letter in the *Times* predict a speedy downfall of the Empire for this apathy of its local guardians. I recited my poem under a tree at the Hindu Mela, and one of my hearers was Nabin Sen, the poet.[15] He reminded me of this after I grew up . . .

Bravery may sometimes have its drawbacks; but it has always maintained a deep hold on the reverence of mankind. In the literature of all countries, we find an unflagging endeavour to keep alive this reverence. So in whatever state a particular set of men in a particular locality may be, they cannot escape the constant impact of these stimulating shocks. We had to be content with responding to such shocks, as best as we could, by letting loose our imagination, coming together, talking tall and singing fervently.[16]

The increased facilities of communication and exchange of thought, the teachings of history, the unity of government, the rise of literature and the efforts of the Congress over a period of time have together begun to make us realize that we belong to one country and are one people; that whether in joy or in sorrow our destiny is one; and that we cannot prosper unless we discover the ties which make us one, and seek to strengthen them.

This consciousness has been growing in us, but it has till now been intermittent and an object of intellectual awareness alone. Because we did not realize this truth with our whole being, we were not able to put our heart into our endeavours or to serve the country with the dedication she demands.

---

[14]Lord Lytton (1831–91), Governor General and viceroy of India, 1876–80, held a ceremonial durbar in 1877 to celebrate the proclamation of Queen Victoria as queen empress of India.

[15]Nabin Chandra Sen (1847–1909), patriot and poet.

[16]*Reminiscences*, p. 142.

Perhaps this state of affairs would have continued long, but suddenly Lord Curzon drew aside the curtain so violently that what was till now hidden could no longer remain so. The moment the order was issued that Bengal should be divided, there arose from east to west one single cry that all Bengalis were one. Never before have we realized so vividly the unity of consciousness in all the limbs of Bengal, based on kinship and the blood bonds of her people.

When the pain of division became intolerable, we thought we would find redress if we made a united appeal to the king. We did not know then that apart from an appeal to the pity of the rulers, there were other ways open to us.

Foreign favour, which is the resort of the helpless, was anyhow denied to us. We had been like the man who was immobile for years as he believed he was lame, but when his house caught fire he discovered that he could move. The stress of our emotions has roused us to the fact that we too have the power of declaring emphatically that we shall not use foreign goods.

Like most discoveries, this discovery came to us out of a particular experience. As we watched, we soon realized that the discovery was greater than the occasion that provoked it. We realized that here was a source of power and wealth. We are troubled today only by the thought that the steam which is being dissipated would have been a source of perennial strength if only we could control and utilize it for a national purpose.[17]

Revolutionary changes have come into our thoughts and attitudes. This is evident in the proposition that those whom social usage has decreed to be untouchables should be given the right to enter temples. There is still a section of the orthodox who seek to justify the temple entry of the casteless on scriptural sanctions, and not moral grounds; but such lopsided advocacy makes little impression. The inner voice of the people has

---

[17]Rabindranath Tagore, 'Presidential Address', Bengal Provincial Congress 1908, *Towards Universal Man*, Reprint, Bombay: Asia Publishing House, 1961, pp. 110-11. (Hereafter, *Towards Universal Man*.)

begun to tell them that neither the scriptures nor tradition nor the force of personality could set a wrong right—the moral standpoint alone counted . . .

When we first became acquainted with English literature, we gained from it not only a new wealth of emotion but also the will to break man's tyranny over man. Our ears rang with the proclamation abolishing the shackles of political slavery. And there was the stern challenge to the attempt to turn human labour into an economic commodity. This was a novel point of view. We had taken it for granted that the accident of birth or the fruits of action pursue us from our past lives and could never be disowned; that the resultant sufferings and the indignities of an inferior status had to be meekly accepted; and that our lot could change only through an accident of rebirth. Even today, in our educated circles, there are people who believe in resisting political denials but ask us to be reconciled to the insult of social and religious disabilities. They forget that the habit of submitting to conditions into which one is born as predestined and inevitable is the strongest link in the chain of our political servitude. However, our contact with Europe has awakened us to the universal laws of cause and effect; and it has given us a set of values against which scriptural dispensation and age-old convention declaim in vain. It is on this ground that we take our stand in trying to improve our political status in spite of all our shortcomings. If, today, we challenge our rulers with demands which we would not have dreamed of presenting to the Mughal Emperor, it is because of the ideal voiced in the words of the poet: 'a man's a man for a' that.'[18]

---

[18]Rabindranath Tagore, 'The Changing Age', Ibid., pp. 344–46.

2

MY BOYHOOD DAYS

Rabindranath was not a pampered boy. There was no question of fancy clothes or even fancy food when he was young. 'The result was,' he wrote, 'that what little we did get we enjoyed to the utmost; from skin to core nothing was thrown away.'[1] He hardly saw his mother, as was typical of a large and traditional Indian household, and his father was often away in the Himalayas. Along with a brother and his sister's son, both just a little older than him, Rabindranath was raised by the family's retinue of servants. He used the term 'servocracy'[2] in his memoirs to describe that period of his life. One of the servants would place him at a certain strategic spot and draw a circle round him, warning of dire consequences if he stepped out. Steeped in stories of the Ramayana and of Sita's punishment for not having heeded a similar warning, the boy stayed well within his boundary, imagining the worst perils possible if he disobeyed. He learnt to amuse himself in his confinement by peering through the Venetian shutters of the window next to him into a public bathing pool and watching the varied rituals of the bathers. When they disappeared at noon, his eyes caught the shadows created by the large banyan tree next to the pool. His childhood memoir, *Chhelebela*, is full of what he called 'pictures' of 'life's memories' rather than 'life's history' about how he spent his time from around the age of four till the time of his first trip abroad in 1878. To him, the pictures were like the 'the original work of an unseen Artist'.[3]

---

[1] *Reminiscences*, p. 10.
[2] Ibid., pp. 24–30.
[3] Ibid., p. 2.

Going out of the house was forbidden to us, in fact we did not have
even the freedom of all its rooms. So we peeped at nature behind
barriers. The limitless thing called the Outside was beyond my reach,
flashes and sounds and scents of which used to come momentarily
and touch me through its interstices. With so many gestures it seemed
to want to play with me through the bars, but it was free and I was
bound, and there was no way of meeting. So the attraction was all
the stronger. The chalk line has been wiped away today, but the
confining ring is still there. The distance is just as distant, the outside
is still beyond me . . .[4]

The Calcutta where I was born was an altogether old-world place. Hackney
carriages lumbered about the city raising clouds of dust, and the whips
fell on the backs of skinny horses whose bones showed plainly their hide.
There were no trams then, no buses, no motors. Business was not the
breathless rush that it is now, and the days went by in leisurely fashion.
Clerks would take a good pull at the hookah before starting for office,
and chew their betel as they went along. Some rode in palanquins, others
joined in groups of four or five to hire a carriage in common, which was
known as a 'share-carriage'. Wealthy men had monograms painted on
their carriages, and a leather hood over the rear portion, like a half-drawn
veil. The coachman sat on the box with his turban stylishly tilted to one
side, and two grooms rode behind, girdles of yaks' tails round their waists,
startling the pedestrians from their path with their shouts of 'Hey-ho!'[5]

The palanquin belonged to the days of my grandmother. It was of ample
proportions and lordly appearance. It was big enough to have needed
eight bearers for each pole. But when the former wealth and glory of the
family had faded like the glowing clouds of sunset, the palanquin bearers,

---

[4]Ibid., pp. 13-14.
[5]Rabindranath Tagore, *My Boyhood Days*, Reprint, Calcutta: Visva-Bharati, 1945, p. 3.
(Hereafter, *Boyhood Days*.)

their gold bracelets, their thick earrings, and their sleeveless red tunics, had disappeared along with it. The body of the palanquin had been decorated with coloured line drawings, some of which were now defaced. Its surface was stained and discoloured, and the coir stuffing was coming out of the upholstery. It lay in a corner of the counting-house veranda as though it were a piece of commonplace lumber.

I was seven or eight years old at that time.

I was not yet, therefore, of an age to put my hand to any serious work in the world, and the old palanquin had been dismissed from all useful service. Perhaps it was this fellow-feeling that so much attracted me towards it. It was to me an island in the midst of the ocean, and I on my holidays became Robinson Crusoe. There I sat with its closed doors, completely lost to view, delightfully safe from prying eyes.

Outside my retreat, our house was full of relatives and other people. From all parts of the house I could hear the shouts of servants at work: Pari the maid returning from the bazaar through the front courtyard, her vegetables in a basket on her hip; Dukhon the bearer carrying Ganga water in a yoke across his shoulder; the weaver woman going into the inner apartments to trade the newest style of sari; Dinu the goldsmith, who received a monthly wage, sitting in the room next to the lane, blowing his bellows and carrying out the orders of the family, now coming to the counting-house to present his bill to Kailash Mukherjee, who has a quill pen stuck behind his ear. The carder sits in the courtyard cleaning the mattress-stuffing on his twanging bow. Mukundalal the durwan is outside rolling on the ground with the one-eyed wrestler, trying out a new wrestling fall. He slaps his thighs loudly, and repeats his movements twenty or thirty times, dropping on all fours. There sits a crowd of beggars waiting for their regular dole.

The day wears on, the heat grows intense, the clock in the gatehouse strikes the hour. Inside the palanquin, however, the day does not acknowledge the authority of the clocks. Our noontime is that of former days, when the drum at the great door of the king's palace would announce the breaking up of the court, and the king would go to bathe in sandal-scented water. On holiday noons, those in charge of me eat their meal and go to sleep. I sit on alone; my palanquin travels on imaginary travels. My bearers, sprung from airy nothing at my bidding, eating the salt of my imagination, carry me wherever my fancy leads. We pass through far, strange lands, and I give each country a name from the books I have read. My imagination has cut a road through a deep forest. Tiger's eyes blaze from the thickets, my flesh creeps and tingles. With me Biswanath the hunter; his gun cracks: boom!—and then all is still. Sometimes my palanquin becomes a peacock-boat, floating on the ocean until the shore is out of sight. The oars dip into the water with a gentle splash, the waves swing and swell around us. The sailors cry to us to beware, a storm is coming. By the tiller stands Abdul the sailor, with his pointed head, shaven moustache and close-cropped hair. I know him for he brings *hilsa*[6] fish and turtle eggs from the Padma for my elder brother.[7]

So much then for my travels in the palanquin. Outside the palanquin there were days when I assumed the role of a teacher, and the railings of the veranda were my pupils. They were all afraid of me and would cower before me in silence. Some of them were very naughty and cared nothing for their books. I told them with dire threats that when they grew up they would be fit for nothing but casual labour. They bore the marks of my beating from head to foot, yet they did not stop being naughty. For it would not have done for them to stop, it would have made an end of my game.

There was another game, too, with my wooden lion. I heard stories of puja sacrifices and decided that a lion sacrifice would be a magnificent thing. I rained blows on his back—with a frail little stick. There had to be a 'mantra', of course, otherwise it would not have been a proper puja:

> Liony, liony, off with your head,
> Liony, liony, now you are dead.
> Woofle the walnut goes clappety clap,
> Snip, Snop, Snap!

---

[6]Hilsa fish is a speciality in Bengal's cuisine, and hilsa from the river Padma was a specially coveted variety.

[7]*Boyhood Days*, pp. 9-10.

I had borrowed almost every word in this from other sources; only the word 'walnut' was my own. I was very fond of walnuts. From the words 'clappety clap' you can see that my sacrificial knife was made of wood. And the word 'snap' shows that it was not a strong one.[8]

There is another piece of vacant land to the north of the house which to this day we call the *golabari* (barn house). The name shows that in some remote past this must have been the place where the year's store of grain used to be kept in a barn. Then, as with brother and sister in infancy, the likeness between town and country was visible all over. Now the family resemblance can hardly be traced.

This *golabari* would be my holiday haunt if I got the chance. It would hardly be correct to say I went there to play—it was the place, not play, that drew me. Why this was so, is difficult to tell. Perhaps it being a deserted bit of waste land lying in an out-of-the-way corner gave it its charm for me. It was entirely outside the living quarters, and bore no stamp of usefulness; moreover, it was as unadorned as it was useless, for no one had planted anything there. It was doubtless for these reasons that this desert spot offered no resistance to the free play of the boy's imagination. Whenever I got any loophole to evade the vigilance of my warders and could contrive to reach the *golabari*, I felt I had a holiday indeed.[9]

In the hot season of *Chaitra* and *Vaisakh*,[10] the hawkers would go about the streets shouting 'I-ii-ce'. In a big pot full of lumps of ice and salt water, were little tin containers of what we called *kulpi*[11] ice—nowadays ousted by the more fashionable ices or ice cream. No one but myself knows how my mind thrilled to that cry as I stood on the veranda facing the street.[12]

---

[8]Ibid., pp. 12-13.

[9]*Reminiscences*, pp. 18-19.

[10]Chaitra is the Bengali month from mid-March to mid-April. Vaisakh or *Baisakh* is the month for mid-April to mid-May.

[11]Kulpi or *kulfi* is a traditional Indian ice cream from Mughal cuisine.

[12]*Boyhood Days*, p. 22.

We used then to spend our evening in the servants' quarters. At that time, English spellings and meanings did not yet lie like a nightmare on my shoulders. My third brother[13] used to say that I ought first to get a good foundation of Bengali and only afterwards to go on to the English superstructure. Consequently, while other school-boys of my age were glibly reciting 'I am up', 'He is down', I had not even started on B, A, D, bad, and M, A, D, mad.

In the speech of the nabobs, the servants' quarters were then called 'tosha-khana'. Even though our house had fallen far below its former aristocratic state, these old high-sounding names, 'tosha-khana', 'daftar-khana', 'baithak-khana', still clung to it.

On the southern side of this 'tosha-khana', a castor oil lamp burned dimly on a glass stand in a big room; on the wall was a picture of Ganesh and a crude country painting of the goddess Kali, round which the wall lizards hunted their insect prey. There was no furniture in the room, merely a soiled mat spread on the floor.

You must understand that we lived like poor people, and were consequently saved the trouble of keeping a good stable. Away in a corner outside, in a thatched shed under a tamarind tree, was a shabby carriage and an old horse. We wore the very simplest and plainest clothes, and it was long time before we even began to wear socks. It was luxury beyond our wildest dreams when our tiffin rations went beyond Brajeswar's inventory and included a loaf of bread, and butter wrapped in a banana leaf.

Brajeswar was the name of the servant who presided over our mat seat.[14]

Day after day, in the evenings, I listened to Brajeswar reciting the seven cantos of Krittivasa's Ramayana. Kishori Chatterjee used to drop in

---

[13]Hemendranath Tagore (1844–84).
[14]*Boyhood Days*, pp. 14-15.

sometimes while the reading was going on. He had by heart *panchali* versions of the whole Ramayana, tune and all.[15] He took possession at once of the seat of authority, and superseding Krittivasa, would begin to recite his simple folk stanzas in great style:

> 'Lakshman O hear me
> Greatly I fear me
> Dangers are near me.'[16]

By and by it would grow late and the assembly on the mat would break up. We would go into the house, to Mother's room, haunted and oppressed on our way by the terror of devils. Mother would be playing cards with her aunt, the inlaid parquet floor gleamed like ivory, a coverlet was spread on the big divan. We would make such a disturbance that Mother would soon throw down her hand and say, 'If they are going to be such a nuisance, auntie, you'd better go and tell them stories.' We would wash our feet with water from the pot on the veranda outside, and climb on to the bed, pulling *didima*[17] with us.

Then it would begin—stories of the magical awakening of the princess and her rescue from the demon city. The princess might wake, but who could waken me? . . . In the early part of the night the jackals would begin to howl, for in those days they still haunted the basements of some of the old houses of Calcutta with their nightly wail.[18]

My initiation into literature had its origin, at the same time, in the books which were in vogue in the servants' quarters. Chief among these

---

[15]Krittivasa (or Krittibas) rendered the Ramayana into Bengali; panchali version is the one used for reciting it.

[16]*Boyhood Days*, pp. 18-19.

[17]Didima is the Bengali term for grandmother.

[18]Ibid., pp. 19-20.

were a Bengali translation of Chanakya's aphorisms,[19] and the Ramayana of Krittivasa.

A picture of one day's reading of the Ramayana comes clearly back to me.

The day was a cloudy one. I was playing about in the long veranda overlooking the road. All of a sudden, Satya,[20] for some reason I do not remember, decided to frighten me by shouting, 'Policeman! Policeman!' My concept of the duties of policemen were of an extremely vague description. One thing I was certain about, that a person charged with crime once placed in a policeman's hands would, as sure as the wretch caught in a crocodile's serrated grip, go under and be seen no more. Not knowing how an innocent boy could escape this relentless penal code, I bolted towards the inner apartments, with shudders down my back for blind fear of pursuing policemen. I broke to my mother the news of my impending doom, but it did not seem to disturb her much. However, not deeming it safe to venture out again, I sat down on the sill of my mother's door to read the dog-eared Ramayana, with a marbled paper cover, which belonged to her old aunt. Alongside stretched the veranda running round the four sides of the open inner quadrangle, on which had fallen the faint afternoon glow of the clouded sky. Finding me weeping over one of its sorrowful situations, my great-aunt came and took away the book from me.[21]

I can recall vividly the winter mornings from my childhood. As night turned into the yellow glow of dawn, I would get out of my blanket quickly. The first light glimmered like dew over the hanging coconut leaves on the east side of our walled garden. Not for a day did I want to be deprived of this beauty. I would, therefore, go out trembling in the cold, wearing a light shirt. On the northern end by the side of the husking-room there was a

[19]Chanakya (Kautilya), intellectual and theorist, belonged to the latter half of the fourth century BC and wrote the *Arthasastra*.

[20]Rabindranath's nephew, Satyaprasad Ganguly (1859–1933).

[21]*Reminiscences*, pp. 7-8.

plum tree and a berry tree. Those hungry for a girlish diet gathered there in the afternoons. There was also a rundown well. In the middle there was a mossy cemented area showing cracks and some very neglected empty space. No other trees come to mind. This was my garden, my all.[22]

I got up while it was still dark and practised wrestling—on cold days I shivered and trembled with cold. In the city was a celebrated one-eyed wrestler, who gave me practice. On the north side of the outer room was an open space known as the 'granary' . . .

It was here that the lean-to shed for wrestling was built against the compound wall. The ground had been prepared by digging and loosening the earth to a depth of about a cubit and pouring over it a maund of mustard oil. It was mere child's play for the wrestler to try a fall with me there, but I would manage to get well smeared with dust by the end of the lesson, when I put on my shirt and went indoors.

Mother did not like to see me come every morning so covered with dust—she feared that the colour of her son's skin would be darkened and spoiled. As a result, she occupied herself on holidays scrubbing me. (Fashionable housewives of today buy their toilet preparations in boxes from Western shops; but then they used to make their unguent with their own hands. It contained almond paste, thickened cream, the rind of oranges and many other things which I forget. If only I had learnt and remembered the recipe, I might have set up a shop and sold it as 'Begum Bilash' unguent, and made at least as much money as the *sandesh-wallahs*.) On Sunday mornings, there was a great rubbing and scrubbing on the veranda, and I would begin to grow restless to get away . . .

When I came in from the wrestling ground I saw a Medical College student waiting to teach me the lore of bones. A whole skeleton hung on the wall of our bedroom, and the bones swayed in the wind and rattled together. But the fear I might otherwise have felt had been overcome by

---

[22]Rabindranath Tagore Manuscript Collection, Ms. Accession no. 190, pp. 8–10, in Bengali. Translated by UDG. (RBA.)

constantly handling it, and by learning by heart the long, difficult names of the bones.

The clock in the porch struck seven. Master Nilkamal was a stickler for punctuality, there was no chance for a moment's variation . . .

Taking my book and slate I sat down before the table, and he began to write figures on the blackboard in chalk. Everything was in Bengali, arithmetic, algebra and geometry. In literature I jumped at one bound from *Sitar Banabas* to *Meghnadbadh Kabya*.[23] Along with this there was natural science. From time to time Sitanath Dutta would come, and we acquired some superficial knowledge of science by experiments with familiar things. Once Heramba Tattvaratna, the Sanskrit scholar, came; and I began to learn the Mugdhabodh Sanskrit grammar by heart, though without understanding a word of it.

In this way, all through the morning, studies of all kinds were heaped upon me, but as the burden grew greater, my mind contrived to get rid of the fragments of it; making a hole in the enveloping net, my parrot-learning slipped through its meshes and escaped—and the opinion that Master Nilkamal expressed about his pupil's intelligence was not of the kind to be made public . . .

At half past four I return from school. The gymnastic master has come, and for about an hour I exercise my body on the parallel bars. He has no sooner gone than the drawing master arrives.

Gradually, the rusty daylight fades away. The many blurred noises of the evening sounds are heard as a dreamy hum resounding over the demon city of brick and mortar. In the study room an oil lamp is burning. Master Aghor has come and the English lesson begins. The black-covered reader is lying in wait for me on the table. The cover is loose; the pages are stained and a little torn; I have tried my hand at writing my name in English in it, in the wrong places, and all in capital letters. As I read I nod, then jerk myself awake with a start, but miss far more than I read. When finally I tumble

---

[23]*Sitar Banabas* is a story in Bengali adapted from the Ramayana by Iswar Chandra Vidyasagar (1820–91); *Meghnadbadh Kabya* (1861) is an epic poem in Bengali by Michael Madhusudan Dutt (1824–73).

into bed I have at last a little time to call my own. And there I listen to endless stories of the king's son travelling over an endless, trackless plain.[24]

In this way, the days passed monotonously on. School grabbed the best part of the day, and only fragments of time in the morning and evening slipped through its clutching fingers.

Now and again, there came to our courtyard a man with a dancing bear, or a snake charmer playing with his snakes. Now and again, the visit of a juggler provided some little novelty. Today the drums of the juggler and snake charmer no longer beat in our Chitpore Road. From afar they have salaamed to the cinema and fled before it to the city.

Games were few and of very ordinary kinds. We had marbles, we had what is called 'bat-ball', a very poor distant relation of cricket, and there were also top-spinning and kite-flying. All the games of the city children were of this same lazy kind. Football, with all its running and jumping about on a big field, was still in its overseas home. And so I was fenced in by the deadly sameness of the days, as though by an imprisoning hedge of lifeless, withered twigs.[25]

I still remember the first magic touch of literature which I experienced when I was a child and was made to struggle across my lesson in a first primer strewn with isolated words smothered under the burden of spelling. The morning hour appeared to me like a once illumined page grown dusty and faded, discoloured into irrelevant marks, smudges and gaps, wearisome in its moth-eaten meaninglessness. Suddenly I came to a sentence of combined words which may be translated thus:

It rains, the leaves tremble.

---

[24]*Boyhood Days*, pp. 39–41, 43-44.
[25]Ibid., pp. 53-54.

At once I came to a world in which I recovered my full meaning. If it were a sentence that informed me of a mere fact, it would fail to rouse up my mind from its boredom. The world of facts pleasant or unpleasant has its restricted range, but freedom is given to us by the world of reality, the reality which is truth made living, which has to be the same assurance of its entity as I myself have to my own self. My mind seemed to touch the eternal realm of truth at the picture of the pattering rain upon the trembling leaves of the forest; and at that moment I was no longer a mere student with his mind muffled by a spelling lesson, enclosed by classroom walls, but one who suddenly realized for himself the unobstructed perspective in which the division between the subject and object vanished in a large harmony of existence. I still remember that morning when that one short sentence rescued me from an endless greyness of obscurity, from the ennui which is the desert haze of inactive imagination.[26]

Looking back on childhood's days, the thing that recurs most often is the mystery which used to fill both life and world. Something undreamt of was lurking everywhere, and the uppermost question every day was: When, oh! When would we come across it? It was as if nature held something in her closed hands and was smilingly asking us: 'What d'you think I have?' What was impossible for her to have was the thing we had no idea of.[27]

---

[26]Rabindranath Tagore Manuscript Collection, Ms. Accession no. 344(A), pp. 3-4, in English. (RBA.)

[27]*Reminiscences*, p. 20.

3

MY FATHER AND MOTHER

Rabindranath was fourteen when his mother died. In his daily life, he had little contact with his mother and his father. But there was once a never-before thrill in store for him when his father took him on a journey to the Himalayas. The grand opportunity came in 1873 just after he was invested with the customary Brahmanical sacred thread. On that journey with his father, he went to Santiniketan and the railway town of Bolpur for the first time. Back in 1863, Debendranath had bought two bighas of land at a short distance from Bolpur. He later built a garden-house on that uninhabited piece of land and named the house Santiniketan, 'abode of peace'. That is how the place came to be called Santiniketan. Debendranath established a Trust Deed to turn Santiniketan into an ashram for Brahmo householders who needed a place for retreat and prayer. Now, on their way to the Himalayas, father and son spent the first few days in the Santiniketan ashram. The boy's joy knew no bounds when he found himself among those incredible open spaces, freed from the confines of his life in Calcutta. 'There was no servant rule here,' he wrote, 'and the only ring which encircled me was the blue of the horizon which the presiding goddess of these solitudes had drawn round them. Within this I was free to move about as I chose.'[1] From Santiniketan, father and son went to Amritsar for a month, visiting the Golden Temple, and then to the Dalhousie hills in the northern Himalayan range. In the words of his biographer, Rabindranath returned home from that journey like 'a little hero from an adventure'.[2]

---

[1] *Reminiscences*, pp. 81-82.
[2] Krishna Kripalani, *Rabindranath Tagore, A Biography*, London: Oxford University Press, 1962, p. 54.

I remember my childhood when the sunrise, like my playfellow,
would burst into my bedside with its daily surprise of morning; when
the faith in the marvellous bloomed like fresh flowers in my heart
every day, looking into the face of the world in simple gladness; when
insects, birds and beasts, the common weeds, grass and the clouds
had their fullest value of wonder; when the patter of rain at night
brought dreams from the fairyland, and mother's voice in the evening
gave meaning to the stars.[3]

Shortly after my birth, my father took to constantly travelling about. So
it is no exaggeration to say that in my early childhood I hardly knew
him. He would now and then come back home all of a sudden, and with
him came foreign servants with whom I felt extremely eager to make
friends . . .

Anyhow, when my father came, we would be content with wandering
round about his entourage and in the company of his servants. We did
not reach his immediate presence . . .

When my father was at home, his room was on the second floor. How
often I watched him from a distance, from my hiding place at the head
of the staircase. The sun had not yet risen, and he sat on the roof, silent
as an image of white stone, his hands folded on his lap.[4]

On one occasion, my father came home to invest the three of us[5] with
the sacred thread. With the help of Pandit Vedantavagish he had collected
the old Vedic rites for the purpose. For days together we were taught to
chant in correct accents the selections from the Upanishads, arranged by
my father under the name of 'Brahmo Dharma', seated in the prayer hall

---

[3]Rabindranath Tagore, 'Crossing', Poem no. 71, *Lover's Gift and Crossing*, London:
Macmillan, 1923, p. 110.

[4]*Reminiscences*, pp. 67-68.

[5]The 'three of us' were Rabindranath, his brother Somendranath, immediately elder to
him, and his nephew Satyaprasad Ganguly.

with Becharam Babu. Finally, with shaven heads and gold rings in our ears, we three budding Brahmins went into a three-day retreat in a portion of the third storey . . .

My shaven head after the sacred thread ceremony caused me one great anxiety. However partial Eurasian lads may be to things appertaining to the Cow, their reverence for the Brahmin is notoriously lacking. So that, apart from other missiles, our shaven heads were sure to be pelted with jeers. While I was worrying over this possibility, I was one day summoned upstairs to my father. How would I like to go with him to the Himalayas? I was asked. Away from the Bengal Academy and off to the Himalayas! Would I like it? Oh, that I could have rent the skies with a shout, that might have given some idea of the How!

On the day of our leaving home, my father, as was his habit, assembled the whole family in the prayer hall for divine service. After I had taken the dust of the feet of my elders, I got into the carriage with my father. This was the first time in my life that I had a full suit of clothes made for me. My father himself had selected the pattern and colour. A gold-embroidered velvet cap completed my costume. This I carried in my hand, assailed with misgivings as to its effect in juxtaposition to my hairless head. As I got into the carriage, my father insisted on my wearing it, so I had to put it on. Every time he looked another way I took it off. Every time I caught his eye it had to resume its proper place.

My father was very particular in all his arrangements and orderings. He disliked leaving things vague or undetermined, and never allowed slovenliness or makeshifts. He had a well-defined code to regulate his relations with others and theirs with him. In this he was different from the generality of his countrymen. Among the rest of us a little laxity this way or that did not signify; so in our dealings with him we had to be anxiously careful. It was not so much the little less or more that he objected to, as the failure to be up to the standard.

My father also had a way of picturing to himself every detail of what he wanted done. On the occasion of any ceremonial gathering, at which he could not be present, he would think out and assign a place for each thing, the duty for each member of the family, the seat for each guest;

nothing would escape him. After it was all over he would ask each one for a separate account and gain a complete impression of the whole for himself. So, while I was with him on his travels, though nothing would induce him to put obstacles in the way of my amusing myself, he left no loophole in the strict rules of conduct which he prescribed for me in other respects.

Our first halt was to be for a few days at Bolpur . . .

The train sped on; the broad fields with their blue-green border trees, and the villages nestling in their shade flew past in a stream of pictures which melted away like a flood of mirages. It was evening when we reached Bolpur. As I got into the palanquin I closed my eyes. I wanted to preserve the whole of the wonderful vision to be unfolded before my waking eyes in the morning light. The freshness of the experience would be spoilt, I feared, by incomplete glimpses caught in the vagueness of the dusk . . .

Though I was yet a mere child, my father did not place any restriction on my wanderings. In the hollows of the sandy soil, the rain water had ploughed deep furrows, carving out miniature mountain ranges full of red gravel and pebbles of various shapes through which ran tiny streams, revealing the geography of Lilliput. From this region, I would gather in the lap of my tunic many curious pieces of stone and take the collection to my father. He never made light of my labours. On the contrary, he waxed enthusiastic.

'How wonderful!' he exclaimed. 'Wherever did you get all these?'

'There are many many more, thousands and thousands!' I burst out. 'I could bring as many every day.'

'That *would* be nice!' he replied. 'Why not decorate my little hill with them?'[6]

We left Bolpur, and making short halts on the way at Sahebganj, Dinapore, Allahabad and Cawnpore we stopped at last at Amritsar . . .

We stayed about a month in Amritsar, and, towards the middle of April,

---

[6]*Reminiscences*, pp. 71, 77–82.

started for the Dalhousie Hills. The last few days in Amritsar seemed as if they would never pass, the call of the Himalayas was so strong upon me.

The terraced hill-sides, as we went up in a *jhampan*,[7] were all aflame with the beauty of the flowering spring crops. Every morning we would make a start after our bread and milk, and before sunset take shelter for the night in the next staging bungalow . . .

My father left his little cash-box in my charge. He had no reason to imagine that I was the fittest custodian of the considerable sums he kept in it for use on the way. He would certainly have felt safer with it in the hands of Kishori, his attendant. So I can only suppose he wanted to train me to the responsibility. One day as we reached the staging bungalow, I forgot to make it over to him and left it lying on a table. This earned me a reprimand.

Every time we got down at the end of a stage, my father had chairs placed for us outside the bungalow and there we sat. As dusk came on, the stars blazed out wonderfully through the clear mountain atmosphere, and my father showed me the constellations or treated me to an astronomical discourse.

The house we had taken at Bakrota was on the highest hill-top. Though it was nearing May it was still bitterly cold there, so much so that on the shady side of the hill the winter frosts had not yet melted . . .

My room was at one end of the house. Lying on my bed I could see, through the uncurtained windows, the distant snowy peaks shimmering dimly in the starlight. Sometimes, at what hour I could not make out, I, half awakened, would see my father, wrapped in a red shawl, with a lighted lamp in his hand, softly passing by to the glazed veranda where he sat at his devotions. After one more sleep I would find him at my bedside, rousing me with a push, before yet the darkness of night had passed. This was my appointed hour for memorizing my Sanskrit declensions. What an excruciatingly wintry awakening from the caressing warmth of my blankets!

By the time the sun rose, my father, after his prayers, finished with me our morning milk, and then, I standing at his side, he would once more hold communion with God, chanting the Upanishads.

---

[7] A carrier used for transporting people on the high hills.

Then we would go out for a walk. But how should I keep pace with him? Many an older person could not! So, after a while, I would give it up and scramble back home through some short cut up the mountain side.

After my father's return, I had an hour of English lessons. After ten o'clock came the bath in icy-cold water; it was no use asking the servants to temper it with even a jugful of hot water without my father's permission. To give me courage, my father would tell of the unbearable freezing baths he had himself been through in his younger days . . .

After our midday meal, lessons began again. But this was more than flesh and blood could stand. My outraged morning sleep *would* have its revenge and I would have been toppling over with uncontrollable drowsiness. Nevertheless, no sooner did my father take pity and let me off, then my sleepiness was off likewise. Then ho! for the mountains.

Staff in hand, I would often wander away from one peak to another, but my father did not object . . .[8]

When evening fell, my father would sit out in the veranda facing the garden. I would then be summoned to sing to him. The moon has risen; its beams, passing through the trees, have fallen on the veranda floor; and I am singing in the *behaga*[9] mode:

O Companion in the darkest passage of life . . .

My father with bowed head and clasped hands is intently listening. I recall the evening scene even now.[10]

My father cherished a synthesis of Hafiz[11] and the Upanishads in his heart. The creation of beauty inspires such a union of opposite elements.

[8]*Reminiscences*, pp. 86, 91–96.
[9]A classical evening raga or melody in Hindustani music.
[10]*Reminiscences*, pp. 88-89.
[11]A Sufi poet in fourteenth-century Persia.

The Creator must be conscious of both the male and female principles without which there can be no Creation.[12]

To the end of his life, I have observed, he never stood in the way of our independence. Many a time have I said or done things repugnant alike to his taste and his judgement; with a word he could have stopped me; but he preferred to wait till the prompting to refrain came from within. A passive acceptance by us of the correct and the proper did not satisfy him; he wanted us to love truth with our own hearts; he knew that mere acquiescence without love is empty. He also knew that truth, if strayed from, can be found again, but a forced or blind acceptance of it from the outside effectually bars the way in.

In my early youth I had conceived a fancy to journey along the Grand Trunk Road, right up to Peshawar, in a bullock cart. No one else supported the scheme, and doubtless there was much to be urged against it as a practical position. But when I discoursed on it to my father he was sure it was a splendid idea—travelling by railroad was not worth the name! With which observation he proceeded to recount to me his own adventurous wanderings on foot and horseback. Of any chance of discomfort or peril he had not a word to say.

Another time, when I had just been appointed Secretary of the Adi Brahmo Samaj, I went over to my father, at his Park Street residence, and informed him that I did not approve of the practice of only Brahmins conducting divine service to the exclusion of other castes. He unhesitatingly gave me permission to correct this if I could. When I got the authority, I found I lacked the power. I was able to discover imperfections but could not create perfection! Where were the men? Where was the strength in me to attract the right man? Had I the means to build in the place of what I might break? Till the right man comes any form is better than none—

---

[12]Rabindranath to Brajendranath Seal, 31 October 1921, Bengali Letters, File: Seal, Brajendranath. Translated by UDG. (RBA.) Brajendranath Seal (1864–1938), friend of Rabindranath, was George V Professor of Mental and Moral Philosophy at Calcutta University, 1912–21.

this, I felt, must have been my father's view of the existing order. But he did not for a moment try to discourage me by pointing out the difficulties.

As he allowed me to wander about the mountains at my will, so in the quest for truth he left me free to select my path. He was not deterred by the danger of my making mistakes, he was not alarmed at the prospect of my encountering sorrow. He held up a standard, not a disciplinary rod.[13]

My father had brought with him some volumes of the Peter Parley series from which to teach me. He selected *The Life of Benjamin Franklin* to begin with.[14] He thought it would read like a storybook and be both entertaining and instructive. But he found out his mistake soon after we began it. Benjamin Franklin was much too business-like a person. The narrowness of his calculated morality disgusted my father. Sometimes he would become so impatient at the worldly prudence of Franklin that he could not help using strong words of denunciation.

Before this, I had had nothing to do with Sanskrit beyond getting some rules of grammar by rote. My father started me on the second Sanskrit reader at one bound, leaving me to learn the declensions as we went on. The advance I had made in Bengali stood me in good stead. My father also encouraged me to try Sanskrit composition from the very outset. With the vocabulary acquired from my Sanskrit reader, I built up grandiose compound words with a profuse sprinkling of sonorous m's and n's, making altogether a most diabolical medley of the language of the gods. But my father never scoffed at my temerity.

Then there were the readings from Proctor's *Popular Astronomy*, which my father explained to me in easy language and which I then rendered into Bengali.

Among the books which my father had brought for his own use, my attention would be mostly attracted by a ten- or twelve-volume edition of

---

[13] *Reminiscences*, pp. 96–98.

[14] Peter Parley is the nom de plume of Samuel G. Goodrich, a nineteenth-century writer of a series of popular books for children. *The Life of Benjamin Franklin* could be a reference to the autobiography of Benjamin Franklin (1706–90) published in 1791.

Gibbon's *Rome*. They looked remarkably dry. 'Being a boy,' I thought, 'I am helpless and read many books because I have to. But why should a grown-up person, who need not read unless he pleases, bother himself so?'[15]

The chains of the rigorous regime which had bound me snapped for good when I set out from home. On my return I gained an accession of rights. In my case my very nearness had so long kept me out of mind; now that I had been out of sight I came back into view.

When I arrived it was not merely a homecoming from travel, it was also a return from my exile in the servants' quarters to my proper place in the inner apartments. Whenever the inner household assembled in my mother's room I now occupied a seat of honour. And she who was then the youngest bride[16] of our house lavished on me a wealth of affection and regard.[17]

After my return from the hills I was the principal speaker at my mother's open-air gatherings on the roof terrace in the evenings. The temptation to become famous in the eyes of one's mother is as difficult to resist as such fame is easy to earn. While I was at the Normal School, when I first came across the information in some reader that the Sun was hundreds and thousands of times as big as the Earth, I at once disclosed it to my mother. It served to prove that he who was small to look at might yet have a considerable amount of bigness about him. I used also to recite to her scraps of poetry used as illustrations in the chapter on prosody or rhetoric of our Bengali grammar. Now I retailed at her evening gatherings the astronomical odds and ends I had gleaned from Proctor.

But the achievement of mine which appealed most to my mother was that while the rest of the inmates of the inner apartments had to be content with Krittivasa's Bengali rendering of the Ramayana, I had been

---

[15]*Reminiscences*, pp. 89–91.

[16]This is a reference to Rabindranath's sister-in-law Kadambari Devi, wife of his fifth brother Jyotirindranath (1849–1925).

[17]*Reminiscences*, pp. 99-100.

reading with my father the original of Maharshi Valmiki himself, Sanskrit metre and all. 'Read me some of that Ramayana, do!' she said, overjoyed at this news which I had given her.

My mother, unable to contain her feelings at my extraordinary exploit, wanted all to share her admiration. 'You must read this to Dwijendra (my eldest brother),' she said.

'In for it!' thought I, as I put forth all the excuses I could think of, but my mother would have none of them. She sent for my brother Dwijendra, and as soon as he arrived, greeted him with: 'Just hear Rabi read Valmiki's Ramayana; how splendidly he does it.'[18]

When my mother died I was quite a child. She had been ailing for quite a long time, and we did not even know when her malady had taken a fatal turn. She used all along to sleep on a separate bed in the same room with us. Then, in the course of her illness, she was taken for a boat trip on the river, and on her return a room on the third storey of the inner apartments was set apart for her.

On the night she died, we were fast asleep in our room downstairs. At what hour I cannot tell, our old nurse came running in weeping and crying: 'Oh my little ones, you have lost your all!' My sister-in-law[19] rebuked her and led her away, to save us the sudden shock at dead of night. Half awakened by her words, I felt my heart sink within me, but could not make out what had happened. When in the morning we were told of her death, I could not realize all that it meant for me.

As we came out into the veranda we saw my mother laid on a bedstead in the courtyard. There was nothing in her appearance which showed death to be terrible. The aspect which death wore in that morning light was as lovely as a calm and peaceful sleep, and the gulf between life and its absence was not brought home to us.

Only when her body was taken out by the main gateway, and we followed the procession to the cremation ground, did a storm of grief pass through

[18]Ibid., pp. 104–06.
[19]Kadambari Devi.

me at the thought that mother would never return by this door and take her accustomed place in the affairs of her household. The day wore on, we returned from the cremation, and as we turned into our lane I looked up at the house towards my father's rooms on the third storey. He was still in the front veranda sitting motionless in prayer.[20]

'Mone Para' (Remembering)

I cannot remember my mother,
only sometimes in the midst of my play
a tune seems to hover over my playthings,
the tune of some song that she used to
hum while rocking my cradle.

I cannot remember my mother,
but when in the early autumn morning
the smell of the *shiuli*[21] flowers floats in the air,
the scent of the morning service in the
temple comes to me as the scent
of my mother.

I cannot remember my mother,
only when from my bedroom window
I send my eyes into the blue of the distant sky,
I feel that the stillness of my mother's
gaze on my face
has spread all over the sky.[22]

When, in later life, I wandered about like a madcap, at the first coming of spring, with a handful of half-blown jessamines tied in a corner of my

---

[20]*Reminiscences*, pp. 255-56.

[21]A fragrant autumnal flower.

[22]Rabindranath Tagore, *Poems*, no. 64, p. 97, Reprint, Calcutta: Visva-Bharati, 2002. Bengali original 'Mone Para', 1921, *Sisu Bholanath*, 1922. (Hereafter, *Poems.*)

muslin scarf, and as I stroked my forehead with the soft, rounded, tapering buds, the touch of my mother's fingers would come back to me; and I clearly realized that the tenderness which dwelt in the tips of those lovely fingers was the very same as that which blossoms every day in the purity of these jessamine buds; and that whether we know it or not, this tenderness is on the earth in boundless measure.[23]

Last night I dreamt that I was the same boy that I had been before my mother died. She sat in a room in a garden-house on the bank of the Ganga. I carelessly passed by without paying attention to her, when all of a sudden it flashed through my mind with an unutterable longing that my mother was there. At once I stopped and went back to her and bowing low touched her feet with my head. She held my hand, looked into my face, and said: 'You have come!'

In this great world we pass by the room where Mother sits. Her storeroom is open when we want our food, our bed is ready when we must sleep. Only that touch and that voice are wanting. We are moving about, but never coming close to the personal presence, to be held by the hand and greeted: 'You have come!'[24]

[23]*Reminiscences*, p. 257.

[24]*Thoughts from Rabindranath Tagore*, London: Macmillan, 1929, p. 3. (Hereafter, *Thoughts*.)

4

A NEW CHAPTER IN MY LIFE

Rabindranath repeatedly acknowledged how much he owed in his upbringing to the personality and activities of his fifth brother Jyotirindranath whom he called Jyotidada. Jyotirindranath was an ardent patriot who went bankrupt over launching and running a steamer service from Khulna to Barisal in East Bengal to rival the British Flotilla Company. He was a painter and musician who played the piano while Rabindranath sang to the melodies he created. Though twelve years older, Jyotirindranath treated his younger sibling as an equal and was one of the 'chief helpers' in his 'literary and emotional training', wrote Rabindranath.[1] His wife Kadambari, whom Rabindranath called *Bouthakrun*,[2] was almost the same age as Rabindranath. Bouthakrun was a lover of literature and quickly became his favourite companion. 'She did not read simply to kill time, but the Bengali books she read filled her whole mind,' he wrote.[3] She was also young Rabindranath's severest critic and did not let him get carried away by the excitement of his early creations. When Jyotirindranath started the Bengali literary journal *Bharati*[4] in 1877, he included his young brother on the editorial staff and allowed him to contribute an 'impudent'[5] criticism of Michael Madhusudan Dutt's epic *Meghnadbadh Kabya* to the first issue. The other articles Rabindranath wrote for *Bharati* were on the Anglo-Saxon and Anglo-Saxon literature, the Norman and Anglo-Norman literature, Petrarch and Laura, Dante and His Poetry, Goethe, and Chatterton. These came out on the eve of his first visit to England in 1878.

---

[1] *Reminiscences*, p. 127.
[2] That is how a sister-in-law is addressed in a traditional Bengali family.
[3] *Reminiscences*, p. 130.
[4] Their eldest brother Dwijendranath was the chief editor.
[5] *Reminiscences*, p. 150.

I had a sister-in-law whose affection I craved for most of all in my
young age. It is since her death that I have grown old rapidly, and I
feel harassed by all this respect and honour shown to me.[6]

I was very lonely—that was the chief feature of my childhood—I was
very lonely. I saw my father seldom: he was away a great deal, but his
presence pervaded the whole house and was one of the deepest influences
on my life. I was kept in the charge of servants of the household after my
mother died, and I used to sit, day after day, in front of the window and
picture to myself what was going on in the outer world.[7]

In the midst of this monotony, there played one day the flutes of festivity.
A new bride came to the house, slender gold bracelets on her delicate
brown hands. In the twinkling of an eye the cramping fence was broken,
and a new being came into view from the magic land beyond the bounds
of the familiar. I circled round her from a safe distance but I did not dare
to go near. She was enthroned at the centre of affection, and I was only a
neglected, insignificant child.

The house was then divided into two suites of rooms. The men lived in
the outer, and the women in the inner apartments. The ways of the nabobs
obtained there still.[8]

---

[6]Rabindranath to Abala Bose, 19 July 1906, *Chitthi Patra*, Volume VI, Calcutta: Visva-
Bharati, 1993, p. 86. Translated by UDG. (Hereafter, *Chitthi Patra* VI.) Abala Bose (1864–
1951), later Lady Abala Bose, wife of the scientist Jagadish Chandra Bose, worked for the
cause of women's education.

[7]Rabindranath to C.F. Andrews, in conversation, London, September 1912, Rabindranath
Tagore, *Letters to a Friend: With Two Introductory Essays on Rabindranath by C.F. Andrews*,
Reprint, New York: Macmillan, 1929, p. 22. (Hereafter, *Letters to a Friend*.) C.F. Andrews
(1871–1940), an Anglican missionary, was a close friend of both Rabindranath and
Mahatma Gandhi, and lived and worked mainly in Santiniketan from 1913 till the end
of his life.

[8]*Boyhood Days*, p. 54.

Write to us at : feedback@travelnews.co.in

- All disputes are subject to jursdiction of Delhi.
- Two or more promotions can not be clubbed at any given time.
- Any merchandize once sold will not be exchanged or returned.

Terms & Conditions:

New Delhi – 110008
Near Metro Station
1/1, East Patel Nagar
Registered Office:

Haryana (India)
Gurgaon – 122002
4ᵗʰ Floor, DLF Cyber City, DLF Phase –
DLF Bu

And when the new bride, adorned with her necklace of gold, came into our house, the mystery of the inner apartments deepened. She, who came from outside and yet became one of us, who was unknown and yet our own, attracted me strangely—with her I burned to make friends. But if by much contriving I managed to draw near, my youngest sister would hustle me off with: 'What d'you boys want here?—get away outside.' The insult, added to the disappointment, cut me to the quick. Through the glass doors of their cabinets one could catch glimpses of all manner of curious playthings—creations of porcelain and glass—gorgeous in colouring and ornamentation. We were not deemed worthy even to touch them, much less could we muster up the courage to ask for any to play with. Nevertheless, these rare and wonderful objects, as they were to us boys, served to tinge with an additional attraction the lure of the inner apartments.[9]

The monsoon rain, rushing down suddenly from the distant mountains, undermines the ancient mountains in a moment, and that is what happened now. The new mistress brought a new regime into the house. The quarters of the bride were in the room adjoining the roof of the inner suite. That roof was under her complete control. It was there that the leaf-plates were spread for the dolls' wedding. On such feast days, boy as I was, I became the guest of honour. My new sister-in-law could cook well, and enjoyed feeding people, and I was always ready to satisfy this craving for playing the hostess. As soon as I returned from school, some delicacy made with her own hands stood ready before me. One day she gave me shrimp curry with yesterday's soaked rice, and a dash of chillies for flavouring and I felt that I had nothing left to wish for.

Sometimes when she went to stay with relatives and I did not see her slippers outside her room, I would go in a temper and steal some valuable object from her room, and lay the foundation of a quarrel. When she

---

[9]*Reminiscences*, pp. 101-02.

returned and missed it, I had only to make such a remark as 'Do you expect me to keep an eye on your room when you go away? Am I a watchman?' She would pretend to be angry and say, 'You have no need to keep an eye on the room. Watch your own hands.'[10]

And so began a new chapter of my lonely Bedouin life on the roof, and human company and friendship entered it. Across the roof garden a new wind blew, and a new season began there. Across the roof kingdom a new wind blew, and a new season began there. My brother Jyotidada played a large part in this change. At that time, my father finally left our home at Jorasanko. Jyotidada settled himself into that outside lower second-floor room, and I claimed a little corner of it for my own.[11]

I said before that in those days there was no bridge of intimacy between adults and children. Into the tangle of these old customs Jyotidada brought a vigorously original mind. I was twelve years younger than he, and that I should come to his notice in spite of such a difference in age is in itself surprising. What was more surprising is that in my talks with him he never called me impudent or snubbed me. Thanks to this, I never lacked courage to think for myself.[12]

A piano appeared in the terrace room. There came also modern varnished furniture from Bowbazar.[13] My breast swelled with pride as the cheap grandeur of modern times was displayed before eyes inured to poverty. At this time, the fountain of my song was unloosed. Jyotidada's hands would stray about the piano as he composed and rattled off tunes in various new styles, and he would keep me by his side as he did so. It was my work to

---

[10]*Boyhood Days*, pp. 54-55.
[11]Ibid., p. 56.
[12]Ibid., p. 57.
[13]Bowbazar in north Calcutta was well known for its furniture shops.

fix the tunes which he composed so rapidly by setting words to them then and there.

At the end of the day, a mat and a pillow were spread on the terrace. Nearby was a thick garland of *bel* flowers on a silver plate, in a wet handkerchief, a glass of iced water on a saucer, and some *chhanchi paan*[14] on a bowl. My sister-in-law would bathe, dress her hair and come and sit with us. Jyotidada would come out with a silk *chadar*[15] thrown over his shoulders, and draw the bow across his violin, and I would sing in my clear treble voice. For Providence had not yet taken away the gift of voice it had given me, and under the sunset sky my song rang out across the house-tops. The south wind came in great gusts from the distant sea, the sky filled with stars.

My sister-in-law turned the whole roof into a garden. She arranged rows of tall palms in barrels and beside and around them *chameli, gandharaj, rajanigandha, karabi* and *dolan-champa*. She considered not at all the possible damage to the roof—we were all alike, unpractical visionaries.

Akshay Chaudhuri[16] used to come almost every day. He himself knew he had no voice, other people knew it even better. In spite of that, nobody could stop the flow of his song. His special favourite was the *behaga* mode.[17]

In infancy the loving care of woman is to be had without the asking, and, being as much a necessity as light and air, is as simply accepted without any conscious response; rather does the growing child often display an eagerness to free itself from the encircling web of women's solicitude. But the unfortunate creature who is deprived of this in its proper season is beggared indeed. This had been my plight. So, after being brought up

---

[14]Chhanchi paan is a special betel-leaf preparation made for chewing.

[15]Shawl.

[16]Akshay Chaudhuri (1850–98), lawyer, writer and poet, a friend of Jyotirindranath whom he accompanied on the piano by putting words to his tunes and also singing them.

[17]*Boyhood Days*, pp. 58-59.

in the servants' quarters, when I suddenly came in for a profusion of
womanly affection I could hardly remain unconscious of it.[18]

A new chapter in the life of the third storey room now opened, as I took
my abode there. Up to that time, it had been merely one of my gypsy
haunts, like the palanquin and the granary, and I roamed from one to
another. But when bouthakrun came, a garden appeared on the roof, and
in the room a piano was established. Its flow of tunes symbolized the
changed tenor of my life.

Jyotidada used to arrange to have his coffee in the mornings in the shade
of the staircase room on the eastern side of the terrace. At such times, he
would read to us the first draft of some new play of his. From time to time,
I also would be called in to add a few lines with my unpractised hand. The
sun's rays gradually invaded the shade, the crows cried hoarsely to each
other as they sat on the roof keeping an eye upon the bread-crumbs. By ten
o'clock the patch of shade had dwindled away and the terrace grew hot.

At midday, Jyotidada used to go down to the office on the ground floor.
Bouthakrun peeled and cut fruit and arranged it carefully on a silver plate,
along with a few sweetmeats made with her own hands, and strewed a few
rose petals over it. In a tumbler was coconut milk or fruit-juice or *tal-
shans* (fresh Palmyra kernels), cooled in ice. Then she covered it with a
silk kerchief embroidered with flowers, put it on a Moradabad tray, and
despatched it to the office at tiffin time, about one or two o'clock.

Just then, *Bangadarshan* was at the height of its fame, and Suryamukhi
and Kundanandini were familiar figures in every house.[19] The whole
country thought of nothing else but what had happened and what was
going to happen to the heroines.

When *Bangadarshan* came, there was no midday nap for anyone in
the neighbourhood. It was my good fortune not to have to snatch for it,

---

[18]*Reminiscences*, p. 100.

[19]Suryamukhi and Kundanandini were the two heroines of Bankim Chandra Chatterjee's
novel *Bisabriksha* (1873).

for I had the gift of being an acceptable reader. Bouthakrun would rather listen to my reading aloud than read for herself. There were no electric fans then, but as I read I shared the benefits of bouthakrun's hand fan.[20]

My sister-in-law was a great lover of literature. She did not read simply to kill time, but the Bengali books she read filled her whole mind. I was a partner in her literary enterprises. She was a devoted admirer of *The Dream Journey*.[21] So was I, the more particularly as, having been brought up in the atmosphere of its creation, its beauties had become intertwined with every fibre of my heart. Fortunately it was entirely beyond my power of imitation, so it never occurred to me to attempt anything like it.

The Dream Journey may be likened to a superb palace of Allegory, with innumerable halls, chambers, passages, corners and niches full of statuary and pictures, of wonderful design and workmanship; and, in the ground around, gardens, bowers, fountains and shady nooks in profusion. Not only do poetic thought and fancy abound, but the richness and variety of language and expression are also marvellous. It is not a small thing, this creative power which can bring into being so magnificent a structure complete in all its artistic detail, and that is perhaps why the idea of attempting an imitation never occurred to me.

At this time, Biharilal Chakravarti's series of songs called 'Sarada Mangal' were coming out in the *Aryadarsan*.[22] My sister-in-law was greatly taken with the sweetness of these lyrics. Most of them she knew by heart. She used often to invite the poet to our house, and had embroidered for him a cushion-seat with her own hands. This gave me the opportunity of making friends with him. He came to have a great affection for me, and I took to dropping in at his house at all times of the day, morning,

---

[20]*Boyhood Days*, pp. 71-72.

[21]Bengali original of *The Dream Journey* is *Swapna Prayana* by Dwijendranath Tagore.

[22]Biharilal Chakravarti (1834–94), leading Bengali poet of that time; *Aryadarsan* (1874), a monthly journal started by the social reformer Jogendranath Bandyopadhyay Bidyabhusan (1845–1904).

noon or evening. His heart was as large as his body, and a halo of fancy
used to surround him like a poetic astral body, which seemed to be his
truer image. He was always full of true artistic joy, and whenever I have
been to him I have breathed in my share of it.

Often have I come upon him in his little room on the third storey, in
the heat of noonday, sprawling on the cool polished cement floor, writing
his poems. Mere boy though I was, his welcome was always so genuine
and hearty that I never felt the least awkwardness in approaching him.
Then, rapt in his inspiration and forgetful of all surroundings, he would
read out his poems or sing his songs to me. Not that he had much of the
gift of song in his voice; but then he was not altogether tuneless, and one
could get a fair idea of the intended melody. When with eyes closed he
raised his voice, its expressiveness made up for what it lacked in execution.
I still seem to hear some of the songs as he sang them. I would also
sometimes set his words to music and sing them to him.

He was a great admirer of Valmiki and Kalidasa. I remember how once
after reciting a description of the Himalayas from Kalidasa with the full
strength of his voice, he said: 'The succession of long *a* sounds here is
not an accident. The poet has deliberately repeated this sound all the way
from *Devatma* down to *Nagadhiraja* as an assistance in realizing the glorious
expanse of the Himalayas.'[23]

At the time, the height of my ambition was to become a poet like Bihari
Babu.[24] I might have even succeeded in working myself up into the belief
that I was actually writing like him, but for my sister-in-law, his zealous
devotee, who stood in the way. She would keep reminding me of a Sanskrit
saying that the unworthy aspirant after poetic fame departs in jeers! Very
possibly she knew that if my vanity was once allowed to get the upper
hand it would be difficult afterwards to bring it under control. So neither
my poetic abilities nor my powers of song readily received any praise

[23]*Reminiscences*, pp. 131–33.
[24]Reference is to Biharilal Chakravarti.

from her; rather she would never let slip an opportunity of praising somebody else's singing at my expense; with the result that I gradually became quite convinced of the defects of my voice. Misgivings about my poetic powers also assailed me, but as this was the only field of activity left in which I had any chance of retaining my self-respect, I could not allow the judgement of another to deprive me of all hope; moreover, so insistent was the spur within me that to stop my poetic adventure was a matter of sheer impossibility.[25]

I remember once composing a poem in the *Payar* and *Tripadi* metres, in which I lamented that as one swims to pluck the lotus it floats further and further away on the waves raised by one's own arms, and remains always out of reach. Akshay Babu[26] took me round to the houses of his relatives and made me recite it to them. 'The boy has certainly a gift for writing,' they said. *Bouthakrun's* attitude was just the opposite. She would never admit that I could ever make a success of writing. She would say mockingly that I would never be able to write like Bihari Chakravarti . . .[27]

Now and again Jyotidada used to go for change of air to a garden-house on the bank of the Ganga. The Ganga shores had then not yet lost caste at the defiling touches of English commerce. Both shores alike were still the undisturbed haunt of birds, and the mechanized dragons of industry did not darken the light of heaven with the black breath of their upreared snouts.

My earliest memory of our life by the Ganga is of a small two-storey house. The first rains had just fallen. Cloud shadows danced on the ripples of the stream, cloud shadows lay dark upon the jungles of the further shore. I had often composed songs of my own on such days, but that day I did

---

[25]*Reminiscences*, pp. 133-34.
[26]Reference is to Akshay Chaudhuri.
[27]*Boyhood Days*, pp. 65-66.

not do so. The lines of Vidyapati[28] came to my mind, *e bhara badara maha bhadara sunya mandira mor.*[29] Moulding them to my own melody and stamping them with my own musical mood, I made them my own. The memory of that monsoon day, jewelled with that music on the Ganga shore, is still preserved in my treasury of rainy season songs. I see in memory the tree-tops struck ever and again by great gusts of wind, till their boughs and branches were tangled together in an ecstasy of play. The boats and dinghies raised their white sails and scudded before the gale, the waves leaped against the *ghat* with sharp slapping sounds. *Bouthakrun* came back and I sang the song to her. She listened in silence and said no word of praise. I must then have been sixteen or seventeen years old. We used to have arguments even then about various matters, but no longer in the old spirit of childish wrangling.[30]

This was the time when my brother Jyotirindra decided to start *Bharati* with our eldest brother as editor, giving us fresh food for enthusiasm. I was then just sixteen, but I was not left out of the editorial staff. A short time before, in all the insolence of my youthful vanity, I had written a criticism of the *Meghnadbadh*. As acidity is characteristic of the unripe mango so is abuse of the immature critic. When other powers are lacking, the power of pricking seems to be at its sharpest. I had thus sought immortality by leaving my scratches on that immortal epic. This impudent criticism was my first contribution to the *Bharati*.

In the first volume, I also published a long poem called *Kavikahini* (The Poet's Story). It was the product of an age when the writer had seen practically nothing of the world except an exaggerated image of his own nebulous self. So the hero of the story was naturally a poet, not the writer as he was, but as he imagined or desired himself to seem. It would hardly

---

[28]Maithili poet who is believed to have lived from about the end of the fourteenth century to the mid-fifteenth century.

[29]. . . *e bhara badara* . . .: 'In this month of *bhadro*, so full with the monsoon rain, my home is empty, devoid of a single soul.' The Bengali month of bhadro corresponds to the period from mid-July to mid-August.

[30]*Boyhood Days*, pp. 73-74.

be correct to say that he desired to be what he portrayed; that represented more what he thought was expected of him, what would make the world admiringly nod and say: 'Yes, a poet indeed, quite the correct thing.' In it was a great parade of universal love, that pet subject of the budding poet, which sounds as big as it is easy to talk about.[31]

With father away in the Himalayas, my brothers were my guardians. Of them I knew Jyotidada best. He never put any restrictions on me. I argued with him and discussed things like an equal. He knew how to respect even a young lad like me. The mental freedom he gave was of great help in my growth. He had immense patience. Had he been patriarchal I would have become something else, broken and twisted into pieces, pleasing to others, but not like myself. I might have become a barrister from England. After all, I had been assured of its material benefits by a friend.[32]

My fifth brother Jyotirindra was one of the chief helpers in my literary and emotional training. He was an enthusiast himself, and loved to evoke enthusiasm in others. He did not allow the difference between our ages to be any bar to my free intellectual and sentimental intercourse with him. This great boon of freedom which he allowed me, none else would have dared to give; many even blamed him for it. His companionship made it possible for me to shake off my shrinking sensitiveness. It was as necessary for my soul after its rigorous repression during my infancy as are the monsoon clouds after a fiery summer.

But for such snapping of shackles I might have been crippled for life. Those in authority are never tired of holding forth the possibility of the abuse of freedom as a reason for withholding it, but without that possibility freedom would not be really free. And the only way of learning how to use a thing properly is through its misuse.

[31] *Reminiscences*, pp. 149–51.

[32] Rabindranath Tagore Manuscript Collection, Ms. Accession no. 100, in Bengali, p. 52. Translated by UDG. (RBA.)

For myself, at least, I can truly say that what little mischief resulted from my freedom always led the way of curing mischief. I have never been able to make my own anything which they tried to compel me to swallow by getting hold of me, physically, or mentally, by the ears. Nothing but sorrow have I ever gained except when left freely to myself.

My brother Jyotirindra unreservedly let me go my own way to self-knowledge, and only since then could my nature prepare to put forth its thorns, it may be, but likewise its flowers. This experience has led me to dread not so much evil itself, as tyrannical attempts to create goodness. Of punitive police, political or moral, I have a wholesome horror. The state of slavery which is thus brought on is the worst form of cancer to which humanity is subject.[33]

---

[33]*Reminiscences*, pp. 127-28.

5

LEAVING HOME:
AHMEDABAD AND ENGLAND, 1878-79

The essays on European literature which appeared in *Bharati* were the fruits of Rabindranath's exploration of his second brother Satyendranath's library. Satyendranath was then a judge in Ahmedabad and expecting to go on furlough to England where his wife and children were staying. It was decided that Rabindranath would accompany him. Rabindranath, therefore, went to Ahmedabad in March 1878 and stayed there for four months to prepare for his journey. Satyendranath sent him to stay in the home of his friend Dr Atmaram Turkhud in Bombay where he could learn about England from Dr Turkhud's daughter Annapurna who had just returned after completing her studies there. Anna was the same age as Rabindranath and they became friends. He called her Nalini, after the heroine in his narrative poem *Kavikahini*, published in 1877. Their friendship was cut short when Rabindranath sailed for England on 20 September 1878, accompanying his brother Satyendranath. On reaching London, the two brothers went to Brighton where Satyendranath's family lived. Afterwards, Rabindranath was brought to London by Satyendranath's friend, Taraknath Palit,[1] and admitted to University College where he studied English literature with Professor Henry Morley. He stayed as a boarder with the Scott family in London. He attended a session of the House of Commons to hear William Gladstone and John Bright speak on India.[2] The letters he wrote from England are a diary of his experiences. They were published in a volume called *Europe Prabasir Patra* in 1881. He regretted the mentality with which he wrote those letters and revised some of his early brash comments.

---

[1]Taraknath Palit (1831–1914), later Sir Taraknath Palit, bar-at-law, was a barrister and a patron of higher education who endowed the University of Calcutta with professorships in physics and chemistry.

[2]John Bright (1811–89), British politician; William Ewart Gladstone (1809–98), politician and prime minister of Britain four times, 1868–74, 1880–85, 1886, and 1892–94.

It is an insult to his humanity if man fails to invoke in his mind a definite image of his own ideal self, of his ideal environment which it is his mission externally to reproduce. It is the highest privilege of man to be able to live in his own creation. His country is not his by the mere accident of birth, he must richly and intimately transform it into his own, make it a personal reality. And what is more, man is not truly himself if his personality has not been fashioned by him according to some mental picture of perfection which he has within. His piled up wealth, his puffed up power can never save him from innate insignificance if he has not been able to blend all his elements into a dynamic unity of presentation. It is for him inwardly to see himself as an idea and outwardly to show himself as a person according to that idea. The individual who is able to do this strongly and clearly is considered to be a character. He is an artist, whose medium of expression is his own psychology. Like all other artists, he often has to struggle hard with his materials to overcome obstructions, inner and outer, in order to make definite his manifestation.[3]

When I was seventeen I had to leave the editorial board of *Bharati*, for it was then decided I should go to England. Further it was considered that before sailing I should live with *mejodada* for a time to get some grounding in English manners. He was then a judge in Ahmedabad, and *mejo-bouthakrun* and her children were in England, waiting for mejodada to get a furlough and join them in England.[4]

I was torn up by the roots and transplanted from one soil to another, and had to get acclimatized to a new mental atmosphere. At first, my shyness was a stumbling block at every turn. I wondered how I should keep my self-respect among all these new acquaintances. It was not easy to habituate myself to strange surroundings, yet there was no means of escape from them; in such a situation a boy of my temperament was bound to find his path a rough one.

---

[3]Rabindranath Tagore Manuscript Collection, Ms. Accession no. 344(J), in English, p. 5. (RBA.)

[4]Mejodada is second brother; mejo-bouthakrun is second sister-in-law.

My fancy, free to wander, conjured up pictures of the history of Ahmedabad in the Mughal period. The judge's quarters were in Shahibagh, the former palace grounds of the Muslim kings. During the daytime, mejodada was away at his work, the vast house seemed one cavernous emptiness, and I wandered about all day like one possessed. In front was a wide terrace, which commanded a view of the Sabarmati river, whose knee-deep waters meandered along through the sands. I felt as though the stone-built tanks scattered here and there along the terrace held locked in their masonry wonderful secrets of the luxurious bathing-halls of the begums.

We are Calcutta people, and history nowhere gives us any evidence of its past grandeur there. Our vision had been confined to the narrow boundaries of these stunted times. In Ahmedabad, I felt for the first time that history had paused, and was standing with her face turned towards the aristocratic past. Her former days were buried in the earth like the treasure of the *yakshas*.[5] My mind received the first suggestion for the story of *Hungry Stones*.[6]

After I had stayed there for some time, mejodada decided that perhaps I should be less homesick if I could mix with women who could familiarize me with conditions abroad. It could also be an easy way to learn English. So for a while I lived with a Bombay family. One of the daughters of the house was a modern educated girl who had just returned with all the polish of a visit to England. My own attainments were only ordinary, and she could not have been blamed if she had ignored me. But she did not do so. Not having any store of book-learning to offer her, I took the first opportunity to tell her that I could write poetry. This was the only capital I had with which to gain attention. When I told her of my poetical gift, she did not receive it in any carping or dubious spirit, but accepted it without question. She asked the poet to give her a special name, and I chose one for her which she found very beautiful. I wanted that name to be entwined with the music of my verse, and I enshrined it in a poem which I made for her. She listened as I sang it in the *bhairavi*[7] mode of

---

[5] A mythological class of ghosts appointed to guard a treasure hidden underground.

[6] The Bengali original of *Hungry Stones* is *Kshudita Pashan* (1900).

[7] Bhairavi is a morning raga or melody in Hindustani classical music.

early dawn, and then said, 'Poet, I think that even if I were on my death-
bed your songs would call me back to life . . .'[8]

When a young Bengali first goes to England there is so much to attract
him there. That is normal and expected. But a tendency towards bravado
can distort feelings. That is what happened to me. I sent out the message
that I was not like others; that I found all of it a trifle beneath me. But I
did not understand at the time that such a reaction is the product of a
mean heart, and also of stupidity . . . The letters I wrote then [*Europe
Prabasir Patra*] were the outcome of a purely audacious defiance. They
were not founded on truth.

I felt ashamed of that collection of letters once I entered the literary
world. With that mentality, I had not only dishonoured the country I
was visiting, I had dishonoured myself . . .

But there is one redeeming feature about the collection and that is its
language. Even if I cannot say it with certainty, I believe this was the first
book in Bengali literature to be written in an informal and colloquial style.
Today the book is sixty years old. My only claim to historicity is that I
wrote those letters in simple Bengali prose.

When I returned to the letters many years later, I sensed there was an
element of respect in them hidden in the disrespect. The disrespect
succeeded in diffusing the respect but not in destroying it. This realization
pleased me very much because I hate loud and empty criticism. I believe
that the capacity to love and respect is God's greatest gift to man. I do
not relish slander; I say that with certainty.[9]

Our ship *Puna* left on 20 September at 5 p.m. We were then standing on
the ship's deck. It was before our eyes that the last outlines of India slowly
faded out. I went into my room and lay down, unable to take the noisy

[8]*Boyhood Days*, pp. 79–82, 85-86.

[9]Rabindranath to Charuchandra Datta, 29 August 1936, *Pashchatyo Bhromon* (Westward
Voyage), Calcutta: Visva-Bharati, Bengali Year 1343 (1936), pp. i–v. Translated by UDG.
Charuchandra Datta (1876–1952), an ICS officer and writer, was a close associate of
Rabindranath.

crowd around me. There is no hiding that my mind was in a state of collapse at the time . . .

I surrendered myself completely to the sea! I alone know how I spent the first six days from the 20th to the 26th. You know what seasickness means, but you don't know how terrible it can be. Even a stone will weep if I describe my suffering in detail. I did not stir out of my bed for six days. My cabin was dark and dinghy. Its windows were tightly shut to stop water getting in from the sea. Thus cut off from the sun and the wind, my body was barely alive at the end of those six days.[10]

Before coming to England, I had imagined like a fool that this small island would be filled with Gladstone's oratory, Max Mueller's explications of the Vedas, Tyndall's scientific theories, Carlyle's deep thoughts and Bain's philosophy.[11] I suppose I was lucky to be disappointed. Just like anywhere else women here are preoccupied with fashions, men with their jobs, and politics is a source of great excitement.

Women want to know whether you went to the ball, if you liked the concert, they will tell you that there is a new actor, that a band will be playing tomorrow somewhere, etc. Men want to know what you think of the Afghan War,[12] they tell you how Londoners honoured the Marquis of Lorne;[13] they tell you that the day is nice, that yesterday was miserable. Women here play the piano, they sing, they sit by the fireside reading novels, they keep the visitor engaged in conversation and, occasionally, they flirt. Unmarried women keep themselves active in public life and speak up on public issues. They can be heard at Temperance meetings or at the Workingmen's Society. But they don't go to work like the men, and there is no question of their raising children. When they become older they

---

[10]First letter from Europe, *Europe Prabasir Patra*, Reprint, Visva-Bharati: 1961, pp. 1–17. Translated by UDG. (Hereafter, *Europe Prabasir Patra*.)

[11]John Tyndall (1820–93) was a distinguished physicist; Thomas Carlyle (1876–1943) was a historian and social reformer; Alexander Bain (1818–1903) was a Utilitarian philosopher and early proponent of scientific psychology.

[12]Afghan War is a reference to the Second Afghan war of the British Empire in Afghanistan, 1879.

[13]Marquis of Lorne, eldest son and heir of the Duke of Argyle, was Queen Victoria's son-in-law.

don't have to go to balls or to flirt. They give their time to public causes, hoping to do some good.

Here, there are wine shops at every door step. When walking, I also come across shoe shops, tailors, meat shops, toyshops, all in plenty, but hardly ever a bookshop. Once when we needed a poetry book we had to order it through a toyshop . . .

I gradually made a few acquaintances. I also realized something funny, that people here think everything has to be explained to me. One day I was going out with Dr—'s brother when we passed by a photo shop. He started to tell me what a photograph is, that it is taken by a machine and not painted by hand. People stood around watching me. Then, when we came near a watch shop, he began to tell me how astonishing a watch was. Once, at an evening party, a lady asked me if I had heard the sound of a piano earlier. In this country they would be able to draw a map of the world beyond death, but they know nothing about India.[14]

We went to a 'Fancy Dress Ball' the other day—so many men and women had turned up to dance in all kinds of costumes. It was in a huge hall, lit by gas lights, with the band playing in all corners. There was an assembly of 600 to 700 handsome men and women with not an inch of empty space anywhere. In each of the rooms, men and women were dancing in each other's arms, in pairs, like mad people. At any time there could have been seventy or eighty pairs of them in a room, packed together, not knowing who might fall on whom. In another room, champagne flowed along with lots of meat and drink, and that room was equally full of people. Some of the girls were dancing for two or three hours without a break.

One of them was dressed as a Snow-maiden, all in white and decked all over with beads twinkling in the lights. Another was there as a Musulmani in red baggy trousers, a woollen top and a head gear—looking rather nice in her attire. One of them was dressed like a native Indian girl in a sari,

[14]Second letter from Europe, *Europe Prabasir Patra*, pp. 17–20. Translated by UDG.

looking better than what she would have looked in English clothing. Another wore the costume of an English maid. I was decked out like a Bengali zamindar in muslin cloth woven with gold thread and also wore a golden headgear.

Last Tuesday, we went to a dance invitation at a gentleman's house. One needs to dress in warm clothing when going out in the evening. But for an evening party one is expected to wear dark clothes with a very clean white shirt, a waist coat on top, a white necktie, and a tailcoat buttoned up to the waist. These tailcoats are not like our *chapkans*[15] coming down to the knees. In a tailcoat, the front comes down to the waist and the back hangs down like a tail. I had to wear a tailcoat like an Englishman. One also has to go in gloves to a dance party, so that a lady's hands or her gloves don't get dirty when holding hands during a dance. It is different when you shake hands with a lady—for that you have to take off your gloves.

The dance began. There were about forty to fifty pairs in a room, neck to neck, even colliding from time to time. The music was playing to the rhythm of the dances and the room was getting quite warm. When the music stops at the end of each dance, the man takes his partner away to get some food and drink from the dining table, or to sit at a corner and talk between themselves. I am no good at mixing with new people and even when I know a dance well, I find it difficult to dance with somebody I don't know. It is like playing cards with a partner you don't like. I quite enjoy dancing with somebody I do know. Women get annoyed if they don't like their dancing partner. My dancing partner must have been wishing for my death when we were dancing. I was much relieved when the dance was over, so was she I am sure.

When I first entered the dance hall, I was taken aback to see an Indian woman among all those white women. My heart jumped with joy to see her. I grew anxious to make her acquaintance. I had not seen a dark face for so long! Moreover, her face had also that gentle and tender Bengali look. I have seen such faces also among English girls but cannot explain where the difference lies. Her hair was done in our native style. On seeing

---

[15]A long north Indian-style coat used on ceremonial occasions.

her I realized how irritable I had become with seeing only the white face and its aggressive immodest beauty day in and day out. Taking everything into account, English women are of a totally different race. I have not learnt enough of English etiquette to be open with them. I don't feel confident enough to cross the limits of expected behaviour . . .

Our Indian clothes occasionally make people on the streets laugh at us. Some are so astonished that they cannot even laugh. But they have so far managed not to get run over when carried away by their curiosity. In Paris, we were once chased by a group of screaming schoolchildren. Some of them laughed at our face when we greeted them and some of them shouted, 'Jack, look at the blackies.'[16]

We went to the House of Commons the other day. We were amazed by the sky-scraping towers of the Parliament, its huge building, its open doors . . .

There were debates on India in the House of Commons last Thursday. Bright and Gladstone tabled Indian petitions on the Civil Service, the tax on cotton and the Afghan War. The session was to begin at four o' clock. We few Bengalis arrived at the House well before four. The House was yet to open and there was a queue of people waiting in the Hall outside. Around the room were busts of Burke, Fox, Chatham, Walpole and so many other great statesmen.

The House opened exactly at four. We had tickets for the Speaker's Gallery. There are five kinds of galleries in the House of Commons: the Strangers' Gallery, Speaker's Gallery, Diplomatic Gallery, Reporters' Gallery, Ladies' Gallery . . .

It was time for the speeches once the question-answer session was over. Most members left the House at that time. After the first couple of speeches, Bright stood up and placed a number of petitions from the Civil Service. I have great respect for Bright; his face is in itself an image of generosity and kindness. Unfortunately, Bright did not make a speech

---

[16]Third Letter from Europe, *Europe Prabasir Patra*, pp. 21–28. Translated by UDG.

that day. After the petitions were tabled, Gladstone came to the floor of the House. There was pin-drop silence when Gladstone arose. Members who had slowly left returned to the hall on hearing Gladstone's voice, and the benches on both sides became full. Every word of his was clearly audible even though Gladstone did not raise his voice. There is something so persuasive about Gladstone and his words inevitably go straight to your heart. He spoke a lot but everything he said was carefully balanced. There was nothing incomplete in what he said. He is forceful but does not ever shout; he gives the feeling that he believes every word he utters.

The House emptied as soon as Gladstone stopped speaking. He was followed by Smollett who made a long speech addressing the empty benches on both sides. I fell asleep while Smollett spoke.[17]

I stayed for a period with my teacher's family. It was a strange family. Mr B, my teacher, was a middle-class man. He knew Latin and Greek very well. He had no children. He, his wife, a maid and I, the four of us stayed in a house. Mr B was an elderly man, very morose, fussy and irritable. He stayed in a small, dark room next to the kitchen and kept his door closed. There was never any question of the sun entering that room for he had a curtain hanging forever drawn on the window. The walls were filled with all kinds of old and torn Greek and Latin books. It was suffocating to be in that room. This was his study where he himself studied and also taught.

He always looked upset about something or the other. He used to get angry with his boots when they were difficult to get into. Everything on earth annoyed him. He tripped and knocked himself here and there, and could seldom find where he put his things. Entering his study one morning, I found him frowning and sighing in his chair with nobody else but him

---

[17]Fourth letter from Europe, *Europe Prabasir Patra*, pp. 28–32. Translated by UDG. The debates Rabindranath is referring to took place on 12 June 1879. Source: *Hansard's Parliamentary Debates*, 3rd ser., vol. 245. Edmund Burke (1729–97), politician and author; Charles Fox (1749–1806), politician; Chatham (1708–78), William Pitt, first earl of Chatham, known as Pitt the elder, prime minister of Britain from 1766 to 1768; Robert Walpole (1676–1745), prime minister of Britain from 1721 to 1742; Patrick Boyle Smollet (1805–95), Member of Parliament.

in the room. But Mr B is actually a good man, he is fussy but not ill-tempered, he is irritable but not quarrelsome.

His wife was a very good person, neither ill-tempered nor arrogant. She was probably pretty to look at when she was young. She now looks older than her age. She does not dress up at all and always wears glasses. She used to do the cooking, she also did all the housework. They had no children so it was not a lot of work. She looked after me with great care. It soon became clear that there was no happiness between them, between husband and wife, but that did not mean they quarrelled with one another. The household was always quiet. Mrs B never went into her husband's study and they saw one another only at mealtimes. At dinner time they used to talk to me but not with each other.[18]

It has been a while since we returned to London from Torquay.[19] Now I am staying with Mr K's family. He, his wife, his four daughters, two sons, three maids, me, and their dog Taby, make up this household. Mr K is a doctor. His hair and beard are grey. He is a strong and handsome man with a genial and good-natured face. Mrs K looks after me with all her heart. She chastises me if I don't wear enough warm clothes. If she thinks I have not eaten enough at mealtimes, she makes me eat more. In England people fear the cough. If perchance I have coughed twice on any day, she stops my bath and makes me take medicines. She also arranges a footbath for me before I go to bed.

I have become very friendly with the younger children of this family. They call me Uncle Arthur. Ethel wants me to be only her Uncle Arthur. If Tom lays a claim on me she will have none of that. Once Tom insisted that I was his Uncle Arthur only to annoy his little sister. Ethel put her arms round my neck and wept.

I have become close friends with this family. The other day their other daughter was telling me how frightened they were when they were first

---

[18]Seventh letter from Europe, *Europe Prabasir Patra*, pp. 62–65. Translated by UDG.
[19]A town in Devonshire, England.

told that an Indian gentleman was coming to stay with them. When I first came, she and her younger sister went away to a relative's house. They did not return for a whole week. They returned when they were told that my face and body were not full of tattoos and my lips were not pierced with jewellery. They recounted all this much later. But they did talk to me when they came back home. They spoke to me without looking at my face. They were perhaps afraid of what they might see. When they saw this face—what then?

I am very happy in this family. In the evenings we sit together entertaining ourselves with songs, music and books. Ethel, in particular, does not want to be away from her Uncle Arthur for a single moment.[20]

One thing struck me when living in this family—that human nature is the same everywhere. We are fond of saying, and I also believed, that the devotion of an Indian wife to her husband is unique, and is not to be found in Europe. But I at least was unable to discern any difference between Mrs Scott and an ideal Indian wife. She was entirely wrapped up in her husband. With their modest means there was no fussing about with too many servants. Mrs Scott attended to every detail of her husband's wants herself. Before he came back home from his work every evening, she would arrange his armchair and woollen slippers and place them in front of the fire with her own hands. She would never allow herself to forget for a moment the things he liked, or the behaviour which pleased him. She would go over the house every morning with their only maid, from attic to kitchen, to get the brass rods on the stairs, the door knobs and other fittings scrubbed and polished till they shone to brightness again. Over and above this domestic routine, there were many calls of social duty. After getting through all her daily duties, she would join with zest in our evening readings and music, for it is not the least of the duties of a good housewife to make real the gaiety of the leisure hour.

---

[20]Thirteenth letter from Europe, *Europe Prabasir Patra*, pp. 202–08. Translated by UDG.

Some evenings I would join the girls in a table-turning séance. We would place our fingers on a small tea-table, and it would go capering about the room. It got to be so that whatever we touched began to quake and quiver. Mrs Scott did not like all this. She would sometimes gravely shake her head and say that she had her doubts about this being right. She bore it bravely, however, not liking to put a damper on our youthful spirits. But one day when we put our hands on Dr Scott's top hat to make it turn, that was too much for her. She rushed up in an agitated state of mind and forbade us to touch it. She could not bear the idea of Satan having anything to do with her husband's headwear, even for a moment . . .

I spent a few months here. Then it was time for my brother to return home, and my father asked me to accompany him back. I was delighted at the prospect. The light of my country, the sky of my country, had been silently calling me back. When I said goodbye, Mrs Scott took me by the hand and wept. 'Why did you come to us,' she said, 'if you must go so soon?'

That household no longer exists in London. Some of the members of the doctor's family have departed to the other world, others are scattered in places unknown to me. But they will always live in my memory.[21]

---

[21]*Reminiscences*, pp. 165–67.

6

MY EDUCATION

Rabindranath's third brother, Hemendranath, was in charge of his education and saw to it that the boy was taught everything from wrestling to grammar to anatomy. All this was part of the boy's 'home studies' for which various tutors came to the house in the mornings and evenings.[1] In addition, he was sent to school during the day. Being truant, he went to a succession of schools: the Oriental Seminary at the age of four in 1865, the Calcutta Training Academy and the Normal School one after the other at age seven, the Bengal Academy and St. Xavier's School when fourteen. He stopped going to school only when his mother died in 1875, unable to face the ordeal any longer. At the Jorasanko house, the boy was surrounded by the activities of a large and buzzing household engaged in linguistic, literary and musical pursuits. Such an atmosphere was central to his education. His elder sister Swarnakumari was the first Bengali woman novelist. His eldest brother Dwijendranath was a poet, philosopher and mathematician who invented the shorthand in Bengali and also musical notations or *swaralipi* for the piano in Bengali. The family was also a hub of patriotic activity and helped to institute an annual fair called the Hindu Mela for displaying national talent and the indigenous arts. Encouraged by his brothers, Rabindranath made his debut as a poet at the Hindu Mela when he was just nine. What was more, his Jyotidada led him to participate in swadeshi ventures and gave him an insight into the spell of 'secret societies' by enrolling him as a junior member of one such society modelled after Giuseppe Mazzini's Carbonari. In 1877, young Rabindranath made his first stage appearance in a comedy written by Jyotirindranath, adapted from French playwright Jean-Baptiste Molière's *Le Bourgeois Gentilhomme*.[2]

[1] *Reminiscences*, pp. 110–16.
[2] Giuseppe Mazzini (1805–72), Italian nationalist leader, founder of the patriotic movement Young Italy (1831); Jean-Baptiste Molière (1622–73), French dramatist whose notable works include *Don Juan* (1665) and *Le Misanthrope* (1666).

So long as I was forced to attend school, I felt an unbearable torture.
I often counted the years before I would have my freedom. My elder
brothers had finished their academic career and were engaged in
life, each in his own way. How I envied them when, after a hurried
meal in the morning, I found the inevitable carriage that took us to
school, ready at the gate. How I wished that, by some magic spell, I
could cross the intervening fifteen or twenty years and suddenly
become a grown-up man. I afterwards realized that what then
weighed on my mind was the unnatural pressure of a system of
education which prevailed everywhere.[3]

In the usual course I was sent to school, but possibly my suffering was
unusually greater than that of most other children. The non-civilized in
me was sensitive; it had great thirst for colour, for music, for movement
of life. Our city-built education took no heed of that living fact. It has its
luggage-van waiting for branded bales of marketable result. The relative
proportion of the non-civilized and civilized in man should be in the
proportion of water and land in our globe, the former predominating.
But the school had for its object a continual reclamation of the non-
civilized. Such a drain of the fluid element caused an aridity which may
not be considered deplorable under city conditions. But my nature
never got accustomed to those conditions, to the callous decency of
the pavement.[4]

I could not have been long at the Oriental Seminary, for I was still of
tender age when I joined the Normal School. The only one of its features
which I remember is that before classes began all the boys had to sit in a
row in the gallery and go through some kind of singing or chanting of
verses—evidently an attempt at introducing an element of cheerfulness
into the daily routine.

---

[3] *Talks*, p. 96.
[4] Rabindranath Tagore, 'A Poet's School', *Santiniketan Vidyalaya*, p. 20.

Unfortunately, the words were English and the tune quite as foreign, so that we had not the faintest notion what sort of incantation we were practising; neither did the meaningless monotony of the performance tend to make us cheerful . . .

The language into which this English resolved itself in our mouths cannot but be edifying to philologists. I can recall only one line:

Kallokee pullokee singill mellaling mellaling mellaling.

After much thought I have been able to guess at the original of a part of it. Of what words *kallokee* is the transformation still baffles me. The rest I think was: . . . full of glee, singing merrily, merrily, merrily![5]

At the age of twelve, I was first coerced into learning English. You will admit that neither its spelling, nor its syntax, is perfectly rational. The penalty for this I had to pay, without having done anything to deserve it, with the exception of being born ignorant.

When in the evening time my English teacher used to come, with what trepidation I waited! I would be yearning to go to my mother and ask her to tell me a fairy story, but instead I had to go and get my text-book, with its unprepossessing black binding, and chapters of lessons, followed by rows of separated syllables with accent marks like soldier's bayonets. As for that teacher, I can never forgive him. He was so inordinately conscientious! He insisted on coming every single evening, there never seemed to be either illness or death in his family. He was so preposterously punctual too.[6]

There was no gas then in the city, and no electric light. When the kerosene lamp was introduced, its brilliance amazed us. In the evening, the house-servant lit castor oil lamps in every room. The one in our study-room had two wicks in a glass bowl.

---

[5]*Reminiscences*, p. 32-33.
[6]Rabindranath Tagore, 'My School', *Santiniketan Vidyalaya*, pp. 10-11.

By this dim light my master taught me from Peary Sarkar's *First Book*. First I would begin to yawn, and then, growing more and more sleepy, rub my heavy eyes. At such times, I heard over and over again of the virtues of my master's other pupil Satin, a paragon of a boy with a wonderful head for study, who would rub snuff in his eyes to keep himself awake, so earnest was he. But as for me—the less said about that the better! Even the awful thought that I should probably remain the only dunce in the family could not keep me awake. When nine o'clock struck I was released, my eyes dazed and my mind drugged with sleep.[7]

After getting through Peary Sarkar's first and second English readers, we entered upon McCulloch's *Course of Reading*. Our bodies were weary at the end of the day, our minds yearning for the inner apartments, the book was black and thick with difficult words, and the subject-matter could hardly have been more uninviting, for, in those days, Mother Saraswati's[8] maternal tenderness was not in evidence. Children's books were not full of pictures then as they are now.[9]

At school we were then in the class below the highest one. At home we had advanced in Bengali much further than the subjects taught in the class. We had been through Akshay Datta's book on Popular Physics, and had also finished the epic of *Meghnadbadh*. We read our physical science without any reference to physical objects, and so our knowledge of the subjects was correspondingly bookish. In fact, the time spent on it had been thoroughly wasted. The *Meghnadbadh* was also not a thing of joy to us. The tastiest dainty may not be relished when thrown at one's head. To employ an epic to teach language is like using a sword to shave with—sad for the sword, bad for the chin. A poem should be taught from the emotional standpoint; inveigling it into

---

[7]*Boyhood Days*, p. 5.
[8]The Hindu goddess of learning and the arts.
[9]*Reminiscences*, pp. 43-44.

service as grammar-cum-dictionary is not calculated to propitiate the divine Saraswati.[10]

The masters and pandits who were charged with my education soon abandoned the thankless task. There was Jnanachandra Bhattacharya, the son of Anandachandra Bhattacharya Vedantabagis, who was a BA. He realized that this boy could never be driven along the beaten track of learning. The teachers of those days, alas! were not so strongly convinced that boys should all be poured into the mould of degree-holding respectability. There was then no demand that rich and poor alike should all be confined within the fenced-off regions of college studies. Our family had no wealth then but it had a reputation, so the old traditions held good, and they were indifferent to conventional academic success. From the lower classes of the Normal School we were transferred to De Cruz's Bengal Academy. It was the hope of my guardians that even if I got nothing else, I should get enough mastery of spoken English to save my face. In the Latin class I was deaf and dumb, and my exercise books of all kinds kept from beginning to end the unrelieved whiteness of a widow's cloth. Confronted by such unprecedented determination not to study, my class-teacher complained to Mr De Cruz, who explained that we were not born for study, but for the purpose of paying our monthly fees. Jnana Babu was of a similar opinion, but found means of keeping me occupied nevertheless. He gave me the whole of *Kumarsambhava* to learn by heart. He shut me in a room and gave me *Macbeth* to translate. Then Pandit Ramsarvasva read *Sakuntala* with me. By setting me free in this way from the fixed curriculum, they reaped some rewards for their labours.[11]

After my promotion to the inner apartments, I felt it all the more difficult to resume my school life. I resorted to all manner of subterfuges to escape

---

[10]Ibid., pp. 56–57.

[11]*Boyhood Days*, pp. 84–85. *Kumarsambhava* is a long poem in Sanskrit by the poet and dramatist Kalidasa (AD 375–455); *Sakuntala* is one of Kalidasa's most well-known plays.

the Bengal Academy. Then they tried putting me at St. Xavier's. But the result was no better . . .

One precious memory of St. Xavier's I still hold fresh and pure . . . this is the memory of Father De Peneranda. He had very little to do with us—if I remember right he had only for a while taken the place of one of the masters of our class. He was a Spaniard and seemed to have an impediment in speaking English. It was perhaps for this reason that the boys paid but little heed to what he was saying. It seemed to me this inattentiveness of his pupils hurt him, but he bore it meekly day after day. I know not why but my heart went out to him in sympathy. His features were not handsome, but his countenance had for me a strange attraction. Whenever I looked on him, his spirit seemed to be in prayer, a deep peace seemed to pervade him within and without.

We had half-an-hour for writing our copybooks; that was a time when, pen in hand, I used to become absent-minded and my thoughts wandered hither and thither. One day, Father De Peneranda was in charge of this class. He was pacing up and down behind our benches. He must have noticed more than once that my pen was not moving. All of a sudden he stopped behind my seat. Bending over me gently laid his hand on my shoulder and tenderly enquired: 'Are you not well, Tagore?' It was only a simple question, but one I have never been able to forget.[12]

When I was thirteen I finished going to school. I do not want to boast about it, I merely give it to you as a historical fact.[13]

I rebelled, young as I was. Of course this was an awful thing for a child to do—the child of a respectable family! My elders did not know how to deal with this phenomenon. They tried all kinds of persuasion, vigorous and gentle, until at last I was despaired of and set free. Through the joy

---

[12]*Reminiscences*, pp. 107–09.
[13]*Talks*, p. 95.

of my freedom, I felt a real urging to teach myself. I undertook the task of playing schoolmaster to myself, and found it to be a delightful game. I poured over any book that came my way, not school-selected text-books that I did not understand, and I filled up the gaps of understanding out of my own imagination. The result may have been quite different from the author's meaning, but the activity itself had its own special value.[14]

One day I discovered, in a library belonging to one of my brothers, a copy of Dickens's *Old Curiosity Shop*. I persisted in reading it, and, with the help of the illustrations supplemented by contributions made by my own imagination, I made out some kind of a story. In this manner, with no help from any teacher, but just as a child learns by sheer guessing, I went on reading and reading and a twilight atmosphere of colourful vision was produced in my mind.[15]

Another time, I had accompanied my father for a trip on the Ganga in his houseboat. Among the books he had with him was an old Fort William edition of Jayadev's *Gita Govinda*.[16] It was in the Bengali character. The verses were not printed in separate lines, but ran on like prose. I did not then know anything of Sanskrit, yet because of my knowledge of Bengali many of the words were familiar. I cannot tell you how often I read that *Gita Govinda*. I can well remember this one line:

The night that was passed in the lonely forest cottage.

It spread an atmosphere of vague beauty over my mind. That one Sanskrit word, *nibhrita-nikunja-griham*, meaning 'the lonely forest cottage', was quite enough for me.

---

[14]Rabindranath Tagore, 'My School', *Santiniketan Vidyalaya*, p. 10.

[15]Ibid., p. 11.

[16]Jayadev or Joydev was a twelfth-century Bengali poet whose *Gita Govinda* is a long poem in twelve cantos and is sung every day at Puri's Jagannath temple.

I had to discover for myself the intricate metre of Jayadev, because its divisions were lost in the clumsy prose form of the book. And this discovery gave me very great delight. Of course I did not fully comprehend Jayadev's meaning. It would hardly be correct to aver that I had got it even partly. But the sound of the words and the lilt of the metre filled my mind with pictures of wonderful beauty, which impelled me to copy out the whole of the book for my own use.

The same things happened, when I was a little older, with a verse from Kalidasa's *Birth of the War-God*.[17] The verse moved me greatly, though the only words of which I gathered the sense were 'the breeze carrying the spray-mist of the falling waters of the sacred Mandakini and shaking the deodar leaves'. These left me pining to taste the beauties of the whole. When, later, a pandit explained to me that in the next two lines the breeze went on 'splitting the feathers of the peacock plume on the head of the eager deer-hunter', the thinness of this last conceit disappointed me. I was much better off when I had relied only upon my imagination to complete the verse.[18]

During my boyhood, Bengali literature was meagre in body, and I think I must have finished all the readable and unreadable books that there were at the time. Juvenile literature in those days had not evolved a distinct type of its own—but that I am sure did me no harm. The watery stuff into which literary nectar is now diluted for being served up to the young takes full account of their childishness, but none of them as growing human beings. Children's books should be such as can partly be understood by them and partly not. In our childhood, we read every available book from one end to the other; and both what we understood and what we did not went on working within us.[19]

---

[17]The English translation of *Kumarsambhava*.
[18]*Reminiscences*, pp. 74-75.
[19]Ibid., pp. 111-12.

Dr Rajendra Lal Mitra used to edit an illustrated monthly miscellany. My third brother had a bound annual volume of it in his bookcase. This I managed to secure, and the delight of reading it through, over and over again, still comes back to me. Many a holiday noontide has passed with me stretched out on my back on my bed, that square volume on my breast, reading about the Narwhal whale or the curiosities of justice as administered by the Kazis of old, or the romantic story of *Krishna-kumari*.[20]

I came across another little periodical in my young days called *Abodhbandhu* (Ignorant Man's Friend).[21] I found a collection of its monthly numbers in my eldest brother's library, and devoured them day by day, seated on the door-sill of his study, facing a bit of terrace to the south. It was in the pages of this magazine that I made my first acquaintance with the poetry of Biharilal Chakravarti. His poems appealed to me the most of all that I read at the time. The artless flute-strains of his lyrics awoke within me the music of fields and forest glades.

Into these same pages I have wept many a tear over a pathetic translation of *Paul and Virginie*.[22] That wonderful sea, the breeze-stirred cocoa-nut forests on its shore, and the slopes beyond lively with the gambols of mountain goats—a delightfully refreshing mirage they conjured up on that terraced roof in Calcutta. And oh! the romantic courting that went on in the forest paths of that secluded island, between the Bengali boy-reader and little Virginie with the many-coloured kerchief round her head![23]

---

[20]*Reminiscences*, pp. 113-14. Rajendra Lal Mitra (1822–91), Indologist and archaeologist, became the first Indian president of the Asiatic Society of Bengal. *Krishna-kumari*, a play by Michael Madhusudan Dutt, based on Lieutenant Colonel James Tod's famous historical work *Annals and Antiquities of Rajasthan* in two volumes (1829, 1832).

[21]*Abodhbandhu* (1866–69), a Bengali monthly, devoted mainly to literature, edited by Biharilal Chakravarti.

[22]A romantic French novel by Bernardin de Saint-Pierre (1737–1814).

[23]*Reminiscences*, pp. 114-15.

The compilations from the old poets by Sarada Mitter and Akshay Sarkar were also of great interest to me.[24] Our elders were subscribers, but not very regular readers of these series, so that it was not difficult for me to get at them. Vidyapati's quaint and corrupt Maithili language attracted me all the more because of its unintelligibility. I tried to make out the sense without the help of the compiler's notes, jotting down in my own notebook all the more obscure words with their context as many times as they occurred. I also noted grammatical peculiarities according to my lights.[25]

I have tried to experience the wealth of beauty in European literature. When I was young I approached Dante,[26] unfortunately through a translation. I utterly failed, and felt it my pious duty to stop, so Dante remained closed to me.

I also wanted to know German literature and, by reading Heine[27] in translation, I thought I had caught a glimpse of the beauty there. Fortunately, I met a missionary lady from Germany and asked her help. I worked hard for some months, but being rather quick-witted, which is not a good quality, I was not persevering. I had the dangerous facility which helps one to guess the meaning too easily. My teacher thought I had almost mastered the language—which was not true. I succeeded, however, in getting through Heine, like a man walking in sleep crossing unknown paths with ease, and I found immense pleasure.

Then I tried Goethe.[28] But that was too ambitious. With the help of the little German I had learnt, I went through Faust. I believe I found my entrance to the place, not like one who has keys for all the doors, but as a casual visitor who is tolerated in some guest room, comfortable but not

---

[24]Sarada Charan Mitter (1848–1917) and Akshay Chandra Sarkar (1846–1917), both lawyers and poets, together compiled a collection of the old poets called *Prachin Kabya Sangraha* which Rabindranath is referring to here.

[25]*Reminiscences*, p. 116.

[26]Dante Alighieri (1265–1321), Italian epic poet.

[27]Heinrich Heine (1797–1856), German poet, some of whose lyrics were put to music by the composers Schubert and Schumann.

[28]Johann Wolfgang van Goethe (1749–1832), German poet, novelist and playwright.

intimate. Properly speaking, I do not know my Goethe, and in the same way many other great luminaries are dark to me. This is as it should be. Man cannot reach the shrine if he does not make the pilgrimage.[29]

This was the experience of my own young days and I believe that a large part of such success or reputations I may have acquired, I owe to that early freedom, won with wilfulness.[30]

If you ask me what gave me boldness, when I was young, I should say that one thing was my early acquaintance with the old Vaishnava poets of Bengal, full of the freedom of metre and courage of expression. I think I was only twelve when these poems first began to be re-printed. I surreptitiously got hold of copies from the desks of my elders. For the edification of the young, I must confess that this was not right for a boy of my age. I should have been passing my examinations and following a path that would lead to failure. I must also admit that the greater part of these lyrics was erotic and not quite suited to a boy just about to reach his teens. But my imagination was fully occupied with the beauty of their forms and the music of their words; and their breath, heavily laden with voluptuousness, passed over my mind without distracting it.[31]

I landed in England, and foreign workmanship began to play a part in the fashioning of my life. The result is what is known in chemistry as a compound. How capricious is Fortune!—I went to England for a regular course of study, and a desultory start was made, but it came to nothing. *Mejo-bouthan* was there, and her children, and my own family circle absorbed nearly all my interest. I hung about around the

[29]Rabindranath Tagore, 'My Life', *A Tagore Reader*, ed. Amiya Chakravarty, Reprint, Boston: Beacon Press, 1966, p. 85. (Hereafter, *Tagore Reader*.)

[30]Rabindranath Tagore, 'My School', *Santiniketan Vidyalaya*, p. 11.

[31]*Talks*, p. 38.

school-room, a master taught me at the house, but I did not give my mind to it.

However, gradually the atmosphere of England made its impression on my mind, and what little I brought back from that country was from the people I came in contact with. Mr Palit[32] finally succeeded in getting me away from my own family. I went to live with a doctor's family, where they made me forget that I was in a foreign land. Mrs Scott lavished on me a genuine affection, and cared for me like a mother. I had then been admitted to London University, and Henry Morley was teaching English Literature. His teaching was no dry-as-dust teaching exposition of dead books. Literature came to life in his mind and in the sound of his voice, it reached our inner being where the soul seeks its nourishment, and nothing of its essential nature was lost. With his guidance, I found the study of the Clarendon Press books at home to be an easy matter and I took upon myself to be my own teacher . . .

I was able to study in the University for three months only, but I obtained almost all my understanding of English culture from personal contacts. The artist who fashions us takes every opportunity to mingle new elements in his creation. Three months of close intimacy with English hearts sufficed for this development. Mrs Scott made it my duty each evening till 11 o'clock to read aloud from poetic drama and history by turn. In this way, I did a great deal of reading in a short space of time. It was not prescribed class study, and my understanding of human nature developed side by side with my knowledge of literature. I went to England but I did not become a barrister. I received no shock calculated to shatter the original framework of my life—rather East and West met in friendship in my own person. Thus it has been given me to realize in my own life the meaning of my name.[33]

---

[32]Reference is to Taraknath Palit. See chapter 5, note 1.
[33]*Boyhood Days*, pp. 85–87.

7

WRITING POETRY

In February 1880, Rabindranath returned home from England with Satyendranath and his family. He immersed himself in writing. While in England, he had begun to write his first drama in verse, *Bhagna Hriday* (The Broken Heart), which, like *Kavikahini* earlier, was about a tormented poet disappointed in love. This was followed by a series of poems called *Sandhya Sangeet* (Evening Songs) published in 1881. He admitted that his life was 'one of utter disorderliness' from the years when he was 'fifteen or sixteen to twenty-two, twenty-three'.[1] He asked his father's permission to return to England and study for the Bar. He and a nephew started on their journey to England on 20 April 1881 but, for some unknown reason, did not proceed after their ship reached Madras. From Madras, Rabindranath went straight to Mussoorie where his father was at the time, and broke the news to him. Relieved that his father was not upset, he went to stay with Jyotirindranath and Kadambari Devi in their villa at Chandernagar on the banks of the Ganga. After a few months, the three of them returned to Calcutta and went to live in a house on Sudder Street, away from Jorasanko. It was here that Rabindranath chanced upon a special and prolonged poetic experience in the rediscovery of a beautiful and happy world, resulting in his famous poem 'Nirjharer Swapnabhanga' (Awakening of the Waterfall). This became the key poem in the series of poems that followed his new poetic experience and was published in the book called *Prabhat Sangeet* (Morning Songs) in 1883.

---

[1]*Reminiscences*, p. 179.

Poetry is a very old love of mine—I must have been engaged to her when I was only Rathi's age.[2] Long ago the recesses under the old banyan tree beside our tank, the inner gardens, the unknown regions on the ground floor of the house, the whole of the outside world, the nursery rhymes and tales told by the maids, created a wonderful fairyland within me. It is difficult to give a clear idea of all the vague and mysterious happenings of that period, but this much is certain, that my exchange of garlands[3] with Poetic Fancy was already duly celebrated.

I must admit, however, that my betrothed is not an auspicious maiden—whatever else she may bring one, it is not good fortune. I cannot say she has never given me happiness, but peace of mind with her is out of the question. The lover whom she favours may get his fill of bliss, but his heart's blood is wrung out under her relentless embrace. It is not for the unfortunate creature of her choice ever to become a staid and sober householder, comfortably settled down on a social foundation.

Consciously or unconsciously, I may have done many things that were untrue, but I have never uttered anything false in my poetry— that is the sanctuary where the deepest truths of my life find refuge.[4]

Absconding from school, never taking a test, never passing one, I was not sure where I stood. My mind wandered everywhere. I discovered then that verses and rhymes were made by ordinary men and women. With the joy of this discovery, I myself began to write. I made and unmade my rhymes sometimes with eight letters, sometimes with six letters or even with ten. Gradually and shamelessly I published them . . .

Thus began my broken rhymes. They were the products of an immature mind and cavalier thoughts. Like wild rain out of an autumn sky, typical of my wayward mind at the time. All this could have gone wrong. But I

---

[2]Rathi, or Rathindranath Tagore (1888–1961), was Rabindranath's elder son and a valued companion in his life and work. Rathi was five years old at the time of this letter.

[3]Exchange of garlands refers to a marriage ritual in Bengal.

[4]Rabindranath Tagore, 8 May 1893, *Glimpses of Bengal*, pp. 100-01.

was saved because fame and infamy were not as plentiful and oppressive at the time. I could, therefore, gather the confidence to slowly go forth into the world with my literary creations.[5]

I could not have been more than eight years old at the time. Jyoti, son of a niece of my father's, was considerably older. He had just gained access to English literature, and would recite Hamlet's soliloquy with great gusto. Why the idea entered his head that a mere child as I was should write poetry I cannot tell, but one afternoon he sent for me and asked me to try and make up a verse after which he explained to me the construction of the *payar* metre of fourteen syllables.[6]

The first feeling of awe once overcome there was no holding me back. I managed to get hold of a blue-paper manuscript book by favour of one of the officers of our estate. With my own hands, I ruled it with pencil lines, at not very regular intervals, and thereon I began to write verses in a large scrawl.

'Like a young deer which butts here, there and everywhere with its newly sprouting horns, I made myself a nuisance with my budding poetry. More so my elder brother, whose pride in my performance impelled him to hunt about the house for an audience.

I recollect how, as the pair of us, one day, were coming out of the estate offices on the ground floor, after a conquering expedition against the officers, we came across the editor of the *National Paper*, Nabagopal Mitra, who had just stepped into the house. My brother tackled him without further ado: 'Look here, Nabagopal Babu! Won't you listen to a poem which Rabi has written?' The reading forthwith followed.

My works had not as yet become voluminous. The poet could carry all his effusions about in his pockets. I was writer, printer and publisher

---

[5]Rabindranath Tagore, Ms. Accession no. 100, in Bengali, p. 52. Translated by UDG. (RBA.)

[6]*Reminiscences*, pp. 34-35.

all in one; my brother, as advertiser, being my only colleague. I had composed some verses on *The Lotus* which I recited to Nabagopal Babu then and there, at the foot of the stairs, in a voice pitched as high as my enthusiasm. 'Well done!' said he with a smile. 'But what is *dwirepha*?'[7]

How I had got hold of this word I do not remember. The ordinary name would have fitted the metre just as well. But this was the one word in the poem on which I had pinned my hopes. It had doubtless duly impressed our officers. But curiously enough Nabagopal Babu did not succumb to it—on the contrary, he smiled! He could not be an understanding man, I felt sure. I never read poetry to him again. I have since then added many more years to my age, but have not been able to improve upon my test of what does or does not constitute understanding in my hearer. However Nabagopal Babu might smile, the word *dwirepha*, like a bee drunk with honey, stuck to its place unmoved.[8]

I remember how, when I was in the lowest class of the *chhatrabritti*,[9] our superintendent Govinda Babu heard a rumour that I wrote poetry. He thereupon ordered me to write, thinking that it would redound to the credit of the Normal School. There was nothing for it but to write, to read my work before my classmates, and to hear the verdict—'this verse is assuredly stolen goods'. The cynics of that day did not know that when I increased in worldly wisdom I should grow shrewd in stealing, not words but thoughts. Yet it is these stolen goods that are valuable.[10]

I cannot claim to have been a passive witness to the spread of my reputation as a poet. Though Satkari Datta was not a teacher of our class, he was very fond of me. He had written a book on Natural History—a fact that will not, I hope, provoke any unkind comment regarding his interest in me. One day he sent for me and asked: 'So you write poetry, do you?' I did

---

[7]An archaic word, meaning bee.

[8]*Reminiscences*, pp. 36–38.

[9]A middle-school examination held formerly in Bengal.

[10]*Boyhood Days*, p. 65.

not attempt to hide it. From that time on he would now and then ask me to complete a quatrain by adding a couplet of my own to give him.[11]

At this time I was blessed with a hearer the like of whom I shall never get again ... Once I had composed a hymn, and had not failed to make the due allusion to the trials and tribulations of this world. Srikantha Babu was convinced that my revered father would be overjoyed at such a perfect gem of a devotional poem. With unbounded enthusiasm he volunteered personally to acquaint him with it. By a piece of good fortune I was not there at the time, but heard afterwards that my father was hugely amused that the sorrows of the world should have so early moved his youngest son to the point of versification.[12]

I have told of my father's amusement on hearing from Srikantha Babu of my maiden attempt at a devotional poem. I am reminded how, later, I had my recompense. On the occasion of one of our *Magh* festivals[13] several of the hymns were of my composition. One of them was

The eye sees thee not, who are the pupil of every eye ...

My father was then bedridden at Chunchura. He sent for me and my brother Jyoti. He asked my brother to accompany me on the harmonium, and got me to sing all my hymns one after the other—some of them I had to sing twice over. When I had finished he said: 'If the king of the country had known the language and could appreciate its literature, he would doubtless have rewarded the poet. Since that is not so, I suppose I must do it.' With which he handed me a cheque.[14]

---

[11]*Reminiscences*, pp. 49-50.

[12]Ibid., pp. 52, 54.

[13]Magh festival or *Maghotsav* refers to an important Brahmo religious event held annually in the month of Magh which is the Bengali month for mid-January–mid-February.

[14]*Reminiscences*, p. 89.

My writings so far had been confined to the family circle. Then was started the monthly called the *Gyanankur* (Sprouting Knowledge), and, as befitted its name, it secured an embryo poet as one of its contributors. It began to publish all my poetic ravings indiscriminately, and to this day I have, in a corner of my mind, the fear that when the day of judgement comes for me, some enthusiastic literary police-agent will institute a search in the inmost zenana of forgotten literature, regardless of the claims of privacy, and bring these out before the pitiless public gaze.[15]

As I have said, I was a keen student of the series of old Vaishnava poems which were being collected and published by Babus Akshay Sarkar and Sarada Mitter. Their language, largely mixed with Maithili, I found difficult to understand; but for that very reason I took all the more pains to get at their meaning . . . While I was so engaged, the idea got hold of me of enfolding my own writings in just such a wrapping of mystery. I had heard from Akshay Chaudhuri the story of the English boy-poet Chatterton. What his poetry was like I had no idea, nor perhaps had Akshay Babu himself. Had we known, the story might have lost its charm. As it happened, the melodramatic element in it fired my imagination; for had not so many been deceived by his successful imitation of the classics? And at last the youth had died by his own hands. Leaving aside the suicide part, I girded up my loins to emulate young Chatterton's exploits.[16]

To my friend mentioned a while ago, I said one day: 'A tattered old manuscript has been discovered while rummaging in the Adi Brahmo Samaj library, and from this I have copied some poems by an old Vaishnava Poet named Bhanu Singha'; with which I read some of my imitation poems to him. He was profoundly stirred. 'These could not have been written

---

[15]Ibid., p. 134. *Gyanankur* (1876-77), a literary monthly, published Rabindranath's long narrative poem 'Banaphul' (1875), The Wild Flower.

[16]Ibid., pp. 136-37. Thomas Chatterton (1752–70) wrote the 'Rowley Poems' at the age of twelve.

even by Vidyapati or Chandidas!' he rapturously exclaimed. 'I really must have that MS to make over to Akshay Babu for publication.'

Then I showed him my manuscript book and conclusively proved that the poems could not have been written by Vidyapati or Chandidas because the author happened to be myself. My friend's face fell as he muttered, 'Yes, yes, they're not half bad.'[17]

While in England I began another poem, which I went on with during my journey home, and finished after my return. This was published under the name of 'Bhagna Hriday' (The Broken Heart). At the time I thought it was very good. There was nothing strange in the writer's thinking so; but it did not fail to gain the appreciation of the readers of the time as well.

About this poem of my eighteenth year, let me set down here what I wrote in a letter when I was thirty:

When I began to write the 'Bhagna Hriday' I was eighteen—neither in my childhood nor in my youth. This borderland age is not illumined with the direct rays of Truth;—its reflection is seen here and there, and the rest is shadow. And like twilight shades its imaginings are long-drawn and vague, making the real world seem like a world of phantasy. The curious part of it is that not only was I eighteen, but everyone around me seemed to be eighteen likewise; and we all flitted about in the same baseless, substanceless world of imagination, where even the most intense joys and sorrows seemed like the joys and sorrows of dreamland. There being nothing real to weigh them against, the trivial did duty for the great.[18]

In the state of being confined within myself, of which I have been telling, I wrote a number of poems which have been grouped together, under the title of *Heart-Wilderness*, in Mohit Babu's edition of my works.

---

[17]Ibid., p. 138. Chandidas is a fourteenth-century Bengali poet.
[18]Ibid., pp. 178–79.

In one of the poems originally published in a volume called *Morning Songs*, the following lines occur:

> There is a vast wilderness whose name is *Heart*;
> Whose interlacing forest branches dandle and rock darkness
>   like an infant.
> I lost my way in its depths.

From which came the idea of the name for this group of poems.

Much of what I wrote, when thus my life had no commerce with the outside, when I was engrossed in the contemplation of my own heart, when my imaginings wandered in many a disguise amidst causeless emotions and aimless longings, has been left out of that edition; only a few of the poems originally published in the volume entitled *Evening Songs* finding a place there, in the *Heart-Wilderness* group.[19]

My brother Jyotirindra and his wife had left home, travelling on a long journey, and their rooms on the third storey, facing the terraced roof, were empty. I took possession of these and the terrace, and spent my days in solitude. While left in communion with myself alone, I do not know how I slipped out of the poetical groove into which I had fallen. Perhaps being cut off from those whom I sought to please, and whose taste in poetry moulded the form I tried to put my thoughts into, I naturally gained freedom from the style they had imposed on me . . .

In the first flood-tide of that joy, I paid no heed to the bounds of metrical form, and as the stream does not flow straight but winds as it lists, so did my verse. Before, I would have held this to be a crime, but now I felt no compunction. Freedom first breaks the law and then makes laws which bring it under true Self-rule.

The only listener I had for these erratic poems of mine was Akshay Babu. When he heard them for the first time he was as surprised

---

[19]Ibid., pp. 199-200.

as he was pleased, and with his approbation my road to freedom was widened.

The poems of Bihari Chakravarti were in a 3-beat metre. This triple time produces a rounded-off globular effect, unlike the square-cut multiple of 2. It rolls on with ease, it glides as it dances to the tinkling of its anklets. I was once very fond of this metre. It felt more like riding a bicycle than walking. And to this stride I had got accustomed. In the *Evening Songs*, without thinking of it, I somehow broke off this habit. Nor did I come under any other particular bondage. I felt entirely free and unconcerned. I had no thought or fear of being taken to task.

The strength I gained by working, freed from the trammels of tradition, led me to discover that I had been searching in impossible places for something which was actually within myself. Nothing but want of self-confidence had stood in the way of my coming into my own. I felt like rising from a dream of bondage to find myself unshackled. I cut extraordinary capers just to make sure I was free to move.

To me, this is the most memorable period of my poetic career. As poems, my *Evening Songs* may not have been worth much, in fact as such they are crude enough. Neither their metre, nor language, nor thought had taken definite shape. But for the first time I had come to write what I really meant, just according to my pleasure. Even if those compositions have no value, that pleasure certainly had.[20]

It was morning. I was watching the sunrise from Free School Lane. A veil was suddenly withdrawn and everything became luminous. The whole scene was one of perfect music—one marvellous rhythm. The houses in the street, the men moving below, the little children playing, all seemed parts of one luminous whole—inexpressibly glorious. The vision went on for seven or eight days. Everyone, even those who bored me, seemed to lose their outer barrier of personality; and I was full of gladness, full of love, for every person and every tiniest thing. Then I went to the Himalayas,

---

[20]Ibid., pp. 200–03.

and looked for it there and lost it . . . That morning in Free School Lane was one of the first things that gave me inner vision, and I have tried to explain it in my poems. I have felt, ever since, that this was my goal: to express the fullness of life, in its beauty, as perfection—if only the veil were withdrawn.[21]

That very day the poem, *The Awakening of the Waterfall*, gushed forth and coursed on like a veritable cascade. The poem came to an end, but the curtain did not fall upon the joy aspect of the Universe. And it came to be so that no person or thing in the world seemed to me trivial or unpleasing . . .

For sometime together I remained in this self-forgetful state of bliss. Then my brother thought of going to the Darjeeling hills. So much the better, thought I. On the vast Himalayan tops I shall be able to look more deeply into what has been revealed to me in Sudder Street; at any rate I shall see how the Himalayas display themselves to my new gift of vision . . .

I wandered about amongst the firs, I sat near the falls and bathed in their waters, I gazed at the grandeur of Kanchenjhunga through a cloudless sky, but in what had seemed to me these likeliest of places I found *it* not. I had come to know it, but could see it no longer. While I was admiring the gem the lid had suddenly closed, leaving me staring at the enclosing casket. But, for all the attractiveness of its workmanship, there was no longer any danger of my mistaking it for merely an empty box.

My *Morning Songs* came to an end, their last echo dying out with *The Echo* which I wrote at Darjeeling. This apparently proved such an abstruse affair that two friends laid a wager as to its real meaning. My only consolation was that, as I was equally unable to explain the enigma to them when they came to me for a solution, neither had to lose any money over it. Alas, the days when I wrote excessively plain poems about *The Lotus* and *A Lake* had gone forever.

---

[21]Rabindranath to C.F. Andrews, in conversation, September 1912, *Letters to a Friend*, p. 24.

But does one write poetry to explain something? Something felt within the heart tries to find outside shape as a poem. So when, after listening to a poem, anyone says he has not understood, I am nonplussed. If someone smells a flower and says he does not understand, the reply to him is: there is nothing to understand, it is only a scent. If he persists, saying: '*that* I know, but what does it all *mean*?' Then one either has to change the subject, or make it more abstruse by telling him that the scent is the shape which the universal joy takes in the flower.

That words have meaning is just the difficulty. That is why the poet has to turn and twist them in metre and verse, so that the meaning can be held somewhat in check, and the feeling allowed a chance to express itself.

This utterance of feeling is not the statement of a fundamental truth, or a scientific fact, or a useful moral precept. Like a tear or a smile, a poem is but a picture of what is taking place within. If Science or Philosophy may gain anything from it they are welcome, but that is not the reason of its being . . .

The Echo was written so long ago that it has escaped attention, and I am now no longer called upon to render an account of its meaning. Nevertheless, whatever its other merits or defects may be, I can assure my readers that it was not my intention in it to propound a riddle, or insidiously convey any erudite teaching. The fact of the matter was that a longing had been born within my heart, and, unable to find any other name, I had called the thing I desired an Echo.[22]

To the uninitiated it might appear that a flower has arrived all of a sudden; the story of its journey from a seed remains unknown . . . The same was true of my poetry, such has been my experience. All my energies and my rejoicing were given to the immediate effort of producing a particular piece, whenever that happened, as if only the immediate mattered in obtaining the result. But I did come to realize that the end-product is merely an occasion, a pretext; it is the creator within oneself who is continuously

---

[22]*Reminiscences*, pp. 217–23.

and unrelentingly providing for future arrivals, without an end in view but with a perpetual meaning for posterity. Like the flute player and his reed pipe. He produces the tunes but the melodies are all in the custody of the perennial musician. Like this verse:

> I was telling you my tale
> I was telling you so many stories of my life
> You put them to flames
> You drowned them in your tears
> That is how you rebuilt me
> As an image after Your heart.

I guess this verse conveys that I set out to write what was straightforward and simple, something just for myself, but it is God's melody which transformed its meaning from the personal to the universal. It is I who put a first stroke on the canvas but it is He who filled it with colours I did not possess.

Does this happen only with *my* poetry, that another poet besides myself is working on my creations from behind the scenes? That is not so. I know it from my life. I know who it is that strings together my life's joys and sorrows, its losses and gains, into one meaningful chain. I know who has woven my life into one whole from all its broken parts and from every impediment that came in the way. Not just that, it is He who has broken down the limits within which my own nature and self had confined me. Cutting across the path of pain and loss, He has connected my life to that which is vast and great.

It is this poet who knows everything about me, my good and my bad, who knows what is right for me and what is not, who steers my life through the propitious and the adverse, whom I call my *jiban-debata*, Lord of my life.[23]

---

[23]*Atmaparichay*, pp. 8-9. Translated by UDG.

8

RESTLESS YEARS, 1883–90

In the summer of 1883, Jyotirindranath, Kadambari Devi and Rabindranath moved to Karwar in south-west India where Satyendranath was posted as district judge. There, Rabindranath wrote his drama in verse called *Prakritir Pratisodh* (Nature's Revenge). In the autumn, the trio moved back to Calcutta. On 9 December 1883, Rabindranath was married. His young bride, Bhavatarini Raichaudhuri, was selected from a Pirali Brahmin family of the provincial town of Jessore in East Bengal. Her old-fashioned name Bhavatarini was changed to Mrinalini, perhaps by Rabindranath himself. He was at that time working on a prose-drama called *Nalini*, a name which resembled Mrinalini. The drama was going to be acted by members of the family. But before it could be produced, the family was overcome by a tragedy. In April 1884, Kadambari Devi suddenly committed suicide. Recalling his shock in his *Reminiscences*, Rabindranath analysed it as his first 'permanent'[1] acquaintance with death. In 1887, he began composing the *Manasi* group of poems and translated one of them into English. At the time, there was a surge of Hindu revivalism in public life. Rabindranath was initially touched by the revivalism, but turned away from it in distaste. He and Bankim Chandra Chatterjee engaged in a heated exchange on the subject of religion. He wrote some biting satires against religious fanaticism and was not in a happy frame of mind. 'I was tormented by a furious impatience, an intolerable dissatisfaction with myself and all around me. Much rather, I said to myself, would I be an Arab Bedouin!'[2]

---

[1] *Reminiscences*, p. 257.
[2] Ibid., p. 269.

This *Nature's Revenge* may be looked upon as an introduction to the whole of my future literary work; or, rather this has been the subject on which all my writings have dwelt—the joy of attaining the Infinite within the finite.

On our way back from Karwar I wrote some songs for the *Nature's Revenge* on board ship. The first one filled me with a great gladness as I sang and wrote it sitting on the deck.

'Mother, leave your darling boy to us,
And let us take him to the field where we graze our cattle.'[3]

Here in Karwar I wrote the *Prakritir Pratisodh* (Nature's Revenge), a dramatic poem. The hero was a *sanyasi* (hermit) who had been striving to gain a victory over Nature by cutting away the bonds of all desires and affections and thus to arrive at a true and profound knowledge of self. A little girl, however, brought him back from his communion with the infinite to the world and into the bondage of human affection. On so coming back, the *sanyasi* realized that the great is to be found in the small, the Infinite within the bounds of form, and the eternal freedom of the soul in love. It is only in the light of love that all limits are merged in the limitless.

The sea beach of Karwar is certainly a fit place in which to realize that the beauty of Nature is not a mirage of the imagination, but reflects the joy of the Infinite and thus draws us to lose ourselves in it. Where the universe is expressing itself in the magic of its laws it may not be strange if we miss its infinitude; but where the heart gets into immediate touch with immensity in the beauty of the meanest of things, is any room left for argument?

Nature took the *sanyasi* to the presence of the Infinite, enthroned on the finite, by the pathway of the heart. In the *Nature's Revenge*, there were shown on the one side wayfarers and the villagers, content with their home-made triviality and unconscious of anything beyond; and on the other, the *sanyasi* busy casting away his all, and himself, into the self-evolved infinite of his imagination. When love bridged the gulf between

---

[3]Ibid., p. 238. Rabindranath had that song addressed to Yashoda, mother of Lord Krishna, by his playmates.

the two, and the hermit and the householder met, the seeming triviality of the finite and the seeming emptiness of the Infinite alike disappeared.

This was to put in a slightly different form the story of my own experience, of the entrancing ray of light which found its way into the depths of the cave into which I had retired, away from all touch with the outer world, and made me more fully one with Nature again . . .

Shortly after my return from Karwar, I was married. I was then twenty two-years of age.[4]

This was the time when my acquaintance with Bankim Babu[5] began. My first sight of him was a matter of long before. The old students of Calcutta University had then started an annual reunion, of which Babu Chandranath Basu[6] was the leading spirit. Perhaps he entertained a hope that at some future time I might acquire the right to be one of them; anyhow I was asked to read a poem on the occasion . . .

While wondering about in the crush at the Student's reunion, I suddenly came across a figure which at once struck me as distinguished beyond that of all the others and who could not have possibly been lost in any crowd. The features of that tall, fair personage shone with such a striking radiance that I could not contain my curiosity about him—he was the only one there whose name I felt concerned to know that day. When I learnt he was Bankim Babu I marvelled all the more, it seemed to me such a wonderful coincidence that his appearance should be as distinguished as his writings . . .

After that I often longed to see him, but could not get an opportunity. At last one day, when he was Deputy Magistrate of Howrah, I made bold to call on him. We met, and I tried my best to make conversation. But I somehow felt greatly abashed while returning home, as if I had acted like a raw and bumptious youth in thus thrusting myself upon him unasked and unintroduced.

[4]Ibid., pp. 236–39.
[5]Reference is to Bankim Chandra Chatterjee.
[6]Chandranath Basu (1854–1910), historian and Hindu revivalist.

Shortly after, as I added to my years, I attained a place as the youngest of the literary men of the time; but what was to be my position in order of merit was not even then settled. The reputation I had acquired was mixed with plenty of doubt and not a little of condescension. It was then the fashion in Bengal to assign each man of letters a place in comparison with a supposed compeer in the West. Thus, one was the Byron of Bengal, another the Emerson and so forth. I began to be styled by some the Bengal Shelley. This was insulting to Shelley and only likely to get me laughed at.

My recognized cognomen was the Lisping Poet. My attainments were few, my knowledge of life meagre, and both in my poetry and in my prose the sentiment exceeded the substance. So that there was nothing there on which anyone could have based his praise with any degree of confidence. My dress and behaviour were of the same anomalous description. I wore my hair long and indulged probably in an ultra-poetical refinement of manner. In a word, I was eccentric and could not fit myself into everyday life like the ordinary man.

From now I began constantly to meet Bankim Babu. He was then living in Bhabani Dutta Street. I used to visit him frequently, it is true, but there was not much of conversation. I was then of the age to listen, not to talk. I fervently wished we could warm up into some discussion, but my diffidence got the better of my conversation . . .

This was the time when Pandit Sashadhar[7] rose into prominence. Of him I first heard from Bankim Babu. If I remember right, Bankim Babu was also responsible for introducing him to the public. The curious attempt made by Hindu orthodoxy to revive its prestige with the help of Western science soon spread all over the country. Theosophy had for some time previously been preparing the ground for such a movement. Not that Bankim Babu ever thoroughly identified himself with this cult. No shadow of Sashadhar was cast on his exposition of Hinduism as it found expression in the *Prachar*[8]—that was impossible.

---

[7]Pandit Sashadhar Tarkachuramani (1851–1928), orthodox Brahmin scholar and Hindu revivalist.

[8]*Prachar* (1884–89), Bengali monthly, which published essays mainly on religion and social issues.

I was then coming out of the seclusion of my corner, as my contributions to these controversies will show. Some of these were satirical verses, some farcical plays, others letters to newspapers. I thus came down from the regions of sentiment and began to spar in right earnest.

In the heat of the fight, I happened to fall foul of Bankim Babu.[9]

It is often said that Bengalis are thinkers, not 'practical', as a people. I am using the English word 'practical', because that *is* the word in use among us. Why attempt a Bengali translation of the word and stick my neck out? In any case, when our people are asked what the word 'practical' means this is what they say: to be 'practical' is to think carefully and weigh the ends before the means, not emphasize high ideals too much, rather to trim the ideals to suit the ends. Just as pure gold has to be adulterated to make good jewellery, not to do so for the sake of the truth is to be 'sentimental'. Those who tell a few lies to get the work done *are* the 'practical' people.

If that is the meaning of the word practical, we Bengalis will not have much difficulty. We are discreet and cowardly by nature. That is why we cannot accomplish anything. We can hold down jobs but cannot get the work done.

In this class of people, the practical and the romantic are a different species. The practical ones have their eye on the results, the romantic get their rewards from doing the work itself. Anyone who loves to learn will always gain from learning. Those who are calculating about learning have so little faith in it that they do not reach the spreading branches; they have to stick out their arm to get at the fruit. But being too short they remain like dwarfs in the world of knowledge.

It is also those that have no faith that are calculating and prudent. Those who have innate faith are courageous and generous and enthusiastic. People start losing their trust as they grow old, and that is also when they refuse to do anything new and adventurous. They are afraid they will not obtain the desired results. This fear is absent in the

---

[9]*Reminiscences*, pp. 246–51.

young, that is why they get things done even when they do not benefit from it themselves.

I am not criticizing discretion or prudence, I am sure they have their uses. But what would it be like when everybody is being prudent or cautious? What is more, there are times when prudence is simply not acceptable. It is only in Bengal that this is a round-the-year phenomenon. Nowhere else. If a child was born cautious it would have remained a child forever. It could not have turned into a human being. Like birds, humans too take flight when their wings grow strong. They then have a large arena in which they can freely move. These are the people who are called 'sentimental' by the infirm—whereas those who have shed their wings, who walk by thrusting a walking stick into the mud with each step are regarded as the epitome of wisdom by the Chanakyas of our society . . .

Man's prime strength is in religion. Man's prime humanity is spiritual. The physical and material in man is dependent on time and space, but not so the spiritual—which is eternal. The realization that we are a part of the eternal, that we are not just scattered little beings, is what makes for spirituality. The individual who feels this from within cannot manipulate and deviate from his ideals. He considers his own interests trivial. He can never compromise with his ideals by finding loopholes to escape from his moral duties. He knows that it is not possible to cheat the eternal. The truth, the eternal, shall always be there. Lies are of man's own making. I can close my eyes and hinder the passage of truth into my life but I cannot turn truth into lies. In other words, I can cheat myself but I cannot cheat truth . . .

The strength of religion flows from the eternal spring; that is why it is not afraid of hindrances, defeat, or even death. Debating and arguing are limited to obtaining results, all argument ends with death. But not so religion.

Can a whole race get its strength only from arguing, generation after generation? A nation's thirst can hardly be quenched by a spring. Even that dries up in high heat. But it is different where there is a free-flowing river which quenches one's thirst, and where the air around it is healthy, because that river is tirelessly cleaning the air of the country's filth . . .

Religion is so vast that in it all races can coexist without polluting the air. Religion is like the endless sky; it can stay clean even with millions and millions of human beings, animals and birds, insects and worms breathing into it. All other things that we depend on shall turn unclean and poisonous with time, sooner or later.

That is why I am making the point that we must never hurt our humanity by compromising our larger ideal for an immediate gain. If we do that, things will turn completely impure before long . . .

Some people can exploit a loophole in the foundations of their society as a means to an end. Presenting themselves as 'practical' men they can put out the notion that even if it is generally bad to tell lies, it is all right to do so for a popular cause. For example, if the English can be insulted by telling a lie, it can be done in the name of a 'big' cause. The question is, which 'big' cause? There is something bigger than all 'big' causes. Teaching a people to take recourse to lies can result in political favours but teaching the truth will enable people to hold their heads high and gain inner strength without fail . . .

Am I reiterating these maxims unnecessarily? It is not my intention to overstate an old truth by repeating it. How shall I put it? Our greatest writer today has openly and unabashedly mixed truth and untruth to publicly deny the full truth while the entire country has stood by in silence. Everybody is busy arguing over the differences in the forms of worship, Brahmo and Hindu. They do not see how this debate can cause irredeemable harm to the foundations of religion. Nobody comes forward to back religion and uphold society. Nobody stops to think how weak must be the hold of religion over society for such an attack to be possible. If lying and cowardliness had not entered our veins, could our foremost writer have got away without the truth?[10]

Nowadays I keep repeating the line: 'Much rather would I be an Arab Bedouin!' A fine, healthy, strong, and free barbarity.

---

[10]Rabindranath Tagore, 'An Old Truth: To Bankim Babu', *Bankim Chandra*, Calcutta, Visva-Bharati, 1977, pp. 58–73. Translated by UDG.

I feel I want to quit this constant ageing of mind and body, with incessant argument and nicety concerning ancient decaying things, and to feel the joy of a free and vigorous life; to have—be they good or bad—broad, unhesitating, unfettered ideas and aspirations, free from everlasting friction between custom and sense, sense and desire, desire and action.

If only I could set utterly and boundlessly free this hampered life of mine, I would storm the four quarters and raise wave upon wave of tumult all around; I would career away madly, like a wild horse, for very joy of my own speed! But I am a Bengali, not a Bedouin! I go on sitting in my corner, and mope and worry and argue. I turn my mind now this way up, now the other—as a fish is fried—and the boiling oil blisters first this side, then that.

Let it pass. Since I cannot be thoroughly wild, it is but proper that I should make an endeavour to be thoroughly civil. Why foment a quarrel between the two?[11]

In the meantime, death made its appearance in our family. Before this I had never met Death face to face. When my mother died I was quite a child . . .

The acquaintance which I made with Death at the age of twenty-four was a permanent one, and its blow has continued to add itself to each succeeding bereavement in an ever-lengthening chain of tears. The lightness of infant life can skip aside from the greatest of calamities, but with age, evasion is not so easy, and the shock of that day I had to take full on my breast.

That there could be any gap in the unbroken procession of the joys and sorrows of life was a thing I had no idea of. I could therefore see nothing beyond, and this life I had accepted as all in all. When of a sudden death came, and in a moment made a gaping rent in its smooth-seeming

---

[11]Shelidah, 31 Jaishtha (12 June) 1892, *Glimpses of Bengal*, pp. 70-71.

fabric, I was utterly bewildered. All around, the trees, the soil, the water, the sun, the moon, the stars, remained as immovably true as before; and yet the person who was as truly there, who, through a thousand points of contact with life, mind and heart, was ever so much true for me, had vanished in a moment like dream. What perplexing self-contradiction it all seemed to me as I looked around! How was I ever to reconcile what remained with that which had gone?

The terrible darkness which was disclosed to me through this rent, continued to attract me night and day as time went on. I would ever and anon return to take my stand there and gaze upon it, wandering what there was left in place of what had gone. Emptiness is a thing man cannot bring himself to believe in; that which is *not*, is untrue; that which is untrue, is not. So our efforts to find something, where we see nothing, are unceasing.

Just as a young plant, surrounded by darkness, stretches itself, as it were on tiptoe, to find its way out into the light, so when death suddenly throws the darkness of negation round the soul, it tries and tries to rise into the light of affirmation. And what other sorrow is comparable to the state wherein darkness prevents the finding of a way out of the darkness?

And yet in the midst of this unbearable grief, flashes of joy seemed to sparkle in my mind, now and again, in a way which quite surprised me. That life was not a stable permanent fixture was itself the sorrowful tidings which helped to lighten my mind. That we were not prisoners for ever within a solid stone wall of life was the thought which unconsciously kept coming uppermost in rushes of gladness. That which I had held I was made to let go—this was the sense of loss which distressed me—but when at the same moment I viewed it from the standpoint of freedom gained, a great peace fell upon me.

The all-pervading pressure of worldly existence compensates itself by balancing life against death, and thus it does not crush us. The terrible weight of an unopposed life-force has not to be endured by man—this truth came upon me that day as a sudden, wonderful revelation.

With the loosening of the attraction of the world, the beauty of nature took on for me a deeper meaning. Death had given me the correct perspective from which to perceive the world in the fullness of its beauty, and as I saw the picture of the Universe against the background of death, I found it entrancing.[12]

At this time, I was attacked with a recrudescence of eccentricity in thought and behaviour. To be called upon to submit to the customs and fashions of the day, as if they were something soberly and genuinely real, made me want to laugh. I *could* not take them seriously. The burden of stopping to consider what other people might think of me was completely lifted off my mind. I have been about in fashionable bookshops with a coarse sheet draped round me as my only upper garment, and a pair of slippers on my bare feet. Through hot and cold and wet I used to sleep out on the veranda of the third storey. There the stars and I could gaze at each other, and no time was lost in greeting the dawn.

This phase had nothing to do with any ascetic feeling. It was more like a holiday spree as the result of discovering the schoolmaster Life with his cane to be a myth, and thereby being able to shake myself free from the petty rules of his school. If, on waking one fine morning, we were to find gravitation reduced to only a fraction of itself, would we still demurely walk along the high road? Would we not skip over many-storied houses for a change, or on encountering the monument take a flying jump, rather than trouble to walk round it? That was why, with the weight of worldly life no longer clogging my feet, I could not stick to the unusual course of convention.

Alone on the terrace in the darkness of night I groped all over like a blind man trying to find upon the black stone gate of death some device or sign. Then when I woke with the morning light falling on that unscreened bed of mine, I felt, as I opened my eyes, that my enveloping haze was becoming transparent; and, as on the clearing of the mist the hills and

---

[12]*Reminiscences*, pp. 257–60.

rivers and forests of the scene shine forth, so the dew-washed picture of the world-life, spread out before me, seemed to become renewed and ever so beautiful.[13]

I am very pained by your letter. When I was your age I had suffered an intense bereavement just like you are suffering today. A very close relative of mine, on whom I was very dependent from my early years, committed suicide. With her death it felt as though the earth had moved away from under my feet and the light had gone out from the sky. My world felt empty and my life dull. I never imagined I would ever get over the delusion of this void. But that tremendous pain set me free for the very first time. I realized gradually that life must be seen through the window of death in order to reach the truth.[14]

'Nishphal Kamona' (Desire for a Human Soul)

> All fruitless is the cry,
> All vain this burning fire of desire.
> The sun goes down to his rest.
> There is gloom in the forest and glamour
>   in the sky.
> With downcast look and lingering steps
> The evening star comes in the wake
>   of departing day
> And the breath of the twilight is deep with
>   the fullness of a farewell feeling.

---

[13]Ibid., pp. 246–61.

[14]Rabindranath to Amiya Chakravarty, 8 Ashar 1324 (22 June 1917), *Chitthi Patra*, Volume XI, Calcutta: Visva-Bharati, 1974, p. 8. (Hereafter, *Chitthi Patra* XI.) Translated by UDG. Amiya Chakravarty (1901–87), modern Bengali poet. Though Rabindranath says 'when I was your age', when referring to Kadambari's death, he was in fact twenty-four at the time. Amiya Chakravarty was seventeen years old when Rabindranath wrote this letter.

I clasp both thine hands in mine,
And keep thine eyes prisoner with my
        hungry eyes;
Seeking and crying, Where art thou,
Where, O, where!
Where is the immortal flame hidden in the
        depth of thee![15]

---

[15]*Poems*, no. 3, p. 15. Bengali original 'Nishphal Kamona', 1887, *Manasi*, 1890.

9

ON THE THRESHOLD OF THIRTY

Around 1890, Rabindranath was asked by his father to take charge of the family's zamindari in East Bengal and Orissa. He therefore came to be stationed at the headquarters in Shelidah for about ten years. Shelidah was situated on the mighty river Padma, a local name for the Ganga. Rabindranath had been to Shelidah earlier, but as a very young boy, when accompanying his brother Jyotirindranath who had been the previous manager.[1] But it was a different experience when he came to the countryside as a mature young man. He wrote, ' A little later, when I was more mature, it was in Shelidah that my nature developed.' *Chhinnapatra*,[2] or the series of letters that he wrote from there mainly to his niece Indira Devi, his brother Satyendranath's daughter, bear testimony to the sensibilities he developed at the time. Recalling how he felt, he wrote, 'My work as zamindar took me on long distances from one village to another, from Shelidah to Patisar, by large and small rivers, and across *beels*.[3] In this way, I saw all aspects of village life and felt a great keenness to understand the daily routine and varied pageant of their lives ... Slowly but surely I began to understand the sorrow and the poverty of the villagers and I grew restless to do something about it. I began to feel ashamed of spending my days simply as a landlord, concerned only with my own profit and loss. So I began to think about what could be done. I did not think helping from outside would help. I began to try and open their minds towards self-reliance.'[4]

---

[1] *Boyhood Days*, pp. 66–70.

[2] The letters collected as *Chhinnapatra* (1912) were written from 1890 to 1895.

[3] A beel is an inlet of the river, like a bay.

[4] Rabindranath Tagore, An Address to Village Workers, Bengali Year 1326 (1919), *Palli Prakriti*, Reprint, Calcutta: Visva-Bharati, 1962, pp. 98-99. Translated by UDG. (Hereafter, *Palli Prakriti*.)

> Marching with the waves of Life Eternal
> we must go forward with Truth as our Polar Star
> and no thought of death.
> Inclement evil days will pour upon our heads,
> but we must struggle on
> to keep our Tryst with Him
> at whose feet we poured the riches of our heart
> from age to age.[5]

When I grew older I was employed in a responsible work in some villages. I took my place in a neighbourhood where the current of time ran slow and joys and sorrows had their simple and elemental shades and lights. The day which had its special significance for me came with all its drifting trivialities of the commonplace life. The ordinary work of my morning had come to its close, and before going to take my bath I stood for a moment at my window, overlooking a marketplace on the bank of a dry river bed, welcoming the first flood of rain along its channel. Suddenly I became conscious of a stirring of soul within me. My world of experience seemed to become lighted, and facts that were detached and dim found a great unity of meaning. The feeling which I had was like that which a man, groping through a fog without knowing his destination, might feel when he suddenly discovers that he stands before his house . . .

In a similar manner, on that morning in the village, the facts of my life suddenly appeared to me in a luminous unity of truth. All things that had seemed like vagrant waves were revealed to my mind in relation to a boundless sea. I felt sure that some Being who comprehended me and my world was seeking his best expression in all my experiences, uniting them into an ever-widening individuality which is a spiritual work of art. To this Being I was responsible; for the creation in me is his as well as mine . . .

---

[5]Poem 'Ebar Phirao Morey', in English translation 'Call Me Back To Work', *Visva-Bharati News*, July 1939, p. 3. Bengali original 'Ebar Phirao Morey', *Chitra*, 1896.

I felt that I had found my religion at last, the Religion of Man, in which the infinite became defined in humanity and came close to me so as to need my love and cooperation.[6]

I am preoccupied with the problems of our village society. I have made up my mind to provide an example of rural reconstruction work in our own zamindari. A few boys from East Bengal have volunteered for the purpose. They are living in the villages and trying to inspire the villagers to organize their own education and sanitation, take measures for the settlement of disputes, etc. The workers have already initiated public works such as the repair of roads and paths, excavation of tanks, cutting of drains and clearing of jungles. A deep despair pervades rural life all over the country. That is why high-sounding phrases like home rule, autonomy, etc., appear ridiculous to me. I feel embarrassed to utter them.[7]

Living in the villages of Shelidah and Patisar, I had made my first direct contact with rural life. Zamindari was then my calling. The tenants came to me with their joys and sorrows, complaints and requests, through which the village discovered itself to me. On the one hand was the external scene of rivers, meadows, rice fields, and mud huts sheltering under trees. On the other was the inner story of the people. I came to understand their troubles in the course of my duties.

I am an urban creature, cityborn. My forefathers were among the earliest inhabitants of Calcutta and my childhood years felt no touch of the village. When I started to look after our estates, I feared that my duties would be irksome. I was not used to such work—keeping accounts, collecting revenue, credit and debit—and my ignorance lay heavy on my mind. I could not imagine that, tied down to figures and accounts, I might yet remain human and natural.

---

[6]*Religion of Man*, pp. 94–96.

[7]Rabindranath to Abala Bose, undated, probably 1905-06, *Prabasi*, Bengali Year 1345 (1938), p. 466. Translated by UDG.

As I entered into the work it took hold of me. It is my nature that whenever I undertake any responsibility I lose myself in it and try to do my utmost. When I once had to teach, I put my whole heart into it and it was a great pleasure. Setting myself to unravel the complexities of zamindari work, I earned a reputation for the new methods I evolved; as a matter of fact, neighbouring landlords began to send their men to me to learn my methods.

The old men on my staff got alarmed. They used to maintain records in a way that I could never have grasped. Their idea was that I should understand nothing more than what they chose to explain. A change of method would create confusion, so they said. They pointed out that, when it came to litigation, the court would be doubtful about the new way the records were kept. I persisted, though, changing things from top to bottom, and the result proved to be satisfactory.

The tenants often came to see me—for them my door was always open, day and night. Sometimes I had to spend the whole day listening to their representations, and mealtimes would slip by. I did all this work with enthusiasm and joy. I had lived in seclusion since boyhood and here was my first experience of the village. I was satisfied and heartened and filled with the pleasure of blazing new trails.[8]

The magistrate was sitting in the veranda of his tent dispensing justice to the crowd awaiting their turns under the shade of a tree. They set my palanquin down right under his nose, and the young Englishman received me courteously. He had very light hair, with darker patches here and there, and a moustache just beginning to show. One might have taken him for a white-haired old man but for his extremely youthful face. I asked him over to dinner, but he said he was due elsewhere to arrange for a pig-sticking party.

As I returned home, great black clouds came up and there was a terrific storm with torrents of rain. I could not touch a book, it was impossible

---

[8]'City and Village', *Towards Universal Man*, pp. 317-18.

to write, so in the I-know-not-what mood I wandered about from room to room. It had become quite dark, the thunder was continually pealing, the lightning gleaning flash after flash, and every now and then sudden gusts of wind would get hold of the great *lichi*[9] tree by the neck and give its shaggy top a thorough shaking. The hollow in front of the house soon filled with water, and as I paced about, it suddenly struck me that I ought to offer the shelter of the house to the magistrate.

I sent off an invitation; then after investigation I found the only spare room encumbered with a platform of planks hanging from the beams, piled with dirty old quilts and bolsters. Servants' belongings, an excessively grimy mat, hubble-bubble pipes, tobacco, tinder, and two wooden chests littered the floor, besides sundry packing-cases full of useless odds and ends, such as a rusty kettle lid, a bottomless iron stove, a discoloured old nickel teapot, a soup-plate full of treacle blackened with dust. In a corner was a tub for washing dishes, and from nails in the wall hung moist dish-cloths and the cook's livery and skull-cap. The only piece of furniture was a rickety dressing-table with water stains, oil stains, milk stains, black, brown and white stains, and all kinds of mixed stains. The mirror, detached from it, rested against another wall, and the drawers were receptacles for a miscellaneous assortment of articles from soiled napkins down to bottle wires and dust.

For a while I was overwhelmed with dismay; then it was a case of send for the manager, send for the storekeeper, call up all the servants, get hold of extra men, fetch water, put up ladders, unfasten ropes, pull down planks, take away bedding, pick up broken glass bit by bit, wrench nails from the wall one by one—the chandelier falls and its pieces strew the floor and out of the window, dislodging a horde of cockroaches, messmates, who dine off my bread, my treacle, and the polish on my shoes.

The magistrate's reply is brought back; his tent is in an awful state and he is coming up at once. Hurry up! Hurry up! Presently comes the shout: 'The sahib has arrived.' All in a flurry I brush the dust off my hair, beard, and the rest of myself, and as I go to receive him in the drawing

---

[9]A seasonal Indian fruit.

room, I try to look as respectable as if I had been reposing there comfortably all the afternoon.

I went through the shaking of hands and conversed with the magistrate outwardly serene; still, misgivings about his accommodation would now and then well up within. When at length I had to show my guest to his room, I found it passable, and if the homeless cockroaches do not tickle the soles of his feet, he may manage to get a night's rest.[10]

Yesterday, while I was giving audience to my tenants, five or six boys made their appearance and stood in a primly proper row before me. Before I could put any question, their spokesman, in the choicest of high-flown language, started: 'Sire! The grace of the Almighty and the good fortune of your benighted children have once more brought about your lordship's auspicious arrival into this locality.' He went on in this strain for nearly half an hour. Here and there he would get his lesson wrong, pause, look up at the sky, correct himself, and then go on again. I gathered that their school was short of benches and stools. 'For want of these wood-built seats,' as he put it, 'we know not where to sit ourselves, where to seat our revered teachers, or what to offer our most respected inspector when he comes on a visit.'

I could hardly repress a smile at this torrent of eloquence gushing from such a bit of a fellow, which sounded specially out of place here, where the *ryots* are given to stating their profoundly vital wants in plain and direct vernacular, of which even the more unusual words get sadly twisted out of shape. The clerks and *ryots*, however, seemed duly impressed, and likewise envious, as though deploring their parents' omission to endow them with so splendid a means of appealing to the zamindar.

I interrupted the young orator before he had done, promising to arrange for the necessary number of benches and stools. Nothing daunted, he allowed me to have my say, then took up his discourse where he had left it, finished it to the last word, saluted me profoundly, and marched off his

---

[10]Shazadpur, 1890, *Glimpses of Bengal*, pp. 5–9.

contingent. He probably would not have minded had I refused to supply the seats, but after all his trouble in getting it by heart he would have resented bitterly being robbed of any part of his speech. So, though it kept more important business waiting, I had to hear him out.[11]

The schoolmasters of this place paid me a visit yesterday.

They stayed on and on, while for the life of me I could not find a word to say. I managed a question or so every five minutes, to which they offered the briefest replies; and then I sat vacantly, twirling my pen, and scratching my head.

At last I ventured on a question about the crops, but being schoolmasters they knew nothing whatever about crops.

About their pupils I had already asked them everything I could think of, so I had to start over again: How many boys had they in the school? One said eighty, another said a hundred and seventy-five. I hoped this might lead to an argument, but no, they made up their difference.

Why, after an hour and a half, they should have thought of taking leave, I cannot tell. They might have done so with as good a reason an hour earlier, or, for the matter of that, twelve hours later! Their decision was clearly arrived at empirically, entirely without method.[12]

I feel a great tenderness for these peasant folk—our *ryots*—big, helpless, infantile children of Providence, who must have food brought to their very lips, or they are undone. When the breasts of Mother Earth dry up they are at a loss what to do, and can only cry. But no sooner is their hunger satisfied than they forget all their past sufferings.

I know not whether the socialistic ideal of a more equal distribution of wealth is unattainable, but if not, the dispensation of Providence is indeed cruel, and man a truly unfortunate creature. For if in this world

---

[11]Kaligram, 1891, Ibid., pp. 12–14.

[12]Shazadpur, June 1891, Ibid., pp. 36-37.

misery must exist, so be it; but let some little loophole, some glimpse of possibility at least, be left, which may serve to urge the nobler portion of humanity to hope and struggle unceasingly for its alleviation.

They say a terribly hard thing who assert that the division of the world's production to afford each one a mouthful of food, a bit of clothing, is only an Utopian dream. All these social problems are hard indeed! Fate has allowed humanity such a pitifully meagre coverlet that in pulling it over one part of the world, another has to be left bare. In allaying our poverty we lose our wealth, and with this wealth what a world of grace and beauty and power is lost to us.[13]

There is another pleasure for me here. Sometimes one or other of our simple, devoted old *ryots* comes to see me—and their worshipful homage is so unaffected! How much greater than I are they in the beautiful simplicity and sincerity of their reverence. What if I am unworthy of their veneration—their feeling loses nothing of its value.

I regard these grown-up children with the same kind of affection that I have for little children—but there is also a difference. They are more infantile still. Little children will grow up later on, but these big children never.

A meek and radiantly simple soul shines through their worn and wrinkled old bodies. Little children are merely simple, they have not the unquestioning, unwavering devotion of these. If there be any undercurrent along which the soul of men may have communication with one another, then my sincere blessing will surely reach and serve them.[14]

All last night the wind howled like a stray dog, and the rain still pours on without a break. The water from the fields is rushing in numberless, purling streams to the river. The dripping *ryots* are crossing the river in the ferry-

[13]Shelidah, 10 May 1893, Ibid., pp. 102-03.
[14]Shelidah, 11 May 1893, Ibid., pp. 104-05.

boat, some with their *tokas*[15] on, others with yam leaves over their heads. Big cargo-boats are gliding along, the boatmen sitting drenched at the helm, the crew straining at the tow-ropes through the rain. The birds remain gloomily confined to their nests, but the sons of men fare forth, for in spite of the weather the world's work must go on.

The river is rising daily. What I could see yesterday only from the upper deck, I can now see from my cabin windows. Every morning I awake to find my field of vision growing larger. Not long since, only the tree-tops near those distant villages used to appear, like dark green clouds. Today the whole of the wood is visible.

Land and water are gradually approaching each other like two bashful lovers. The limit of their shyness has nearly been reached—their arms will soon be round each other's necks. I am fidgeting to give the order to cast off.[16]

A little gleam of light shows this morning. There was a break in the rains yesterday, but the clouds are banked up so heavily along the skirts of the sky that there is not much hope of the break lasting. It looks as if a heavy carpet of cloud has been rolled up to one side, and at any moment a fuzzy breeze may come along and spread it over the whole place again, covering every trace of blue sky and golden sunshine.

What a store of water must have been laid up in the sky this year. The river has already risen over the low *char*-lands,[17] threatening to overwhelm all the standing crops. The wretched *ryots*, in despair, are cutting and bringing away in boats sheaves of half-ripe rice. As they pass my boat, I hear them bewailing their fate. It is easy to understand how heart-rending it must be for cultivators to have to cut down their rice on the very eve of its ripening, the only hope left them being that some of the ears may possibly have hardened into grain.

---

[15]Head covers made with a particular kind of straw.

[16]Shelidah, 3 July 1893, *Glimpses of Bengal*, pp. 107–09.

[17]Char-lands are old sandbanks consolidated by the deposit of a layer of cultivable soil.

There must be some element of pity in the dispensations of Providence, else how did we get our share of it? But it is so difficult to see where it comes in. The lamentations of these hundreds of thousands of unoffending creatures do not seem to get anywhere. The rain pours on as it lists, the river still rises, and no amount of petitioning seems to have the effect of bringing relief from any quarter. One has to seek consolation by saying that all this is beyond the understanding of man. And yet, it is so vitally necessary for man to understand that there are such things as pity and justice in the world.

However, this is only sulking. Reason tells us that creation never can be perfectly happy. So long as it is incomplete it must put up with imperfection and sorrow. It can only be perfect if it ceases to be creation, and is God. Do our prayers dare go so far?

The more we think over it, the oftener we come back to the starting point—Why this creation at all? If we cannot make up our minds to object to the thing itself, it is futile complaining about its companion, sorrow.[18]

To try to help villagers from outside could do no good. How to kindle a spark of life in them—that was my problem. It was so difficult to help them because they did not have much respect for themselves. 'We are curs,' they would say, 'only the whip can keep us straight.'

One day, a fire broke out in a village nearby. The people were so utterly dazed that they could do nothing. Then the men from a neighbouring Muslim village came rushing and fought the fire. There was no water and thatched roofs had to be pulled down to stifle the flames. The stricken ones had to be beaten up before they would let this be done. You have to use force in order to do good! And they came to me saying, 'What luck that our roofs were dismantled—that is how we have been saved.' They were happy that the beating benefited them; but I was filled with shame by their submissiveness.

I planned to put up a small building for them at the centre of the

---

[18]Shelidah, 4 July 1893, *Glimpses of Bengal*, pp. 109–12.

village, where at the day's end they could get together, read newspapers, listen to the Ramayana and Mahabharata—it would be a sort of club. For, I had been unhappy, thinking of their cheerless evenings; it was as if the same tedious line of verse was being endlessly sung. In course of time the building was erected. But, then, it was never used. I engaged a teacher, but the pupils kept away with all kinds of excuses.

In contrast, the Muslims from the other village came to me and said, 'Will you give us a teacher? We are ready to bear the expense.' I agreed and a school was set up in the village . . . In my village, nothing could be done, its inhabitants had lost all faith in themselves.

The habit of dependence has come down to us from time immemorial. In the olden days, one rich man used to be the mainstay of the village and its guide. Health, education and all else were his responsibility. I have praised that system, but it is also true that because of it the common man's capacity for self-reliance was enfeebled.

In my estate, the river was far away and lack of water was a serious problem. I said to my tenants, 'If you dig a well, I shall get it cemented.' They replied, 'You want to fry the fish in the oil of the fish itself! If we dig the well you shall go to heaven through the accumulated virtue of having provided water for the thirsty, while we shall have done the work.' The idea, obviously, was that an account of all such deeds was kept in heaven and while I, having earned great merit, could go to the seventh heaven, the village people would simply get some water. I had to withdraw my proposal.

Let me give another example. I had built a road from our estate office up to Kushtia. I told the villagers who lived close to the road, 'The upkeep of this road is your responsibility. You can easily get together and repair the ruts.' It was, in fact, their ox-cart wheels that damaged the road and put it out of use during the rains. They replied, 'Must we look after the road so that gentlefolk from Kushtia can come and go with ease?' They could not bear the thought that others should also enjoy the fruits of their labour. Rather than let that happen, they would put up with inconveniences.

The poor in our villages have borne many insults, the powerful have done many wrongs. On the other hand, the powerful have had to do all the welfare work. Caught between tyranny and charity, the village people have been emptied of self-respect. They ascribe their miseries to sins committed in previous births, and believe that, to have a better life, they must be reborn with a greater fund of merit. The conviction that there is no escape from suffering makes them helpless.[19]

---

[19]'City and Village', *Towards Universal Man*, pp. 318–20.

10

MY WIFE AND CHILDREN

Rabindranath's young family was at the centre of his life. He was deeply upset to leave them in order to go to England in August 1890. A letter that he wrote to his wife from the ship says it all. 'On Sunday night I felt my spirit leave the body to come and see you . . . I shall ask you when I return from my travels if you saw me too.'[1] His eldest daughter Madhurilata, nicknamed Bela, was four years old at the time, and his eldest son Rathi was two. He speedily returned home from England in November 1890. But he could not take his family with him when he first went to live in Shelidah on zamindari work. Their house was not yet built. He lived in the old family houseboat called the *Padma-boat*. He moved his wife and children to Sholapur in Maharashtra where Satyendranath was posted at that time. He wrote very frequently to his wife and, as his letters show, he waited anxiously and longingly for her reply. His letters tell us how closely he communicated with her, how much he wanted his family near him. The concerns he was sharing were about their togetherness, her happiness, his life, their children's future, and the marriages of their daughters. He explains in the letters why he got them married early, thus conforming to the social expectation of those times. Reasoning how different they were as a family, he was anxious for the girls to integrate with their husbands' homes as painlessly as possible when young. Both Bela and his second daughter Renuka, or Rani, were married in 1901 when they were fourteen and twelve years old, respectively. He worried especially about Rani's ability to make the transition, he wrote.[2]

---

[1]Rabindranath to Mrinalini Devi, 29 August 1890, *Chitthi Patra*, Volume I, Reprint, Calcutta: Visva-Bharati, 1966, p. 11. Translated by UDG. (Hereafter, *Chitthi Patra* I.)

[2]Rabindranath to Mrinalini Devi, 20 July 1901, Ibid., pp. 67–69.

Rabindranath and Mrinalini Devi at the
time of their marriage

Mrinalini Devi

Birds build their nests with straw. It matters little to them to leave
their homes and go. But we build ours with our minds. That becomes
an invisible shelter in all that we do, in our work, our reading and
writing, our thinking. Just as a cart makes grooves on its journey
which we can feel in the swaying of our bodies, a mind involuntarily
settles into the grooves it makes with the mind's eye. And we don't
want to get out of them even when there is occasion for it.[3]

Your letter was prompted by my scolding, wasn't it? Just shows. This is
not the age for being gentle! Pleading gets me nothing, but scolding
certainly does . . .

All morning I had lawyers and teachers with me. That is why I could
not open your letter till they were gone. I am trying to get my books
included in the school lists. This is now in progress. But do you know
where the books are? They have not yet reached me. I gave away my copy
of *Rajarshi* to the inspector of schools. I also gave him Nawdidi's[4]
Galpasalpa. I even gave him some homeopathic pills for his bad throat.
He should be pleased with that even if his throat does not improve. See
what I am doing to earn a bit more! I have sat down to write from early
in the morning. Even if it does not pay for the printing cost it will at least
leave me with ten to twelve rupees more. This is the only way to make
money. All *you* know is how to spend money—but can you earn even a
single paisa?

My sahib will turn up day after tomorrow. So will my memsahib. They
might come to dine with me, but they might not. He might say, 'Babu, I
have no time.' But he might be tempted by the food.

I feel very restless at times when my mind turns to Beli and Khoka.[5]
Give Beli a couple of 'odd' on my behalf. I am sure she does not get

---

[3]Rabindranath Tagore, Ms. Accession no. 23, in Bengali, p. 16. (RBA.) Translated by
UDG.

[4]Refers to Rabindranath's fourth sister Swarnakumari Devi (1885–1932).

[5]Beli is an affectionate derivative of Bela, and Khoka is the common Bengali address for
the boy-child of the family. Here, it is used as an affectionate reference to his son Rathi.

to eat many things when I am not around. Do also remember me to Khoka . . .[6]

We shall be at a place called Aden today. But we shall not be able to land there for fear of catching infectious diseases. We shall have to change ships at Aden. This time I have been quite seasick. My nausea was such that I could not eat a thing for three days. I was also very dizzy and could not get out of bed. I don't know how I survived.

On Sunday night, I felt my spirit leave my body to come and see you. I saw you sleeping on one side of the large bed, next to you were Beli and Khoka. I caressed you and whispered in your ears, '*Chhoto-bou*,[7] please remember that on this Sunday night I left my body to come and see you. I shall ask you on my return from England if you saw me too.' Then I kissed Beli and the baby, and returned.

Did you think of me when I was ill on the ship? I was dying to return home to you. These days I am convinced there is no place like home. I am not going anywhere after I get back from this trip. I have taken a bath today after a whole week. It is no fun to bathe in salty water. One's hair gets all knotted and the body feels sticky. I have decided not to bathe again till I leave the ship.

We have one more week to reach Europe. It will be such a relief to be on land again. I am tired of being on the sea day and night. However, the sea is now calm and I am no longer sick. I lie on a deckchair on the ship's deck all day long, talking to Loken[8] or at times just reading or thinking. I hardly stay in my cabin, it feels so uncomfortable. I lie out on the deck even in the night. Last night it rained a lot—I had to move my bed to stay out of the rain. It has rained ever since but now the sun is out.

---

[6]Rabindranath to Mrinalini Devi, January 1890, Shazadpur, *Chitthi Patra* I, pp. 9-10. Translated by UDG. 'Odd' must have been a kind of candy of those times.

[7]Meaning 'my little wife'; also an address for the youngest bride in the family in Bengali households.

[8]Loken Palit (1865–1915), member of the Indian Civil Service (1886) and close friend of Rabindranath.

There are a couple of small girls in our ship whose mother is no more. They are going to England with their father. My heart goes out to them. Their father watches over them closely—they don't know how to look after themselves. They dash out into the rain and if their father asks them not to, they insist they like it in the rain. Their father smiles. I guess he feels sad to deprive them of their fun. They remind me of our children. I saw Beli in a dream last night. I saw that she is on the ship, looking splendid. What shall I bring them from England? If you answer this letter as soon as it reaches you I might get it before I leave. Don't forget the post to England leaves on Tuesdays. Kiss the children for me, will you?[9]

I wrote to you day before yesterday, I am writing again today. You may get both these letters on the same day, what is the harm? We shall be landing tomorrow—all the more reason for writing to you today. I will be able to write again on reaching England. In case there is a slight delay in my writing to you over all this movement, please don't be upset. It is not difficult to write from the ship—but once we have landed it is not always predictable where we shall be. There may be a day or two when I may not be able to write. We shall be in Europe from tomorrow.

We can at times see Europe's coast at a distance. There is Greece on our left and an island on our right as our ship goes down the middle. The island seems very close to us—there are hills and houses and a large town somewhere—I can see the houses quite clearly through the binoculars. The town looks rather nice with its white houses in the middle of the blue hills. Do you not wish to see all this, chhoto-bou? One day you must come too. Are you feeling happy to think of that day? What you see will be beyond your dreams.

It has been a bit chilly over the last two days, but not much. It feels a little cold if I sit out on the deck when there's a strong wind. I have started to wear light woollens. I do not sleep out on the deck these

---

[9]Rabindranath to Mrinalini Devi, 29 August 1890, on board the SS *Shyam*, *Chitthi Patra* I, pp. 11-12. Translated by UDG.

Rabindranath and Mrinalini Devi with baby
Rathi, 1888

From left to right: Mira, Rathindranath, Rabindranath, Protima Devi (daughter-
in-law) and Bela

days. Loken has got a swollen tooth from sleeping out. We shall get a lot of cold weather now—like it is in Darjeeling. It will get colder by the time we leave.

I have sent some clothes for you and some quilts with mejo-bouthan. Have you got them? If you haven't, do ask for them. I have also sent a sari and a border for Beli with mejo-bouthan—a bright red sari. I think Beli-buri[10] will look nice in it—the border is quite an unusual one, is it not? Mejo-bouthan also has a sari for Beli, a blue and white one. That should suit Beli and also Rani. I hope Rani likes it—the fusspot that she is. Does she ever ask about me? Who knows how grown Khoka will be when I see him on my return. By then he may have started to say a few words. I am sure he will not recognize me. I may turn into such a sahib that none of you may recognize me.

Remember that cut on my finger? It has left two gaping holes—it was a really bad cut. I took a bath yesterday and also the day before after not being able to for some time. I shall have to arrange to take a bath after arriving in Paris day after tomorrow. That will be a Turkish bath—which is a good way to get clean. You may have read about it in my *Europe Prabasir Patra*. If I find the time I shall take a bath there. I am feeling quite well. There is so much food served on the ship that I may have put on some weight. I hope to see you looking well and fat when I am back, chhoto-bou. The car is now with you, I hope you go out in it every day. Don't just lend it to others. Last night there was a drama on board our ship—there are quite a few fun things happening. Tonight is our last night here.[11]

It has just been one month since I came to stay here. I have found that I can barely manage a month away from home, and that too only if I have plenty to do. I long to return home after that.

There was a storm here last night. I could not sleep for a long time with the noise of the howling winds. You may also have got this storm. It

---

[10]Beli-buri or 'little-old Beli' was Rabindranath's affectionate reference to his daughter Bela.

[11]Rabindranath to Mrinalini Devi, 6 September 1890, on board the SS *Masilia*, *Chitthi Patra* I, pp. 13–15. Translated by UDG.

rained a lot yesterday. The waters have risen considerably. The mustard fields are all submerged. One foot more and the same would happen to our garden . . .

Please tell me if you are taking a walk on the roof twice daily. And tell me also if you are able to do the other things required for your health. But I rather suspect you are just comfortably stretched out on an armchair with a novel. Have your headaches gone?[12]

I got your letter just as I was leaving Shelidah this morning. It made me sad. But the thought of your returning to Calcutta cheered me up. Otherwise, I would not have come to Calcutta now. I am not feeling too well either and wishing that you were with me. I was sure in my mind that it would be for the best that all of you stay in Sholapur for as long as possible. I had hoped that the children would study well there and grow up healthy. Anyway, not everything can be in one's control. We have to make do with what comes our way and dutifully do the best we can under those circumstances. That is all that is humanly possible.

Please don't nurse any discontent within yourself, chhoto-bou; that does more harm than good. Let us just carry on resolutely with contentment and a smile. With my brooding temperament I know that I suffer unnecessarily. I want you to stay happy, otherwise our prospect looks bleak. You know, my dear, how intense I am by nature. But you don't know how hard I work to keep calm. Please help me overcome my discontent, and please never join me in it.

If you are already on your way, I shall see you when I am in Calcutta this time. I shall try to arrange for you to come with me to Orissa. It is a very healthy place. I have already told father what I want to do, I think he understands. I may get my way if I talk to him once or twice more—still it is best not to raise our hopes. I have a feeling this letter may reach you while you are still in Sholapur. It may be eight or ten days more before you can start. Let's see.

---

[12]Rabindranath to Mrinalini Devi, Shazadpur, 1891, Ibid., p. 19. Translated by UDG.

My boat is slowly moving along the whole day. It is already evening but we have not yet made it to Pabna. Once we are there we shall have to go on for many more miles by palanquin.[13]

Yesterday, I received from Dickinson's a bill for Rs 182, together with a reminder for payment. I shall have to borrow from Satya[14] again. I shall then owe him nine hundred rupees. Has he given you four hundred rupees? He has not written to me about it yet. There is news of you in Bibi's[15] letter today. She writes that you often visit them—that our little one makes all kinds of gestures and sounds in mejo-bouthan's lap. I so long to see her. She will have changed a lot if I spend the whole month of *ashar*[16] in the country. Is Khoka also learning to sing along with Beli? Is his voice shaping well? He should be taught not just the *sa re ga ma* for voice training but also a song as a start. Otherwise he will soon lose interest. When I was a boy I disliked being taught *sa re ga ma* by Bishnu. I used to be so happy on the days he taught me a song. Why don't you also learn singing with the children? You and I can sit together on a rainy day and talk of music when I am back home. What do you feel?[17]

You know from my letter to Bela that I was not able to come today. I have stayed home. The post arrived, there were three letters but none from you. I did not expect one but wondered if by divine chance you could have written one by mistake! The joy of living separately is in writing letters to one another. It *can* be more rewarding than being together. When we write letters we can come closer to each other with only a few words, and get as much of each other as possible by way of those few words. What we

---

[13]Rabindranath to Mrinalini Devi, Shelidah, 1892, Ibid., pp. 28-29. Translated by UDG.

[14]Reference is to Satyaprasad Ganguly, Rabindranath's nephew, who was a finance manager of sorts for the Jorasanko household.

[15]His niece Indira or Indira Devi Chaudhurani.

[16]The Bengali month corresponding to mid-June to mid-July.

[17]Rabindranath to Mrinalini Devi, Shelidah, June–July 1893, *Chitthi Patra* I, pp. 32-33. Translated by UDG.

say to each other when we meet can fade away in the instant excitement of meeting each other. Really and truly, writing letters can become a deeper and more intimate experience of knowing ourselves than just seeing each other. Don't you agree?[18]

I do constantly try not to worry about our children. It is our duty to see to it that they are well behaved and that they get a good education. Beyond that it is a mistake to dwell on them. They will grow up to do their life's work in their own way be it good, bad, or indifferent. It is, of course, true they are *our* children, but they are also individuals in their own right. We will not have much control over the way they live their lives. Let us do our duty by them but let us not expect too much from them. It is in God's hands how they turn out as human beings. It is from a certain vanity that we expect the best from our own progeny. We have no right to do that. After all, are we all that concerned about other children who have hard lives?

The future is uncertain no matter how we live. Therefore, it is only sensible that we should simply do our duty and not think of the outcome. We have to forever learn to take both good and bad—and we must restrain ourselves every time there is an urge to deviate from that path. We have to understand that we do not belong only to this life of ours. We have our past, and we can have no prior knowledge about our future. Therefore, all that is possible is to do our work diligently, wherever we are and whatever the work is. We must also try to be happy and make others happy. If after that we fail it should not matter to us. We must accept and remember that the results are in God's hands once we have done our part. We must at least try to free our minds from expectations.[19]

I am so delighted to get all of two letters from you today. Unfortunately, I am unable to respond . . . because I must go to Bolpur today. I have

[18]Rabindranath to Mrinalini Devi, 1899, Ibid., p. 41. Translated by UDG.

[19]Rabindranath to Mrinalini Devi, Calcutta, December 1900, Ibid., pp. 43-44. Translated by UDG.

read out to father my address for the *Seventh of Pous* celebrations.[20] He has asked me to expand it a bit here and there. I have to get down to that now. There is only an hour left to finish it.

Please don't work any harder for my happiness. Your love is enough. But it would be very nice if you and I could work together and think together with one mind. I know that cannot always happen even if we wish it. It will make me happy if you could join me in all that I do—and give me much joy if you agree to learn what I want to learn . . . It is easier to move forward if we are as united. I don't wish to leave you out of anything I do, but I hesitate to thrust my will on you. Everyone has the right to do things their way, as they would like to. It may not be possible for you to agree with my wishes and inclinations every time—I would not worry about it. It is good enough if you spare me sadness wherever possible, and sweeten my life the way you do with your love.[21]

I am back to my writing at the end of the festivities. I am just like a fish back in its own habitat when I can return to my writing. The solitude of this place has given me perfect shelter; none of the trivialities of daily life can touch me any more, so I am able to forgive my enemies easily. I can well understand how this solitude may not appeal to you. I would have been so happy if only I could have given you even a portion of my *feeling* for solitude. But such things cannot be given. I can understand how you would miss the hustle and bustle of Calcutta in the first few days when you come here. I can also imagine that it may not be easy for you to cope with so much quiet even after you get used to it.

But what can I do if I can't stand the atmosphere of our Calcutta household any better? When I am there I feel a continuous irritation over every little thing, and lose my peace of mind. Besides, I know that Rathi will not get an adequate education there since everybody around

[20]Seventh of Pous is the foundation day of the Santiniketan ashram. Pous corresponds to the period mid-December to mid-January; seventh of Pous will be around 22 December.

[21]Rabindranath to Mrinalini Devi, Calcutta, 21 December 1900, *Chitthi Patra* I, p. 49. Translated by UDG.

is so restless. You will, therefore, have to accept this exile till I am able to move you to a better place. I cannot surrender my inherent nature to live in Calcutta.

The whole sky is thick with clouds and it has just begun to rain. I have closed the glass windows in my room and I am enjoying the rain while I sit and write to you. You don't have this grand view from your room on the second storey. It is so beautiful to see this new rain falling on the rice fields on all sides. I am writing an essay on *Meghdut* . . .[22]

I have left Bela at her husband's home. Things are not what you imagine them to be from far away. Bela seems quite happy to be there. I believe she is enjoying her new life. She does not need us in the same way now. It is important for a newly married girl to be away from her parents so that she gets time and space to feel comfortable in her new home. The proximity of parents can hinder this process because the two families are inevitably different in habit and taste. Even in little ways. With parents around, it is difficult for a girl to forget her earlier life. If she must be given away, why cling on? It is her happiness and peace we must ensure, not ours. If that is more important, why must we burden her with more attachment?

Believe me, Bela is all right. We should find peace in the thought that she is happy. Things would not have been good if we had not let go of her and her husband. We will continue to love her as before, even more, now that she is far away. We shall enjoy a new and expectant love when they come to us for the pujas, or when we visit them on occasion. Distance is important in all love. Simply surrounding each other may not necessarily be for the good. We will do the same for Rani after her marriage. She must of course stay with us for the first couple of years but when the time is right she must be sent away for her own well-being.

Our family is very different from other Bengali families in culture and taste, language and mentality. That is all the more reason why our girls

---

[22]Rabindranath to Mrinalini Devi, Shelidah, June 1901, Ibid., pp. 59-60. Translated by UDG. Rabindranath's essay *Meghdut* was based on Kalidasa's epic poem.

must stay away from us after they are married. Otherwise, small matters about the husband's family will begin to tell on their nerves and weaken respect and feeling. We must be particularly mindful about Rani, given her temperament. She will change once she leaves us behind.

Just think back about yourself. If I had stayed on at Phultala[23] after our marriage, your personality and your behaviour would have been so different. We must forget our own joy and sorrow where our children are concerned. They are not in the world merely for our happiness. We must make room for them so that they can mould their lives in their own way. Yesterday, my mind went back to Bela's childhood time and again. I raised her with such loving care. I remember how she would play with the pillows in bed and jump on to the little toys that came her way. How greedy she could be, and still so good-natured. I remembered how I used to bathe her in our Park Street house, and when we were in Darjeeling how I used to wake her up and feed her with warm milk in the nights. Those early days of having her so close keep haunting me. But she does not know this. It is better that she doesn't, so that she can now fill her life painlessly with affection and adoration for her new family. This is not something we should ever regret.[24]

I have arrived here after quite a dangerous journey. There were whirlwinds during the first three days which made it impossible for the boat to move. When we finally but slowly started out we fell into a beel. As you know, a beel is like a sea—everywhere there is a lot of water. All one could see was submerged grain peeping out above the water, or villages looking like small islands as they tried to stay afloat. The cows cannot graze, people have no ground to walk on. They move from village to village by boat. You cannot imagine such a scene from Bolpur. Everywhere there is moss floating on the waters, the lotus, the blue flower, also black weed—all producing such a rotten smell. I see kites flying over our heads to catch fish. My mind

---

[23]Mrinalini Devi's home town in the Jessore district of East Bengal.

[24]Rabindranath to Mrinalini Devi, Santiniketan, 20 July 1901, *Chitthi Patra* I, pp. 67–69. Translated by UDG.

turns wistful in the evenings on these endless still waters. Things are much more varied when one is on the sea. Also, the sea makes a noise—that is not so here. It is absolutely quiet all around. Just the sound of the water from the passing ferry boats.

When the faint moonlight falls on this scene, I really wonder if I am in the world of the dead. I switch off my light, draw my armchair out near the window, and sit absolutely still in the moonlight. The peace of these massive waters touches my heart fully. Day before yesterday, there was a storm over this beel from clouds gathering on the western sky. Luckily for us, our boat was floating on a rice field, so that we could drop anchor quickly and somehow manage to cling to the earth below. We started out as soon as the storm was over. But as our luck would have it there was another storm suddenly. This time, too, we found a safe place by God's grace. Or else there was no knowing where the storm would have taken us.

On arrival here I was informed that I shall have to appear in court this coming Monday. So I must set out tomorrow. I may not get the time to write to you while I am in Calcutta given that there is always so much going on there. That is why I am writing from here. I feel better for having lived on the waters these few days in absolute quiet and peace. If I want to recover my broken health, the only way for me is to surrender to these waters. Yet another storm has arisen while I am writing to you. Topsi is dropping anchor rather volubly. I hope to get news of you once I am in Calcutta.[25]

---

[25]Rabindranath to Mrinalini Devi, Kaligram, 1901, Ibid., pp. 70-71. Translated by UDG. Topsi was his boatman's name.

11

LETTERS TO MY CHILDREN

Sadly, Rabindranath's family was short-lived. Mrinalini Devi died after a brief illness in 1902. He wrote the *Smaran* poems to enshrine her memory. In 1903, Renuka (Rani) died, nine months after her mother's death. In 1907, the same fate befell his youngest child Samindranath (Sami). Sami was then only eleven years old and died of cholera while on a visit to Monghyr in Bihar. While nursing Rani in Almora in her last days, Rabindranath wrote the *Sisu* poems to amuse Sami who had to be left with relatives. Bela died in 1918. The only two children who lived were his elder son Rathindranath (Rathi) and his youngest daughter Mira. In 1906, he sent Rathi to the University of Illinois at Urbana to study agriculture so that he would have the expertise on his return to work for the improvement of rural life. The following year, he arranged Mira's marriage to Nagendranath Ganguli,[1] whom too he sent to Urbana to study agriculture. The marriage did not last, and Rabindranath did not compel Mira to return to her husband. If anything, as is evident from his letters in this context, he blamed himself for getting Mira married young. He worried about Mira and was heartbroken when her son Nitindranath (Nitu), his only grandson, died at the prime of his life in 1932, aged twenty-one. Rabindranath once suffered a nervous breakdown of which the only record is a letter he wrote to Rathi, very probably in 1915. In spite of all that went wrong in his life, he continued with every activity and kept his personal pain to himself. The letters he wrote to Bela, Rathi and Mira show how much he thought about them in the midst of his very busy life.

---

[1]Nagendranath Ganguli (1889–1954), agricultural scientist, became professor of agriculture and rural economics at the University of Calcutta in 1921.

Something has happened to me lately which I find difficult even to mention. I very seldom speak about it to anybody. It is the death of my eldest daughter Bela. She was exceptionally beautiful in body and mind, and I cannot but think that all things that are real in this world cannot afford to lose the intense reality of life and yet remain the same. We can only see the one side of truth from the point where we live and miss the meaning of death, but there must be another side where it is in harmony with life, like the setting sun whose meaning is not in its disappearance but in the sunrise in the new morning outside our ken.[2]

I would like you to stay at the school. There are a number of distractions at the Santiniketan house. You must never forget that you are a student of the school. You will only harm your future if you take things easy now because there is no examination to prepare for. You must study regularly. You must continue your training in English composition from Satish. You will forget what you have learnt if you don't keep it up. You have a truly skilled teacher in literature. It will be sad if you still cannot develop a love of literature.

You are old enough to protect yourself from all kinds of evil and learn to take responsibility for yourself . . . You must be your own judge in good and bad. I hope you can hold on to your ideals no matter what others say. You must not let the greed for material things overwhelm you. Let your life be simple whether you are in the company of the rich or of the poorest of the poor. You must never be ashamed of your simplicity. You must imbibe India's eternal ideal of inner fulfilment.[3]

[2]Rabindranath to William Rothenstein, 1 June 1918, *Imperfect Encounter: Letters of William Rothenstein and Rabindranath Tagore 1911–1941*, edited by Mary Lago, Cambridge: Harvard University Press, 1972, p. 248. (Hereafter, *Imperfect Encounter*.) William Rothenstein (1872–1945), English painter who introduced Rabindranath to literary circles in Britain and saw to the first publication of *Gitanjali* in 1912.

[3]Rabindranath to Rathindranath, Calcutta, 17 May 1903, Bengali Letters, File: Tagore, Rathindranath. (RBA.) Translated by UDG. Satish Chandra Ray (1882–1904), teacher of English literature at the Santiniketan school.

Miru, I am so glad to know you are starting to settle down in Shelidah. But you should not live anywhere far. That will make it difficult for you to move around. Going everywhere by palanquin will become a problem. It will be best if you live close by. I would love to see the plan of your house. Make sure the house is built in such a way that it does not become damp in the rains and make you ill. The foundation must be made damp-proof right from the start. The damp cannot rise because of a capillary pull if the plinth is packed with ashes and sand . . .

Don't forget to sit down to your studies regularly. Your mind will not stay tuned otherwise . . .

How is your mother-in-law liking Shelidah? Give her my regards. God bless you.[4]

Miru, I have just got your letter. We are getting ready for our first of Baisakh[5] celebrations. I think there may be many visitors on the day. Ramananda Babu's daughters and other women from the Brahmo Samaj are coming for the occasion.[6] I am happy about this growing connection between girls and our ashram. I believe the girls are benefiting from it . . .

I wrote to Rathi a couple of days back to send us some melon from the Shelidah garden for the first of Baisakh celebrations. This idea of getting things cheaply has won me such an elevated reputation among the people around that I am almost embarrassed by it. It will become memorable in the school's history. Specially now that the course of my life is being discussed, whether secretly or openly, this aspect of my character may feature in it too! So, ask your brother not to send the melon now.[7]

[4]Rabindranath to Mira, Santiniketan, Phalgun 1317 (1910), *Chitthi Patra*, Volume IV, Calcutta: Visva-Bharati, Bengali Year 1350 (1943), pp. 17-18. Translated by UDG. (Henceforth, *Chitthi Patra* IV.)

[5]First of Baisakh is Bengali New Years' Day, which falls on 14 or 15 April.

[6]Ramananda Chatterjee (1865–1943), Brahmo leader, journalist and professor of English, also founder-editor of *Prabasi* (1901) and the *Modern Review* (1907). His daughters, Santa and Sita, became active Brahmos and writers themselves.

[7]Rabindranath to Mira, Santiniketan, Chaitra 1317 (1910), *Chitthi Patra* IV, pp. 19–21. Translated by UDG.

Miru, I am happy to hear from you after a long time. Is Rathi reading out Ball's *Astronomy* to you? I remember I liked the book so much that I went without food or sleep while reading it. I think *bouma* also likes it very much. Is she being taught from the book, *The Fairy Land of Science*? She will be able to learn a lot from it. I found she has quite a natural inclination for science. I hope her studies are not suffering because her teacher has fled to Calcutta. Why don't you give her lessons?

I hope you are keeping well. Your *mejoma* wants to take you to stay with her in Ranchi. It is a nice place and healthy too. I think you will like it there. I don't know whether she has already spoken about this to Nagen. He must be back in Shelidah by now.[8]

Miru, your *dada* and *boudi* have written proposing that I go with them to Singapore. I am not feeling too well and it might help me to forget all my worries by going away for a while. But I am wondering if it will be worth taking a sea voyage just for twenty-two days? That will probably be more trouble than anything else, and the seasickness may get me down. So I have written to him today asking if he is willing to take three months off so that we might go to Japan instead. That would account for a substantial change of air. I might feel a bit restored by leaving all my burdens behind while on a long trip. Do mention this to your mejoma. Let's see what her advice is. Ashu has sent me a cable. But I have come down again with an attack of piles. I am not fit enough now to take a rail journey. That is why I could not go to their meeting. In any case, it is time I stopped going to meetings—I am quite unable to meet the demands of people . . .

Autumn is in the air here—filling the sky with the scent of shiuli flowers—and the sun is shining through the moving clouds. I like it very

---

[8]Rabindranath to Mira, 1 August 1911, Ibid., p. 25. Translated by UDG. Stewart Stawell Ball (1840–1913), astronomer and mathematician, wrote a series of popular books on astronomy; *The Fairy Land of Science* (1878) by Arabella Buckley was a children's book about the latest thinking on science. Bouma is daughter-in-law and mejoma is second aunt; Nagen refers to Nagendranath Ganguli.

much. There was a full moon last night, so I spent a long time out in the field sitting on a bench.[9]

All my weariness and an intolerable weakness have vanished on coming here. I have not felt so comfortable for a long time. It is strange how I have travelled far and wide for a little rest from my worldly distractions when there was somewhere to go so close by. For a while I have been feeling as if death has been stalking me, as if it is time to depart from this life. But the One who is the shadow of death is also the harbinger of the immortal. It is after a long time that I am again conscious of the immortal.[10]

Bel, I remain very worried to know that you are not too well. You don't reply to my letters and I hardly get any news of you. Please write me a postcard occasionally. How is Sarat's[11] health now?

I have been confining myself to this small town called Urbana after coming to America and keeping to myself for a while. But people love to listen to lectures, so they have really been pressing me to give lectures. I was not responding because I was convinced that it would hurt my self-respect to give lectures in English. Following Chanakya's example, I was simply sitting dumb. Ultimately, I could not turn down an invitation to speak at a club called the Unity Club.[12] It is a small club with just a few members, and therefore, less daunting. I wrote an essay for the lecture. Their hall was packed with people on the day. From then on there was no stopping me. They were very satisfied. As a result, I gained confidence and read out as many as five essays to them, one after the other, on separate

---

[9]Rabindranath to Mira, Bhadra 1318 (September 1911), Ibid., pp. 29-30. Translated by UDG. Dada and boudi are addresses in Bengal for elder brother and his wife.

[10]Rabindranath to Rathindranath, Shelidah, 1912, *Chitthi Patra*, Volume II, Calcutta: Visva-Bharati, Bengali Year 1349 (1942), p. 21. Translated by UDG. (Hereafter, *Chitthi Patra* II.)

[11]Sarat Kumar Chatterjee was Bela's husband.

[12]Unity Club of Urbana-Champaign was affiliated to the Unitarians who had links with the Brahmo Movement.

occasions. Since then I have received many invitations to lecture. My hesitation is gone after the lecture I gave at Chicago University. At Rochester, I spoke to this year's annual Congress of Religious Liberals on the subject of 'Race Conflict' for a bare twenty minutes. Rochester is close to Boston. Having come this far I wanted to include Boston which is home to the largest university here called Harvard University. That is where I am now. I gave a lecture there yesterday, and have three more to give. I am not sure where I shall be going from here . . .

How was maghotsav? I still have not had any word about it. I had to miss it after many years. Five of us Bengalis celebrated the seventh of Pous in one corner of our living room at Urbana. That was no big gathering but I liked it all the same.[13]

Bel, I hope you are not ill from staying late that night at our house. I remain very worried for you. I would like to suggest a homeopathic medicine, will you try it out once? It is Sulphur 200—I am sending you a single dose with this letter. I think it might help your feeling of feverishness in the afternoons and the burning sensation in your legs. Let me know if it helps so that I can give you another dose in eight or ten days' time.

I think you will greatly benefit if you can come for a few days to stay on the boat with me. It will make me very happy. But I guess you may not be able to move now. Your health would improve even if you come only for five or six days.[14]

I have come to Shelidah . . . sounds of the stream, the green fields and the quiet have restored truth within me. I wish to stay on here for as long as I can. I am in absolute need of nature's care in its splendid isolation. That is why I am forever restless to break out of this worldly life and go far, far away. It must be that I need the peace of the unknown. That must be why

[13]Rabindranath to Bela, Urbana, postmarked 19 February 1913, *Chitthi Patra* IV, pp. 5–9. Translated by UDG.

[14]Rabindranath to Bela, Shelidah, Chaitra 1321 (March 1914), Ibid., pp. 1-2. Translated by UDG.

those invitations from Japan keep coming to me despite so many obstacles. I no longer want to resist; it is high time that I fulfil my life in the few days left to me.

If I stay on for some more time in Shelidah I will need a few more books. I have brought only a few with me. Please send me as many as you can from the list below:

1. Viscount Haldane's *The Pathway to Reality*, 2 Vols. The Gifford Lectures.

2. *The Interpretation of Radium*, by Frederick Soddy.

3. *Recent Advances in the Study of Variation, Heredity and Evolution*, by Robert H. Lock.

The publisher is John Murray. You will not get them at Newman. Please try at Thacker.[15]

Sometime ago, Nagen wrote an angry letter which I showed to Mira. She sought my advice on what she should do, whether she should return to Nagen. In other words, she will go back to him if I tell her to. But how can I be so cruel to Mira when it was I who had dealt the first blow in her life by marrying her off without thinking carefully enough about it? I was terribly anxious when I arranged her marriage. I remember how on the night of her marriage a cobra had raised its hood at her as she was going down to her husband's room. Sometimes I think in despair that she might have been spared this cruelty if the cobra had got her.

There is a barbarity about Nagen which Mira has come to dread. That is why she could not love him. There might have been a solution if they could live as friends even without being in love. But that is not possible. Mira is incapable of prevaricating, and Nagen cannot control his temper. When once they stayed with me in Madras, I observed them at close quarters and realized how troubled their married life was. How can I let her return to such a predicament? How can she raise her children with all

[15]Rabindranath to Rathindranath, Shelidah, 18 July 1915, *Chitthi Patra* II, pp. 33-34. Translated by UDG. Newman and Thacker were prominent bookstores in central Calcutta near the Great Eastern Hotel which was then the hub of central Calcutta. Newman still exists there but on a diminished scale.

of that insult and anger and cruelty? She will not be able to hide any of this from the servants and from her relatives. That itself would be hurtful to the children even more than to Mira. However, if Nagen insists on taking his children away, we cannot stop him. We can think of that if the occasion arises. For the time being, she must never feel that we want to send her away. I cannot throw her into that fire and kill her. Her life is already destroyed, now it is for me to protect her and make her as happy as possible. I must bear as much pain for it as I can because I am responsible for her misery.[16]

It is now becoming clear to me that I have been suffering from acute anxiety for a while. There are two reasons why I think so. First, I know for certain that I had suffered a breakdown sometime ago. At that time, I used to have a pain in my ear and also on the left side of my head. I reckoned it was not a good sign. But I forced myself to go on. I used to feel very gloomy and depressed for no reason that I knew of.

The Unani doctor gave me Aurum in 'high dilution' for my condition. I still don't know why he gave me this. Kanai Babu warned me the medication could be harmful. It cured me of my earache but it left some sort of effect on my mind. Let me describe the symptoms.

'Melancholy, with inquietude and desire to die. Irresistible impulse to weep. Sees obstacles everywhere. Hopeless, suicidal, desperate. Great anguish. Excessive scruples with conscience. Despair of oneself and others. Grumbling, quarrelsome humour. Alternate peevishness and cheerfulness.'

The above description from the *Materia Medica* fits my condition. I was hounded by a death wish day and night. I felt I have been a failure all my life. I experienced a sense of great despair and could not trust anyone. Then, when I was in Ramgarh, I felt guilty thinking I had not done my duty to my school, to my zamindari, my family, my country. I told myself I should have renounced everything and forced my family to do the same. I was overcome by disgust for my failure and thought that it was better to end this life and start all over again with a new resolve. The turmoil

---

[16]Rabindranath to Rathindranath, undated, Bengali Letters, File: Tagore, Rathindranath. (RBA.) Translated by UDG.

within me led me to behave abominably with all those I loved most, such as yourself and bouma. I have always believed in the goodness and beauty of your and bouma's life together. I have always wished you well and trusted in bouma's goodness. When those feelings began to change I feared I was in a hostile environment. I was convinced that whatever you do for me was out of compulsion, not from love.

I had never known such anxiety ever. I have never been nervous by nature. I hardly worried about any of you. That is why I could give you so much freedom in your childhood. Now my mind is so full of apprehensions that I worry even when you go out on a bicycle. When you are late coming home I fear you are in some sort of danger. It is incredible how all this anxiety has taken over my free and detached temperament. I know it is both wrong and ludicrous of me to cling to you so desperately. I had never even tried to 'impose' my 'ideal' on you, believing firmly that each of you must develop in your own individual way.

Last evening I felt I was finally coming out of this dark state of mind and returning to my former self. That is why I looked up Aurum in the *Materia Medica* and was amazed to find those symptoms described from which I was suffering. It was a kind of *suicide* for me. There was no joy left in me. I rejected whatever I touched. This was a new 'experience' for me. It was like a bad dream. But have no fear, I will get out of this state and overcome. Its cure is within me.

Tell bouma to bear with me as if I were a sick child and to put her trust in me. She must know that I am not responsible for my acts in my present state. It haunts me to think that I hurt her feelings, but she must realize that I have not been the same person.

Don't worry for me any longer. I will spend a few days very quietly on my terrace at Surul and regain my sanity. I am confident I shall find my way out of the dark caves of death to witness the light of day again.[17]

[17]Rabindranath to Rathindranath, undated (1915?), *Chitthi Patra* II, pp. 27–32. Translated by UDG. *Materia Medica* is a sourcebook for medical practitioners; Surul is a village at a distance of around two miles from Santiniketan where Rabindranath had bought some land and a house in 1912 to start the work of rural reform in the area.

You have been in my mind a lot these days. You cannot possibly be comfortable where you are. I would have been unbearably miserable if somebody had kept me caged in a house in Calcutta. In fact, I feel quite oppressed at times under London's cloudy sky, and among its crowds. I crave to return home every day. I know how much you love the fields of Bolpur and the light of its sky. I know how much you cherish the freedom of the place. Yet, no living creature on this earth is as subservient as man. Man knows the value of freedom but is deprived of it at every stage. This is specially true of women, and my mind revolts when I think of it. We men have been policing women for ages and we have no sense of the cruelty this involves.

I suffer badly because I could not make you happy. I hoped at least to enable you to stay in the open air of Bolpur. Even that seems beyond me. I can only pray God gives you forbearance, that He takes His place within you, that your suffering leads you to radiance and purity. After coming here I can see how the world has been divided into two camps, one of them armed, the other helpless. The helpless will triumph. Those who have always used force will break under the weight of their own force. Meanwhile, we shall all have to suffer. May those who suffer be given the strength to endure. Pain and suffering are unavoidable in life. We human beings must learn to accept them by lighting the flame of sacrifice in us. We can say to the Almighty, 'I am offering myself to you through this suffering, may Your guidance prevail.'

> *Sukham va yadi va duhkham—*
> *Priyam va yadi va'priyam*
> *Praptam praptam upasita hrdayenaparajitah.*[18]

[18]Rabindranath to Mira, London, June 1920, *Chitthi Patra* IV, pp. 89-90. Translated by UDG. The sloka '*Sukham va yadi va duhkham…*' is from the Mahabharata, Santi-parban, Bengal recension, 174.39. It was a favourite with Rabindranath. He translated it into Bengali and used it in his letters more than once. The English translation, provided by Professor Abhijit Ghosh, is as follows: Be it happiness or sorrow/Be it agreeable or disagreeable/Let us accept our destinies, undaunted in mind.

I loved Nitu dearly. My heart goes out to you. But I don't want to make a public show of my grief. I don't want to upset my daily routine. I don't want to make anybody wait on me. Let everybody go where they normally would, I shall go along too. Someone asked me if the performance of *Barsha Mangal* should be postponed. I vetoed that. My loss is my very own, how can anybody really know what it means from the outside? They must simply accept that a public mourning is not for me. At the outset I feared people would come to console me, so I asked that nobody should see me for a few days. I have been otherwise working normally without stopping anything at all. It is not self-respecting to put one's private life over public duty.

I have prayed to my Almighty friend for protection. Perhaps He has protected me. But it is a weakness to pray for such things. Nobody can escape the rules of the universe. It is irrational to hope that those rules will not apply for me, and cowardly to expect to be spared the common human experience of suffering. When Sami died, I prayed with all my heart that he would pass unhindered into the Eternal existence, that my sorrow would not hold him back. With Nitu's death, similarly, I kept telling myself that I can only wish him well in his Eternal abode. Our nursing cannot reach him there, but our love can. How else can we explain this lingering love?

I was on a train the night after Sami died and saw how the sky was flooded with moonlight, how it had not dimmed one bit, how it shone as bright as on all other moonlit nights. I came to realize how everything remained as full as ever, how I was a part of that fullness. Let me again take courage and not give in to weariness, let me accept gracefully what has happened and do all that remains to be done for as long as I live.

I am not sure that this letter will reach you if I send it to Aden. Let me send it to Bombay.[19]

---

[19]Rabindranath to Mira, Santiniketan, 28 August 1932, *Chitthi Patra* IV, pp. 150–53. Translated by UDG.

12

STARTING MY SCHOOL
AT SANTINIKETAN, 1901

Shelidah became a turning point in Rabindranath's life. His troubled conscience expressed itself in his classic poem of 1894, 'Ebar Phirao Morey' (Call Me Back to Work). It was a call to turn away from a life of ease to a life of struggle in the service of his people. In the summer of 1901, he moved with his family to his father's ashram in Santiniketan. On 22 December 1901, he established a school there as his response to constructive nationalism. He wrote, 'Starting the school at Bolpur is an endeavour to take education into our own hands and make it as indigenous as possible.'[1] He started the school with his own meagre funds and, in the beginning, took no fees from the students on the model of the ancient Indian *guru-sishya* hermitages. He realized soon enough the problem of finding teachers and students for such an idealistic school. Describing his father's struggle, Rathindranath wrote, 'Very few realized the struggle with which Father had to carry on his educational experiment in Santiniketan. When the school was established he had difficulty in getting pupils and those that came were mostly of the difficult type. People looked down upon the institution and ridiculed Father's attempt to introduce new ideas in education ... Considered from a worldly point of view it was foolhardy of Father to have launched into this misadventure when he hardly had enough to support himself and his family and was actually in debt over the failure of the Kushtia business.[2] He had to dispose of everything he possessed including the jewellery belonging to my mother, in order to start the school.'[3]

---

[1]Rabindranath to Dinesh Chandra Sen, 17 November 1905, Bengali Letters, File: Dinesh Chandra Sen. (RBA.) Translated by UDG. Dinesh Chandra Sen (1866–1939), literary historian, author of *A History of Bengali Language and Literature* (1919).

[2]In 1895, a family business in storing grain, baling jute, and crushing sugarcane was started in Kushtia. Rabindranath's nephews Balendranath (1870–99) and Surendranath (1872–1940) were partners in this venture named Tagore and Co. This went bankrupt after 1899 and left Rabindranath with large debts.

[3]Rathindranath Tagore, *On the Edges of Time*, Reprint, Calcutta: Visva-Bharati, 1981, p. 154.

> Because the growth of this school was the growth of my life and not
> that of a mere carrying out of my doctrines, its ideals changed with its
> maturity like a ripening fruit that not only grows in its bulk and deepens
> in its colour, but undergoes change in the very quality of its inner pulp.[4]

Fortunately for me, I had a place ready to my hand where I could begin my work. My father, in one of his numerous travels, had selected this lonely spot as the one suitable for his life of communion with God. This place, with a permanent endowment, he dedicated to the use of those who seek penance and seclusion for their meditation and prayer. I had about ten boys with me when I came here and started my new life with no previous experience whatsoever.[5]

All round our ashram is a vast open country, bare up to the line of the horizon except for sparsely growing stunted date palms and prickly shrubs struggling with ant-hills. Below the level of the field, there extend numberless mounds and tiny hillocks of red gravel and pebbles of all shapes and colours, intersected by narrow channels of rainwater. Not far away towards the south near the village can be seen through the intervals of a row of palm trees the gleaming surface of steel-blue water, collected in a hollow of the ground. A road used by the village people for their marketing in the town goes meandering through the lonely fields, with its red dust staring in the sun. Travellers coming up this road can see from a distance on the summit of the undulating ground the spire of a temple and the top of a building, indicating the Santiniketan ashram, among its *amlaki* groves and its avenue of stately *sal* trees.[6]

[4]Rabindranath Tagore, 'My School', *Santiniketan: 1901–51*, Calcutta: Visva-Bharati, 1951, pp. 6-7.

[5]Rabindranath Tagore, 'My School', *Personality*, Reprint, London: Macmillan, 1959, pp. 130-31. (Hereafter, *Personality*.)

[6]Ibid., p. 131. Amlaki is a pungent-tasting seasonal fruit; sal is a tall evergreen tree.

I am trying hard to start a school in Santiniketan. I want it to be like the ancient hermitages we know about. There will be no luxuries, the rich and poor alike will live like ascetics. But I cannot find the right teachers. It is proving impossible to combine today's practices with yesterday's ideals. Simplicity and hard work are not tempting enough. I wonder why the English school system has not shaped us into dedicated workers. We have Tilak and Paranjpye in Maharashtra, but hardly anyone as selfless and hard-working here. Asceticism must begin at a young age for us to become genuine Hindus. We are becoming spoilt by wasteful pleasure and the lack of self-control. Not being able to accept poverty is at the root of our defeat. I hope I have your support in starting this work.[7]

I sold all my books, my copyrights, everything I had, in order to carry on with the school. I cannot really tell you what a struggle it was, and what difficulties I had to go through. At first the object in view was purely patriotic, but later on it grew more spiritual. Then in the midst of all these outer difficulties and trials, there came the greatest change of all, the true *Varsha Sesha*,[8] the change in my own inner life.[9]

There are men who think that by the simplicity of living introduced in my school I preach the idealization of poverty which prevailed in the medieval age. The full discussion of this subject is outside the scope of this paper, but seen from the point of view of education, should we not admit that poverty is the school in which man had his first lessons and his best training?

---

[7]Rabindranath to Jagadish Chandra Bose, undated, (August 1901), *Chitthi Patra* VI, pp. 35–36. Translated by UDG. Jagadish Chandra Bose (1858–1937), renowned physicist and close friend of Rabindranath from their younger years. Bal Gangadhar Tilak (1856–1920), also known as the Lokamanya, was a freedom fighter. Raghunath Purushottam Paranjpye (1876–1966), later Sir Raghunath Purushottam Paranjpye, educationist and social reformer, principal of Fergusson College, Poona, 1902–24.

[8]Varsha Sesha or *barsho sesh* is a phrase in Bengali for the end of the old year.

[9]Rabindranath to C.F. Andrews, in conversation, London, September 1912, *Letters to a Friend*, pp. 28-29.

Even a millionaire's son has to be born helplessly poor to begin his lesson of life from the beginning. He has to learn to walk like the poorest of children, though he has the means to afford to be without the appendage of legs. Poverty brings us into complete touch with life and the world, for living richly is living mostly by proxy, thus living in a lesser world of reality. This may be good for one's pleasure and pride, but not for one's education. Wealth is a golden cage in which the children of the rich are bred into artificial deadening of their powers. Therefore, in my school, much to the disgust of the people of expensive habits, I had to provide for this great teacher—this bareness of furniture and materials—not because it is poverty, but because it leads to personal experience of the world . . .

What tortured me in my school days was the fact that the school had not the completeness of the world. It was a special arrangement for giving lessons. It could only be suitable for grown-up people who were conscious of the special need of such places and ready to accept their teaching at the cost of disassociation from life. But children are in love with life, and it is their first love. All its colour and movement attract their eager attention. And are we quite sure of its wisdom in stifling this love? Children are not born ascetics, fit to enter at once into the monastic discipline of acquiring knowledge. At first they must gather knowledge through their love of life, and then they will renounce their lives to gain knowledge, and then again they will come back to their fuller lives with ripened wisdom.

But society has made its own arrangements for manipulating men's minds to fit its special patterns. These arrangements are so closely organized that it is difficult to find gaps through which to bring in nature. There is a serial adjustment of penalties which follows to the end one who ventures to take liberty with some part of the arrangements, even to save his soul. Therefore, it is one thing to realize truth and another to bring it into practice where the whole current of the prevailing system goes against you. This is why when I had to face the problem of my own son's education I was at a loss to give it a practical solution. The first thing I did was to take him away from the town surroundings into a village and allow him the freedom of primeval nature as far as it is available in modern days. He had a river, noted for its danger, where he swam and rowed without check from the anxiety of his elders. He spent his time in the fields and on the trackless sandbanks, coming late for his meals without being questioned. He had none of those luxuries that are not only customary but are held as proper for boys of his circumstance. For which privations, I am sure, he was pitied and his parents blamed by the people for whom society has blotted out the whole world. But I was sure that luxuries are burdens to boys. They are the burdens of other people's habits, the burdens of the vicarious pride and pleasure which parents enjoy through their children.

Yet, being an individual of limited resources, I could do very little for my son in the way of educating him according to my plan. But he had freedom of movement, he had very few of the screens of wealth and respectability between himself and the world of nature. Thus, he had a better opportunity for a real experience of this universe than I ever had. But one thing exercised my mind more than anything else as the most important.

The object of education is to give man the unity of truth. Formerly, when life was simple, all the different elements of man were in complete harmony. But when there came the separation of the intellect from the spiritual and the physical, the school education put entire emphasis on the intellect and on the physical side of man. We devote our sole attention to giving children information, not knowing that by this emphasis we are accentuating a break between the intellectual, the physical and the spiritual life.

I believe in a spiritual world—not as anything separate from this world—but as its innermost truth. With the breath we draw we must always feel this truth, that we are living in God. Born in this great world, full of the mystery of the infinite, we cannot accept our existence as momentary outburst of chance drifting on the current of matter towards an eternal nowhere. We cannot look upon our lives as dreams of a dreamer who has no awakening in all time. We have a personality to which matter and force are unmeaning unless related to something infinitely personal, whose nature we have discovered, in some measure, in human love, in the greatness of the good, in the martyrdom of heroic souls, in the effable beauty of nature which can never be a mere fact nor anything but an expression of personality.[10]

I wrote to you in a hurry day before yesterday. This is because I am working six hours a day for my school and, in the time remaining, trying to write something for the coming *nabo barsho*, the New Year. I have to finish that piece in a day or two. I don't get into any discussions because I cannot afford to get distracted. I wrote brief notes to both you and Suren. I am trying hard not to let my worries pull me down.

It will be such a relief if you can get forty or fifty thousand rupees for me. Suren has written today mentioning another source from where he can get the money, but the person giving it may not be in a position to do so without breaking into one of his investments and losing some money in the process. So I am trying to get it from some other source. I am writing to Suren to get in touch with you.

It will be nice if you could come over nabo barsho. That is a festive day for the school. This will be a good time to visit if you are curious about the school. It will also give us the opportunity to discuss things.[11]

Can you not come this way? Do I really need to go for the paperwork? I am expecting some volunteers here to help my school. They are offering a month's labour to it. It will be discourteous of me if I am not here when they come, nor will they be well looked after in my absence. I have given power of attorney to Suren—he can sell my house or donate it, if needed.[12]

---

[10]Rabindranath Tagore, 'My School', *Personality*, pp. 121–27.

[11]Rabindranath to Priyanath Sen, Santiniketan, 6 April 1902, *Chitthi Patra*, Vol. VIII, Reprint, Calcutta: Visva-Bharati, Bengali Year 1399 (1992), pp. 195–96. Translated by UDG. (Hereafter, *Chitthi Patra* VIII.) Priyanath Sen (1854–1916), writer, translator and a close friend of the Tagore family as well as of Rabindranath. Suren refers to Surendranath Tagore, Rabindranath's nephew.

[12]Rabindranath to Priyanath Sen, Santiniketan, 21 April 1902, Ibid., p. 199. Translated by UDG.

I was ill—what is more, I was substituting for two schoolteachers who were on leave. As a result, I had no time to write about the money. My mind does not function well when I have to attend to money matters. I have therefore left the decision to Suren. I am sitting back quietly . . . God keeps me at peace even with these burdens and difficulties. I have not succumbed to them. In fact, I don't think of the present state as a crisis because I know He is preparing me for all possible disasters and disappointments.[13]

I seem to have set the boat of my life afloat on stormy seas, I do not know when I can drop anchor safely. My children are scattered here and there, there is also my school, while I am somewhere else coping distractedly with illnesses. I long to pull together my scattered life into one whole.[14]

I had to rush here on receiving a cable about Renuka's critical condition. I did not expect to see her alive. The doctors were treating her repeatedly with Strychnine and brandy. On reaching, I found they had given up all hope. I have stopped all her stimulants. I have put her on homeopathy. She is no longer spitting blood. Her cough and fever are also down, as is the discomfort in her stomach. She has stopped hallucinating, her chest pain is gone. She seems stronger and is talking normally. I am hopeful she has got over the crisis.[15]

But there seems to be no end to my worries over my school. I can't look after it from here. I had to leave everything and come over here. I have no idea when I can return. What can I say but to implore you and Mohit Babu and Ramani to take charge of the school—to treat it as your own. My problem is that I am alone in this endeavour. It will not work if you don't join hands with me. Please inform the newly appointed teachers

---

[13]Ibid., p. 198. Translated by UDG.

[14]Rabindranath to Priyanath Sen, Almora, 30 May 1903, Ibid., p. 205. Translated by UDG.

[15]Renuka's crisis was 'over' only for a brief interlude. She succumbed to her illness in September that year.

of their duties, and see that the boys eat and behave properly. We must have rules both for the teachers and the students. Otherwise there will be indiscipline in the future and the school will lose its reputation. Once that happens, all our efforts will come to naught. There are many newly admitted students and we don't know what their characters are like. We shall regret it if they spread any evil influences in the school. Don't delay any further. Mohit Babu knows the arrangements in the school. Ask him to come immediately and show him my letter. Renuka needs to be nursed day and night. I have little time to write letters. That is why I haven't written to Mohit Babu. I know he will do his best if he knows how worried I am. I have worked him very hard in the past and I am about to do so again. All of you must make the school your own.

I really should be resting instead of writing letters. But the school has taken away my sleep. Will I ever get some rest?[16]

Meanwhile, a man of meagre means has donated a thousand rupees to my school. I cannot adequately say how much it has meant to me. Just this one instance has brought God closer to me. I feel this is His work bringing in its own successes. We are merely the links. He alone knows what I am doing. What more can I say? The donor does not want to give his name, so his name shall remain embedded in my heart.[17]

The school has reopened today, and all the work with it. During the holidays there were only a few boys—I was giving them some lessons. Today the place has turned from empty to full. From now my rest will come out of this work, rest *and* cure for my mind and body. I know now

---

[16]Rabindranath to Jagadish Chandra Bose, 30 June 1903, *Chitthi Patra* VI, pp. 50-51. Mohit Babu refers to Mohit Chandra Sen (1870–1906), teacher of the school at Santiniketan who also edited and published a collected edition of Rabindranath's poetical works (1903); Ramani refers to Ramani Mohan Chattopadhyaya (1859–1919), trustee of the Santiniketan Trust established by Debendranath, closely associated with the activities of the Brahmo Samaj.

[17]Rabindranath to Priyanath Sen, undated, probably 1903, *Chitthi Patra* VIII, p. 204. Translated by UDG.

it does not help me to be away from it because I don't get any peace of mind when I am away.[18]

My life has followed various directions. But in all my distractions, inwardly or outwardly, I have been conscious of a continuous companionship with God which expressed itself in gladness. There has been a meeting of my faith and His poetry. Thus I came to know myself.

Is there then no connection between God and my practical work? Yes, there is. I have proof of it but not by any mechanical route. The work I began in Santiniketan was His field for poetry. It is there that I sought help from the elements to establish my enterprise and, in my gladness, tried to instil in the student's minds songs of the seasons and the celebration of nature. The ashram grew from a creative spirit and not from any custom-made religion. The school was conceived to free the students' minds from blind superstition, leading them to a state of creative unity where they would respect human beings irrespective of caste and creed.[19]

It is also a surprise to me how I had the courage to start an educational institution for our children, for I had no experience in this line at all. But I had confidence in myself. I knew that I had very profound sympathy for children. And about my knowledge of psychology I was very certain. I felt that I could help them more than the ordinary teachers.

I selected a beautiful place, far away from the contamination of town life . . .

I knew that the mind has its hunger for the ministrations of mother-nature, and so I selected this spot where the sky is unobstructed to the verge of the horizon. There the mind could have its fearless freedom to create its own dreams, and the seasons could come with all their colours

---

[18]Rabindranath to Abala Bose, probably October 1903, *Chitthi Patra* VI, p. 84. Translated by UDG.

[19]Rabindranath Tagore, Ms. Accession no. 190, in Bengali, pp. 12-13. Translated by UDG. (RBA.)

and movements and beauty into the very heart of the human dwelling. And there I got a few children around me and I taught them. I was their companion. I sang to them. I composed musical pieces, operas and plays, and they took part in the performances. I recited to them our epics, and this was the beginning of this school.

I had only about five or six students at that time. People did not have any confidence in a poet for bringing up their children and educating them. And so I had very few students to begin with.

My idea was that education should be part of life itself, and must not be detached from it and be made into something abstract. And so when I brought these children around me, I allowed them to live a complete life. They had perfect freedom to do what they wished, as much liberty as was possible for me to give them. And in all their activities, I tried to put before them something which would be interesting to them.

I tried to arouse their interest in all things, in nature's beauty and the surrounding villages, and also in literature. I tried to educate them through play-acting, through listening to music in a natural manner, and not merely by class teaching.

They knew when I was employed in writing a drama, and they took an interest as it went on and developed, and in the process of their rehearsals they acquired a real taste for literature, more than they could get through formal lessons in grammar and class teaching. And this was my method. I knew the children's mind. Their subconscious mind is more active than the conscious one, and therefore the important thing is to surround them with all kinds of activities which could stimulate their minds and gradually arouse their interest.

I had musical evenings—not merely music classes, and those boys who at first did not have any special love of music would, out of curiosity, listen to our songs from outside, and gradually they too were drawn into the room and their taste for music developed. I had some of the great artists of our land, and while they went on with their work, the boys could watch them and they saw day by day how those great works of art developed.

An atmosphere was created, and what was important, this atmosphere provided the students with a natural impulse to live in harmony with it.

In the beginning it was easier to feel this, when I had only a few students; I was then almost their only companion and teacher and it was truly the golden age of our school . . .

But as their number grew, it became more and more expensive for me to carry on the school in my own way.

According to the old tradition of our country, it was the responsibility of the teacher to give education to those who came to him to be taught, and in our country students used to have free tuition and also free lodging in the teacher's house. The teachers acknowledged their responsibility: they themselves had the privilege of being educated, and they owed it to society that they should help their students in return, and should not claim anything in the shape of fees or remuneration.

And I also began like that. Free tuition, lodging and boarding and all necessities of life, I supplied to my students out of my own poor resources. But as you can easily imagine that under modern conditions of life it was not possible to continue like this, because now you have to get the help of teachers whose salaries are high, and there are other expenses which daily seem to increase.

I could not maintain the old tradition that it was the duty and the privilege of the teacher to impart education to his students, and that an educational institution was not a shop where you could buy commodities with money. I was compelled to give up this idea and now it has taken the shape of an ordinary school . . .

But I believe that an atmosphere has been created and it is there. The school has grown. The number of students is increasing year by year, which is not always an advantage. But it cannot be helped.

Another feature, which is of later growth, is that the number of girls has been increasing. The coeducation system is quite a new thing in India. But it is working perfectly in my school. We have had no cause for complaint. Very often the boys and girls go out together on excursions; the boys help the girls by bringing fuel and fetching water, and the girls cook the dinners for the boys and everything is arranged by mutual help. That is a great education in itself.

There is another factor which I consider to be important. I always try to get from Europe and from the Far East, lecturers, who come to the school with our students. This contributes to the creation of a favourable atmosphere. Our boys are very natural in their relationship with the foreign guests and visitors. My idea is that the mind should find its freedom in every respect, and I am sure that our children have, through early training, freedom from the barriers of country and race, creeds and sects. It is always difficult to get rid of these prejudices after we grow up. It is often sedulously cultivated in our school-books, and also by the patriots who wish the boys to be proud of the exploits of their own country by running down other countries. In this way, nationalistic prejudices are cultivated. With the help of my visitors from abroad I have tried my best to make our boys' minds hospitable to the guests who come to us, and I think I have been successful.[20]

---

[20]Rabindranath Tagore, 'Conversations in Russia', September 1930, *English Writings*, Volume III, pp. 932–34.

13

MY EXPERIENCE OF THE SWADESHI MOVEMENT

Rabindranath opposed the Congress policies of petitioning the government for favours and pressed for an alternative way—that of self-reliance. By 1904, he drew up a clearly stated programme of action in his essay 'Swadeshi Samaj'. In it, he called for swadeshi work in the following ways: abandoning the politics of 'begging' from the government, reviving the traditional *samaj* or society and channelling all constructive work through it, and empowering educated volunteers to live and work among villagers. In this period, Rabindranath was temporarily lured to the movement for Hindu revivalism and put his hopes in Hindu religion and society as a means of uniting the country. Stirred by these ideas, he plunged into the Swadeshi Movement in 1904-05 and contributed several patriotic songs to it. He even took part in street processions. But he was shocked when the Swadeshi Movement broke out into communal violence. What he had not taken into account was the fact that traditional Hindu samaj never included in its fold Muslims and low-caste Hindus. Confronted with this reality, he turned away from the ideology of Hindu revival for all time and concluded that the only path to swadeshi lay in constructive work, not religion nor samaj. Withdrawing from the political movement, Rabindranath turned his passion to a scheme of rural reform for the Hindu and Muslim tenants in his family's estates. He was convinced that in his country social change was more urgent than political freedom and blamed the political leaders for shifting the focus.

I seemed choked for breath in the hideous nightmare of our present time, meaningless in its petty ambitions of poverty, and felt in me the struggle of my motherland for awakening in spiritual emancipation. Our endeavours after political ambition seemed to me unreal to the core, and pitifully feeble in their utter helplessness. I felt that it is a blessing of providence that begging should be an unprofitable profession, and that only to him that hath shall be given. I said to myself that we must seek for our own inheritance, and with it buy our true place in the world.[1]

Here are a few clues to the history of the Swadeshi Movement:

Initially, the English-educated Bengali students were overcome by an anti-swadeshi feeling. Intoxicated with western influences they felt ashamed of our art, literature, history, religion and were convinced of the superiority of the West's culture. Ignorant of our ancient scriptures, and out of sheer contempt, many became atheists while some turned to Christianity.

At that time, Debendranath Tagore, a follower of Ram Mohan Roy, started exploring the shastras with a view to presenting them in a scientific manner. Although Debendranath had abandoned the customary Hindu rituals through the Brahmo Movement, he never doubted the authenticity of the shastras and regarded them as fundamental for religious advancement.

Debendranath began to publish discourses on the Vedas and the Upanishads in Bengali in the *Tattwabodhini Patrika*. He also published in foreign scientific journals. This was a strategy of the Adi Brahmo Samaj to attract educated Indians to their own religion and away from the lure of Christianity.

Although Keshab Babu and his followers brought about a split between the Brahmo Samaj and Hindu society by joining the Brahmo Movement,

---

[1]Rabindranath Tagore, 'Introduction', in W.W. Pearson, *Santiniketan: The Bolpur School of Rabindranath Tagore*, New York: Macmillan, 1916, pp. 18-19. W.W. Pearson (1881–1923) came from the London Missionary Society to Calcutta and joined the school at Santiniketan as a teacher in 1914 and worked there till his death in a train accident when travelling in Italy.

Debendranath remained loyal to the shastras throughout. He insisted that the Brahmo Dharma was an integral part of the Hindu Dharma. This was also his way to influence educated society towards swadeshi.

In Debendranath's family, there was a synthesis between swadeshi sentiment and modernity. The Hindu Mela arose from that premise. Dwijendranath and Ganendranath helped Nabagopal Mitra to establish the Hindu Mela for the display of swadeshi art and craft, swadeshi wrestling, and swadeshi games, also swadeshi songs and swadeshi poetry.

At this time, Bankim's *Bangadarshan* was nourishing contemporary Bengali literature and encouraging educated Bengalis to contribute to their national literature in their mother tongue. Sashadhar's appearance also deserves mention in this period. Our family was at that time seriously cultivating swadeshi enterprise helped by the elderly Rajnarain Basu. We were secretly making swadeshi matchsticks and improved weaving looms. In his fervour, Jyotirindranath even established a steamer service for ferrying people from Khulna to Barishal to rival an English steamer company. Swadeshi groups in Barishal tried to lure passengers away from the English ferry. You can imagine what might have happened if we did this in Fuller's time.

But the Congress chose to put its faith in the efficacy of petitioning the government for favours to educated Indians. We appealed in the pages of the *Sadharani* to abandon petitions and work for self-reliance instead. Balendranath and many others in our family started the Swadeshi Stores.

The Indian Stores was founded on the remains of the Swadeshi Stores.

At the Provincial Conference of Rajshahi and later in Dhaka, proceedings were conducted in Bengali under Satyendranath's leadership. He made the point that our duty did not end with merely presenting our problems in English to the British Raj.

All these efforts for change were intimately linked to the Swadeshi Movement. As in religion so also in politics, the Adi Brahmo Samaj tried to draw the people's attention to their country. The educated elite of those early years took no interest in their shastras, nor in serving their people. Similarly, today's 'agitation'-wallahs all plead with the government instead of tackling the basic problems of the country.

The new series of *Bangadarshan* is making a valiant attempt to turn our minds to the value of self-reliance and swadeshi feeling. The Bolpur [Santiniketan] school is a step in that direction with its objective of taking education into our own hands. Vidyasagar was a pioneer in this regard. He started English-type schools that were run by Bengali teachers. My goal is to make my school at Santiniketan as indigenous as possible.

Congress leader Jogesh Chowdhury has been organizing art exhibitions at the Congress sessions every year to inspire swadeshi sentiment within the Congress and to wean their minds away from the policy of begging the government for favours. Ashu Chowdhury was greeted with brickbats at the Burdwan conference for challenging the politics of begging. Swadeshi was definitely catching on in the country when the Partition gave the movement an impetus. It would not be fair to say that boycott was the mainstay of the movement.[2]

I remember the day, during the Swadeshi Movement in Bengal, when a crowd of young students came to see me in the first floor of our Bichitra House. They said to me that if I would order them to leave their schools and colleges they would instantly obey. I was emphatic in my refusal to do so, and they went away angry, doubting the sincerity of my love for my motherland. And yet, long before this popular ebullition of excitement, I myself had given a thousand rupees, when I had not five rupees to call my own, to open a swadeshi store and courted banter and bankruptcy.

---

[2]Rabindranath to Dinesh Chandra Sen, Bolpur, 17 November 1905, *Chitthi Patra*, Volume X, Calcutta: Visva-Bharati, 1967, pp. 30–33. Translated by UDG. (Hereafter *Chitthi Patra* X.) Keshab Babu or Keshab Chandra Sen (1838–84), religious reformer and founder of a new movement within the Brahmo Samaj called Nababidhan ('new dispensation'); Ganendranath Tagore, see chapter 1, note 2; Sashadhar refers to Sasadhar Tarkachuramani, see chapter 8, note 7; Sir (Joseph) Bampfylde Fuller (1854–1935), administrator in India and author; Iswar Chandra Vidyasagar (1820–91), writer, social reformer and educator; Rajnarain Basu (1826–99), patriot and professor of English; Jogesh Chowdhury (1864–1951), lawyer and Congress activist; Ashutosh Chowdhury (1860–1924), later Sir Ashutosh Chowdhury, lawyer and founder-member of the Bengal Landholder's Association; *Sadharani* (1873), a Bengali weekly founded by the lawyer and writer Akshay Chandra Sarkar (1846–1917); Swadeshi Stores sold goods made from swadeshi enterprise only; Khulna, Barishal, Rajshahi and Dhaka are towns in present-day Bangladesh, erstwhile East Bengal, Dhaka being the capital of Bangladesh.

The reason for my refusing to advise those students to leave their schools was because the anarchy of a mere emptiness never tempts me, even when it is resorted to as a temporary measure. I am frightened of an abstraction which is ready to ignore living reality. These students were no mere phantoms to me; their life was a great fact to them and to the All. I could not lightly take upon myself the tremendous responsibility of a mere negative programme for them which would uproot their life from its soil, however thin and poor that soil might be.[3]

In my paper called *Swadeshi Samaj*, written in 1905, I discussed at length the ways and means by which we could make the country of our birth more fully our own. Whatever may have been the shortcomings of my words then uttered, I did not fail to lay emphasis on the truth that we must win our country, not from some foreigner, but from our own inertia, our own indifference. Whatever be the nature of the boons we may be seeking for our country at the door it only makes our inertia more densely inert. Any public benefit done by the alien Government goes to their credit not to ours. So whatever outside advantage such public benefit might mean for us, our country will only get more and more completely lost to us thereby. That is to say, we shall have to pay out in soul value for what we purchase as material advantage. The *rishi* has said: 'The son is dear, not because we desire a son, but because we desire to realize our own soul in him.' It is the same with our country. It is dear to us because it is the expression of our own soul. When we realize this, it will become impossible for us to allow our service of our country to wait on the pleasure of others.

These truths I then tried to press on my countrymen, which were not particularly new, nor was there anything therein which need have grated on their ears; but whether anyone else remembers it or not, I at least am not likely to forget the storm of indignation which I roused. I am not merely referring to the hooligans of journalism whom it pays to be

---

[3]Rabindranath Tagore, 'Reflections on Non-cooperation and Cooperation', in *The Mahatma and the Poet*, edited by Sabyasachi Bhattacharya, New Delhi: National Book Trust, 1997, p. 58. (Hereafter, *Mahatma and Poet*.)

scurrilous. But even men of credit and courtesy were unable to speak of me in restrained language.

There were two root causes of this. One was anger, the second was greed.

Giving free vent to angry feelings is a species of self-indulgence. In those days there was practically nothing to stand in the spirit of the destructive level which spread all over the country. We went about picketing, burning, placing thorns in the path of those whose way was not ours, acknowledging no restraints in language and behaviour—all in the frenzy of our wrath. Shortly after it was all over, a Japanese friend asked me: 'How is it you people cannot carry on your work with calm and deep determination? This wasting of energy can hardly be of assistance to your object.' I had no help but to reply: 'When we have the gaining of the object clearly before our minds, we can be restrained, and concentrate our energies to serve it; but when it is a case of venting our anger, our excitement rises and rises till it drowns the object and then we are spendthrift to the point of bankruptcy.'

However that may be, there were my countrymen encountering, for the time being, no check to the overflow of their outraged feelings. It was like a strange dream. Everything seemed possible. Then all of a sudden it was my misfortune to appear on the scene with my doubts and my attempts to divert the current into the path of self-determination. My only success was in diverting their wrath on to my own devoted head.

Then there was our greed. In history, all people have won valuable things by pursuing difficult paths. We had hit upon the device of getting them cheap, not even through the painful indignity of supplication with folded hands, but by proudly conducting our beggary in threatening tones. The country was in ecstasy at the ingenuity of the trick. It felt like being at a reduced price sale. Everything worth having in the political market was ticketed at half-price. Shabby-genteel mentality is so taken up with low prices that it has no attention to spare for quality and feels inclined to attack anybody who has the hardihood to express doubts in that regard. It is like the man of worldly piety who believes that the judicious expenditure of coin can secure, by favour of the priest, a direct passage to heaven. The daredevil who ventures to suggest that not heaven but dreamland is likely to be his destination must beware of a violent end.

Anyhow, it was the outside *maya* which was our dream and our ideal in those days. It was a favourite phrase of one of our leaders of the time that we must keep one hand at the feet and the other at the throat of the Englishman—that is to say, with no hand left free for the country! We have since perhaps got rid of this ambiguous attitude. Now we have one party that has both hands raised to the foreigner's throat, and another party which has both hands down at his feet; but whichever attitude it may be, these methods still appertain to the outside maya. Our unfortunate minds keep revolving round and round the British Government, now to the left, now to the right; our affirmations and denials alike are concerned with the foreigners.

In those days, the stimulus from every side was directed towards the heart of Bengal. But emotion by itself, like fire, only consumes its fuel and reduces it to ashes; it has no creative power. The intellect of man must busy itself, with patience, with skill, with foresight, in using this fire to melt that which is hard and difficult into the object of its desire. We neglected to rouse our intellectual forces, and so were unable to make use of this surging emotion of ours to create any organization of permanent value. The reason of our failure, therefore, was not in anything outside, but rather within us. For a long time past we have been in the habit, in our life and endeavour, of setting apart one place for our emotions and another for our practices. Our intellect has all the time remained dormant, because we have not dared to allow it scope. That is why, when we have to rouse ourselves to action, it is our emotion which has to be requisitioned, and our intellect has to be kept from interfering by the hypnotism of some magical formula—that is to say we hasten to create a situation absolutely inimical to the free play of our intellect . . .

In the heat of the enthusiasm of the Partition days, a band of youths attempted to bring about the millennium through political revolution. Their offer of themselves as the first sacrifice to the fire which they had lighted makes not only their own country, but other countries as well, bare the head to them in reverence. Their physical failure shines forth as the effulgence of spiritual glory. In the midst of the supreme travail, they realized at length that the way of bloody revolution is not the true way; that where there is no politics, a political revolution is like taking a short cut to nothing; that the wrong way may appear shorter, but it does not reach the goal, and only grievously hurts the feet. The refusal to pay the full price for a thing leads to the loss of the price without the gain of the thing. These impetuous youths offered their lives as the price of their country's deliverance; to them it meant the loss of their all but alas! the price offered on behalf of the country was insufficient. I feel sure that those of them who still survive must have realized by now that the country must be the creation of all its people, not of one section alone. It must be the expression of all their forces of heart, mind and will.

This creation can only be the fruit of that *yoga*, which gives outward form to the inner faculties. Mere political or economical *yoga* is not enough; for that all the human powers must unite.[4]

Our real problem in India is not political. It is social. This is a condition not only prevailing in India, but among all nations. I do not believe in an exclusive political interest. Politics in the West have dominated Western ideals, and we in India are trying to imitate you. We have to remember that in Europe, where peoples had their racial unity from the beginning, and where natural resources were insufficient for the inhabitants, the civilization has naturally taken the character of political and commercial aggressiveness. For on the one hand they had no internal complications, and on the other they had to deal with neighbours who were strong and rapacious. To have perfect combination among themselves and a watchful attitude of animosity against others was taken as the solution of their problems. In former days, they organized and plundered, in the present age the same spirit continues—and they organize and exploit the whole world.

But from the earliest beginnings of history, India has had her own problem constantly before her—it is the race problem. Each nation must be conscious of its mission and we, in India, must realize that we cut a

[4]Rabindranath Tagore, 'The Call of Truth', *Mahatma and Poet*, pp. 71–74.

poor figure when we are trying to be political, simply because we have not yet been finally able to accomplish what was set before us by providence.

This problem of race unity which we have been trying to solve for so many years has likewise to be faced by you here in America. Many people in this country ask me what is happening as to the caste distinctions in India. But when this question is asked me, it is usually done with a superior air. And I feel tempted to put the same question to the American critics with a slight modification, 'What have you done with the Red Indian and the Negro?' For you have not got over your attitude of caste towards them. You have used violent methods to keep aloof from other races, but until you have solved the question here in America, you have no right to question India.

In spite of our great difficulty, however, India has done something. She has tried to make an adjustment of races, to acknowledge the real differences between them where these exist, and yet seek for some basis of unity. This basis has come through our saints, like Nanak, Kabir, Chaitanya and others, preaching one God to all races of India . . .

The most important fact of the present age is that all the different races of men have come close together. And again we are confronted with two alternatives. The problem is whether the different groups of peoples shall go on fighting with one another or find out some true basis of reconciliation and mutual help; whether it will be interminable competition or cooperation.

I have no hesitation in saying that those who are gifted with the moral power of love and vision of spiritual unity, who have the least feeling of enmity of others, will be the fittest to take their permanent place in the age that is lying before us, and those who are constantly developing their instinct of fight and intolerance of aliens will be eliminated. For this is the problem before us, and we have to prove our humanity by solving it through the help of our higher nature. The gigantic organizations for hurting others and warding off their blows, for making money by dragging others back, will not help us. On the contrary, by their crushing weight, their enormous cost and their deadening effect upon the living humanity, they will seriously impede our freedom in the larger life of a higher civilization . . .

India has never had a real sense of nationalism. Even though from childhood I had been taught that the idolatry of Nation is almost better than reverence for God and humanity, I believe I have outgrown that teaching, and it is my conviction that my countrymen will gain truly their India by fighting against that education which teaches them that a country is greater than the ideals of humanity.

The educated Indian at present is trying to absorb some lessons from history contrary to the lessons of our ancestors. The East, in fact, is attempting to take unto itself a history which is not the outcome of its own living. Japan, for example, thinks she is getting powerful by adopting Western methods but, after she has exhausted her inheritance, only the borrowed weapons of civilization will remain to her. She will not have developed herself from within.

Europe has her past. Europe's strength therefore lies in her history. We, in India, must make up our minds that we cannot borrow other people's history, and that if we stifle our own, we are committing suicide. When you borrow things that do not belong to your life, they only serve to crush your life.

And therefore I believe that it does India no good to compete with Western civilization in its own field. But we shall be more than compensated if, in spite of the insults heaped upon us, we follow our own destiny.[5]

My experience in the West, where I have realized the immense power of money and of organized propaganda—working everywhere behind screens of camouflage, creating an atmosphere of distrust, timidity, antipathy— has impressed me deeply with the truth that real freedom is of the mind and spirit; it can never come to us from the outside. He only has freedom who ideally loves freedom himself and is glad to extend it to others. He who cares to have slaves must chain himself to them; he who builds walls

---

[5]Rabindranath Tagore, 'Nationalism in India', *Nationalism*, New York: Macmillan, 1917, pp. 97–101, 106-07. Guru Nanak Dev (1469–1539), founder of the Sikh religion; Kabir (1398–1518), universalist poet–saint who openly criticized all sects. His philosophy, expressed in his poetry, represented an unique synthesis of Hindu and Muslim concepts. A collection of his poems was translated into English by Rabindranath with the assistance of the British poet Evelyn Underhill; Sri Chaitanya (b.1486) founded the new non-sectarian Bhakti Movement.

to create exclusion for others builds walls across his own freedom; he who distrusts freedom in others loses his moral right to it. Sooner or later he is lured into the meshes of physical and moral servility.

Therefore, I would urge my own countrymen to ask themselves if the freedom to which they aspire is one of external conditions. Is it merely a transferable commodity? Have they acquired a true love of freedom? Have they faith in it? Are they ready to make space in their society for the minds of their children to grow up in the ideal of human dignity, unhindered by restrictions that are unjust and irrational?

Have we not made elaborately permanent the walls of our social compartments? We are tenaciously proud of their exclusiveness. We boast that, in this world, no other society but our own has come to finality in the classifying of his living members. Yet in our political agitations we conveniently forget that any unnaturalness in the relationship of governors and governed which humiliates us, becomes an outrage which is artificially fixed under the threat of military persecution.

When India gave voice to immortal thoughts, in the time of fullest vigour of vitality, her children had the fearless spirit of the seekers of truth. The great epic of the soul of our people—the Mahabharata—gives us a wonderful vision of the overflowing life, full of the freedom of enquiry and experiment. When the age of the Buddha came, humanity was stirred in our country to its uttermost depth. The freedom of mind which it produced expressed itself in a wealth of creation, spreading everywhere in its richness over the continent of Asia. But with the ebb of life in India, the spirit of creation died away. It hardened into an age of inert construction. The organic unity of a varied and elastic society gave way to a conventional order which proved its artificial character by its inexorable law of exclusion.

Life has its inequalities, I admit, but they are natural and in harmony with our vital functions. The head keeps its place apart from the feet, not through any external arrangement or any conspiracy of coercion. If the body is compelled to turn somersaults for an indefinite period, the head never exchanges its relative function for that of the feet. But have our social divisions the same inevitableness of organic law? If we have the hardihood to say 'yes' to that question, then how can we blame an alien people for subjecting us to a political order which they are tempted to believe eternal?[6]

Till we can achieve something, let us live incognito, say I. So long as we are only fit to be looked down upon, on what shall we base our claim to respect? When we have acquired a foothold of our own in the world, when we have had some share in shaping its course, then we can meet others smilingly. Till then let us keep in the background, attending to our own affairs.

But our countrymen seem to hold the opposite opinion. They set no store by our more modest, intimate wants which have to be met behind the scenes—the whole of their attention is directed to momentary attitudinizing and display.[7]

[6]Rabindranath Tagore, 'The Spirit of Freedom: A Letter from New York to My Own Countrymen', *Creative Unity*, pp. 136–38.

[7]*Glimpses of Bengal*, p. 95.

14

GITANJALI AND THE NOBEL PRIZE, 1913

Rabindranath wrote the poems of *Gitanjali* between 1907 and 1910. Being in poor health for some time, he was advised a trip to the West to recover his health. He was ready to leave on 19 March 1912 when he fell critically ill the night before and was unable to travel. He went instead to rest in Shelidah on the banks of his beloved Padma. It was there that he began to translate the *Gitanjali* poems into English. He took the translations with him when he was finally able to sail for England on 27 May 1912. On his arrival in London, he gave the poems to the English painter William Rothenstein whom he had met in Calcutta in 1911. Rothenstein had wanted to read Rabindranath's work in English. Struck by the poems, Rothenstein gave them to the poet W.B. Yeats to read. Much taken with their beauty, Yeats read them out to a circle of their literary and artistic friends one evening in London. Some of them decided to get a collection published by the India Society of London after Yeats made a selection of the poems and wrote an introduction to the collection. That is how *Gitanjali* (*Song Offerings*) was first published in 1912. From London, Rabindranath went to America for the first time and stayed at the University of Illinois in Urbana-Champaign where his son was enrolled for graduate studies in agricultural sciences. In April 1913, all of them returned to England and then sailed for India in September 1913. News of the Nobel Prize reached Rabindranath in Santiniketan on 14 November 1913.

My elder sister has sent me her translation of her novel *Phuler Mala* (The Flower Garland). If she knew the literary market here, she would understand why her writing will not be appreciated. What they are looking for here is 'reality'. We on the other hand have very little truck with 'reality'—we don't even miss it when it is absent. But I will be misunderstood if I say this, because my own compositions have been accepted. If you ask me why, I will tell you that in my case I was not consciously writing poetry when writing the songs of *Gitanjali*. They were an expression of my inmost feelings, they were my humblest prayers, my sincerest *sadhana*, and a reflection of my joys and sorrows.[1]

You have alluded to the English translation of *Gitanjali*. I have not been able to imagine to this day how people came to like it so much. That I cannot write English is such a patent fact that I never had even the vanity to feel ashamed of it. If anybody wrote an English note asking me to tea, I never felt equal to answering it. Perhaps you think I have got over that delusion. On the day I was to board the ship, I fainted due to my frantic efforts at leave-taking and the journey itself was postponed. Then I went to Shelidah to take rest. But unless the brain is fully active, one does not feel strong enough to relax completely; so the only way to keep calm was to take up some light work.

It was then the month of *Chaitra* (March-April), the air was thick with the fragrance of mango-blossoms and all hours of the day were delirious with the song of birds. When a child is full of vigour, he does not think of his mother. It is only when he is tired that he wants to nestle in her lap. That was exactly my position. With all my heart and with all my holiday I seemed to have ensconced myself comfortably in the arms of Chaitra, without missing a particle of its light, its air, its scent and its song. In such a state one cannot remain idle. It is an old habit of mine, as you know, that when the air strikes my bones, they tend to respond in music. Yet I

[1]Rabindranath to Indira Devi Chaudhurani, London, 6 May 1913, Bengali Letters, File: Chaudhurani, Indira Devi. Translated by UDG. (RBA.)

had not the energy to gird up my loins and sit down to write. So I took up the poems of *Gitanjali* and set myself to translate them one by one. You may wonder why such a crazy ambition should possess one in such a weak state of health. But believe me, I did not undertake this task in a spirit of reckless bravado. I simply felt an urge to recapture through the medium of another language the feelings and sentiments which had created such a feast of joy within me in the days gone by. The pages of a small exercise book came to be filled gradually, and with it in my pocket I boarded the ship. The idea of keeping it in my pocket was that when my mind became restless on the high seas, I would recline on a deckchair and set myself to translate one or two poems from time to time. And that is what actually happened. From one exercise-book I passed on to another. Rothenstein already had an inkling of my reputation as a poet from another Indian friend. Therefore, when in the course of conversation he expressed a desire to see some of my poems, I handed him my manuscript with some diffidence. I could hardly believe the opinion he expressed after going through it. He then made over the manuscript to Yeats. The story of what followed is known to you. From this explanation of mine you will see that I was not responsible for the offence, which was due mainly to the force of circumstances.[2]

Last night I had dinner with the poet Yeats. He read out from the prose translations of my poems. He read beautifully, and in the correct tone. I have hardly any confidence in my English—but he definitely said that anybody who thought my English needed improving had no sense of literature.

My work has been received with great enthusiasm here, so much so that I can barely take it all in. I feel they expect nothing much from our part of the world, and that is why they are so overwhelmed. Anyway, Yeats himself has undertaken to edit my poems, write an introduction to

---

[2]Rabindranath to Indira Devi Chaudhurani, on the genesis of *Gitanjali* in English, London, 6 May 1913, *Indian Literature*, Volume II, no. 1, October 1958–March 1959, New Delhi, Sahitya Akademi, pp. 3-4. Translated by Indira Devi Chaudhurani.

them, and see to their publication. I feel very elated by all this but also a bit overwhelmed myself. I do not enjoy being in this limelight and want to escape to Germany. But I ask myself whether this is the handiwork of my God who brought me all the way to this country—at my age—to bring the world closer. It is through literature and art that countries come to know one another. I feel He must be happy with my writing and wants others to share that happiness. It is something like our taking delight in the lotus we offer Him because He delights in it. I feel He has brought me from East to West to demonstrate His pleasure in my work. I should learn to receive this honour with humility and gratitude.[3]

It has been a great joy to me to think that things I wrote in a tongue not known to you should at last fall in your hands and that you should accept them with so much enjoyment and love. When, in spite of all obstacles, something seemed to impel me to come to this country I never dreamt that it was for this that I was taking my voyage. What my soul offered to my master in the solitude of an obscure corner of the world must be brought before the altar of man where hearts come together and tongues mingle like the right and the left palms of hands joined in the act of adoration. My heart fills with gratitude and I write to you this letter to say that appreciation from a man like you comes not only as a reward for my lifelong devotion to literature but as a token that my songs have been acceptable to Him, and He has led me over the sea to this country to speak to me His approval of my works through your precious friendship.

We intend to leave England in the beginning of November. I do hope I shall be able to see you before that, and, if possible, to have a sight of my translations published with your introduction.

I hope you will kindly accept from me a copy of the English translation

---

[3]Rabindranath to Kshitimohan Sen, London, 20 June 1912, in *Desh*, Calcutta, 6 December 1986, pp. 15-16. Translated by UDG. Kshitimohan Sen (1880–1960), early teacher of the school at Santiniketan and later head of Visva-Bharati's Department of Advanced Studies called Vidya-Bhavana.

of my father's *Autobiography* which I left with Mr Rothenstein to be sent
to your address.[4]

I am so glad to know that you are now in Santiniketan. It is impossible
to describe to you my longing to join you there.

The time has come at last when I must leave England; for I find that
my work here in the West is getting the better of me. It is taking up too
much of my attention and assuming more importance than it actually
deserves. Therefore, I must, without delay, go back to that obscurity where
all living seeds find their true soil for germination.

This morning, I am going to take a motor-ride to Rothenstein's country
house, and if I delay any longer I may not have the time to write to my
other correspondents by this mail, so I must close this letter.[5]

I have gone through a period of difficulty. My life had appeared to me
lonely and burdened with responsibilities too heavy for a single man to
bear. Evidently, my mind has gone into a habit of leaning too much upon
my friends whom I had acquired in England, and letting most of its
current flow outward. Therefore, coming to my own country, where the
contact of humanity is not so close as in the West, I felt suddenly stranded
and in a desolation, wherein every individual has to struggle through his
own problem unaided. For some length of time, solitariness weighed upon
my heart like a heavy load, till I gained my former mental adjustment and
felt again the current turn inward from the world outside. Now I feel the
flood-tide of life and companionship. It sweeps the burden from off my
shoulders and carries me along with it on its joyous course.

In India, the range of our lives is narrow and discontinuous. This is the
reason why our minds are often beset with provincialism. In our Ashram
at Santiniketan, we must have the widest possible outlook for our boys,

[4]Rabindranath to W.B. Yeats, London, 2 September 1912, *Selected Letters*, pp. 93-94.
[5]Rabindranath to C.F. Andrews, London, 16 August 1913, *Letters to a Friend*, pp. 37-38.

and universal human interests. This must come spontaneously—not merely through the reading of books, but through dealings with the wider world.[6]

I hope we are friends and you will not misunderstand me. I have done a wrong to you and I must ask your pardon for it. While you were minutely going over my ms, your very kindness embarrassed me and prevented me from being frank with you—which was foolish on my part and absurdly oriental—and for which I have been feeling ashamed ever since. The *Gitanjali* poems are intimately personal to me and the pleasure I have of polishing their English version is of a different nature than that of an author revising his works for publication. Every line of these should be as closely my own as possible though I must labour under the disadvantage of not being born to your language. In such a case, I have to be guided by my instinct, allowing it to work almost unconsciously without being hindered by more than casual suggestions from outside. I think that the method that Yeats followed while editing my book was the right one in selecting those poems that required least alterations and rejecting others in spite of their merits. There is a great risk of my overlooking crudities of language— the evidence of which you will find in *The Gardener*—but still I must go on with my work unaided till I have done what is in my power to do.[7]

. . . My days are riddled all over with interruptions, they are becoming perfectly useless to me. I am worn out writing letters, distributing thanks by handfuls and receiving visitors. I cannot tell you how unsuitable this sudden eruption of honour is to a man of my temperament. The winter sun is sweet, the green is luxuriant all around me—I want to be gloriously idle and let my thoughts melt and mingle in the blue of the space. I am beginning to envy the birds that sing and gladly go without honour. I was

---

[6]Rabindranath to C.F. Andrews, 11 October 1913, Ibid., p. 38.

[7]Rabindranath to Edward Thompson, Santiniketan, 18 November 1913, *Difficult Friendship*, p. 52.

watching a calf this morning, tired of browsing, basking in the sun on the grass, supinely happy and placid; it made my heart ache with the desire to be one with the great life that surrounds this earth and to be able to be peacefully joyous in the simple enjoyment of the wealth lavished everywhere without being asked. But my mind is invaded and my time is wasted with things that are of the least significance to the inner [life]. Perhaps you will smile and think this mood of mine absurdly oriental—but still it has its truth which must not be overlooked.[8]

My ordeal is not yet over. I still have dinners to attend to, and listen to speeches in praise of my genius, and to answer them in a becoming spirit of modesty. This has brought me to Calcutta and kept me in our Jorasanko lane, while the mustard fields are in bloom in Shilida [Shelidah] and wild ducks have set up their noisy households in the sandbanks of the Padma. I have already raised a howl of protests and vilifications in our papers by saying in plain words what was in my mind to a deputation who had come to Bolpur to offer me congratulations. This has been a relief to me—for honour is a heavy enough burden even when it is real but intolerable when meaningless and devoid of sincerity. However, I must not complain. Let me patiently wait for the time when all this tumult will be a thing of the past and truth will shine and peace will come even to a man whom the West has thought fit to honour.[9]

My destiny is furiously amusing herself showering upon me dry leaves of correspondence thick and fast—and when, hidden among them, come down by a chance a few stray flowers of friendship I have very little breath left to receive them with any show of welcome. Your last letter is of such a kind lying on my table in apparent neglect. I know you will pardon me and will have some sympathy for a poet whose latest acquisition in the

---

[8]Rabindranath to William Rothenstein, Shelidah, 10 December 1913, *Imperfect Encounter*, p. 143.

[9]Rabindranath to William Rothenstein, Calcutta, 16 December 1913, Ibid., pp. 143-44.

shape of honour can, by no means, be described as a feather in his cap, judged by its weight. But still I must bear it proudly, rejoicing in the fact that the East and the West ever touch each other like twin gems in the circlet of humanity, that they have met long before Kipling was born and will meet long after his name is forgotten.[10]

I have been polishing the English versions of some of my narrative poems since we last met. I find it difficult to impart to them the natural vigour of the original poems. Simplicity appears anaemic and spectre-like when she lacks her ruddy bloom of life, which is the case with these translations of mine. Some of these, with my latest revisions, have already appeared in the *Nation* in England, and as for the remaining ones are they worth the trouble of publishing?[11]

I am still suffering from Nobel Prize notoriety and I do not know what nursing home there is where I can go and get rid of this my latest and greatest trouble. To deprive me of my seclusion is like shelling my oyster—the rude touch of the curious world is all over me. I am pining for the shade of obscurity. I hope you have not already tired of my name being discussed in every newspaper and you do not despise me who has been dragged from his nest of dreams into the most crowded market of public applause. Why do I not have a word of sympathy from you in my time of distress?[12]

---

[10]This is a reference to Rudyard Kipling's couplet 'But there is neither East nor West, Border, nor Breed, nor Birth/When two strong men stand face to face, tho' they come from the ends of the earth!' Kipling is often quoted for having written that the East and West shall *never* meet. But his poem here shows that he, in fact, believed it is possible to overcome the gulf between the East and West. Rudyard Kipling (1865–1936), British novelist and poet. Author of *The Jungle Book* and *Kim*. Received the Nobel Prize for Literature in 1907.

[11]Rabindranath to Harriet Monroe, Santiniketan, 31 December 1913, *Selected Letters*, p. 136. Harriet Monroe (1860–1936), founder and long-time editor of *Poetry: A Magazine of Verse* which published six lyrics of Rabindranath in its issue of December 1912. That was the first time he was published in America.

[12]Rabindranath to Harriet Moody, Santiniketan, 22 January 1914, Ibid., p. 137. Harriet Moody (1857–1932), wife of the American poet William Vaughan Moody, who became a very kind friend to Rabindranath. He dedicated *Chitra* to Harriet Moody.

An incident will show you how the award of the Nobel Prize has roused up antipathy and suspicion against me in certain quarters. A report has reached me from a barrister friend of mine who was present on the occasion when, in a meeting of the leading Mohammedan gentlemen of Bengal, Valentine Chirol told the audience that the English *Gitanjali* was practically a production of Yeats. It is likely he did not believe it himself, it being merely a political move on his part to minimize the significance of this Nobel Prize affair which our people naturally consider to be a matter for national rejoicing. It is not possible for him to relish the idea of Mohammedans sharing this honour with Hindus. Unfortunately for me, there are signs of this antagonism in England itself which may be partly due to the natural reaction following the chorus of praise that *Gitanjali* evoked and partly, as you have said in your letter, to the bitterness of disappointment in the minds of the partisans of the candidates for the Nobel Prize. You know it had been the source of a rare great pleasure for me while in England to be able to admire your manly power of appreciation which was without a tinge of meanness or jealousy. I could have gladly sacrificed my Nobel Prize if I could be left to the enjoyment of this strong friendliness and true-hearted admiration.[13]

I take this opportunity to tell you how touched I was by the kind welcome you gave me when I met you in Oxford. Although for a poet neglect is hard to bear yet appreciations always come to him as a surprise. Because a poet's work is really no work—it is an outcome of his life. It is like the expression of love by a lover for which he never expects praise simply because it is so vital to him. Life is not self-conscious in my country where there is no such world as a literary world where poets' are given a conventional value by appraisers expert in their trade. We have our share

[13]Rabindranath Tagore to Thomas Sturge Moore, Shelidah, 17 February 1914, Sturge Moore Papers, Senate House Library, London University. Thomas Sturge Moore (1870–1944), poet and book designer, one of Rabindranath's close circle of friends in England. He did the cover for Rabindranath's *Crescent Moon* (1913). Valentine Chirol (1852–1929), later Sir Valentine Chirol, British journalist and author.

of praise, no doubt, but it is simple like the warmth of the sun, it gives you pleasure but it has no market value. The reputation I earned in the West was sudden, as well as great—but being brought up in a different atmosphere my mind was not trained to imbibe it and be filled with it to a saturation point. That is why every piece of genuine kindness I had from you is precious to me for the hearty goodwill and gift of friendship it brings to me from you. Next time I go to England I should like nothing better than to take shelter in your home for a while and be protected from the whirlwind of the Nobel Prize notoriety.[14]

I have greatly enjoyed two of my *Gitanjali* poems done into verse by your friend and thank you for sending them to me. It was the want of mastery in your language that originally prevented me from trying English metres in my translations. But now I have grown reconciled to my limitations through which I have come to know the wonderful power of English prose. The clearness, strength and the suggestive music of well-balanced English sentences make it a delightful task for me to mould my Bengali poems into English prose form. I think one should frankly give up the attempt at reproducing in a translation the lyrical suggestions of the original verse and substitute in their place some new quality inherent in the new vehicle of expression. In English prose there is a magic which seems to transmute my Bengali verses into something which is original again in a different manner. Therefore it not only satisfies but gives me delight to assist my poems in their English rebirth though I am far from being confident in the success of my task.[15]

---

[14]Rabindranath to Robert Bridges, Santiniketan, 8 July 1914, Bridges Papers, Western Manuscripts Department, Bodleian Library, Oxford University. Robert Bridges (1844–1930), poet laureate from 1913 to 1930, who included a poem by Rabindranath in his anthology of British verse titled *The Spirit of Man: An Anthology of Verse* (1915).

[15]Rabindranath to James Drummond Anderson, Calcutta, 14 April 1918, English Letters, File: Anderson, J.D. Copy. (RBA.) J.D. Anderson (1852–1920), lecturer in Bengali at Cambridge University, corresponded closely with Rabindranath.

. . . You remind me of those early days of *Gitanjali*.

Poets are proverbially vain and I am no exception. Therefore, if I cherish even an exaggerated notion of the value of my own poems which are in Bengali I am sure you will half humorously tolerate it. But I am no such fool as to claim an exorbitant price for my English which is a borrowed acquisition coming late in my life. I am sure you remember with what reluctant hesitation I gave up to your hand my manuscript of *Gitanjali*, feeling sure that my English was of that amorphous kind for whose syntax a schoolboy could be reprimanded. The next day you came rushing to me with assurance which I dared not take seriously and to prove to me the competence of your literary judgement you made three copies of those translations and sent them to Stopford Brooke, Bradley and Yeats. The letter which Bradley sent to you in answer left no room for me to feel diffident about the merit of those poems and Stopford Brooke's opinion also was a corroboration. These were enthusiastic as far as I remember. But even then I had no doubt that it was not the language but the earnest feeling expressed in a simple manner which touched their hearts. That was enough for a foreigner and the unstinted praise offered to me by those renowned critics was a great deal more than I could ever expect. Then came those delightful days when I worked with Yeats and I am sure the magic of his pen helped my English to attain some quality of permanence. It was not at all necessary for my own reputation that I should find my place in the history of your literature. It was an accident for which you were also responsible and possibly most of all was Yeats. But yet sometimes I feel almost ashamed that I, whose undoubted claim has been recognized by my countrymen to a sovereignty in our own world of letters, should not have waited till it was discovered by the outside world in its own true majesty and environment, that I should ever go out of my own way to court the attention of others having their own language for their enjoyment and use. At least it is never the function of a poet to personally help in the transportation of his poems to an alien form and atmosphere, and be responsible for any unseemly risk that may happen to them. However, you must own that you alone were to blame for this and not myself. To the end of my days, I should have felt happy and contented to think that the translations I did were merely for private recreation and never for public display if you did not bring them before your readers. Please thank Yeats once again on my behalf for the help which he rendered to my poems in their perilous adventure of a foreign reincarnation and assure him that I at least never underrate the value of his literary comradeship. Latterly I have written and published both prose and poetry in English, mostly translations, unaided by any friendly help, but this again I have done in order to express my ideas, not for gaining any reputation for my mastery in the use of a language which can never be mine.[16]

---

[16]Rabindranath to William Rothenstein, Santiniketan, 26 November 1932, *Imperfect Encounter*, pp. 345-46. Stopford Brooke (1832–1916), preacher and writer, author of *The Theology of the English Poets* (1872); Andrew Cecil Bradley (1851–1935), literary scholar.

15

MY TRAVELS IN JAPAN
AND THE USA, 1916-17

Rabindranath felt the gloom of the impending World War of 1914 when he went to England in 1912. He had believed for some time now that the fratricidal conflict in Europe was dividing races. He wanted to think of an alternative. With the award of the Nobel Prize, and his admission into the world community, he began earnestly to pursue his idea of establishing a centre for East–West fellowship in Santiniketan. But well before all this, Santiniketan received its first international student in 1903. This was Hori San from Japan, a scholar of Sanskrit, sent to Santiniketan by the savant Kakuzo Okakura[1] who was a friend of the Tagore family. Rabindranath and his friend Jagadish Chandra Bose made plans to send Hori San to copy the Sanskrit documents in the temples of China and Japan and bring back the copies to India in the interest of historical research.[2] In 1916, Rabindranath decided to visit Japan and to communicate with the thinkers there about his idea of starting a centre for the study of Eastern and Western civilizations. The Japanese were frequently inviting him to their country to honour him for his Nobel Prize. At this time, Rabindranath was also negotiating for a lecture tour in the USA to take his ideas there. He sailed for Japan in May 1916, reaching Kobe in June. In Japan, he gave lectures criticizing militant nationalism. His reception in Japan cooled off after his comments against Japanese militarism. The Japanese press ridiculed his lectures and dismissed them as the verdict of a defeated nation. After spending four months in Japan, he sailed for America and gave the same lectures there from September 1916 to January 1917.

---

[1]Kakuzo Okakura (1863–1913), also known as Okakura Tenshin, Japanese scholar who contributed to the development of the arts in Japan, and author of *The Ideals of the East* (1903) where be declared 'Asia is one'.

[2]Uma Das Gupta, *Rabindranath Tagore: A Biography*, New Delhi: Oxford University Press, 2004, pp. 29-30.

The West in the voice of her thundering cannon had said at the door of Japan, Let there be a Nation—and there was a Nation. I am just coming from my visit to Japan, where I exhorted this young nation to take its stand upon the higher ideals of humanity and never to follow the West in its acceptance of the organized selfishness of Nationalism as its religion, never to gloat upon the feebleness of its neighbours, never to be unscrupulous in its behaviour to the weak, where it can be gloriously mean with impunity, while turning its right cheek of brighter humanity for the kiss of admiration to those who have the power to deal it a blow.[3]

I was restless to go somewhere. Just like I was when going to England last time. I kept asking myself: where shall I go? The war had closed doors to the West but when I got a telegram from America inviting me, I thought to myself that this was my call from the world.

I have realized that God does not intend me for the life of a householder. Therefore I am a constant traveller, unable to set up home anywhere. The world has received me with open arms, I want to do the same with the world.[4]

We reached Rangoon yesterday after a huge storm. There was a big crowd at the shore in the evening. On spotting me, they began to shout 'Bande Mataram' and 'Jai Rabindranath ki Jai'. They kept running behind our car for about three miles. The people on the streets and in the shops were stunned. I almost died of embarrassment.

There is a reception for me this evening in their Jubilee Hall. It will be a noisy affair. Since I can't help it, I must simply put up with it. The situation could have been salvaged if I could have at least kept quiet—but no, I have also to say something. There was a storm the other day, but what is happening here is worse than a storm! Our ship is due to leave tomorrow, Tuesday, in the evening. It is a very nice ship—we can do as we like. The captain is very amiable, and we are happy and comfortable.[5]

We were expected to arrive at Hong Kong last night. But to begin with, the current has been against us and then there was such a squall that we could not make it even this morning. We may be able to in the afternoon.

I hardly ever sleep in my cabin. I have got into such a habit of lying out on the deck that I feel suffocated when I go down to the cabin. Last night it rained so heavily that I could hardly find a sheltered spot on the deck. I kept dragging my bedroll from this end to that—then I kept standing and singing for some time, waiting for the storm to pass. I finally gave up at 1.30 in the night and had no alternative left but to go down and sleep in the cabin.

It is still pouring this morning—I cannot see myself getting down at Hong Kong in this rain. Pearson and Mukul will surely go and look around the city, rain and storm notwithstanding. It is possible that a friend will get hold of me here in Hong Kong. If that happens I shall also go and take a quick look at the city. It is possible that a Japanese reporter might seek me out.

The ship will sail from Hong Kong to Shanghai and then to Kobe. It will be another nine or ten days before we are in Japan. Our captain has said we shall reach Japan on the first of June. I don't mind if we are delayed. On the whole, I am enjoying the sea voyage, but not the rain and storm. My days are peaceful and comfortable. I have translated *Bisarjan* as well as *Raja o Rani*. Of course, I have abridged them greatly and made changes to them. If I stayed longer on such a sea voyage I could translate many more of my pieces. I don't think I shall get much time to write lectures once I am in Japan. I have written out the discussions I had with the purser of this ship and am sending you a typed copy. If you find it 'interesting', you may get it published in *Sabuj Patra*.[6]

[5]Rabindranath to Mira Devi, 8 May 1916, Ibid., pp. 72-73. Translated by UDG.

[6]Rabindranath to Rathindranath Tagore, 9 Jaishtha 1323 (22 May 1916), *Chitthi Patra* II, pp. 39–41. Translated by UDG. Pearson refers to W.W. Pearson, see chapter 13, note 1; Mukul Dey (1885–1989) was an art student at Santiniketan, who later became principal of

I was given a reception today at a Buddhist temple here. Tomorrow I have an invitation to Yokohama. There will be a reception there too. On getting into the car today after leaving the temple I saw a few girls assembled on the road. I greeted them with a namaskar which delighted them no end. They started running after the car. When we stopped the car they encircled it and made a lot of fuss. I like the girls of this country. They are simple, gentle and devoted.

At the temple I was asked to speak in Bengali. Kimura translated it into Japanese. Among those most enthusiastic about me are the Japanese students. Everyone around is saying that my presence and my talks will usher a fresh breeze into Japan. People here seem quite excited over my lectures. I spoke impromptu at an art school yesterday. I am sending it to you to read . . .[7]

Immediately on arriving, I was caught in the midst of a cyclone of greetings and kind hospitality, together with which the newspapermen created a furore around me. I had almost given up hope of seeing anything of Japan through the loopholes in this wall. They crowd around you on board ship, they follow you in the streets, they crash into your room.

Pushing our way through this inquisitive crowd, at last we arrived in Tokyo town. Here we found asylum in the home of our artist friend Yokoyama Taikan. Now we began to become acquainted with the heart of Japan. First of all, we had to take off our shoes at the door. We were given to understand that shoes are for the street, and only the feet for the house. We also found that dust was a thing of the world outside! There was none of it in their houses. All the rooms and corridors were covered with mats under which were mattresses of hard straw, so that no dust enters their rooms, so that no footfalls are heard. The doors are sliding doors, so that there is no chance of their rattling in the wind.

---

the Government School of Art, Calcutta. *Bisarjan* (1890), drama in verse; *Raja o Rani* (1889), drama in verse; *Sabuj Patra* (1914), literary monthly started by the essayist Pramatha Chaudhuri (1868–1946).

[7]Rabindranath to Rathindranath Tagore, 31 Jaishtha 1323 (13 June 1916), Ibid., pp. 42-43. Translated by UDG.

Another thing is, their houses are not very large. There are as few walls and beams and windows as possible. That is to say, that the house does not exceed the householder, but is completely within his grasp, and easily amenable to washing and scrubbing, cleaning and polishing . . .

When I took my seat at early dawn on a mat by the window, I realized that not only are they Japanese master-painters but they have reduced the whole of man's life to an art. They know this much, that a thing which is valuable, which has worth, must be allowed a sufficient amount of space around it. Emptiness of space is most necessary for fullness of perception. A crowd of material is most inimical to the unfolding of life. In the whole of this house, there is not a single corner which is uncared for, which is superfluous. The eye is not offended by any unnecessary object; the ear is not annoyed by any unwanted sound. The mind of man can spread itself out as much as it likes, and does not have to trip over things at every step.[8]

When I came to Japan, I had a chance of observing something that deeply hurt my mind. I saw the trophies won from the Chinese people being exhibited there. It was just after China had been humiliated by the Japanese people. It struck me as vulgar and vainglorious that these people should forget everything and show this spirit of bragging. It was almost childish that a self-respecting nation should indulge in such a thing. It came to me very strongly owing to the fact that naturally the Japanese are very courteous and take an immense amount of trouble to make life beautiful and poetical. Because of this intense nationalism in abstract form, humanity is obscured, and that is why the Japanese did not see the shame of indulging in such a display. I feel that nationalism smothers the higher spirit of man which you often find in the individual.[9]

---

[8]Rabindranath Tagore, 'In Japan', Amiya Chakravarty, ed., *A Tagore Reader*, Boston: Beacon Books, 1966, pp. 5-6. (Hereafter, *Tagore Reader*.) Yokoyama Taikan (1868–1958), Japanese painter.

[9]Rabindranath Tagore, 'International Goodwill', *English Writings*, Volume III, p. 646.

The first thing which is uppermost in my heart is the feeling of gratitude which we all owe to you—we whose home is in Asia. The worst form of bondage is the bondage of dejection which keeps men hopelessly chained in loss of faith in themselves. We have been repeatedly told, with some justification, that Asia lives in the past—it is like a rich mausoleum which displays all its magnificence in trying to immortalize the dead. It was said of Asia that it could never move in the path of progress, its face was so inevitably turned backwards. We accepted this accusation and came to believe it. In India, I know, a large section of our educated community, grown tired of feeling the humiliation of this charge against us, is trying with all its resources of self-deception to turn it into a matter of boasting. But boasting is only a masked shame, it does not truly believe in itself.

When things stood like this . . . Japan rose from her dreams and in giant strides left centuries of inaction behind, overtaking the present time in its foremost goal. This has broken the spell under which we lay in torpor for ages, taking it to be the normal condition of certain races living in certain geographical limits . . .

And Japan, the child of the Ancient East, has also fearlessly claimed all the gifts of modern age for herself. She has shown her bold spirit in breaking through the confinements of habits, useless accumulations of the lazy mind, which seeks safety in its thrift and its locks and keys. Thus she has come in contact with the living time and has accepted with an amazing eagerness and aptitude the responsibilities of modern civilization.

This it is which has given heart to the rest of Asia . . .

I, for myself, cannot believe that Japan has become what she is by imitating the West. We cannot simulate strength for long, nay, what is more, a mere imitation is a source of weakness. For it hampers our true nature; it is always in our way . . .

But at the initial stage of our schooling we cannot distinguish between the essential and the non-essential, between what is transferable and what is not . . .

I earnestly hope that Japan may never lose her faith in her own soul in the mere pride of her own foreign acquisition. For that pride itself is a humiliation, ultimately leading to poverty and weakness.

The whole world waits to see what this great Eastern nation is going to do with the opportunities and responsibilities she has accepted from the hands of modern time. If it be a mere reproduction of the West, then the great expectation she has raised will remain unfulfilled. For there are grave questions that Western civilization has presented before the world but not completely answered. The conflict between the individual and the state, labour and capital, the man and the woman; the conflict between the greed of material gain and the spiritual life of man, the organized selfishness of nations and the higher ideals of humanity; the conflict between all the ugly complexities inseparable from giant organizations of commerce and state and the natural instincts of man crying for simplicity and beauty and fullness of leisure—all these have to be brought to a harmony in a manner not yet dreamt of . . .

I do not for a moment suggest that Japan should be unmindful of acquiring modern weapons of self-protection. But this should never be allowed to go beyond her instinct of self-preservation. She must know that the real power is not in the weapons themselves, but in the man who wields these weapons; and when he, in his eagerness for power, multiplies his weapons at the cost of his own soul, then it is he who is in even greater danger than his enemies . . .

What is dangerous for Japan is not the imitation of the outer features of the West, but the acceptance of the motive force of Western nationalism as her own . . .

I know my voice is too feeble to raise itself above the uproar of this bustling time, and it is easy for any street urchin to fling against me the epithet of 'unpractical'. It will stick to my coat-tail, never to be washed away, effectively excluding me from the consideration of all respectable persons. I know what a risk one runs from the vigorously athletic crowds in being styled an idealist in these days, when thrones have lost their dignity and prophets have become an anachronism, when the sound that drowns all voices is the noise of the marketplace. Yet when, one day, standing on the outskirts of Yokohama town bristling with its display of its modern miscellanies, I watched the sunset in your southern sea, and saw its peace and majesty among your pine-clad hills—with the great Fujiyama growing faint against the golden horizon, like a god overcome with his own radiance—the music of eternity welled up through the evening silence, and I felt that the sky and the earth and the lyrics of the dawn and the dayfall are with the poets and idealists, and not with the marketmen robustly contemptuous of all sentiment—that, after all the forgetfulness of his divinity, man will remember again that heaven is always in touch with his world, which can never be abandoned for good to the hounding wolves of the modern era, scenting human blood and howling to the skies.[10]

One thing strikes the eye. There are crowds of people in the streets, but no confusion whatsoever. It is as if these people do not know how to shout; they even say the children of Japan do not cry. On going through the street in a car, when one is sometimes held up by rickshaws, the chauffeur waits quietly, never shouting or abusing anybody. Suddenly in the middle of the road a bicycle nearly collided with our car, under which circumstances an Indian chauffeur could not have refrained from abusing the cyclist to his heart's content, but our man took not the slightest notice. I am told by the Bengalis here that even when there is an injury caused by a collision between two vehicles in the streets, both parties, instead of shouting and abusing each other, brush the dust off and walk away.[11]

I have nearly come to the end of my visit to Japan. I had my idea of Japan of the bookland—the Japan which had no soul of her own therefore had no difficulty in getting into the bodies belonging to others. I fully expected to find here one monotonous mist of the Modern everywhere and very little Japan behind it. But to my surprise I find that the mist is not continuous and Japan is still visible. Her features are still distinct— and what is more, she is human. She is not a mask of modern science and organization with no living face inside. I can see that Japan has all the

[10]Rabindranath Tagore, 'Nationalism in Japan', *Nationalism*, pp. 49–93.

[11]Rabindranath Tagore, 'Japan', *Tagore Reader*, p. 4.

advantage of the smallness of her area, security of her sea and homogeneity of her inhabitants. She is like a skilful gardener having a small piece of land, compelled to take recourse to intensive culture, making every inch of the ground yield its best. She has not been burdened with a bulk which breeds slowness and negligence. It is wonderful to see how the mind of a whole people has been trained to love beauty in nature and bring it out in art. It has been their conscious endeavour to make their daily life in all its details perfect in rhythm of beauty. There is no sign of oversight or vulgar display in their houses or their manners. The reticence in their taste shows their natural sensibility for the beautiful. Because their enjoyment is true, for them the enough is better than the more and right proportion better than profuseness.

This has been made possible because for their expression they seem to have concentrated all their resources in the picturesque. Their genius has taken the course of the definite—they revel in the rhythm of proportion in lines and movements. But music is lacking in them and the deeper currents of poetry which deal with the ineffable. They have acquired a perfect sense of the form at some cost of the sense of the spirit. Their nature is solely aesthetic and not spiritual. Therefore, it has been easier for them to make their ideals almost universal in their peoples. For these ideals are more in the sense of the decorum and deftness of mind and fingers than in the sense of the infinite in man—they are more of the dress than of the health. However, it is wonderful to see perfection achieved and made the common property of a whole race of men.

My next move is towards America where I shall spend my winter on a lecturing tour, hoping that by that time the war will be over and the next spring will find me in England. You know that I was not born for the career of the lecturer but life is a combination of what one is and what one is not, in which the latter predominates in quantity in the same proportion as the water is to the land in the composition of the earth.[12]

[12]Rabindranath to William Rothenstein, Yokohama, 2 August 1916, *Imperfect Encounter*, pp. 231-32.

I have received a cable from America offering me $12,000 for my lectures. I have responded, saying that I shall plan the lectures once I am there. Now that I will not have to worry about the living expenses, I have decided to go. Andrews must come with me otherwise it will be too much for me to arrange things. I shall take the Pacific route. Going via Japan will make it easier and less costly. Do enquire quickly about getting us berths on a Japanese vessel. I want to leave just after the first of Baisakh. Ask for those boats where one can get a berth for two hundred rupees.[13]

I am moving from one town to another, giving lectures. My agents have been doing this job for two generations. They say they have hosted many lecturers earlier but never before have they seen such crowds. People have had to go away because of lack of even standing room. I feel that my God has brought me here at the right moment. My words may have an influence on the students. I am happy to see their enthusiasm . . .

It is exhausting to be so much on the move. But I am willing because it is by God's will that I bring my message here. I hope that the school at Santiniketan will become the link between India and the world. We will have to establish there a centre for humanistic research concerned with all the world's peoples. The age of narrow chauvinism is coming to an end for the sake of the future, and the first steps towards that great meeting of world humanity will have to be taken on those very fields of Bolpur. I am determined to plant that seed of world humanity, and throw out the geographical limits of nations as a thing of the past. It is the task of my old age to put a stop to national chauvinism. That is why my God has steered my boat to these shores without prior notice. I accept His will.[14]

[13]Rabindranath to Rathindranath Tagore, undated (1916?), *Chitthi Patra* II, p. 35. Translated by UDG.

[14]Rabindranath to Rathindranath Tagore, Los Angeles, 11 October 1916, Ibid., pp. 54–56. Translated by UDG.

I got your letter today. I am staying in Mrs Moody's house. I shall not be here for long because I have more lectures to give. People seem to want them even though my arguments go against the prevailing opinion here. Nobody has raised objections at least up till now. I hope my words will resonate in the minds of some people even after I have left. I will continue for another five months here, till April. After that I have invitations to lecture in Honolulu. I will return to India from Honolulu if the war in Europe is not over by then. I don't see any signs of the war ending soon. I wanted to go to England and read my lectures there before returning to India. That does not seem likely to happen.

I was writing to you regularly. But I felt discouraged to write when I was told that my letters from Singapore took so long to reach you.

Having been subjected unjustly to censorship makes me even more resolute to say all I am here to say, in the West. Nobody can stop me from expressing my thoughts. I have made the world my own. I too am accepted by the world, more than I am in my own country. I feel blessed by a sense of oneness with the world before my time comes to depart from it. We must not forget that a world-consciousness reached the corners of Bengal. It was there that Ram Mohan founded a religion for all humanity. That was the dawn of Bengal's renaissance. The melody of that world-consciousness is our song—the song of man's future.[15]

---

[15]Rabindranath to Rathindranath Tagore, Chicago, 28 October 1916, Ibid., pp. 57-58. Translated by UDG.

16

RENOUNCING THE KNIGHTHOOD, AND MY ARGUMENTS AGAINST NON-COOPERATION

In his lectures on nationalism, Rabindranath made three major points. First, that war and misery were caused by the *cult* of the nation; second, that the British government was entirely impersonal, with the result that there was no affection between them and their colonial subjects; third, that Indians should not claim equality among nations until they could remove their own social injustices of caste and untouchability. He came in touch with Mahatma Gandhi in 1915. They grew to be lifelong friends, sharing closely their common concern for humanity. But their actions took different paths. On 12 April 1919, two days after the declaration of martial law in the Punjab, Rabindranath wrote a long and intimate letter to Gandhi cautioning him about the use of 'passive resistance' as a political weapon without preparing the minds of the masses for the responsibility. He did not join Gandhi's Non-cooperation Movement. The Jallianwallah Bagh massacre took place on 13 April 1919, when British troops opened fire on a peaceful gathering at an enclosed space called Jallianwallah Bagh in Amritsar. Hundreds of unarmed Indians who had come to protest against the Rowlatt Act were killed or wounded. Shocked by the crime, Rabindranath decided to renounce his knighthood which he had accepted from the government in 1915. Surrendering the honour, he wrote to the viceroy of India on 31 May 1919, 'The time has come when badges of honour make our shame glaring.' He returned to Santiniketan on 17 June and, at the request of Romain Rolland,[1] signed *Le Declaration pour l'independence de l'esprit* along with many pacifists of the world.

---

[1]Romain Rolland (1866–1944), French litterateur and pacifist, awarded the Nobel Prize for Literature in 1915.

Those of us in India who have come under the delusion that mere political freedom will make us free have accepted their lessons from the West as the gospel truth and lost their faith in humanity. We must remember that whatever weakness we cherish in our society will become the source of danger in politics. The same inertia that leads us to our idolatry of dead forms in social institutions will create in our politics prison-houses with immovable walls. The narrowness of sympathy which makes it possible for us to impose upon a considerable portion of humanity the galling yoke of inferiority will assert itself in our politics in creating the tyranny of justice.[2]

Power in all its forms is irrational, it is like the horse that drags the carriage blindfolded. The moral element in it is only represented in the man who drives the horse. Passive resistance is a force which is not necessarily moral in itself; it can be used against truth as well as for it. The danger inherent in all force grows stronger when it is likely to gain success, for then it becomes temptation.

I know your teaching is to fight against evil by the help of the good. But such a fight is for heroes and not for men led by impulses of the moment. Evil on one side naturally begets evil on the other, injustices leading to violence and insult to vengefulness. Unfortunately, such a force has already been started and either through panic or through wrath, our authorities have shown us their claws whose sure effect is to drive some of us into the secret path of resentment and others into utter demoralization.

In this crisis, you as a great leader of men have stood among us to proclaim your faith in the ideal which is both against the cowardliness of hidden revenge and the cowed submissiveness of the terror-stricken. You have said, as Lord Buddha has done in his time and for all time to come:

Akkodhena jine kodhan asadhum sadhuna jine.
Conquer anger by the power of non-anger and evil by the power of good.

---

[2]Rabindranath Tagore, *Nationalism*, p. 123.

This power of good must prove its truth and strength by its fearlessness, by its refusal to accept any imposition, which depends for its success upon its power to produce frightfulness and is not ashamed to use its machines of destruction to terrorize a people completely disarmed. We must know that moral conquest does not consist in success, that failure does not deprive it of its dignity and worth. Those who believe in spiritual life know that to stand against wrong which has overwhelming material power behind it is victory of the active faith in the ideal in the teeth of evident defeat.

I have always felt, and said accordingly, that the great gift of freedom can never come to a people through charity. We must win it before we can own it. And India's opportunity for winning it will come to her when she can prove that she is morally superior to the people who rule her by their right of conquest. She must willingly accept her penance of suffering, the suffering which is the crown of the great. Armed with her utter faith in goodness, she must stand unabashed before the arrogance that scoffs at the power of the spirit.

And you have come to your motherland in the time of her need to remind her of her mission, to lead her in the true path of conquest, to purge her present-day politics of its feebleness which imagines that it has gained its purpose when it struts in the borrowed feathers of diplomatic dishonesty.

This is why I pray most fervently that nothing that tends to weaken our spiritual freedom may intrude into your marching line, that martyrdom for the cause of truth may never degenerate into fanaticism for mere verbal forms, descending into self-deception that hides itself behind sacred names.

With these few words for an introduction, allow me to offer the following as a poet's contribution to your noble work:

I

Let me hold my head high in this
faith that thou art our shelter,
that all fear is mean distrust of thee.
Fear of man? But what man is there
in this world, what king, O King of kings

who is thy rival, who has hold of me
for all time and in all truth?
What power, is there in this world to rob
me of my freedom? For do not the arms reach
the captive through the dungeon-walls bringing
unfettered release to the soul?
And must I cling to this body in fear of
death, as a miser to his barren treasure?
Has not this spirit of mine the eternal call
to the feast of everlasting life?
Let me know that all pain and death are
shadows of the moment; that the dark force
which sweeps between me and thy truth is but the
mist before the sunrise; that thou alone art
mine forever and greater than all pride of
strength that dares to mock my manhood with
its menace.

II

Give me the supreme courage of love, this is
my prayer, the courage to speak, to do, to
suffer at thy will, to leave all things or to be
left alone.
Give me the supreme faith of love, this is
my prayer, the faith of the life in death,
of the victory in defeat, of the power hidden in
the frailness of beauty, of the dignity of pain
that accepts hurt, but disdains to return it.[3]

---

[3]Rabindranath to Mahatma Gandhi, Santiniketan, 12 April 1919, *Mahatma and the Poet*, pp. 49–51.

The enormity of the measures taken by the Government in the Punjab for quelling some local disturbances has, with a rude shock, revealed to our minds the helplessness of our position as British subjects in India. The disproportionate severity of the punishments inflicted upon the unfortunate people and the methods of carrying them out, we are convinced, are without parallel in the history of civilized governments, barring some conspicuous exceptions, recent and remote. Considering that such treatment has been meted out to a population, disarmed and resourceless, by a power which has the most terribly efficient organization for destruction of human lives, we must strongly assert that it can claim no political expediency, far less moral justification. The accounts of our insults and sufferings undergone by our brothers in the Punjab have trickled through the gagged silence, reaching every corner of India, and the universal agony of indignation roused in the hearts of our people has been ignored by our rulers—possibly congratulating themselves for imparting what they imagine as salutary lessons. This callousness has been praised by most of the Anglo-Indian papers, which have in some cases gone to the brutal length of making fun of our sufferings, without receiving the least check from the same authority—relentlessly careful in smothering every cry of pain and expression of judgement from the organs representing the sufferers. Knowing that our appeals have been in vain and that the passion of vengeance is blinding the nobler vision of statesmanship in our Government, which could so easily afford to be magnanimous as befitting its physical strength and moral tradition, the very least I can do for my country is to take all consequences upon myself in giving voice to the protest of millions of my countrymen, surprised into a dumb anguish of terror. The time has come when badges of honour make our shame glaring in their incongruous context of humiliation, and I for my part wish to stand, shorn of all special distinctions, by the side of those of my countrymen, who, for their so-called insignificance, are liable to suffer a degradation not fit for human beings.

These are the reasons which have painfully compelled me to ask Your Excellency, with due deference and regret, to relieve me of my title of

Knighthood, which I had the honour to accept from His Majesty the King at the hands of your predecessor,[4] for whose nobleness of heart I still entertain great admiration.[5]

I find our countrymen are furiously excited about Non-cooperation. It will grow into something like our Swadeshi Movement in Bengal. Such an emotional outbreak should have been taken advantage of in starting independent organizations all over India for serving our country.

Let Mahatma Gandhi be the true leader in this; let him send his call for positive service, ask for homage in sacrifice, which has its end in love and creation. I shall be willing to sit at his feet and do his bidding if he commands me to cooperate with my countrymen in service and love. I refuse to waste my manhood in lighting fires of anger and spreading it from house to house.

It is not that I do not feel anger in my heart for injustice and insult heaped upon my motherland. But this anger of mine should be turned into the fire for lighting the lamp of worship to be dedicated through my country to my God.

It would be an insult to humanity if I use the sacred energy of my moral indignation for the purpose of spreading a blind passion all over my country. It would be like using the fire from the altar of sacrifice for the purpose of incendiarism.[6]

Your letter gives wonderful news about our students in Calcutta. I hope that this spirit of sacrifice and willingness to suffer will grow in strength; for to achieve this is an end in itself. This is the true freedom! Nothing is of higher value—be it national wealth or independence—than disinterested faith in ideals, in the moral greatness of man.

The West has its unshakeable faith in material strength and prosperity;

[4]The reference is to Lord Hardinge, viceroy of India (1910–16).

[5]Rabindranath to Lord Chelmsford, viceroy of India (1916–21), Calcutta, 31 May 1919, English Letters, File: Knighthood. (RBA.); also see *Modern Review*, Calcutta, July 1919, p. 105.

[6]Rabindranath to C.F. Andrews, Paris, 18 September 1920, *Letters to a Friend*, pp. 95-96.

therefore, however loud grows the cry for peace and disarmament, its ferocity grows louder, gnashing its teeth and lashing its tail in impatience. It is like a fish, hurt by the pressure of the flood, planning to fly in the air. Certainly the idea is brilliant, but it is not possible for a fish to realize. We, in India, shall have to show to the world, what is that truth, which not only makes disarmament possible but turns it into strength.

The truth that moral force is a higher power than brute force will be proved by the people who are unarmed. Life, in its higher development, has thrown off its tremendous burden of armour and a prodigious quantity of flesh; till man has become the conqueror of the brute world. The day is sure to come, when the frail man of spirit, completely unhampered by arms and air fleets, and dreadnoughts will prove that the meek is to inherit the earth.

It is in the fitness of things that Mahatma Gandhi, frail in body and devoid of all material resources, should call up the immense power of the meek that has been lying waiting in the heart of the destitute and insulted humanity of India. The destiny of India has chosen for its ally the power of soul, and not that of muscle. And she is to raise the history of man from the muddy level of physical conflict to the higher moral attitude . . .

Our fight is a spiritual fight, it is for Man. We are to emancipate Man from the meshes that he himself has woven round him—these organizations of national egoism. The butterfly will have to be persuaded that the freedom of the sky is of higher value than the shelter of the cocoon. If we can defy the strong, the armed, the wealthy, revealing to the world power of the immortal spirit, the whole castle of the Giant Flesh will vanish in the void. And then Man will find his *Swaraj.*

We, the famished, ragged ragamuffins of the East, are to win freedom for all Humanity. We have no word for Nation in our language. When we borrow this word from other people, it never fits us.[7]

Lately I have been receiving more and more news and newspaper cuttings from India, giving rise in my mind to a painful struggle that presages a period of suffering which is waiting for me. I am striving with all my power

[7]Rabindranath to C.F. Andrews, Chicago, 2 March 1921, Ibid., pp. 127-28.

to tune my mood of mind to be in accord with the great feeling of excitement sweeping across my country. But deep in my being why is there this spirit of resistance maintaining its place in spite of my strong desire to remove it? I fail to find a clear answer, and through my gloom of dejection breaks out a smile and a voice saying, 'Your place is on the seashore of worlds with children; there is your peace, and I am with you there . . .'

But where am I among the crowd, pushed from behind, pressed from all sides? And what is this noise about me? If it is a song, then my own sitar can catch the tune and I join in the chorus, for I am a singer. But if it is a shout, then my voice is wrecked and I am lost in bewilderment. I have been trying all these days to find in it a melody, straining my ear, but the idea of non-cooperation with its mighty volume of sound does not sing to me, its congregated menace of negation shouts. And I say to myself, 'If you cannot keep step with your countrymen at this great crisis of their history, never say that you are right and the rest of them wrong; only give up your role as a soldier, go back to your corner as a poet, be ready to accept popular derision and disgrace . . .'

The idea of non-cooperation is political asceticism. Our students are bringing their offering of sacrifices to what? Not to a fuller education but to non-education. It has at its back a fierce joy of annihilation which is at best asceticism, and at its worst is that orgy of frightfulness in which the human nature, losing faith in the basic reality of normal life, finds a disinterested delight in an unmeaning devastation as has been shown in the late war and on other occasions which came nearer to us. [8]

. . . Today, at this critical moment of the world's history cannot India rise above her limitations and offer the great ideal to the world that will work towards harmony and cooperation between the different peoples of the earth? Men of feeble faith will say that India requires to be strong and rich before she can raise her voice for the sake of the whole world. But I

[8]Rabindranath to C.F. Andrews, Chicago, 5 March 1921, Ibid., pp. 128–31.

refuse to believe it. That the measure of man's greatness is in his material resources is a gigantic illusion casting its shadow over the present-day world—it is an insult to man. It lies in the power of the materially weak to save the world from this illusion and India, in spite of her penury and humiliation, can afford to come to the rescue of humanity . . .

I feel that the true India is an idea and not a mere geographical fact. I have come into touch with this idea in faraway places of Europe and my loyalty was drawn to it in persons who belonged to different countries from mine. India will be victorious when this idea wins victory—the idea of *purusham mahantam aditya-varnam tamasah parastat*, the Infinite Personality whose Light reveals itself through the obstruction of Darkness. Our fight is against this Darkness. Our object is the revealment of the Light of the Infinite Personality in ourselves. This Infinite Personality of man is not to be achieved in single individuals, but in one grand harmony of all human races. The darkness of egoism which will have to be destroyed is the egoism of the Nation. The idea of India is against the intense consciousness of the separateness of one's people from others, and which inevitably leads to ceaseless conflicts. Therefore, my one prayer is: let India stand for the *cooperation* of all peoples of the world.[9]

My difficulty is that when, in my environment, some intense feeling of pride or resentment concentrates its red light within a certain limited area, I lose my true perspective of life and the world, and it hurts deeply my nature. It is not true that I do not have any special love for my own country, but when it is in its normal state it does not obstruct outside reality; on the contrary, it offers a standpoint and helps me in my natural relationship with others. But when that standpoint becomes a barricade, then something in me asserts that my place is somewhere else.

I have not yet attained that spiritual altitude from which I can say, with perfect assurance, that such barricading is wrong, or even unnecessary; but

[9]Rabindranath to C.F. Andrews, New York, 13 March 1921, Ibid., pp. 133–35.

some instinct in me says that there is a great deal of unreality in it, as there is in all passions that are generated through contraction of consciousness, through rejection of a great part of truth.

I remember you wondering why Christ gave no expression to His patriotism which was so intense among the Jewish people. It was because the great truth of man, which He realized through His love of God, would only be cramped and crushed within that enclosure. I have a great deal of the patriot and politician in me, and therefore I am frightened of them; and I have an inner struggle against submitting myself to their sway.

But I must not be misunderstood. There is such a thing as a moral standard of judgement. When India suffers from injustice, it is right that we should stand against it; and the responsibility is ours to right the wrong, not as Indians, but as human beings. There your position is higher than most of our countrymen's. You have accepted the cause of India for the sake of humanity. But I know that most of our people will accept your help as a matter of course and yet reject your lesson. You are fighting against the patriotism whereby the West had humiliated the East—the patriotism which is national egoism. This is a comparatively later growth in European history and a far greater cause of misery and injustice in the human world than the bloodthirsty ferocity, the nomadic savagery, in the primitive history of man.

The Pathans came to India, and the Mughals, and they perpetrated misdeeds in their heedlessness; but because they had no taint of patriotism they did not attack India at the very root of her life, keeping superciliously aloof. Gradually they were growing one with us; and just as the Normans and Saxons combined into one people, our Mohammedan invaders would ultimately have lost their line of separateness and contributed to the richness and strength of Indian civilization.

We must remember that Hinduism is not the original Aryanism; in fact, a great portion of it is non-Aryan. Another great mixture had been awaiting us, the mixture with the Mohammedans. I know there were difficulties in its way. But the greatest of difficulties was lacking—the idolatry of Geography. Just see what hideous cries are being committed by British patriotism in Ireland! It is a python which refuses to disgorge this living creature which struggles to live its separate life. For patriotism is proud of its bulk, and in order to hold in a bond of unity the units that have their own distinct individualities, it is ever ready to use means that are inhuman. Our own patriots would do just the same thing, if the occasion arose. When a minority of our population claimed its right of inter-caste marriage, the majority cruelly refused to allow it that freedom. It would not acknowledge a difference which was natural and real, but was willing to perpetrate a moral torture far more reprehensible than a physical one. Why? Because power lies in number and in extension. Power, whether in the patriotic or in any other form, is no lover of freedom. It talks of unity, but forgets that the true unity is that of freedom. Uniformity is unity of bondage.

Suppose, in our *swaraj*, the anti-Brahmin community refuses to join hands with us; suppose, for the sake of its self-respect and self-expression, it tries to keep an absolute independence—patriotism will try to coerce it into an unholy union. For patriotism has its passion of power; and power builds its castle upon arithmetic. I love India, but my India is an Idea and not a geographical expression. Therefore, I am *not* a patriot—I shall ever seek my compatriots all over the world. You are one of them, and I am sure there are many others.[10]

---

[10]Rabindranath to C.F. Andrews, on board the SS *Rhyndam*, undated, probably July 1921, Ibid., pp. 142–45.

17

'A WORLD IN ONE NEST': VISVA-BHARATI UNIVERSITY, SANTINIKETAN

With the War of 1914–18 in the West and the politics of conflict in India, Rabindranath was in no doubt about the need for global cooperation. On 22 December 1918, he called a special meeting of students, teachers and well-wishers of the school at Santiniketan to explain his ideas about creating an institution for East–West fellowship and the study of cultures. The name Visva-Bharati dates from that time and also its motto, *yatra visvam bhavati ekanidam*, taken from a Sanskrit Vedic text meaning 'where the world meets in one nest'. In 1919, he toured extensively in southern India to spread word about the newly established Visva-Bharati, reading his lecture on 'The Centre of Indian Culture' for the first time. He followed it up with a tour of western India. During 1920-21, he went to Europe and America to raise funds and to enlist support for the institution. In Europe, he met many scholars who showed a keen interest in the study of cultures and who shared his views on and hopes for the unity of the human race. With Professor Sylvain Levi of Sorbonne University accepting his invitation to come as a visiting professor to Visva-Bharati in the autumn of 1921, the institution got off to a brilliant start. Returning to Santiniketan in July 1921, Rabindranath began to organize the arrangements. But raising funds was neither easy nor honourable, with many a disappointment in store. He was more than a little surprised to discover that some powerful sections in the West were even suspicious of his venture because he spoke out against militant nationalism. His letters reveal the humiliation he felt of belonging to a subject race in those circumstances.

I say again and again that I am a poet, that I am not a fighter by
nature. I would give everything to be one with my surroundings.
I love my fellow beings and I prize their love. Yet I have been
chosen by destiny to ply my boat there where the current is against
me. What irony of fate is this that I should be preaching
cooperation of cultures between East and West on this side of
the sea just at the moment when the doctrine of non-cooperation
is preached on the other side?[1]

The geographical segregation of races has been removed by the
help of science but the psychological barriers solidly built upon
time-honoured tradition still stand firm, in fact are being raised
higher and more strongly buttressed on all sides.[2]

When I left you I was labouring under the delusion that my mission was
to build an Indian university in which Indian cultures would be
represented in all their variety. But when I came to the continental Europe
and fully realized that I had been accepted by the Western people as one
of themselves I realized that my mission was the mission of the present
age. It was to make the meeting of the East and West fruitful in truth.[3]

The world of learning must be illuminated by a festival of lights, a festival
to which every race brings its own light. The whole world suffers if even
a single race is left out of it.

Once upon a time we possessed a mind of our own in India. It was a
living entity. It thought, it felt, it expressed itself. It was receptive as well
as productive. We have evidence that India used her mind to reflect seriously
on the world's problems and to find solutions. The test of our education
today lies in our ability to explore the truth and give it expression

---

[1]Rabindranath to C.F. Andrews, 5 March 1921, *Letters to a Friend*, p. 132.
[2]Rabindranath Tagore, Ms. Accession no. 314, 'National Unity', 1917, in English. (RBA.)
[3]Rabindranath to C.F. Andrews, 17 December 1921, English Letters, Collection: C.F. Andrews.
(RBA.)

creatively. Imitation and repetition can do us no good. A simple machine can do that.

There was unity among us when the Indian mind was actively engaged in creative thinking. But now we are divided, disunited. The branches are no longer connected to the root. Separation of the limbs is dangerous for the body and mind. The Indian mind is now divided into the Hindu, Buddhist, Jain, Sikh, Muslim and Christian branches. We are neither able to see ourselves as a composite whole nor contribute something worthy to the composite whole. Just as our ten fingers must be together when we make an offering, so they must be when we receive an offering. The Indian heart will again be full when our education is a blend of the Vedic, Puranic, Buddhist, Jain and Islamic minds. That is how India will grasp the unity in its diversity. We must rediscover ourselves in this connected way or else our education will not be our own. No nation can thrive on imitation.

Education can flourish in an environment where scholarship can grow and spread its wings. That is the purpose of a university. To fulfil this purpose, it is essential to invite intellectuals and scholars who are contributing to the world of learning and creativity. A meeting of minds makes a university true. This cannot happen by mere imitating.

In every nation education has to be intimately associated with the life of the people. But in our case, modern education has served only to turn out clerks, lawyers, doctors, magistrates, munsifs and policemen. These are the few favourite professions of the English-educated Indian elite. This new education has not reached the farmer, the oil-grinder, the potter. That is precisely why it has been a disaster for our society. Our modern universities have not germinated from the soil but have been parasites feeding on foreign oaks. The only way to change things is to apply our newly acquired knowledge of economics, agriculture, health and all other everyday sciences in the neglected villages. We must mix and match new knowledge with the old. The old and the new will make our schools genuinely and creatively Indian. Such schools must practise agriculture, dairy-keeping and weaving on the best modern methods and also adopt cooperative methods to generate financial resources. All must be roped into the enterprise—teachers, students, and the ordinary people.

I have proposed to call this ideal school Visva-Bharati.[4]

I depend on all of you to make Visva-Bharati happen. I am planning it in a big way, but I can succeed only if you—my friends at home—help me in the effort. My guests from the West must be made welcome here. I am simply a messenger delivering the invitations. The rest is in your hands.

There was a time in India's history when guests would come from far and wide. That was when this country was connected with the world. But that guesthouse has long been closed and its foundation destroyed. We have to rebuild it now with what we have in our mothers' stores. I can only announce everywhere that we have enough. The proof of it lies with you.

I am confident that our invitation will be accepted. All we have to ensure is that their hearts are not starved when they are with us. Being a poet I can merely play the flute at the gate. But I don't have strength enough to look after them once they are with us. I need your help.[5]

Today is the first meeting of the Visva-Bharati Society even though the work began sometime ago. I am offering it to the public today. I know that those who believe in its ideals will not hesitate to receive it. They are our well-wishers. I offer it to them.[6]

I wish to associate those present with us today with the inner ideal of Visva-Bharati. It will reveal itself gradually as individual departments of the institution develop and grow. At this stage I hesitate to talk about the larger ideal because it might not remain as pristine when we give it shape and form. This can lead to disappointment . . .

Many have received Visva-Bharati's ideal with respect even at this initial stage. That has been encouraging for us. But many have not. There are

[4]Rabindranath Tagore, 1919, *Visva-Bharati*, pp. 7–10. Translated by UDG.

[5]Rabindranath to Kshitimohan Sen, 30 November 1920, Bengali Letters, File: Sen, Kshitimohan. Translated by UDG. (RBA.)

[6]Rabindranath Tagore, 8 Poush 1328 (22 December 1921), *Visva-Bharati*, p. 20. Translated by UDG.

some who are working for it without being able to see its inner truth. They, therefore, regret their association with us. A reason for this is that such an ideal is not suited to the present environment. Many today are engaged in enterprises where they do not feel the need for a different kind of goal. But it could also just be my failure to attract them to my ideas.[7]

Our university—Visva-Bharati—has already been started. Its international character has been emphasized by Prof. Sylvain Levi's coming here and helping us with his cooperation. If there is any possibility of your visiting India once again we shall be most glad to make every suitable arrangement for the occasion. Prof. Winternitz of Prague University has accepted our invitation for the next winter season and we are earnestly hoping that there will be no prohibition from the Indian Government in his case.[8]

Sometimes my Western friends ask me if they will be accepted by my countrymen. I reply emphatically in the affirmative. I say to them we will never turn you away.

I know that Bengal takes a pride in education. I am also sure that Bengal will not reject Western scholarship. Whatever the politics, Bengalis, more than all other Indians, have an inborn respect for learning. Even the very poor among them long to go to school. Bengalis know that they will not attain social status without education. That is why even the poorest widow in Bengal undertakes every hardship possible for her child's education. I am, therefore, confident that Bengalis will not turn their backs to learning and the learned. I assured my friends that they will be received lovingly.

My assurance will be put to the test in Visva-Bharati.[9]

[7]Rabindranath Tagore, 1 Bhadra 1329 (18 August 1922), Ibid., pp. 34-35. Translated by UDG.

[8]Rabindranath to Sten Konow, Santiniketan, 14 May 1922, English Letters, File: Konow, Sten. Copy. (RBA.) Sten Konow (1867–1948), linguist and professor of Indian philology, University of Oslo. Sylvain Levi (1863–1935), French Orientalist who wrote on Eastern religion, literature and history; Moritz Winternitz (1863–1937), professor of Indology at the German University of Prague, came as visiting professor to Visva-Bharati in 1922.

[9]Rabindranath Tagore, 1922, Visva-Bharati, p. 57. Translated by UDG.

We have guests here from many parts of the world. If we can warm their hearts with our hospitality we will become a pilgrim spot for the new age. In Bengal, many rivers flow into the sea. It is from that confluence that Bengal has evolved its distinctive character. If our ashram here can freely give its heart to our guests, they will surely find their place among us. There will then be a meeting of truths here. Pilgrims go on pilgrimages with a vision and purity of heart. That is how they make their pilgrimages truthful. What is it that we can expect from this ashram where we have come—the mantra *yatra visvam bhavati ekanidam*, 'where the whole world meets in one nest'. Wherever we go, we see man within his racial limits and not as part of one mankind. Let our ashram be the one place in the world where we can mingle without the differences in religion, language and race. Surely, that *must* be the way forward to the new age.[10]

Geographical boundaries have lost their significance in the modern world. Peoples of the world have come closer. We must realize this and understand that this closeness must be founded on love. I don't deny that nations are hurting one another, that they are exploiting one another. Still, the East and West must join hands in the pursuit of truth.[11]

My dear friend, when I sent my appeal to Western people for an International Institution in India I made use of the word 'University' for the sake of convenience. But that word not only has an inner meaning but outer associations in minds of those who use it, and that fact tortures my idea into its own rigid shape. It is unfortunate. I should not allow my idea to be pinned to a word like a dead butterfly for a foreign museum. It must be known not by a definition, but by its own life growth. I saved my Santiniketan from being trampled into smoothness by the steamroller of your education department. It is poor in resources and equipment but it has the wealth of truth that no money can ever buy. I am proud of the fact that it is not a machine-made article perfectly modelled in your

[10]Rabindranath Tagore, 1923, Ibid., p. 65. Translated by UDG.

[11]Rabindranath Tagore, 4 March 1922, Ibid., pp. 31-32. Translated by UDG.

workshop—it is our very own. If we must have a university it should spring from our own life and be sustained by it. You may say that such freedom is dangerous and that a machine will help to lessen our personal responsibility and make things easy for us. Yes, life has its risks and freedom its responsibility—and yet they are preferable for their immense value and not for any other ulterior results. Now I am beginning to discover that it was more an ambition than an ideal that dragged me to the door of the rich West. It must have been the vision of a big undertaking that lured me away from my seclusion in search of big means and big results. And I am being punished deep in my heart. So long as I have been able to retain my perfect independence and self-respect because I had faith in my own resources and proudly worked within their sovereign limits ... I know that the idea of an International University is complex, but I must make it simple in my own way.[12]

My dear friend, when I was in America, the British agency thwarted me in my appeal to the people for the proposed university. An American friend, who is struggling against obstacles to raise funds for this object has lately informed me that the British consul in his own town is hindering him. I am not trusted. How can I be certain that this mistrust that has nearly killed my mission by its antagonism will not kill it by its help? But possibly your point is that trying to be independent will not further my cause. That is true. It would be presumptuous for me to imagine that my project can thrive against the suspicion lurking in the minds of the British authorities. At the same time, I feel strongly that it is far better to allow it openly to be strangled by that mistrust than to be fettered by its help. I remember you suggesting to me once in course of conversation that exuberant protestation of friendliness towards me on the part of the continental people of Europe was easy because they had no responsibility with regard to such demonstrations. You were right. For disinterested relationship is the only pure channel through which sympathy and cooperation can have a clear

---

[12]Rabindranath to William Rothenstein, Boulogne-sur-Seine, 24 April 1921, *Imperfect Encounter*, pp. 283-84.

flow. Possibly these very people would also be wisely suspicious in a similar case where they had their own interest to consider. I have often heard that when the French people tried to be hospitable to our Indian soldiers in the late war, the British officers in charge of them were alarmed. It was easier for the French to be human and grateful towards those foreigners who came to fight for them than for the British officers who had their own anxieties about these soldiers which were not purely human. Similarly, when I, who belong to a subject race under British rule, am too warmly received in America or in other Western countries, the British agency may feel uneasy— for their interest in me and my cause is not purely human and simple. Your contention is that the man who is sober in mind accepts such facts as facts and deals with them accordingly and that it is a sign of moral drunkenness to be able to think that one can ignore them in pride of his self-sufficiency. But of one thing you may be certain, that I have a natural power of resistance in me against intoxication produced by praise, and my mind in the present moment is not in a dazed state of drunkenness. I am not in the least oblivious of the fact that the breath of official suspiciousness can blight in a moment my cherished scheme.[13]

My fate still appears to be in the hands of Saturn. The stars do not favour my destiny yet. They never will till the sun sets on my life. We were almost dying of exhaustion on our journey here; I was in bed for two days. This morning I wrote a letter to the Raja of Mahmudabad, from which I quote:

> I must let you know how deeply I was touched by the warm expression of sympathy with which you accepted my appeal for the Visva-Bharati. It has delighted me particularly because there is hardly any understanding of its ideals among my countrymen. They almost rudely refuse to face the true nature of their country's problems and reach out to the populace. Please accept my heartfelt thanks not only for the ready welcome you accorded to the ideals I try to represent in my life's work but also because you had sufficient respect for my

---

[13]Rabindranath to William Rothenstein, Geneva, 8 May 1921, Ibid., pp. 285-86.

personality not to hurt my cause with an impatient gesture of an
indifferent charity made all the more conspicuous by the high position
which you and your peers in Oudh hold in India.

I'll be most grateful if every now and again you remind him of his promise
to me. He promised me also to write to his friend Madho Lal, the Raja of
Benaras, about endowing a Chair of Sanskrit at Visva-Bharati. He offered
to discuss the matter in Delhi when he goes there at the end of March. As
of now, we need to do two things urgently: appoint Brajen Babu as professor
of Sanskrit and build a guesthouse for the visiting Indian scholars who
want to come but cannot be provided with accommodation.[14]

... I have formed the nucleus of an International University in India, as
one of the best means of promoting mutual understanding between the
East and the West. This Institution, according to the plan I have in mind,
invites students from the West and the Far East to study the systems of
Indian philosophy, literature, art and music in their proper environment,
encouraging them to carry on research work in collaboration with the
scholars already engaged in this task.

India has her renaissance. She is preparing to make her contribution
to the world of the future. In the past she produced her great culture,
and in the present age she has an equally important contribution to make
to the culture of the New World which is emerging from the wreckage of
the Old. This is a momentous period of her history, pregnant with
precious possibilities, when any disinterested offer of cooperation from
any part of the West will have an immense moral value, the memory of
which will become brighter as the regeneration of the East grows in vigour
and creative power.

The Western universities give their students an opportunity to learn
what all the European peoples have contributed to their Western culture.

---

[14]Rabindranath to Atul Prasad Sen, Bengali Letters, File: Sen, Atul Prasad. Translated by
UDG. (RBA.) Atul Prasad Sen (1871–1934), writer and composer of Bengali songs who
lived in Lucknow and knew the Raja of Mahmudabad. Brajen Babu refers to Brajendranath
Seal, see chapter 3, note 12.

Thus the intellectual mind of the West has been luminously revealed to the world . . .

There was a time when the great countries of Asia had, each of them, to nurture its own civilization apart in comparative seclusion. Now has come the age of coordination and cooperation. The seedlings that were reared within narrow plots must now be transplanted into the open fields. They must pass the test of the world-market if their maximum value is to be obtained.

But before Asia is in a position to cooperate with the culture of Europe, she must base her own structure on a synthesis of all the different cultures which she has. When, taking her stand on such a culture, she turns towards the West, she will take, with a confident sense of mental freedom, her own view of truth from her own vantage-ground and open a new vista of thought to the world. Otherwise, she will allow her priceless inheritance to crumble into dust, and, trying to replace it clumsily with feeble imitations of the West, make herself superfluous, cheap and ludicrous. If she thus loses her individuality and her specific power to exist, will it in the least help the rest of the world? Will not her terrible bankruptcy involve also the Western mind? If the whole world grows at last into an exaggerated West, then such an illimitable parody of the modern age will die, crushed beneath its own absurdity.

In this belief it is my desire to extend by degrees the scope of this University on simple lines, until it comprehends the whole range of Eastern cultures—the Aryan, Semitic, Mongolian and others. Its object will be increasingly to reveal the Eastern mind to the world.

Of one thing I felt certain during my travels in Europe, that a genuine interest has been roused there in the philosophy and the arts of the East, from which the Western mind seeks fresh inspiration of truth and beauty.[15]

---

[15]Rabindranath Tagore, *An Eastern University*, Santiniketan: Visva-Bharati Bulletin Number 6, 1927, pp. 3-4.

18

VISVA-BHARATI 'SRINIKETAN': A SCHEME
FOR VILLAGE RECONSTRUCTION

S tarting scientific agriculture in the surrounding villages and instituting
a comprehensive plan of rural reconstruction were fundamental to
Visva-Bharati's goals. An Institute of Rural Reconstruction was established
in 1922 at a village called Surul, within two miles of Santiniketan. It was
named Sriniketan, Abode of Well-Being. In 1921, Rabindranath invited
Leonard Elmhirst from England to lead the Sriniketan Institute of Rural
Reconstruction. He had met Elmhirst during his travels in America in
1920–21 when Elmhirst was graduating in agricultural studies at Cornell
University. Rabindranath had two objectives in his village work: educate
the villager in self-reliance, and bring back 'life in its completeness' to the
villages with music and readings from the epics as in the past. Due to his
meagre resources, he was willing to limit the experiment to 'one or two'
villages if necessary. He hoped that success with even a single village might
serve as an ideal for the whole country. Given the problems of over three
hundred million people, he hoped at least to touch the hearts of his village
neighbours at Santiniketan. He had begun this work in his family estates
at the time of the Swadeshi Movement. Sriniketan was a continuation of
the same principles. Dorothy Whitney Straight, daughter of an American
millionaire who later married Leonard Elmhirst, put Sriniketan on its feet
financially by endowing it with a permanent fund. Rabindranath dedicated
his book *The Religion of Man* to Dorothy. There was a period in Visva-
Bharati's history when idealists from all over the world joined hands with
the Sriniketan villagers to bring hope and action to their lives.[1]

---

[1]Leonard Knight Elmhirst (1893–1974), agricultural economist, led Visva-Bharati's scheme
of rural reconstruction from 1921 to 1923. He and his wife Dorothy Straight later founded
the Dartington Trust in Devonshire, England, inspired by Rabindranath's ideas of education.

It is not enough to try to remove wants; you can never remove them completely from the outside; the far greater thing is to rouse the will of the people to remove their own wants.[2]

We have started in India, in connection with our Visva-Bharati, work of village reconstruction, the mission of which is to retard the process of race suicide. If I try to give you the details of our work, they will look small. But we are not afraid of smallness, for we have confidence in life. We know that if as a seed it represents the truth that is in us, it will overcome opposition and conquer space and time. According to us, the poverty problem is not the most important, the problem of unhappiness is the great problem. Wealth, which is the synonym for the production and collection of things, men can make use of ruthlessly. They can crush life out of the earth and flourish. But, happiness, which may not compete with wealth in its list of materials, is final, it is creative; therefore, it has its source of riches within itself.

Our object is to try to flood the choked bed of village life with the stream of happiness. For this, the scholars, the poets, the musicians, the artists, have to collaborate, to offer their contributions. Otherwise they must live like parasites, sucking life from the people and giving nothing back to them. Such exploitation gradually exhausts the soil of life, which needs constant replenishing, by the return to it of life, through the completion of the cycle of receiving and giving back.

Most of us, who try to deal with the poverty problem, think of nothing but a greater intensive effort of production, forgetting that this only means a greater exhaustion of materials as well as of humanity. This only means giving exaggerated opportunity for profit to a few, at the cost of the many. It is food which nourishes, not money; it is fullness of life which makes one happy, not fullness of purse. Multiplying materials intensifies the inequality between those who have and those who have not, and this

---

[2]Rabindranath Tagore, *The Growth of Visva-Bharati 1901–1921*, Santiniketan: Visva-Bharati Bulletin No. 8, April 1928, p. 6.

yields a fatal wound to the social system, through which the whole body is eventually bled to death.[3]

I used to sit in my house and watch the farmers come to plough their small fragmented and scattered fields—with their bullocks and ploughs. Each man ploughed his own land only. I thought how needlessly they were wasting their strength. I called them and said, 'Plough all the land together; pool your capital and resources, and you will be able to get a tractor and get your plowing done easily. If you all work together, the insignificant differences in the land can be neglected, and you can portion out whatever profit there is among you. You can store all your harvest in one place in the village, and the merchants can buy from there for the right price.' They listened and said, 'A very good idea, but who will carry it out?'

If I had had the necessary knowledge, I would have undertaken it, for they knew and trusted me. But we cannot help merely by our willingness to help. There is nothing so dangerous as inexpert service. In our country nowadays the young students of the towns have taken up village service. The villagers laugh at them. How can they help them? They don't know their language and have no acquaintance with their minds.

From that time I made up my mind that I must do some village work. I sent my son and Santosh abroad to learn agriculture and animal husbandry and began to turn over all kinds of plans in my mind.[4]

What was it that hindered us from taking upon ourselves the full responsibility of our own education, sanitation, prevention of crimes, and such other duties that God himself, and not Montagu[5] or British

[3]Rabindranath Tagore, 'City and Village', Visva-Bharati Bulletin No. 10, December 1928, pp. 24-25.

[4]Rabindranath Tagore, 'City and Village', *Towards Universal Man*, p. 321. Santosh Chandra Majumdar (1886–1926), student of the first batch at the Santiniketan school who also went to the University of Illinois to study agriculture.

[5]Edwin Montagu (1879–1924), Secretary of State for India, 1917–22.

Parliaments, had given us to perform entirely according to our own way? The sacred responsibility had been lying before our own door wearily waiting, not for any passing of a Bill, but for real sacrifice from ourselves.

The *power* is where there is right, and where there is the dedication of love. It is a *maya* to imagine that the gift of self-government is somewhere outside us. It is like a fruit that the tree must produce itself through its own normal function, by the help of its inner resources. It is not a Chinese lantern, flimsily gaudy, that can be bought from a foreign second-hand shop to be hung on the tree to illuminate its fruitlessness.

All this I tried to explain in 'Swadeshi Samaj'—and when I found that nobody took me at all seriously, and when pedants discovered to their utter disgust discrepancies between my proposal and some doctrine of John Stuart Mill, then I took up unaided my village organization work, which at the present moment is throbbing out its last heart throbs in a remote corner of Bengal. Certainly, I was more successful in writing the song on that occasion—'If nobody cares to come in answer to thy call, walk alone'.

Of course turning out songs is my proper work. But those who are unfortunate cannot afford to limit their choice to the works they *can* do; they must also bear the burdens of the tasks they can *not* do![6]

It is hard to imagine a life as cheerless as in our rural areas.

I could hardly see a way out. It is not easy to do something for people who have cultivated weakness for centuries and don't know what self-help is. But I had to anyhow make a start.[7]

I was one of the principal organizers of the National Fund and my conscience hurts to even think about it now. Our countrymen became excited with hope whenever some big plan was announced. Inevitably,

---

[6]Rabindranath Tagore, 'On Constructive Work—A Letter', *Modern Review*, Calcutta, March 1921, pp. 355-56. John Stuart Mill (1806–73), British political economist.

[7]Rabindranath Tagore, 'Abhibhasan', Address to the Visva-Bharati Sammilani, 1922, *Palli Prakriti*, p. 121. Translated by UDG.

what followed were disillusionment and disgrace. I concluded early enough that these endeavours were utterly futile. I told myself the best thing is to start something on a very modest scale, single-handedly, and to build it up away from the public gaze. There was no other alternative, particularly for those of us who are compelled to work in a miserly fashion because our resources and our ability to bear initial losses are limited.[8]

I have never treated village people disrespectfully. But our *bhadralok* class often does that. It doesn't even know how to behave though it regards itself educated because of its university degrees. Yet our shastras say: *shraddyeya deyam*, 'when you give, give with respect'.[9]

When our college students study economics and ethnology, they rely entirely on European scholarship to learn about their own villages. The rural people mean nothing to us because we regard them as *chhotolok*, meaning, literally, small people. Given such contempt for their own village people, it is not surprising that educated Indians prefer to learn about their country's history and society from the Europeans. There have been many an ethnological 'movement' among our common people. Our educated class is ignorant about those. It takes no interest in its native environment because it does not have to study it to pass examinations.[10]

There was a time when our villages were in intimate contact with the manifold culture of this land. Towns were administrative centres serving

---

[8]Rabindranath to Rathindranath Tagore, 7 April 1910, Bengali Letters, File Tagore, Rathindranath. Translated by UDG. (RBA.)

[9]Rabindranath to Santosh Chandra Majumdar, Santiniketan, undated, probably September 1916, Bengali Letters, File: Majumdar, Santosh Chandra. Translated by UDG. (RBA.) Bhadralok refers to the white-collared upper and middle classes in Bengali society.

[10]Rabindranath Tagore, 'Palli-Seva', 1926, *Palli Prakriti*, pp. 64-65. Translated by UDG. Chhotolok refers to the lower or menial classes in Bengal.

special purposes mostly of an official and professional character while for the complete purposes of the people's life the villagers were cherished and served by all the capable persons of the land with the most of their means and the best that their minds produced.

Today, for various reasons, villages are fatally neglected. They are fast degenerating into serfdom, compelled to offer to the ungrateful towns cheerless and unintelligent labour for work carried on in an unhealthy and impoverished environment. The object of Sriniketan is to bring back life in its completeness into the villages, making them self-reliant and self-respectful, acquainted with the cultural tradition of their own country, and competent to make an efficient use of the modern resources for the improvement of their physical, intellectual and economic condition.[11]

We must see that a force from within the people starts functioning. When I was writing *Swadeshi Samaj* the same idea had struck me. What I wanted to say then was that we did not have to think of the whole country; we could make a start with one or two villages. If we could free even one village from the shackles of helplessness and ignorance, an ideal for the whole of India would be established. That is what occurred to me then and that is what I still think. Let a few villages be rebuilt in this way, and I shall say they are my India. That is the way to discover the true India.[12]

I have an institution in Santiniketan that is mainly academic, but so many of the villages around it are in decay. Their culture is failing, their social life is deteriorating, their economic base is disintegrating. These villages are Hindu, Muslim and Santali. Except that we employ a number of these village folk for various menial tasks in my school, we have no intimate contact with them at all inside their own communities. Some years ago, I

[11]Rabindranath Tagore, *Sriniketan: The Institute of Rural Reconstruction*, Visva-Bharati Bulletin No. 11, December 1928, p. 1.

[12]Rabindranath Tagore, 'City and Village', *Towards Universal Man*, p. 322.

bought from the Sinha family a farm just outside the village of Surul, a little over a mile from Santiniketan. I hear that you might be interested in going to live and work on such a farm in order to find out more clearly the causes of this decay.[13]

Speaking of the villages that I know of personally, I may say they are absolutely appalling in their total joylessness. Gone without trace are *jatra*, *kathakata*, *kirtan* and other aids to folk education and folk entertainment. Those who patronized these have either left the village or their sense of values has undergone complete reorientation. The village folk are no more able to benefit from what knowledge we have acquired or amassed; or rather, we are no more able to plough back our stored knowledge into the soil of their mind. Their mental life is no longer enlivened with music and ballads and tales. It is these plain and simple fares which constitute those organic elements with which to enrich their mind and heart. Without them life ceases to be worth living. The sad anomaly is that our cities hardly make for social contacts in the real sense. Here, lanes and bye-lanes separate us and walls rear up their heads forbiddingly. In the city, it is hardly ever possible to establish those simple and natural relations which should obtain amongst the members of a community. Such intercourse can take place only in the rural setting. But, then *bhadraloks* are finding it increasingly onerous to spend time in the villages. They complain that there they do not get food material in sufficient quantities, and, as far as food of the mind is concerned, the less said the better. They seem to overlook the fact that it is because they deserted their villages that the villages have now become a desert.

Nobody seems to go deep into the problems that the village faces today, and even if they do they are reluctant to formulate their findings in clear terms. The way to our survival does not lie only in our non-cooperation with the foreigner. In order to live we must coexist with our rural brethren. Few among us know or realize the sad state of affairs that are allowed to flourish in the village. Some of the communities there indulge in atrocious

---

[13]Rabindranath to Leonard Elmhirst, in conversation, New York, 1921, Leonard Elmhirst, ed., *Poet and Plowman*, Calcutta: Visva-Bharati, 1975, p. 16. (Hereafter, *Poet and Plowman*.)

travesties in the name of their ancient faiths and religions—a tragic fact which does not even bear talking about.[14]

Your letter has delighted me. Every day I am getting more and more envious of your swaraj at Surul, especially when I hear of your hens contributing their dues to the commonwealth. Plato had no place for poets in his Republic—I hope your Swaraj of Chashas do not cultivate platonic ideals in their election of members. I am proud to be able to remind you of the fact that my poet's contribution reached you weeks earlier than that of the most conscientious and capable of your hens. I do not know what has happened to that poem of mine which I had to copy twice over—please take that to be my petition of candidature for poet-laureateship of your Swaraj if you have the good sense to acknowledge that the culture of imagination is not altogether superfluous for the purpose of agriculture. Please take it seriously when I say that my whole heart is with you in the great work you have started. I wish I were young enough to be able to join you and perform the meanest work that can be done in your place, thus getting rid of that flimsy web of respectability that shuts me off from the intimate touch of mother dust. It is something unclean like prudery itself to have to ask a sweeper to serve that deity who is in charge of the primal cradle of life. I wonder if you fully realize how great is your mission and what a future it has before it. But the small beginnings which you have made of this institution [in] a remote corner of the world carries in it a truth for which men today are groping in bewilderment. It is the truth of Peace. Real peace comes from a wealth which is living, which has the blessings of nature's direct touch, which is not machine-made—let us seek humbly, coming down to the soil, dealing with forces of life which are beautiful and bounteous.[15]

---

[14]Ibid., pp. 170–72. Jatra refers to a form of folk theatre or street drama, kathakata to a battle of wits, and kirtan to devotional songs. All three forms of entertainment belong to the folk tradition of Bengal.

[15]Rabindranath to Leonard Elmhirst, Shelidah, 31 March 1922, English Letters, File: Elmhirst, L.K. Photocopy. (RBA.)

My days have been strenuous and though often I have felt that I am not
strong enough to bear the strain, I do not repent. I am the sower of seeds,
the soil is not barren and I am sure the harvest will be reaped in my time.

You know my heart is with Surul. I feel that it has life in it—it does
not deal with abstractions, but has its roots deep in the heart of living
reality. You may be absolutely certain that it will be able to weather all
storms and spread its branches wide. I shall have a good talk with you
about the questions you have raised in your letter when I return sometime
in the first week of December.[16]

It has been my earnest desire for long that we in this country should deal
with the problems of agriculture in a big way. I had sent some of our young
men abroad to study agriculture so that on their return home they might
tackle this problem and thus serve their motherland. During those days, I
had said in my article entitled *Swadeshi Samaj* that we have to reconstruct
our national life with the village as the centre. To bring completeness to
the village has been a dream of mine of long standing. That must have
been the reason why I shared this dream with Mr Elmhirst when I met
him for the first time in the States. I had told him that if he could come to
India there would be no dearth of work to do and that he might be of help
in bringing to the Indian village the kind of fulfilment that I had envisaged.
He readily agreed to my proposal.[17]

It is well known that the education which is prevalent in our country
is extremely meagre in the spread of its area and barren in its quality.
Unfortunately, this is all that is available for us and the artificial standard
set up is proudly considered respectable. Outside the bhadralok class,
pathetic in its struggle to affix university labels to the names of its members,

---

[16]Rabindranath to Leonard Elmhirst, Trivandrum, 13 November 1922, Ibid., Photocopy.
(RBA.)

[17]Rabindranath Tagore, Introduction to Elmhirst's Lecture 'The Robbery of the Soil',
delivered to the Visva-Bharati Sammilani at the Ram Mohan Library, Calcutta, 28 July
1922, *Poet and Plowman*, p. 166.

there is a vast obscure multitude who cannot even dream of such a costly ambition. With them we have our best opportunity if we know how to use it there, and there only can we be free to offer to our country the best kind of all-round culture not mutilated by the official dictators. I have generally noticed that when the charitably minded city-bred politicians talk of education for the village folk they mean a little leftover in the bottom of their cup after diluting it copiously. They are callously unmindful of the fact that the kind and amount of food that is needful for the mental nourishment must not be apportioned differently according to the social status of those that receive it . . . Our people need more than anything else a real scientific training that could instil in them the courage to experiment and initiative of mind which we lack as a nation. Sriniketan should be able to provide for its pupils an atmosphere of rational thinking and behaviour which alone can save them from stupid bigotry and moral cowardliness.[18]

Man's civilization has grown in its several departments by the conjunction of his own intellect with the gifts of Nature. These two must work in partnership throughout. Whenever man's intellect, feeling secure by locking up its acquisitions in some strong-room of habit, has fallen asleep, his wealth has left him. For, the store that is not added to goes on dwindling. We cannot afford to live on the accumulations of a bygone age for long, in fact, we have already come to the end of our resources.

Science has given man immense power. The golden age will return when it is used in the service of humanity. The call of that supreme age is already heard. Man must be able today to say to it, 'May this power of yours never grow less; may it be victorious in works and in righteousness!' Man's power is Divine power; to repudiate it is blasphemy.

This latest manifestation of man's power must be brought into the heart of the villages. It is because we have omitted to do so that our water-courses and pools have run dry; malaria and disease, want and sin and crime stalk the land; a cowardly resignation overwhelms us. Whichever way we turn,

---

[18]Rabindranath to Leonard Elmhirst, 19 December 1937, English Letters, File: Elmhirst, L.K. Photocopy. (RBA.)

there is the picture of defeat, of the penury due to the depression of defeat. Everywhere our countrymen are crying, 'We have failed.' From our dried-up hollows, our fruitless fields, our never-ceasing funeral pyres, rises the wail, 'We have failed; we have failed; we own defeat!' If we can but gain the science that gives power to this age, we may yet win, we may yet live.[19]

I am sure you will be able to help our Visva-Bharati by the experience you gain in your European tour. We specially want you to study for us Agricultural Cooperation in Ireland and let us know how far its methods can be adapted to our condition. We shall be very thankful if you can persuade some experienced man who has worked with AE to come and help us in our village work for about six months or more if it is possible. Of course, on our side we shall be only too glad to offer to you the pecuniary help you need so much, the amount of which will be fixed in our committee meeting according to our financial capacity and communicated to you without delay.[20]

---

[19]Rabindranath Tagore, 'City and Village', Santiniketan: Visva-Bharati Bulletin No. 10, December 1928, pp. 9-10.

[20]Rabindranath to James H. Cousins, undated, (1924?), English Letters, File: Cousins, J.H. (RBA.) James Henry Cousins (1873–1956) was a poet and educator who came to India from Ireland in 1915. AE was the pseudonym of Irish author and active member of the Irish Nationalist Movement, George Russell (1867–1935), who worked for Irish agricultural improvement through the Cooperative Movement.

19

IN CHINA, 1924

Rabindranath wanted to draw scholars from other countries to Visva-Bharati. In 1923, the Lecture Association of Peking invited him to China. They had earlier invited Bertrand Russell and John Dewey on the same lecture programme. Rabindranath welcomed the prospect of this visit because it would give him an opportunity to associate Visva-Bharati with China and also renew cultural ties between the two countries. Although the invitation was made to him personally, he arranged for Kshitimohan Sen of Visva-Bharati's Indology Department and Nandalal Bose of the Art School or Kala Bhavana to come with him. Leonard Elmhirst also accompanied them. Together they set out from Calcutta by SS *Ethiopia* on 24 March 1924. Jugal Kishore Birla donated twenty thousand rupees to Visva-Bharati to pay for this tour. Rabindranath gave lectures in the cities of Shanghai and Peking as well as in five of the country's twenty-four provincial capitals—Hangchow, Nanking, Tsinan, Taiyuan and Wuchang. His lectures were well received in general but China's youth challenged his views about the greatness of the ancient Chinese civilization. They distributed a leaflet against him in the Chinese language after his second lecture in Peking in which they wrote, 'Since he has come to indoctrinate us we must express the displeasure his lectures create in us.'[1] He stayed in China just under seven weeks and gave more than two dozen talks. He sailed for Japan on 30 May. In Japan, he reiterated his opposition to militant nationalism. He returned to India after four weeks in Japan.[2]

---

[1]Stephen Hay, *Asian Ideas of East and West: Tagore and His Critics in Japan, China, and India*, Cambridge: Harvard University Press, 1970, pp. 162-63, 389. (Hereafter, *Asian Ideas.*)

[2]Bertrand Russell (1872–1970), philosopher and political campaigner; John Dewey (1859–1952), philosopher and pragmatist; Nandalal Bose (1882–1966), painter and art teacher who headed Santiniketan's Kala Bhavana; Jugal Kishore Birla (1883–1967), Congress activist and elder brother of the business tycoon Ghyanshyam Das Birla.

> I have a kind of civil war constantly going on in my own nature
> between my personality as a creative artist, who necessarily must be
> solitary, and that as an idealist who must realize himself through works
> of a complex character needing a large field of collaboration with a
> large body of men . . . I earnestly hope that I shall be rescued in time
> before I die—in the meantime I go to China, in what capacity, I do
> not know. Is it as a poet or as a bearer of good advice and sound
> common sense?[3]

The time is not at all favourable in India for me to persuade our people
of the importance of the reconciliation of the East and West. They all
seem to think that it can wait till we are powerful enough to negotiate
with the West on equal terms, till the Western people are compelled for
the sake of expediency to come to a mutual understanding. It is the pride
of nationalism which stands in the way of a spiritual ideal. It is very
much like saying that until we are rich we need not be honest, that first
we must have material power and then we shall be in a position to seek
spiritual perfection. Unfortunately, such has been the brutal lesson of
facts in the history of all powerful nations of the world, and the idealists
have to fight against tremendous odds when they have to assert that there
are truths which transcend all facts . . .

, All the same, the fact is that man is man and we must keep reminding
him of it by constantly appealing to his humanity. I have taken that task
in my country though the time is unfavourable, the minds of the people
being overcome with storm clouds of resentment.[4]

When the invitation from China reached me, I felt that it was an invitation
to India herself, and as her humble son, I must accept it . . . In the midst

---

[3]Rabindranath to Romain Rolland, 28 February 1924, English Letters, File: Rolland,
Romain. (RBA.)

[4]Rabindranath to William Rothenstein, Colombo, 20 October 1922, *Imperfect Encounter*,
pp. 296-97.

of strife and conflict of contending commerce and politics, of monstrous greed and hatred, of wholesale destruction, India has still her message of salvation to offer to the world . . . She has kept her faith in the unity of man and boldly asserted that he only knows truth who knows the unity of all beings in spirit . . .

Visva-Bharati has accepted this ideal as its own and is asking the whole world to share in all that is great and true in the common heritage of man. I am hoping that our visit will re-establish the cultural and spiritual connections between China and India. We shall invite scholars from China and try to arrange an exchange of scholars. If I can accomplish this, I shall feel happy.[5]

My friends, I have come to ask you to reopen the channel of communion which I hope is still there; for though overgrown with weeds of oblivion, its lines can still be traced. I shall consider myself fortunate if, through this visit, China comes nearer to India and India to China—for no political or commercial purpose, but for disinterested human love and for nothing else.

It is not difficult at all for me to know the beauty of your lakes and your hills, why then should it be difficult for me to know you yourselves? Being a man I want to know you as men, not in order to improve your minds or your morals. When we realize this unity, which is natural only when it is for no ulterior purpose either good or bad, then all the misunderstanding in the human world will be removed. For that I ask your help to make it easy for us. We in India are a defeated race; we have no power, political, military or commercial; we do not know how to help or injure you materially. But, fortunately we can meet you as your guests, your brothers and your friends; let that happen.[6]

---

[5]Kalidas Nag, ed., *Tagore and China*, Calcutta: 1945, p. 34.
[6]*Talks*, pp. 64-65.

I am a poet, not a politician nor a diplomat, and can only say what I feel most sincerely in my heart. I feel that China is now going the same way as India. I love culture, I love life. I cannot bear to see Chinese culture endangered day by day. Therefore, I sincerely warn you: know that happiness is the growth of the power of the soul. Know that it is absolutely worthless to sacrifice all spiritual beauty to obtain the so-called material civilization of the West![7]

When I first visited Japan I had the opportunity of observing where the two parts of the human sphere strongly contrasted; one, on which grew up the ancient continents of social ideal, standards of beauty, codes of personal behaviour; and the other part, the fluid element, the perpetual current that carried wealth to its shores from all parts of the world. In half a century's time, Japan has been able to make her own the mighty spirit of progress which suddenly burst upon her one morning in a storm of insult and menace. China also has had her rousing, when her self-respect was being knocked to pieces through series of helpless years, and I am sure she also will master before long the instrument which hurt her to the quick.[8]

We travelled up from Shanghai to this town along your great river, Yang Tse. All through the night I often came out from my bed to watch the beautiful scene on the banks, the sleeping cottages with their solitary lamps, the silence spreading over the hills, dim with mist. When morning broke, what was my delight to find fleets of boats coming down the river—their sails stretching high into the air, a picture of life's activity with its perfect grace of freedom. It moved my heart deeply. I felt that my own sail had caught the wind, and was carrying me from my captivity, from the sleeping past, bringing me out into the world of man.

[7] *Asian Ideas*, p. 152.
[8] *Religion of Man*, pp. 152-53.

It brought to my mind different stages in the history of Man's progress.

In the night, each village was self-centred, each cottage stood bound by the chain of unconsciousness. I knew, as I gazed on the scene, that vague dreams were floating about in this atmosphere of sleeping souls, but what struck my mind more forcibly was the fact that when men are asleep they are shut up within the very narrow limits of their own individual lives. The lamps exclusively belonged to the cottages, which in their darkness were in perfect isolation. Perhaps, though I could not see them, some prowling bands of thieves were the only persons awake, ready to exploit the weakness of those who were asleep.

When daylight breaks, we are free from the enclosure and the exclusiveness of our individual life. It is then that we see the light which is for all men and for all times. It is then that we come to know each other and come to cooperate in the field of life. This was the message that was brought in the morning by the swiftly moving boats. It was the freedom of life in their outspread sails that spoke to me; and I felt glad. I hoped and prayed that morning had truly come in the human world and that the light had broken forth.

This age to which we belong, does it not still represent night in the human world, a world asleep, whilst individual races are shut up within their own limits, calling themselves nations, which barricade themselves, as these sleeping cottages were barricaded, with shut doors, with bolts and bars, with prohibitions of all kinds? Does not all this represent the dark age of civilization, and have we not begun to realize that it is the robbers who are out and awake? . . .

This age, that still persists, must be described as the darkest age in human civilization. But I do not despair. As the early bird, even while the dawn is yet dark, sings out and proclaims the rising of the sun, so my heart sings to proclaim the coming of a great future which is already close upon us. We must be ready to welcome this new age. There are some people who are proud and wise and practical, who say that it is not in human nature to be generous, that men will always fight one another, that the strong will conquer the weak, and that there can be no real moral foundation for man's civilization. We cannot deny the facts of their assertion: the strong have their rule in the human world: but I refuse to accept this as a revelation of truth . . .

We should know this, that Truth—any truth that man acquires—is for all. Money and property belong to individuals, to each of you, but you must never exploit truth for your personal aggrandizement—that would be selling God's blessing to make profit. Science also is truth. It has its own place, in the healing of the sick, and in the giving of more food, more leisure for life. But when it helps the strong to crush the weak, to rob those who are asleep, that is using truth for impious ends and those who are so sacrilegious will suffer and be punished, for their own weapons will be turned against them.[9]

The time for taking leave has come, leave from friends with whom I have lived and at whose hands I have received much kindness. I cannot tell you how much I have felt at home with those who have taken the trouble to introduce me to this great land and its people. Yet I feel today a discontent, as of something not accomplished, as of my mission not completed. But it is not I who am to blame. The present age is the great obstacle . . .

It has become so easy for us to approach each other. We have come to you in only a few days' time. But this very ease of communication takes away from our minds the realization of the fact. Our visit becomes a picnic. We attend parties, amuse one another, hold teas, lectures, and keep engagements. Then we go back. It is all too easy.

But things that are valuable you have to pay for. Our ancestors had a great ideal of the spiritual relationship between peoples, but there were no end of difficulties in their way; they could not carry their message in a comfortable manner. Nevertheless, a thousand years ago, they could speak in your language. Why? Because they realized the importance of the work in hand—how invaluable was this bond of unity among nations, which could surmount the difference of languages. It is the one bond that can

<hr />

[9]Rabindranath Tagore, 'To Students at Nanking', *Talks*, pp. 81–85.

save humanity from the utter destruction with which it is threatened today, through the selfishness which is torturing mankind and causing misery in the world.

Is it not marvellous how these men at all arrived, and having come, translated their metaphysical ideas into Chinese, a language so utterly different from Sanskrit that the difficulties thereby encountered were far more insurmountable than the mountains they climbed, the deserts they traversed, the seas they navigated?

Our ancestors, thus, had to pay for the truth they served. I never had to pay—everything is made so easy and comfortable for me. I have spoken to you, I have read a few lectures, I have enjoyed travelling in your railway carriages which have hurried me to my destination. I have had no opportunity to know my fellow travellers who, in the days of the caravans, would have been real to me. As for my audience—are they not mere shadows? Do I ever know them, or they me? Every man has his own language—do they, can they, understand mine? For three quarters of an hour I pour down a torrent of words on their hapless heads. It is this that civilization has made so easy.

But ideas, to be fruitful, must have the collaboration of hearer and speaker. All real union consists of a binding of two hearts. If I could live among you, I could speak to you and you to me, and our thoughts would live through our close contact. They would bear fruit not immediately, but in the process of time. Obstacles would vanish, misunderstanding would not be possible. Our relationship would no longer be one-sided. We would work and produce together from the mutual contact of our hearts and minds. But our professors and schoolmasters demand lectures, from which no deep impression remains but only some faint outlines upon the memory—merely events, which find their paragraphs in the newspapers, but do not leave their mark on the hearts of men.

The truths that we received when your pilgrims came to us in India, and ours to you—that is not lost even now. We may feel that those ideas have to be adapted to the present changed conditions, and we cannot accept in their totality the thoughts and teachings of thousands of years ago. We may even grow angry over them and consider them mischievous, but we can never forget them completely because they were mutually assimilated to our lives. They are there for good or for evil, the result of a real meeting for which our ancestors paid . . .[10]

Let me confess this fact that I have my faith in higher ideals. Through them we can best serve the higher purpose of life. At the same time, I have a feeling of delicacy in giving utterance to them, because of certain obstacles which make it almost a disreputable thing to be frank and free in the expression of ideas . . .

Never think that this is a complaint at not having found a place in your hearts . . . My stay here has been made pleasant, beautiful, and I am happy. But in the depth of my heart there is pain—I have not been serious enough. I have had no opportunity to be intensely, desperately serious about your most serious problem. I have been pleasant, nice, superficial, when I ought to have come as one making penance, to take up the heart of life, to prove that I was sincere, not merely literary and poetical.

But it is true I have not had the opportunity; I have missed it. At the same time, I hope that something has been done, that some path has been opened up which others may follow, and along this path I also hope that some of you will find your way to India.

I have this one satisfaction that I am at least able to put before you the mission to which these last years of my life have been devoted. As a servant of the great cause, I must be frank and strong in urging upon you this mission. I represent in my institution an ideal of brotherhood, where men of different countries and different languages can come together. I believe in the spiritual unity of man and therefore I ask you to accept this task from me. Unless you come and say, 'We also recognize this ideal', I shall know that this mission has failed. Do not merely discuss me as a guest, but as one who has come to ask your love, your sympathy and your faith

---

[10]Ibid., pp. 106–10.

in the following of a great cause. If I find even one among you who accepts it, I shall be happy.[11]

This meeting reminds me of the day I came to China, when I had my first reception in this garden. I had come a comparative stranger and I hardly knew any of those who came to welcome me. I kept wondering whether China was at all like the pictures I had in my mind and whether I should ever be able to enter the heart of the country. My mind was full of anxiety that day, thinking all the time that your expectation would probably be exaggerated in regard to one who for you belonged to a region of mystery, who had a reputation founded upon rumour. So in order to let you know I had my limitations, I immediately confessed to you that I was nothing more than a mere poet.

I knew that you have had great men from all parts of the world to visit you, great philosophers and great scientists from across the sea, and I felt very small when I came among you, you who had the chance of hearing their words of wisdom. I was very shy that day, for I thought that I was receiving your attention almost under a false personation. I was reminded of the woman Chitra in my play who had the boon of beauty given to her by the God of Love. When through this divine illusion she succeeded in winning her lover's heart, she rebelled against this beauty, crying that all the caresses which her heart craved from her lover were intercepted by this disguise.

I have come to the end of my stay in China and if you are still ready to receive me and to shower upon me such kind words as you have spoken, I can accept them: for I have been put upon my trial and I have come through. Today I have come ever greedy of your love and sympathy and praise. You may lavish your friendship now, so that when I am away I shall remember this evening of my stay which, like some extravagant sunset, has generously spent its full store of colours. Still, however, I have some misgivings. Those of you who have travelled along with me have not yet spoken.

---

[11]Ibid., pp. 112-13.

The speaker of this meeting, who has praised me, has been ill all the time since he met me on the first day. So his imagination about me had no chance of meeting disaster through my personal companionship. Therefore, I am still waiting to hear friends who had the unfortunate disadvantage of having been too much with me.

Meanwhile I can say one thing. On the first day I also had my expectations. I had in my mind my own vision of China, formed when I was young, China as I had imagined it when reading my *Arabian Nights*, the romantic China, as well as the China of which I had caught glimpses when I was in Japan.

My host there had a great collection of Chinese paintings, marvels of beauty, and he would display them casually to me one by one, surprising me into making chance acquaintanceship with great masterpieces. Thus I built my China on the basis of the great works of your artists of the older days. I used to say to myself: These people are a great people. They have created a world of beauty . . .

Of course, you know, such a vision, created from the best product of your history, and your past, does not represent the complete life of your people. Yet I firmly believe that it is from the ideal that we get the best aspect of the real, and these two should be seen together. I must admit it is difficult for a stranger to discover that innermost truth, that hidden store of your strength and resources which will have to be worked out over a series of centuries and brought to perfection.

One thing I have felt, and it has often been spoken of by foreigners I have met in your land. You are very human. I too have felt the touch of the human in you, and I have come, or at least I hope I have come, close to your heart. I myself am filled, not with a feeling of mere admiration or wonder, but with a feeling of love, especially for those persons with whom I have come into close touch. This personal touch is not an easy thing to obtain.

Some people say that you have the gift of accepting things as they are, that you can take your joy in a naked presentation of reality, which you value, not because it has any association with something outside itself, but simply because it is before you, attracting your attention. May be it is because of this gift that you have been willing to accept me as I am, not as a poet, not, as some foolish people think, as a philosopher or, as still more foolish people think, as a prophet, but as very much of an individual.

Some of my younger new friends have become quite familiar with me, taking me to be of their own age and show but scant respect for my great age, or for my reputation. There are so many who would deprive me of the contact of reality by trying to turn me into an idol. I feel certain that God himself is hurt because men keep their daily love for their fellow beings in their homes, and only their weekly worship for Him in the Church. I am glad that my young friends never made these mistakes and treated me as their fellow human being.

You have asked me to offer some frank criticisms on this day of my departure. I absolutely refuse to accede to your request. You have critics innumerable, and I do not want to be added to their ranks. Being human myself, I can make allowance for your shortcomings, and I love you in spite of them. Who am I to criticize? We people of the Orient possess all kinds of qualities of which others do not approve—then why not let us be friends.

You shall have no criticisms from me, and please refrain from criticizing me in return. I hope my friends in China will not have the heart to probe into my failings. I never posed as a philosopher, and so I think I ought to be left alone. Had I been accustomed to living on a pedestal, they could have pulled me down and damaged my spine, but since I have been living on the same level, I trust I am safe.

The day when I first came here, your welcome was offered to me on credit. I hope I have been able to pay the price to your satisfaction but if you think I have been overpaid at the very start, do not blame me: blame your own folly. You should have been more carefully circumspect and not lavished so much praise in anticipation.

I have done what was possible, I have made friends. I did not try to understand too much, but to accept you as you were, and now on leaving I shall bear away the memory of this friendship. But I must not delude myself with exaggerated expectations. My evil fate follows me from my own country to this distant land. It has not been all sunshine of sympathy for me. From the corners of the horizon have come the occasional growlings of angry clouds.

Some of your patriots were afraid that, carrying from India spiritual contagion, I might weaken your vigorous faith in money and materialism. I assure those that thus feel nervous that I am entirely inoffensive; I am powerless to impair their career of progress, to hold them back from rushing to the marketplace to sell the soul in which they do not believe. I can even assure them that I have not convinced a single sceptic that he has a soul, or that moral beauty has greater value than material power. I am certain that they will forgive me when they know the result.[12]

---

[12]Rabindranath Tagore, 'Farewell Speech', Ibid., pp. 114–20.

20

AN UNEXPECTED STOP IN ARGENTINA

On his return from China and Japan, Rabindranath stayed home barely two months before he was travelling again. This time he went to Peru on an invitation from the Republic of Peru to attend the centenary celebrations of their independence. Leonard Elmhirst was once more his companion on this tour. Rabindranath fell ill on the voyage and they had to halt in Buenos Aires, where they were received by the Argentine writer and literary activist Victoria Ocampo (1890–1979). She arranged for Rabindranath to rest and recuperate in her villa at San Isidro on the River Plate. This is what she wrote about the event in a memoir: 'In September 1924 it was announced that Rabindranath Tagore would pass through Buenos Aires on his way to Peru, and from that moment we who knew his poems in the French translation of Gide, the English of Yeats or the Spanish of Zenobia Camprubi (wife of our Juan Ramon Jimenez) anxiously awaited the Poet's arrival which for us would be the great event of the year.'[1] Rabindranath stayed in San Isidro for a month and twenty days because his trip to Peru was cancelled. On his return voyage from Argentina, he stopped briefly in Italy. The poems he wrote during his stay at San Isidro, along with some that he wrote earlier, were published as *Purabi* in 1925 and dedicated to Victoria Ocampo whom he called 'Vijaya'. They met once again in Paris in 1930. But she could never come to Santiniketan. When Rabindranath left San Isidro, she had his favourite armchair shipped to go with him. He loved to use the chair in Santiniketan and wrote a poem about it when he was too ill to use it in his last days.

---

[1]Victoria Ocampo, 'Tagore on the banks of the River Plate', in *Rabindranath Tagore: A Centenary Volume 1861–1961*, Reprint, New Delhi: Sahitya Akademi, 1987, p. 27. Andre Gide (1869–1951), Nobel Prize winning French writer, was Rabindranath's first French translator; Juan Ramon Jimenez (1881–1958), Spanish poet and winner of the Nobel Prize for Literature in 1956.

Sometime ago I was invited to China. The people there wanted me
to speak to them on profound matters. In other words, it was an
invitation for the learned. This time I have an invitation from South
America asking me to join them in their centenary celebrations. So
I can travel light. I will not have to pose either as a scholar or as a
learned man. I see that the more I lecture the more lost I feel, as if
enveloped in mist. That is never how I feel as a poet.[2]

We leave on 29 December and reach Peru in the second half of January.
We shall have to sail via the Andes as the doctor has forbidden me to take
a rail journey over the mountains. But the further south we go by the sea,
the closer we will be to the South Pole. It will get very cold but there are
arrangements for heating on board. Besides, it will be summer here at
the end of December. The weather was supposed to have warmed up by
this time, but this year it is still cold. Thanks to medical advice, I have been
able to live quietly. I have not yet had to give lectures. Pity, there has been
no news from home, nor any letters.[3]

Last night when I offered you my thanks for what is ordinarily termed as
hospitality, I hoped that you could feel that what I said was much less
than what I meant.

It will be difficult for you to realize fully what an immense burden of
loneliness I carry about me, the burden that has specially been imposed upon
my life by my sudden and extraordinary fame. I am like an unfortunate
country where on an auspicious day a coal mine has been discovered, with
the result that its flowers are neglected, its forests cut down and it is laid
bare to the pitiless gaze of a host of treasure-seekers. My market price has
risen high and my personal value has been obscured. This value I seek to

---

[2]Rabindranath Tagore, 24 September 1924, *Paschim Jatrir Diary*, Reprint, Calcutta: Visva-
Bharati, Bengali Year 1368 (1961), p. 2. Translated by UDG.

[3]Rabindranath to Rathindranath Tagore, San Isidro, December 1925, Bengali Letters,
File: Tagore, Rathindranath. (RBA.) Translated by UDG.

realize with an aching desire which constantly pursues me. This can be had only from a woman's love and I have been hoping for a long time that I do deserve it.

I feel today that this precious gift has come to me from you and that you are able to prize me for what I am and not for what I contain. This has made me so glad and yet I know that I have come to that period of my life when in my travel across a desert I need my supply of water more than ever before but I neither have the means nor strength to carry it and therefore can only thank my good fortune when it is offered to me and then take my leave.[4]

Vijaya, under a grey sky my days are repeated in rhymes that are monotonous, like a perpetual telling of beads. I pass most part of my day and a great part of my night deeply buried in your armchair which, at last, has explained to me the lyrical meaning of the poem of Baudelaire that I read with you. I had hoped that I should be able to do some writing while crossing the interval between two shores—but the wind has veered and my manuscript book lies idle, its virgin pages looking like the sandy beach of a distant island unexplored. My day is divided into 2/3rd part of sleep and 1/3rd part of reading. I am completamente surrounded by a deep atmosphere of laziness as befits a human male in an ideal condition of life. In these two days I have been able to understand why Chinamen must smoke opium in order to realize intensely for a few moments the profound dignity of the male, his natural birthright of inutile passiveness of which he is forcibly deprived the rest of his waking hours . . . I only wish you could see how greatly Leonard has improved since he has got his leisure on this ship (not shiiiiip). He has suddenly turned an astronomer, haunting the upper deck, waiting for the chance of meeting some star of the first magnitude belonging to the southern hemisphere. You know, human males as secretaries are inefficient, but as astronomers they know how to make their opportunities

[4]Rabindranath to Victoria Ocampo, San Isidro, 14(?) November 1924, K.K. Dyson, ed., *In Your Blossoming Flower-Garden: Rabindranath Tagore and Victoria Ocampo*, New Delhi: Sahitya Akademi, 1988, p. 374. (Hereafter, *Tagore and Ocampo*.)

rich and shining. I suppose you know that also for me astronomy has a great attraction, but being a poet I have my chart of stars in my memory which I can study even when I am confined in my cabin. I have been advised never to joke with a woman but I am afraid that some of the observations in this letter show signs of frivolity. You will excuse me when you know that a man who is not a prophet and yet who is treated as a prophet must give vent to his fit of laughter even at the risk of misunderstanding.[5]

I am drifting farther and farther away from your shore and now it has become possible for me to set the vision of my everyday surroundings at San Isidro against a background of separation. I am not a born traveller—I have not the energy and strength needed for knowing a strange country and helping the mind to gather materials from a wide area of new experience for building its foreign nest. And therefore, when I am away from my own land, I seek for some individuals who may represent to me the country to which they belong. For me the spirit of Latin America will ever dwell in my memory incarnated in your person. You rescued me from the organized hospitality of a reception committee and allowed me to receive through yourself the personal touch of your country. Unfortunately, there was the barrier of language that prevented a free enough communication of minds between us, for you never felt fully at home in the only European language I happen to know. It was unfortunate because you have a richness of mind which naturally longs to offer its own tribute to those whom you accept as your friends, and I fully understand the pain which you must have suffered for not being able to reveal adequately to me your deeper thoughts and to dissolve the fog that screened off the world of your intellectual life from my vision. I am deeply sorry it has not been possible for me to have an acquaintance of your complete personality—the difficulty having been enhanced owing to the literary character of your mind. For such a mind has its aristocratic code of honour about its manner of self-expression, choosing to remain dumb than to send out its thoughts dressed in rags.

[5]Rabindranath to Ocampo, 5 January 1925, English Letters, File: Ocampo, Victoria. Photocopy. (RBA.)

But never for a moment imagine that I failed to recognize that you had a mind. To me it was like a star that was distant and not a planet that was dark. When we were together we mostly played with words and tried to laugh away our best opportunities to see each other clearly. Such laughter often disturbs the atmosphere of our mind, raising dust from its surface which only blurs our view. One thing most of my friends fail to know that where I am real I am profoundly serious. Our reality is like treasure, it is not left exposed in the outer chamber of our personal self. It waits to be explored and only in our serious moments it can be approached. You have often found me homesick—it was not so much for India, it was for that abiding reality in me in which I can have my inner freedom. It becomes totally obscured when for some reason or other my attention is too much directed upon my own personal self. My true home is there where from my surroundings comes the call to me to bring out the best that I have, for that inevitably leads me to the touch with the universal. My mind must have a nest to which the voice of the sky can descend freely, the sky that has no other allurements but light and freedom. Whenever there is the least sign of the nest becoming a jealous rival of the sky, my mind, like a migrant bird, tries to take its flight to a distant shore. When my freedom of light is obstructed for some length of time, I feel as if I am bearing the burden of a disguise, like the morning in its disguise of a mist. I do not see myself—and this obscurity, like a nightmare, seems to suffocate me with its heavy emptiness. I have often said to you that I am not free to give up my freedom—for this freedom is claimed by my Master for his own service. There have been times when I *did* forget this and allowed myself to drift into some easeful captivity—but every time it ended in catastrophe and I was driven by an angry power to the open, across broken walls.

I tell you all this because I know you love me. I trust my Providence. I feel certain—and I say this in all humility—that he has chosen me for some special mission of his own and not merely for the purpose of linking the endless chain of generation. Therefore, I believe that your love may, in some way, help me in my fulfilment. It will sound egoistic, only because the voice of our ego has in it the same masterful cry of insistence as the voice of that which infinitely surpasses it. I assure you that through me a claim comes that is not mine. A child's claim upon its mother has a sublime origin—it is not a claim of an individual, it is that of humanity. Those who come on some special errand of God are like that child, if they ever attract love and service it should be for a higher end than merely their own enjoyment. Not only love, but hurts and insults, neglect and rejection come not to grind them into dust but to kindle their life into a brighter flame.

Your friendship has come to me unexpectedly. It will grow to its fullness of truth when you know and accept my real being and see clearly the deeper meaning of my life. I have lost most of my friends because they asked me for themselves, and when I said I was not free to offer away myself—they thought I was proud. I have deeply suffered from this over and over again—and therefore I always feel nervous whenever a new gift of friendship comes in my way. But I accept my destiny and if you also have the courage fully to accept it we shall ever remain friends.[6]

Tomorrow we shall reach Barcelona and the day after Genoa. I am about to leave my easy chair in my cabin. That chair has been my real nest for these two weeks giving me rest and privacy and a feeling that my happiness is of value to somebody. I do not know when it will be possible for me to write to you again but I shall always remember you. Farewell.[7]

Dear Vijaya, the same old stupid joke of fate, I have fallen ill again and am compelled to give up all my engagements and hasten home. It is a great pity, for I have been deeply touched by the genuine feeling of regard for me by the people of this country. I must come back to them and fulfil their expectation. Leonard is working with our friends here to find a suitable place for me. I shall be very happy indeed to have my European

[6]Rabindranath to Ocampo, on board the SS *Giuleo Cesaro*, 13 January 1925, English Letters, File: Ocampo, Victoria. Photocopy. (RBA.)

[7]Rabindranath to Ocampo, on board the SS *Giuleo Cesaro*, 17 January 1925, English Letters, File: Ocampo, Victoria. Photocopy. (RBA.)

nest in this delightful country which is so friendly to me. I am sure to visit Italy next September and October if everything is settled before that time. I remember you said you also would come to Europe at that time— so you will once again have me for your guest under your own roof. I am writing to you lying on bed—I hope you will be able to decipher my scrawl. Leonard is sure to write to you a detailed description of my visit to Italy.[8]

I shall sail for India tomorrow. Leonard will arrange with our friends here some quiet place where I may spend some part of my year. I remember, you wished to come to Europe some time next autumn, therefore I decided to meet you here about the middle of September, remaining here till the third week of October. If you are compelled to change your plan, let me know it beforehand. Italy has been very gracious to me and I feel that the Italian sun and the warmth of the Italian heart will do me good. Goodbye.[9]

I have just reached India. The tired feeling still persists. The doctor in Venice strongly advised me to be very careful in spending the small remnant of my energy and I already feel that India is sure to make an extravagant claim upon it and exhaust my resources sooner than it could be helped. I am seriously thinking of leaving for Europe next April and spend the hot months there. Elmhirst has left me for a sphere completely out of my reach. It will be difficult for me to find some companion equally helpful who can fill up the gap. I shall cable to you if I can start for Europe this summer.

Have you decided, the money which I earn from my writings in the *Nacion*, to reach me through Elmhirst and not directly? The programme for myself which I have in my mind will to a certain extent depend upon this contribution and therefore I am anxious to receive it regularly and without much circumlocution. For the first year, at least, in his married

[8]Rabindranath to Ocampo, Italy, possibly end of January 1925, English Letters, File: Ocampo, Victoria. Photocopy. (RBA.)

[9]Rabindranath to Ocampo, Venice, 1 February 1925, English Letters, File: Ocampo, Victoria. Photocopy. (RBA.)

life Elmhirst's mind is not likely to be in its normal state of sanity and therefore he should not be burdened with any responsibility in which a third party is concerned. However, I should not trouble myself too much about this matter knowing for certain that you will look after my interest and I can have an absolute trust in any arrangement you make for my sake.

I do not know how long a letter takes in reaching you from India—but I do hope it will be before the time I start for Europe. If you do not receive any cable from me know that I am prevented from sailing from India and that my departure for Europe has been postponed.

Though you may not get letters from me too often, be sure that I remember you with my *bhalobasa*.

I have some misgivings about the continuity of my relationship with *La Nacion*—some day it may be felt as unnecessary—and in that case please never force my writings upon them trying to tie them to their promise. As for my own necessity, it is not at all important.[10]

There are some animals which feign death in order to save animals from the danger of death. I am advised by my doctors to follow their example and must never move, never talk, never meet people—in fact, behave in every way as if I am dead. Therefore, I shall completely have to surrender myself to your easy chair which has followed me from shore to shore. Thus I shall be saving my energy with a miserly care till I leave India once again for Italy next May the first. My cabin has been secured on the same boat 'Cracovia' which had brought me to India. I hope that by that time I shall have strength enough to carry out my plan and sail for the shore where the people are expecting me with all their wealth of welcome. The other day I met with a remarkable French woman who has been travelling in Tibet for some years and who has been able to love the people. She asked my opinion about *La Nacion*, the Editor having asked for some

---

[10]Rabindranath to Ocampo, Bombay, 19 February 1925, English Letters, File: Ocampo, Victoria. Photocopy. (RBA.) 'Bhalobasa' means love in the Bengali language.

contribution from her. I have assured her of the respectability of the paper and have referred her to you. You are likely to receive a letter from her.

I am writing this letter against the prohibition of the doctor who has advised me to keep to my reclining position on an easy chair and never to sit at the desk to do any writing. I am allowed to dictate but I take the risk of writing to you personally and lose a fraction of my vitality much more readily than sending my message to you through somebody else's handwriting.

My bhalobasa.[11]

I am writing this, reclining on your armchair, which, I am afraid, will keep me within its enclosure much longer than what I calculated. I am much worse than I was when you saw me and I am certain it will not be possible for me to leave India before August. I have asked my son to cancel my passage this summer.

I am sending you some of my short stories, translations of which I hope will be acceptable for *La Nacion*. If not, make any use you like, for they have not yet been published.

I suppose you have, by this time, heard from Italian sources how cordially I was received there. This has been a further inducement for me for seeking my European home somewhere in Italy. I hope Elmhirst has been successful in cho[o]sing a suitable place. Have you heard from him?

I must close my letter here—my body refuses to work.

Bhalobasa.[12]

My weakness has not yet forsaken me. I am asked to keep still, and I am only too willing to do so, but there are others who in their dealings with me are guided by a motive which has an object contrary to mine. My

[11]Rabindranath to Ocampo, 27 February 1925, English Letters, File: Ocampo, Victoria. Photocopy. (RBA.)

[12]Rabindranath to Ocampo, Santiniketan, 4 March 1925, English Letters, File: Ocampo, Victoria. Photocopy. (RBA.)

time in this country is constantly pelted with petty claims by numerous individuals, each of whom believes that he is the only one who deserves to be attended to. There is no escape from them unless I run away from India. Romain Rolland has thought of a sanatorium near his own place in Switzerland where he will arrange to intern me as long as doctor advises. Our steamer sailing on the 15th August will reach Genoa somewhere about the beginning of September. I wish you could be there to welcome me. But I suppose it is not going to happen. Now that I have vast stretches of leisure, chiefly employed in cultivating dreams, a swarm of details from my memory of San Isidro repeatedly comes to hum and hover around my thoughts. You express regret in your letter that I could not continue my stay at that beautiful house near the river till the end of the summer— you do not know how often I wish I could do so. It was some lure of duty which drove me from that sweet corner with its inspiration for seemingly futile idling; but today I discover that my basket, while I was there, was being daily filled with shy flowers of poems that thrive under the shadow of lazy hours. I can assure you most of them will remain fresh long after the time when the laboriously built towers of my beneficent deeds will crumble into oblivion. Very few people will know that they ought also to thank you for this gift of lyrics which I am about to offer to them. My bhalobasa.[13]

I do not like to talk about my illness which has become a bore in its endless monotony. I am wearily waiting for the summer to come when I shall make another attempt to visit Europe in order to get proper medical treatment.

I am sending to you a Bengali book of poems[14] which I wish I could place in your hand personally. I have dedicated it to you though you will never be able to know what it contains. A large number of poems in this book were written while I was in San Isidro. My readers who will understand

---

[13]Rabindranath to Ocampo, 2 August 1925, English Letters, File: Ocampo, Victoria. Photocopy. (RBA.)

[14]*Purabi* (1925).

these poems will never know who my Vijaya is with whom they are associated. I hope this book will have the chance of a longer time with you than its author had.

Bhalobasa.[15]

'Atithi' (Guest)
Buenos Aires, 1924

Woman, thou hast made my days of exile
    tender with beauty,
and has accepted me to thy nearness
    with a simple grace
that is like the smile with which the
    unknown star welcomed me
when I stood alone at the balcony and
    gazed upon the southern night.

There came the voice from above: 'We
    know you,
For you come as our guest from the dark of
    the infinite, the guest of light.'
Even in the same great voice thou hast
    cried to me: 'I know you.'
And though I know not thy tongue,
    Woman, I have heard it uttered in
    thy music,—
'You are ever our guest on this earth,
    poet, the guest of love.'[16]

[15]Rabindranath to Ocampo, Calcutta, 29 October 1925, English Letters, File: Ocampo, Victoria. Photocopy. (RBA.)

[16]*Poems*, no. 72, p. 108. Bengali original, 'Atithi', *Purabi*, 1925.

'Shunyo Chowki' (The Empty Chair)

The sun is blazing hot,
>> this lonely hour of the noon;
>> the empty chair is disconsolate.

Out of the depths of its heart
>> rise words of utter despair
>> voice of emptiness laden with sorrow,
>> whose depth none can sound.

Like a dog pining with sad eyes
>> for his lost master
>> his heart wailing with a blind sorrow,
>> not knowing what happened and why
>> seeking everywhere with unavailing eyes . . .

More sad than his pain
>> is the voice of the chair
>> as its wordless grief
>> pervades the room
>> bereft of the dear one.[17]

---

[17]The poem 'The Empty Chair' is in File: Ocampo, Victoria, English Letters, (RBA.); Bengali original, 'Roudro tap jha jha karey', *Sesh Lekha*, 1941. The Bengali original was initially published with the title 'Shunyo Chowki' in the journal *Bangalakshmi* in 1941. Translated as 'The Empty Chair', the poem was enclosed in a letter to Victoria Ocampo from Rathindranath Tagore in which he wrote: 'Dear Madam, I am enclosing with this the translation of the poem which father wrote a few days before his death. The translation being literal misses all the pathos in the original.' Rathindranath Tagore to Victoria Ocampo, Santiniketan, 3 November (1941?), File: Ocampo, Victoria, English Letters. Photocopy. (RBA.) Ketaki Kushari Dyson states that the poem was 'not written a few days before his death but more than four months before the event: on 26 March 1941'. See *Ocampo and Tagore*, p. 464.

21

GANDHIJI AND I

Mahatma Gandhi came to Santiniketan on Rabindranath's return from Argentina. He wanted to discuss the cause of spinning for swaraj with Rabindranath. In 1924, the Congress moved a resolution under Gandhi's recommendation enlisting its members to spin a certain quantity of cloth on the charka as a monthly contribution. The idea was to give the movement countrywide publicity, and also to make spinning a means of bonding between the masses and the politicians. Rabindranath was wholly opposed to the idea and explained his position in an essay called 'The Cult of the Charka' in 1925. He argued that there could be no short-cut to reason and hard work if anything was to succeed; that nothing worthwhile could be achieved by 'mass conversion' to an idea; that our poverty was a complex phenomenon which could not be solved by the application of spinning and weaving. Was our poverty due to the 'lack of sufficient thread', he asked, or was it rather due to 'our lack of vitality, our lack of unity'?[1] He also objected to the burning of cloth. He argued that it effectively forced the poor to sacrifice even the little they possessed for their dignity and survival. He added that buying and selling cloth from Manchester should be a matter left to the realm of economics. Gandhi agreed with Rabindranath on the need to be patient for swaraj. But he did not accept his argument against the burning of cloth. 'In burning *my* foreign clothes I burn my shame,' Gandhi wrote, adding that any 'economics' which hurts the well-being of an individual or a nation was 'immoral and therefore sinful'.[2]

[1] Rabindranath Tagore, 'The Cult of the Charka', *Mahatma and Poet*, p. 103.
[2] M.K. Gandhi, 'The Great Sentinel', Ibid., p. 90.

It is extremely distasteful to me to have to differ from Mahatma Gandhi in regard to any matter of principle or method. Not that, from a higher standpoint, there is anything wrong in so doing; but my heart shrinks from it. For what could be a greater joy than to join hands in the field of work with one for whom one has such love and reverence? Nothing is more wonderful to me than Mahatmaji's great moral personality. In him divine providence has given us a burning thunderbolt of *shakti*. May this shakti give power to India—not overwhelm her—that is my prayer![3]

The discussion so far has proceeded on the assumption that the large-scale production of homespun thread and cloth will result in the alleviation of the country's poverty. But after all, that is a gratuitous assumption. Those who ought to know have expressed doubts on the point. It is however better for an ignoramus like me to refrain from entering into this controversy. My complaint is that by the promulgation of this confusion between swaraj and *charka*, the mind of the country is being distracted from swaraj.

We must have a clear idea of the vast thing that the welfare of our country means. To confine our idea of it to the outsides, or to make it too narrow, diminishes our own power of achievement. The lower the claim made on our mind, the greater the resulting depression of its vitality, the more languid does it become. To give the charka the first place in our striving for the country's welfare is only a way to make our insulted intelligence recoil in despairing action. A great and vivid picture of the country's well-being in its universal aspect, held before our eyes, can alone enable our countrymen to apply the best of head and heart to carve out the way along which their varied activities may progress towards that end. If we make the picture petty, our striving becomes petty likewise. The great ones of the world who have made stupendous sacrifices for the land of their birth, or for their fellowmen in general, have all had a supreme vision of

---

[3]Rabindranath Tagore, 'The Cult of the Charka', Ibid., p. 112.

the welfare of country and humanity before their mind's eye. If we desire
to evoke self-sacrifice, then we must assist the people to meditate thus
on a grand vision. Heaps of thread and piles of cloth do not constitute
the subject of a great picture of welfare. That is the vision of a calculating
mind; it cannot arouse those incalculable forces which, in the joy of a
supreme realization, cannot only brave suffering and death, but reck
nothing either of obloquy and failure.

The child joyfully learns to speak, because from the lips of father and
mother it gets glimpses of language as a whole. Even while it understands
but little, it is thereby continually stimulated and its joy is constantly at
work in order to gain fullness of utterance. If, instead of having before it
the exuberance of expression, the child had been hemmed in with grammar
texts, it would have to be forced to learn its mother tongue at the point of
the cane, and even then could not have done it so soon. It is for this reason
I think that if we want the country to take up the striving for swaraj in
earnest, then we must make an effort to hold vividly before it the complete
image of that swaraj. I do not say that the propositions of this image become
immensely large in a short space of time; but we must claim that it be
whole, that it be true. All living things are organic wholes at every stage
of their growth. The infant does not begin life at the toe-end nor get its
human shape after some years of growth. That is why we can rejoice in it
from the very first, and in that joy bear all the pains and sacrifices of
helping it to grow. If swaraj has to be viewed for any length of time only
as homespun thread, that would be like having an infantile leg to nurse
into maturity. A man like the Mahatma may succeed in getting some of
our countrymen to take an interest in this kind of uninspiring nature for a
time because of their faith in his personal greatness of soul. To obey him
is for them an end in itself. To me it seems that such a state of mind is
not helpful for the attainment of swaraj.

I think it to be primarily necessary that, in different places over the
country, small centres should be established in which expression is given
to the responsibility of the country for achieving its own swaraj—that is
to say, its own welfare as a whole and not only in regard to its supply of

homespun thread. The welfare of the people is a synthesis comprised of many elements, all intimately interrelated. To take them in isolation can lead to no real result. Health and work, reason, wisdom and joy, must all be thrown into the crucible in order that the result may be fullness of welfare. We want to see a picture of such welfare before our eyes, for that will teach us ever so much more than any amount of exhortation. We must have before us, in various centres of population, examples of different types of revived life abounding in health and wisdom and prosperity. Otherwise we shall never be able to bring about the realization of what swaraj means simply by dint of spinning threads, weaving *khaddar*, or holding discourses. That which we would achieve for the whole of India must be actually made true even in some small corner of it—then only will a worshipful striving for it be born in our hearts. Then only shall we know the real value of self-determination, *na medhaya na bahudha srutena*, not by reasoning nor by listening to lectures, but by direct experience. If even the people of one village of India, by the exercise of their own powers make their village their very own, then and there will begin the work of realizing our country as our own.

Fauna and flora take birth in their respective regions, but that does not make any such region belong to them. Man creates his own motherland. In the work of its creation as well as of its preservation, the people of the country come into intimate relations with one another, and a country so created by them, they can love better than life itself. In our country its people are only born therein: they are taking no hand in its creation; therefore between them there are no deep-seated ties of connection, nor is any loss sustained by the whole country felt as a personal loss by the individual. We must reawaken the faculty of gaining the motherland by creating it. The various processes of creation need all the various powers of man. In the exercise of these multifarious powers, along many and diverse roads, in order to reach one and the same goal, we may realize ourselves in our own country. To be fruitful, such exercise of our powers must begin near home and gradually spread further and further outwards. If we are tempted to look down upon the initial stage of such activity as too small, let us remember the teaching of

Gita: swalpamasaya dharmosya travate mahato bhayat, by the least bit of dharma (truth) are we saved from immense fear. Truth is powerful, not in its dimensions but in itself.

When acquaintance with, practise of, and pride in cooperative self-determination shall have spread in our land, then on such broad abiding foundation alone may swaraj become true. So long as we are wanting therein, both within and without and while such want is proving the root of all our other wants . . . want of food, of health, of wisdom—it is past all belief that any programme of outward activity can rise superior to the poverty of spirit which has overcome our people. Success begets success; likewise swaraj alone can beget swaraj.

The right of God over the universe is His swaraj . . . the right to create it. In that same privilege, I say, consists our swaraj, namely our right to create our own country. The proof of such right, as well as its cultivation, lies in the exercise of the creative process. Only by living do we show that we have life.

It may be argued that spinning is also a creative act. But that is not so: for, by turning its wheel man merely becomes an appendage of the charka; that is to say, he but does himself what a machine might have done: he converts his living energy into a dead turning movement. The machine is solitary, because being devoid of mind it is sufficient unto itself and knows nothing outside itself. Likewise, alone is the man who confines himself to spinning, for the thread produced by his charka is not for him a thread of necessary relationship with others. He has no need to think of his neighbour—like the silkworm his activity is centred round himself. He becomes a machine, isolated, companionless. Members of Congress who spin may, while so engaged, dream of some economic paradise for their country, but the origin of their dream is elsewhere; the charka has no spell from which such dreams may spring. But the man who is busy trying to drive out some epidemic from his village, even should he be unfortunate enough to be all alone in such endeavour, needs must concern himself with the interests of the whole village in the beginning, middle and end of his work, so that because of this very effort he cannot help realizing within himself the village as a whole, and at every moment consciously rejoicing in its creation. In his work, therefore, does the striving for swaraj make a true beginning. When the others also come and join him, then alone can we say that the whole village is making progress towards the gain of itself which is the outcome of the creation of itself. Such gain may be called the gain of swaraj. However small the size of it may be, it is immense in its truth.

The village of which the people come together to earn for themselves their food, their health, their education, to gain for themselves the joy of so doing, shall have lighted a lamp on the way to swaraj. It will not be difficult therefore to light others, one after another, and thus illuminate more and more of the path along which swaraj will advance, not propelled by the mechanical revolution of the charka, but taken by the organic processes of its own living growth.[4]

I remember that many of our women used to go about almost naked in the villages. Mahatma Gandhi said, the use of impure cloth was like using a piece of cloth used by a leper. I remember this made me feel very angry and when Mahatmaji came to see me I asked him, 'Do you seriously mean to say that foreign cloth is really impure?' He kept silent and did not give a definite reply but merely remarked that he believed in idolatry. I suppose he believed that idolatry is needed for our people. Idolatry is to make an idol of an idea. I have no doubt that he felt fully justified in making use of this idolatry. I felt that by this means he was merely increasing the blind hatred of the English. Although it was almost dangerous to have opposed Mahatmaji in those days, I said, 'It is a worse calamity to lose our freedom of mind than not to gain our political freedom.' I told Mahatmaji, 'If what you say is true, then our people cannot accept truth unless it is presented to them in the form of falsehood.' To my mind this is our real problem and not foreign subjection. This is the greatest evil and an evil from which nobody can save us. Even in politics we do the same thing. We criticize the British Government saying that a particular law or a particular event was objectionable. We dare not boldly say that foreign government must go.

---

[4]Rabindranath Tagore, 'Striving for Swaraj', 1925, Ibid., pp. 118–21.

Last year I said to Mahatmaji when he came to Santiniketan, 'You have not defined swaraj. Do you mean by it complete independence?' He again kept silent and avoided a direct answer and remarked that he has very great faith in the character of the British people. I gather from that remark that he wanted the British connection to be severed . . .

What is fundamentally wrong in India is that our people live like a crowd. There is no common unifying activity of creation. Our land is merely occupied by us. We do not do anything to make it our own. The real problem in India is that we must make the whole country a creation of our own. A creation in which all the communities and individuals will participate. I myself have started an organization with the villagers in the neighbourhood of Santiniketan. There are both Hindus and Mohammedans. We make no distinction between them. We are giving them training for improving sanitation, in organizing medical relief, in building village schools and also in creating cooperative organizations, in which both Hindus and Mohammedans take part and work for the common good. A very significant incident took place during the Calcutta riots. A large number of Mohammedan rowdies from outside were imported to Bolpur and a mischievous rumour was spread that a Hindu temple would be destroyed and demolished. The strange thing, however, was that we had no need to seek police help. We went to our own Mohammedan villagers who had been working for the common good and had no separate communal jealousy and hatred. The Mohammedan villagers prevented the Mohammedan rowdies who came from outside from doing any mischief and actually turned them away from the surrounding country.

In India, this is our task. We must set up organizations through which we can actively win back our own country. They must be human and not merely mechanical. Here I differ from Mahatmaji. He thinks that charka alone will do. I want to take the whole life of the village. My little experiment in Santiniketan has convinced me that if we succeed it will be an object lesson to the whole of Bengal. The village boys, some Mohammedan, some Brahmin, some of the lower caste, all work together for the good of the village. They live and grow in an atmosphere of common activity. They are the future villagers and if you can succeed in enlightening them to a sensation of common good, the problem will be solved . . . It will take time but that is the only way. I am sure that after the first difficulties are over, if the work is once successful, it will spread like fire. The first ten years will be difficult and we must wait patiently.

When people asked me why I did not join Mahatmaji, I did not care to give a formal reply. I know in my heart that I will prepare my answer in the slow work in the villages where I am hoping to reach a final solution of our problem.[5]

A shadow is darkening today over India like a shadow cast by an eclipsed sun. The people of a whole country are suffering from a poignant pain of anxiety, the universality of which carries in it a great dignity of consolation. Mahatmaji, who through his life of dedication has made India his own in truth, has commenced his vow of extreme self-sacrifice.

> I appeal to my countrymen that they must not delay a moment effectively to prove that they are in earnest to eradicate from their neighbourhood untouchability in all its ramifications. The movement should be universal and immediate, its expressions clear and indubitable. All manner of humiliation and disabilities from which any class in India suffers should be removed by heroic efforts and self-sacrifice. Whoever of us fails in this time of grave crisis to try his utmost to avert the calamity facing India would be held responsible for one of the saddest tragedies that could happen to us and to the world.

Samskara Samiti,   Rabindranath Tagore
Visva-Bharati
22 September 1932

---

[5]Rabindranath to Romain Rolland, in conversation, June 1926. See 'A Diary of Rabindranath Tagore's Tour in Europe in 1926', recorded and compiled by Prasanta Chandra Mahalanobis, Archives of the Indian Statistical Institute, Calcutta. (Hereafter, 'Europe Tour Diary, 1926'.) Also see *Rabindra-Biksha*, Volume 38, Calcutta: Rabindra Bhavana, 2000.

General Appeal

> *Ya eko varno bahudha saktiyogat*
> *Varnana anekan nihitartho dadhati*
> *Vichaiti chante visvamadan sa devah*
> *Sa na buddhya subhaya samyunakto*
>   Svetasvatara Upanishad

He who is one, and who dispenses the inherent needs of all peoples and all times, who is in the beginning and the end of all things, may He unite us with the bond of truth, of common fellowship, of righteousness.

Object of our work:

We have long been suffering from the grave social inequities which we have allowed to grow unchecked. Mutual distrust and hatred are the root cause of our misery. That is why Mahatma Gandhi has been compelled to resort to the extreme form of penance for our sins—to take the vow of fasting unto death if this curse of social discrimination is not removed from our midst. It is our imperative duty immediately to eradicate the evils that poison the sources of our humanity.

We resolve that:

1. We shall not look down upon any person as inferior to us in status because of his caste, or the community to which he may belong.

2. All public temples, places of worship, schools, and social gatherings, water tanks etc. will be made accessible to all irrespective of caste and creed. Untouchability in all its forms shall be discarded; we shall be constantly engaged in trying to remove this evil from our neighbourhood, and from all places wherever we may find ourselves.

3. We shall tolerate nothing in our society which wounds the feeling of others.[6]

---

[6]Rabindranath Tagore, 'An Appeal to my Countrymen: After Mahatma Gandhi's Epic Fast', 20 September 1932, *Mahatmaji and the Depressed Humanity*, Calcutta, Visva-Bharati, 1932, Appendix, pp. 3–9.

After my return from some months' touring in the West, I found the whole country convulsed with the expectation of an immediate Independence— Gandhiji had promised swaraj in one year—by the help of some process that was obviously narrow in its scope and external in its observance.

Such an assurance, coming from a great personality, produced a frenzy of hope even in those who were ordinarily sober in their calculation of worldly benefits; and they angrily argued with me that in this particular case it was not a question of logic, but of a spiritual phenomenon that had a mysterious influence and miraculous power of prescience. This had the effect of producing a strong doubt in my mind about Mahatmaji's wisdom in the path through satisfying an inherent weakness in our character which has been responsible for the age-long futility of our political life.

We, who often glorify our tendency to ignore reason, installing in its place blind faith, valuing it as spiritual, are ever paying for it with the obscuration of our mind and destiny. I blamed Mahatmaji for exploiting this irrational force of credulity in our people, which might have had a quick result in a superstructure, while sapping the foundation. Thus began my estimate of Mahatmaji, as the guide of our nation, and it is fortunate for me that it did not end there.

Gandhiji, like all dynamic personalities, needed a vast medium for the proper and the harmonious expression of his creative will. This medium he developed for himself, when he assumed the tremendous responsibility of leading the whole country to freedom past countless social ditches and fences and the unlimited dullness of barren politics. This endeavour has enriched and mellowed his personality and revealed what was truly significant in his genius. I have since learnt to understand him, as I would understand an artist, not by the theories and fantasies of the creed he may profess, but by that expression in his practice which gives evidence to the uniqueness of his mind. In that only true perspective, as I watch him, I am amazed at the effectiveness of his humanity.

An ascetic himself, he does not frown on the joy of others, but works for the enlivening of their existence day and night. He exalts poverty in his own life, but no man in India has striven more assiduously than he for the material welfare of his people. A reformer with the zeal of a revolutionary, he imposes severe restraints on the very passions he provokes. Something of an idolator and also an iconoclast, he leaves the old gods in their dusty niches of sanctity, and simply lures the old worship to better and more humane purposes. Professing his adherence to the caste system, he launches his firmest attack against it where it keeps its strongest guards, and yet he has hardly suffered from popular disapprobation as would have been the case with a lesser man who would have much less power to be effective in his efforts.

He condemns sexual life as inconsistent with the moral progress of man, and has a horror of sex as great as that of the author of *The Kreutzer Sonata*, but, unlike Tolstoy, he betrays no abhorrence of the sex that tempts his kind.[7] In fact, his tenderness for woman is one of the noblest and most consistent traits of his character, and he counts among the women of his country some of his best and truest comrades in the great movement he is leading.

He advises his follower to hate evil without hating the evil-doer. It sounds an impossible precept, but he has made it as true as it can be made in his own life. I had once occasion to be present at an interview he gave to a certain prominent politician who had been denounced by the official Congress party as a deserter. Any other Congress leader would have assumed a repelling attitude, but Gandhiji was all graciousness and listened to him with patience and sympathy, without once giving him occasion to feel small. Here, I said to myself, is a truly great man, for he is greater than the party he belongs to, greater even than the creed he professes.

This, then, it seems to me to be the significant fact about Gandhiji. Great as he is as a politician, as an organizer, as a leader of men, as a moral reformer, he is greater than all these as a man, because none of these aspects and activities limits his humanity. They are rather inspired and sustained by it. Though an incorrigible idealist and given to referring all conduct to certain pet formulae of his own, he is essentially a lover of men and not of mere ideas; which makes him so cautious and conservative in his revolutionary schemes. If he proposes an experiment for society, he must

---

[7]Leo Tolstoy (1828–1910), Russian novelist and moral philosopher, author of *War and Peace* and *Anna Karenina*. His novel *The Kreutzer Sonata* was published in 1889.

first subject himself to its ordeal. If he calls for sacrifice, he must first pay its price himself. While many Socialists wait for all to be deprived of their privileges before they would part with theirs, this man first renounces before he ventures to make any claims on the renunciation of others.

There are patriots in India, as indeed among all peoples, who have sacrificed for their country as much as Gandhiji has done, and some who have had to suffer much worse penalties than he has ever had to endure; even in the religious sphere, there are ascetics in this country compared to the rigours of whose practices Gandhiji's life is one of comparative ease. But these patriots are mere patriots and nothing more; and these ascetics are mere spiritual athletes, limited as men by their very virtues; while this man seems greater than his virtues, great as they are.

Perhaps none of the reforms with which his name is associated was originally his in conception. They have almost all been proposed and preached by his predecessors or contemporaries. Long before the Congress adopted them, I had myself preached and written about the necessity of a constructive programme of rural reconstruction in India; of handicrafts as an essential element in the education of our children; of the absolute necessity of ridding Hinduism of the nightmare of untouchability. Nevertheless, it remains true, that they have never had the same energizing power in them as when he took them up; for now they are quickened by the great life-force of the complete man who is absolutely one with his ideas, whose visions perfectly blend with his whole being.

His emphasis on the truth and purity of the means, from which he has evolved his creed of non-violence, is but another aspect of his deep and insistent humanity; for it insists that men in their fight for their claims must only so assert their rights, whether as individuals or as groups, as never to violate their fundamental obligation to humanity, which is to respect life. To say that, because existing rights and privileges of certain classes were originally won and are still maintained by violence, they can only be destroyed by violence, is to create an unending circle of viciousness; for there will always be men with some grievance, fancied or real, against the prevailing order of society, who will claim the same immunity from moral obligation and the right to wade to their goal through slaughter.

Somewhere the circle has to be broken, and Gandhiji wants his country to win the glory of first breaking it.

Perhaps he will not succeed. Perhaps he will fail as the Buddha failed and as Christ failed to wean men from their iniquities, but he will always be remembered as one who made his life a lesson for all ages to come.[8]

---

[8]Rabindranath Tagore, 'Gandhi The Man', *Mahatma Gandhi*, Calcutta: Visva-Bharati, 1963, pp. 11–17.

22

IN EUROPE AGAIN, 1926

Rabindranath stopped in Italy for the first time when he was returning from Argentina in January 1925. But he could not keep his engagements there due to ill health. Later that year, Carlo Formichi[1] of the University of Rome came to Visva-Bharati as visiting professor with a gift of books on Italian art and culture from President Benito Mussolini of Italy. Encouraged by this generosity towards Visva-Bharati, Rabindranath sailed for Italy on 15 May 1926. Mussolini said to him on their meeting in Rome, 'I am an Italian admirer of yours who has read every one of your books translated into the Italian language.'[2] During the visit, Italian and European newspapers began to publish interviews with Rabindranath. But humanist friends in Europe became concerned over the reports they published. Romain Rolland was among them. Rabindranath went to meet Rolland in Villeneuve as soon as his commitments in Italy were over. Rolland personally translated those newspaper reports which discussed Rabindranath's attitude to fascism. He also arranged for Rabindranath to meet some of the Italian victims of fascist atrocities. Faced with all this evidence, Rabindranath wrote a letter denouncing fascism and explaining the developments to C.F. Andrews in India. The letter was published in the English daily *Manchester Guardian* on 5 August 1926. This infuriated the Italians who damned him in their press. Despite this setback, Rabindranath continued with his travels in Europe. He went to England, Scandinavia, Germany, and met Albert Einstein in Berlin. From there on he travelled to Czechoslovakia, Hungary, Rumania and, on his way back home, made stops also in Athens, Cairo and Alexandria.

---

[1] Carlo Formichi (1871–1943), Indologist and professor of Sanskrit at the University of Rome.
[2] 'Europe Tour Diary, 1926', *Rabindra-Biksha*, vol. 38, p. 19.

I need not go into detail about the communications that were poured upon me by the victims of Fascism when I came out of Italy. I felt bound to assure my friends that the rumour which spread the impression that I supported Fascism as an ideal was unjust to me, that I still decried the despotic intimidation of spirit that humiliates the inner man in order to decorate him with a costly semblance of an outer glory.[3]

On the eve of the departure of Professor Carlo Formichi, may I be allowed to send you through him our message of deep and cordial appreciation of what Italy has contributed to the growth of Visva-Bharati? Professor Formichi came with a rich gift of a library of Italian Classics and of books on art, the value of which will be gratefully inscribed in the memory of successive generations of our students. Professor Formichi's own stay at Santiniketan has been fruitful not only in the formation of lasting bonds of cooperation between him and the scholars who worked with him in his subject, but also in the creation of intimate links of friendship with others who happened to come into his contact.

We are very thankful too that Professor Guiseppe Tucci did at last come to Santiniketan and introduce our students to the study of Italian language and literature. Professor Tucci's brilliant versatility of talents has made him an invaluable colleague of those of our scholars who pursue studies in Buddhism through Tibetan and Chinese texts. Visva-Bharati scholars recognize with feelings of gratitude the help he has rendered them and earnestly hope that his services may be available to them for a number of years to come. I am confident that if the duration of Professor Guiseppe Tucci's stay here be extended to a sufficient long period of years, we shall be able to consolidate the work which he has begun with admirable energy and the fruits of which promise to be of great mutual benefit in the history of cultural relations between Italy and India.[4]

---

[3]Rabindranath Tagore, 'Open Letters, Speeches, Tributes', *English Writings*, Volume III, p. 776.

[4]Rabindranath Tagore to His Excellency President Benito Mussolini, Santiniketan, 10 March 1926, English Letters, File: Mussolini, Benito. Copy. (RBA.)

I send you a copy of the letter which I have sent to Andrews. This will give you my idea about my attitude towards Fascism. I have been forced to give my explanation because not only in Europe, but in India the rumour has been circulated that I have advocated the doctrine of Fascism and I have taken up the mission of defending it when I go to India.

In the meantime, the evidence from the other side is pouring down upon me—and some of the facts are of a disturbing character. I cannot tell you what a great suffering it has caused me—for I have a deep love for your people. Also, I realize that my expressed opinion on this political movement will hurt you and this thought is constantly oppressing my mind. Our cause of Visva-Bharati will receive a setback in Italy—which is a matter of very great regret for me. And yet I cannot help taking the step I have taken—for I do represent certain ideals for which I have faced unpopularity in my own country and derision in some parts of the West. The report which appeared in the Indian newspapers last year after my return from Italy contained extracts from the Fascist papers fiercely attacking me for my humanitarian ideals. I feel certain that my espousing the cause of Fascism would be a kind of moral suicide. But exactly that is being widely believed by peoples of all shades of opinion in Europe and other continents. I find it absolutely impossible to let it go uncontradicted and with a great feeling of pain I have allowed myself to express my opinion about my position with regards to this movement.

I fervently hope that you will understand the situation and forgive me and still consider me as one of your best friends.[5]

My mind is passing through conflict. I have my love and gratitude for the people of Italy. I deeply appreciate their feeling of admiration for me which is so genuine and generous. On the other hand, the Italy revealed in Fascism alienates herself from my own ideal picture of that great country which I should love to cherish in my heart. I fervently hope that this movement is not in harmony with the true nature of Italy, and that it is only a momentary eruption of her surface life. The painful facts about

---

[5]Rabindranath to Carlo Formichi, Vienna, 21 July 1926, English Letters, File: Formichi, Carlo. Photocopy. (RBA.)

this movement that are daily coming to my notice since I have left Italy make it almost a matter of personal grievance for me because of the assurance I have had from the people of that land of their regards for my own self.

You know I had my first introduction to Italy when I was invited to Milan last year. It takes long to study the mind of a people but not to feel their heart when that heart opens itself. I was in the town only for a very few days and in that short time I realized that the people really loved me. One can claim, rightly or wrongly, praise as one's dessert, but love is a surprise every time it comes. I was strongly moved by that surprise when I found loving friends and not merely kind hosts in the people of Italy. It grieved me deeply, and I felt almost ashamed, when I suddenly fell ill and had to sail back home before I could fulfil my engagements in all other towns.

Then followed the magnificent gift from Mussolini, an almost complete library of Italian literature, for my institution. It was a great surprise to me. In this greeting I felt the touch of a personality which could express itself in this direct manner in an appropriate action of unstinted magnificence.

This helped me to make up my mind to visit Italy once again in spite of my misgivings created by the reports reaching us in India about the character of the Fascist Movement.

I could gather from the literature that had come to my notice that the Fascist Movement contained in it elements that were against my ideals, that its success was borne by tortured lives and exiled aspirations, that it was tainted by conspiracy dealing its blows in secret, driving the corrupt politics of Europe towards barefaced barbarity. But lately we have lost our faith in all reports from the West in which the representatives of a people are accused of public crimes. For it is an open secret that along with the army and navy and aircrafts, the Western nations maintain their organizations of worldwide propaganda of misrepresentation. Neither did I have any qualification nor the inclination to dabble in politics which specially concerns any of the European countries. And this was why I wanted to keep my mind neutral when I came to Italy. But we live in a whirlwind of talk today and an individual like myself is compelled to contribute to that universal noise, dragged by the chain of *karma* as we say in our country.

I allowed myself to fall victim to this relentless karma with its ever lengthening coil of consequence when I succumbed to the importunity of the interviewers in Italy.

An interview is a dangerous trap in which our unwary opinions are not only captured but mutilated. Words that come out of a moment's mood are meant to be forgotten, but when they are snap-shotted, most often our thoughts in them are presented in a grotesque posture which is an irony of accident. The camera in this case being also a living mind, the picture becomes a composite one in which two dissimilar features of mentality have a misalliance that is likely to be unhappy and undignified.

My interviews in Italy were the products of three personalities, that of the reporter, the interpreter and mine. Over and above that, there evidently was a hum in the atmosphere of another insistent and universal whisper which without our knowing mingled in all our talks. Being ignorant of Italian I had no means of checking the result of this concoction. The only precaution which I could take was to repeat emphatically to all my listeners that I had no opportunity yet to study the history and character of Fascism.

But since then I have had the chance of knowing the contents of some of these interviews from the newspaper cuttings that my friends have gathered and translated for me. And I was not surprised to find in them what was inevitable. Through misunderstanding, wrong emphasis, natural defects in the medium of communication, and the preoccupation of the national mind, some of these writings have been made to convey that I have given my deliberate opinion on Fascism, expressing my unqualified admiration.

This time it was not directly the people of Italy whose hospitality I enjoyed, but that of Mussolini himself as the head of the Government. This was, no doubt, an act of kindness, but somehow unfortunate for me. For, always and everywhere official vehicles, though comfortable, move only along a chalked path of programme too restricted to lead to any places of significance, or persons of daring individuality. They are for providing visitors only with specially selected morsels of experience.

The opinions which I could gather in an atmosphere of distraction were enthusiastically unanimous in the praise of Mussolini for having rescued Italy in a most critical moment of her history from the brink of ruination. In Rome I came to know a professor, a genuinely spiritual character, a seeker of peace who was strongly convinced not only of the necessity but of the philosophy of Fascism. About the necessity, I am not competent to discuss, but about the philosophy I am doubtful. For it costs very little to fashion a suitable philosophy in order to mitigate the rudeness of facts that secretly hurts one's conscience. One thing which surprised me most, coming from the mouth of fervent patriots, was that the Italian people, owing to their unreasoning impulsive nature, had proved their incapacity to govern themselves, and therefore in the inevitable logic of things they lent themselves to be governed from the outside by strong hands.

However, these are the facts that immediately and exclusively concern Italy herself, the validity of even which has sometimes been challenged by European critics. But whatever may be the case, the methods and the principle of this Fascism concern all humanity, and it is absurd to imagine that I could ever support a movement which ruthlessly suppresses freedom of expression, enforces observances that are against individual conscience, and walks through a bloodstained path of violence and stealthy crime. I have said it over and over again that the aggressive spirit of nationalism and Imperialism, religiously cultivated by some of the Nations of the West, is a menace to the whole world. The demoralization which it produces in European politics is sure to have disastrous effects especially upon the peoples of the East who are helpless to resist the Western methods of exploitation. It would be most foolish, if it were not almost criminal, for me to express my admiration for a political ideal which openly declares its loyalty to brute force as the motive power of civilization. That barbarism is not altogether compatible with material prosperity may be taken for granted, but the cost is terribly great—it is fatal. This worship of unscrupulous force as the vehicle of nationalism keeps ignited the fire of international jealousy which is for universal incendiarism, a fearful orgy of devastation. The mischief of the infection of this moral aberration is great because today the human races have come close together and any process of destruction once set going does its work in an enormously wholesale manner. Knowing all this, could I be credited to having played my fiddle while an unholy fire was being fed with human sacrifice?

I was greatly amused in reading in a Fascist organ how the writer, vehemently decrying pantheistic philosophy of the passive and meditative East, comparing with it the vigorous self-assertion and fury of efficiency which he acknowledges to have been borrowed by his people from their modern schoolmasters in America. This has suggested to my mind the possibility of the idea of Fascism being an infection from across the Atlantic.

The unconscious irony in this paper lies in the fact of the writer's using with unction the name of Christianity in this context, the religion which had its origin in the East. He evidently does not realize that if Christ were born again in this world he would forcibly have been turned back from New York had he come there from outside, if for nothing else, at least for the want of the necessary amount of dollars to be shown to the gatekeeper. Or, if he had been born in that land, Ku Klux Klan[6] would secretly have knocked him to death or have lynched him. For did he not give utterance to the political blasphemy that blessed are the meek, thus insulting the Nordic right to rule the world? And the economic heresy that blessed are the poor? Would he not have been put into prison for twenty or more years for saying that it was as easy for the prosperous to reach the kingdom of heaven as for the camel to pass through the eyes of a needle? The Fascist professor deals a pen-thrust against what he calls our pantheism which as a word has no synonym in our language nor as a doctrine any place in our philosophy. He does not seem to have realized that the Christian idea that God remains essentially what he is while manifesting himself in the son's being belongs to the same principle as our principle of immanence. The divinity of God according to it accepts humanity for its purpose of self-revelation and bridges the infinite gulf

---

[6]An extremist right-wing society in the US, originating after the Civil War, advocating white supremacy and anti-semitism.

between them. This idea has glorified all human beings, has had the effect in the Christian West to emancipate individuals from the thraldom of absolute power. This has trained that attitude of mind which is the origin of the internal politics of Western people. It has helped to distribute the power of government all over the country and thus given it a permanent foundation which cannot be tampered with or destroyed by the will of one individual or whim of a group of them. This consciousness of the dignity of the individual has encouraged in the West the freedom of conscience and thought. We in the East come to Europe for this inspiration. We are also dreaming of the time when the individuals belonging to the people of India will have the courage to think for themselves and express their thoughts, feel their strength, know their rights and take charge of their own government.

The Fascist organ is evidently fascinated by the prospect of economic self-aggrandizement of the nation at the cost of moral self-respect of the people. But it is the killing of the goose for the sake of the golden eggs. In the olden civilizations, the slavery of the people did build for the time being stupendous towers of splendour. But this spirit of slavishness constantly weakened the foundations till the towers came down to the dust, offering as their sole contribution to humanity ruins haunted by venerable ghosts.

In bygone days in India, the state was only a part of the people. The mass of the population had its own self-government in the village community. Dynasties changed but the people always retained the power to manage all that was vital to them. This has saved them from sinking into barbarism, this has given our culture a community through centuries of political vicissitude.

Our Western rulers have destroyed this fundamental structure of our civilization, the civilization based upon obligations of intimate human relationship. And therefore nothing today has been left for the people through which they can express their collective mind, their creative will, realize the dignity of their soul, except the political instrument, the foreign model of which is always before their envious gaze. We come to Europe for our lesson in the mastery of this instrument, as Japan has done and has been successful in her purpose. But must our friend, the Fascist philosopher, come to us to copy our political impotence, the result of the surrender of freedom for centuries to the authority of some exclusive reservoir of concentrated power, while rejecting our great ideal of spiritual freedom which has its basis upon the philosophy that infinite truth is everywhere, and that it is for everyone to reach it by removing the obstruction of the self that obscures light?

I am sure you will be interested to know the impression that I have carried away from my interview with Mussolini. We met only twice and our meetings were extremely brief owing very likely to our mutual difficulty of communication through the slow and interrupted medium of an interpreter.

In the hall which emphasized its bigness by the unusual bareness of its furniture, Mussolini has his seat in a distant corner. I believe this gives him the time and space to observe visitors who approach him, and makes him ready to deal with them. I was not sure of his identity while he was walking towards me to receive me, for he was not tall in proportion with his fame that towers high. But when he came near me I was startled by the massive strength of the head. The lower part of the face, the lips, the smile revealed a singular contradiction to the upper one, and I have often wondered since then, if there was not a secret hesitation in his nature, a timid doubt which is human. Such an admixture of vacillation in a masterful personality makes his power of determination all the more vigilant and strong because of the internecine fight in its own character. But this is a mere surmise.

For an artist it is a great chance to be able to meet a man of personality who walks solitary among those who are fragments of a crowd which is always on the move, pressed from behind. He is fully visible in his integrity above the lower horizon obstructed by the dense human undergrowth. Such men are the masters of history and one cannot but feel anxious lest they might miss their eternity by using all their force in capturing the present by its throat, leaving it killed for all future. Men have not altogether been rare who furiously created their world by trampling human materials into the shape of their megalomaniac dreams, at last to burden history with the bleached bones of their short-lived glory while there were others, the serene souls, who with their light of truth and magic of love have made deserts fruitful along endless stretches of grateful years. . . .

My letter has run on to a great length. But I hope you will bear with it knowing that it has helped me in making my thoughts clear about my experience in Italy and also explaining the situation in which I have been placed. This letter which I write to you I shall make use of in removing the misunderstanding that has unfortunately been created in the minds of those who are in harmony with my ideals about the problems of the present age.[7]

Ever since I left Villeneuve I have been cherishing the thought that the last few days of my stay in Europe must be spent with you. While I was wandering from place to place in a rate of speed too quick for realizing the meaning of things or the touch of man I felt like a derelict human planet that cried for its lost orbit. All the time I had a longing to have a good talk with you in the atmosphere of your companionship. I have passed that period of my life when letter-writing was natural, when mutual communication between friends could easily flow through the channel of alphabet. Because the old age, like the evening hours, has its own inevitable solitude, it craves for the intimacy of conversation—the living music of thoughts, to fill the silence of the day's end. Our mind begins its career in speech in childhood when it is in bud; then through the intermediate discipline of reading and writing it finds at last its speech as a mature fruit. There was a time when I used to feel real pleasure in writing, like the water which in its freezing stage seems to take delight in its hieroglyphics of crystalline characters. But now no longer do I feel the necessity, and my mind only wishes to express itself in a flow, which like a stream speaks as it moves. And therefore, on these few days when my mind came to a close neighbourhood of years, I had

[7]Rabindranath to C.F. Andrews, Vienna, 20 July 1926, Xerox copies of English Letters, 1926–29. Collection: Andrews, C.F. (RBA.) Also published in *Manchester Garden*, 5 August 1926.

the profound pleasure of a quickening of thoughts by listening and speaking to you face to face and heart to heart. I shall always remember them.

It may be that you know from the newspapers that lately I fell ill owing to overstrain. Doctors advise me to take the shorter Eastern route to India after a few days' rest. And so my long cherished plan to come to you before my final departure is not to be realized. In most of the places of Europe where I travelled I was surprised to discover what great love people have for me. In course of time a bankruptcy of reputation may happen to me in the West where the people get angry at their discarded favourites when they imagine that they had cheated themselves by overpayment. And yet even if what I have experienced does belong to the moment, it is amazing in itself. I am not ambitious and therefore do not set much value on any immediate reward. But I am confident that I have left enough legacy in my own language which has a permanent worth. And therefore, in spite of the certainty of a reaction against this sudden popularity of mine, I feel that I have the right to what has been offered to me by the West, that most of my works will bear testimony to the fact that I have truly loved and therefore I can truly claim love not only for today but for the days to come.[8]

'Nai Nai Bhoy' (Fear Not)

Fear not, for thou shalt conquer,
thy doors will open, thy bonds break.
Often thou losest thyself in sleep,
and yet must find back thy world
again and again.
The call comes to these from the earth
    and sky

---

[8]Rabindranath to Romain Rolland, Balatonfured, 6 November 1926, English Letters, File: Rolland, Romain. Photocopy. (RBA.)

the call from among men,
the call to sing of gladness and pain,
of shame and fear.
The leaves and the flowers,
the waters that fall and flow,
ask for thy notes to mingle with their
     own,
the darkness and light
to tremble in the rhythm of thy song.[9]

My Tree

When I am no longer on this earth, my tree,
let the ever-renewed leaves of thy spring
murmur to the wayfarers:
'The poet did love while he lived.'[10]

---

[9]*Poems*, no. 78, p. 115, Munich, 1926. Bengali original 'Nai Nai Bhoy', *Gitabitan*, 1926.
[10]Rabindranath Tagore Manuscript Collection, Ms. Accession no. 20, (Balatonfured, November 1927), in English. (RBA.)

23

AN UNEASY THOUGH VERSATILE
PERIOD, 1927–31

The episode over Mussolini was a setback for Visva-Bharati. Rabindranath began to have doubts about his mission for international cooperation. In July 1927, he took another cultural journey, this time to the East. He went to British Malaya, Java, Bali, and Siam. In 1928, he was invited to Oxford University to give the Hibbert Lectures but had to postpone it due to ill health. It so happened that things were not going well at his institution. He was glad to have stayed back to look after things. In 1929, the other Italian visiting professor, Guiseppe Tucci, who came after Carlo Formichi, criticized the Visva-Bharati community for not treating him well. Rabindranath realized that his long absences from Santiniketan had been harmful, that he needed to give his time and energy to the work he had begun. Fighting his disappointments on more than one front, he found a new outlet for his creative activity in painting. In March 1929, he was invited to a conference on education in Vancouver by the Canadian National Council of Education. In May 1930, he went to Oxford to give the postponed Hibbert Lectures. From there he went to Paris, Birmingham, London, Berlin with exhibitions of his paintings. In Berlin, he had long discussions with Albert Einstein which were published in 1931 along with his Hibbert Lectures titled *The Religion of Man*. In September 1930, he was invited to visit Russia by the Soviet government. His paintings were exhibited in Moscow during that visit. He gave talks about his paintings in Moscow and later in Geneva. Turning seventy on 8 May 1931, he gave a talk to the Santiniketan community about how he saw his own life.

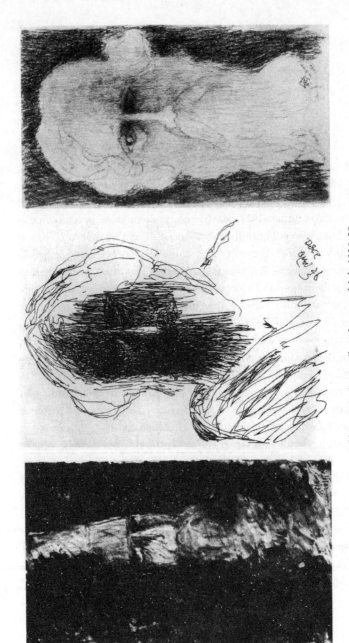

Self-portraits in pencil, and pen-and-ink, 1936–38

We should not ignore the difficulties. They must be faced. I myself think these will be, some day or other, tackled by the idealists who are not shackled by the weight of old traditions, by things that are already dead, but which still cling to life. The young are trying to shake off all that, though their minds are immature, it will come, these problems will be brought before them.

My hope is with the young people of the West, the vigorous-minded, full of enthusiasm and youth. Those who are powerful and prosperous are suspicious of ideals, and men of practical politics. Therefore I find difficulty.[1]

This time I have been able to see the state of things in Europe that has filled my mind with misgivings. There was a time when ideals of Justice, love of freedom could find their voice from some corner or other of this continent. But today all the big nations seem to have gone half seas over in their reckless career of political ambition and adventures of greed. None of them has the natural privilege today to stand for the right when any great wrong is done to humanity. The standard of life has become so complex and costly that these people cannot help thinking that righteousness is a luxury that can only be indulged in when all claims [by] their insatiable self [are] fairly satisfied. They are ashamed of the sentiments that help to keep life green and tender and in its place they cultivate the sneering spirit of cynicism brilliant and barren. Europe has got her science not as complimentary to religion but as its substitute. Science is great, but it only affords us knowledge, power, efficiency, but no ideal of unity, no aspiration for the perfect—it is non-human, impersonal, and therefore is like things that are inorganic, useful in many ways but useless as our food of life. If it is allowed to go on extending its sole dominion in the human world then the living flesh of men will wither away and his skeleton will reign supreme in the midst of his dead wealth. I have very strongly felt this time

---

[1]Rabindranath Tagore Manuscript Collection, Ms. Accession no. 329, 'Talks in Geneva', 1930, in English, p. 41. (RBA.)

that the European countries have found themselves [in] a vicious circle of mutual hatred and suspicion and they do not know how to stop, however much they may wish. Their passion of greed has been ignited to a terrible intensity and magnitude through the immense possibility of power that science has offered to them and they appear like a star suddenly flaring up into rapid and fatal brilliancy through some enormous accession of materials. The present European atmosphere has been very oppressive to me, making me think over and over again what a terrible menace man has been for man.[2]

I am thankful to my infirmity for having brought me back at last to my own true orbit. Latterly I have too often been away from my proper place and the consequent punishment has proved to be a blessing that has restored me to my own place. The work which is natural to me is not primarily moral but creative. I am apt to lose myself among the crowd when instead of producing ideas and giving form to them I go about hawking them from door to door. Anything that does not grow fresh from a living source within myself is a burden that exhausts me. My cure is not in a cessation of work but in work which is one with my life.

You know how I offered my ashram to the public, an abstraction that could only receive gifts through a machine of constitution. I foolishly assured myself that from then I could claim my release from all obligations with regard to it. After a long absence when I had time to come and watch it, I found that it was something different from what I had made over to my people. It was merely an institution whose principle was efficiency and no living force, whose movements were not of growth but of repetition. Only limbs of our ashram that remained living were Kala Bhavana and Sriniketan, the rest was rigidly immobile.

I must blame myself for having forgotten, when I thought I had my call outside India, that the ashram was waiting for my help to complete

──────────
[2]Rabindranath to Leonard Elmhirst, Balatonfured, 7 November 1926, English Letters, File: Elmhirst, L.K. Photocopy. (RBA.)

the initial stage of its life cycle in order to be able to proceed on its final career of fulfilment by its own inner impulse.[3]

I have just received an invitation from Vancouver, through our Viceroy, asking me to attend the meeting of the National Council of Education which will be held in the beginning of April. It means a long sea voyage across the Pacific and at least during the voyage a better place of safety than my second storey room. I hope Andrews will be able to help me while I am in Canada, rescuing me from engagements that may suck me down into an eddy of talk. I wish you were by me. This wish often comes to me with some other wishes of life that show no sign of exhaustion in spite of being consistently starved of hope.

I had my Hibbert Lectures engagement in England. I hoped I should be able to write them before they were expected. But it became impossible, owing to the fact that lately I have taken up in all earnest my work in Santiniketan. During my prolonged absence, our institution was going off the track, heading towards the realm of *nirvana* where responsibility ceases and material resources vanish. I am proud to say that things are looking brighter now—but all this time other duties outside the range of Santiniketan have had no chance. My Canada engagement will cover a little over our summer vacation and my absence will not be felt.[4]

I have come to that stage of life when one gets fond of idly rummaging among the hoarded treasures of past days . . .

I think you are the only one who came close to me when I was young and old at the same time, when my aspirations had the sureness of maturity and, not having passed through the buffetings of experience, were youthful in their ferment and unbounded expectancy. Since then the burden of

[3]Rabindranath to Leonard Elmhirst, Santiniketan, 7 November 1928, Ibid. Photocopy. (RBA.)

[4]Rabindranath to Leonard Elmhirst, Santiniketan, 15 January 1929, Ibid. Photocopy. (RBA.)

responsibility has grown heavy and its path intricate. I have come to know the inevitable limitations of ideas when solidified in an institution.[5]

If ever I get an opportunity I should like to show you some pictures that I have done myself with the hope of once again being startled with your appreciation as in the case of *Gitanjali*.[6]

I find that you already know that of late I have suddenly been seized with the mania of producing pictures. The praise they had won from our own circle of artists I did not take at all seriously till some of them attracted notice of a Japanese artist of renown whose appreciation came to me as a surprise. Some European painters who lately visited our ashram strongly recommended me to have them exhibited in Berlin and Paris. Thus I have been persuaded to bring them with me, about four hundred of them. I still feel misgivings and I want your advice. They certainly possess psychological interest, being products of untutored fingers and untrained mind. I am sure they do not represent what they call Indian Art, and in one sense they may be original, revealing a strangeness born of my utter inexperience and individual limitations. But I strongly desire to have your opinion before they are judged by others in Europe.[7]

Oxford lectures are over. Some American friends have come to settle my programme in the United States. This has brought me once again to Woodbrooke. In the meantime, I have got an invitation from Atul Chatterji to meet Wedgwood Benn at his house next Friday for lunch. I had been hoping to arrange a meeting with these people through you. Can you come

[5]Rabindranath to Leonard Elmhirst, Santiniketan, 10 July 1930, Ibid. Photocopy. (RBA.)

[6]Rabindranath to William Rothenstein, Calcutta, 22 February 1929, *Imperfect Encounter*, p. 325.

[7]Rabindranath to William Rothenstein, 30 March 1930, Ibid., p. 326.

there after lunch at Sir Atul's place? I am asked to be there about half past eleven and lunch with them.

My pictures are going to be exhibited at Birmingham next Monday. I shall have to come back for that day and the next day I must be in London for PEN Club dinner. Then I hope I shall be free and come to your place. You can't imagine how busy I have been these days and I need rest very badly.[8]

In Germany my pictures have found a very warm welcome which was far beyond my expectation. Five of them have got their permanent place in Berlin National Gallery, and several invitations have come from other centres for their exhibition. This has a strange analogy with the time which followed the *Gitanjali* publication—it is sudden and boisterous like a hill stream after a shower and like the same casual flood may disappear with the same emphasis of suddenness.[9]

I have been asked to talk about my pictures. This is a subject which is new to me. It came only two years ago, suddenly. I had no training whatever before that time. I have been occupied with literary work, and always had the idea that outside these limits I had not the right to enter. Even when I began working on it, it was just at odd moments to while away the time, on pieces of paper on my desk. My pictures do not represent any external fact, or any inner vision, they occur out of accidents, just a play with lines, and when lines do not find their proper balance, my mind works upon them until satisfied that they have reached their finality. It does

---

[8]Rabindranath to Leonard Elmhirst, Woodbrooke Settlement, Birmingham, 27 May 1930, English Letters, File: Elmhirst, L.K. Photocopy. (RBA.) Atul Chandra Chatterji (1874–1955), later Sir Atul Chandra Chatterji, was India's High Commissioner in Britain from 1925 to 1931; William Wedgwood Benn (1877–1960), British Liberal MP; the PEN Club was founded to defend freedom of expression, resist censorship worldwide and maintain the conscience of world literature.

[9]Rabindranath to William Rothenstein, Geneva, 24 August 1930, *Imperfect Encounter*, pp. 328-29.

Rabindranath, seated on the stage, watching a performance of his dance-drama *Mayar Khela* (Play of Dreams), 1939

not matter what is represented, bird or animal, what does matter is this,— these lines must have their perfect ultimate balance, their cadence and feeling for rhyme. This is the only urge which I have within me which does produce something.

When I brought these to Europe, I was urged and encouraged by some European artists, who insisted on exhibiting these pictures in Berlin and Paris, certain that people would understand and not bother about asking me what are their meanings. Many people asked me if these pictures had mystic meaning. You have to realize that the whole world outside the human world of this earth is dumb, the stars do not utter words, nor the planets and clouds and trees, the green grass and flowers, they do not lecture as I am doing now. They are silent, the whole world, the greater part of it whose expression is expression of gesture, it has no other meaning, and we think it must have some deeper truth of existence. We don't ask a rose to explain itself, to justify its existence, we don't ask 'what is your philosophy of life or your ultimate meaning!' We are satisfied with a rose as a rose, that is to say it contains within itself a perfect harmony of its parts and its surroundings. The lines and colours have also ultimate value of perfection and therefore they have a value of reality which is in themselves. We don't bother a rose about any meaning. Of course Botany is helpful to know that in the rose is the same general principle as in all flowers, but that is nothing to do with the rose itself, and so the artist in a similar manner creates rather like that rose. So I think that is the explanation which I can give about my pictures.[10]

I thank you for your warm welcome and the words of appreciation. I know that the best communication between nations is the communication of mind and heart. The best products of each country belong to all humanity. This is the proper field of exchange—the field of culture. And I shall be only too glad to show you what I have done in this latest manifestation of my own creative mind.

---

[10]Rabindranath Tagore Manuscript Collection, Ms. Accession no. 329, 'Talks in Geneva', 1930, in English, pp. 47-48. (RBA.)

It came to me all of a sudden without any training or preparation, and so it has its psychological value, I believe. In other parts of Europe I must confess, however, those who are very critical of art or are producers of art, have given me assurance that my pictures not only have a psychological interest, but also a higher interest of art, and they have acknowledged me as an artist, for which I feel very proud. I want now to know what you think of my attempts, because I value your opinion of art very highly indeed.

I have felt a need to bring my pictures to you also because through pictures I can come into direct touch with your mind. I cannot do this with my words owing to the barrier of language. But my pictures, they will speak to you without the medium of an interpreter.[11]

All sorts of people are walking along the streets of Moscow. Nobody is well-dressed: one knows at once that the leisured class has disappeared altogether; everybody has to earn his living by his own hands: the refinements of luxury are nowhere in evidence. I had to call on a high official, Dr Petrov, in his office in a building which once belonged to an old aristocrat, but the office itself has little furniture and no sign of neatness. It has the bare, unkempt and unwashed appearance of a house in our country at the time of mourning when all social obligations are in abeyance. The arrangement for food and comfort at the place where I am staying is highly inappropriate for a place called the Grand Hotel, but no one bothers because everyone is in the same state . . .

What has pleased me most here is the complete disappearance of the vulgar conceit of wealth. For this reason alone the self-respect of the people has been restored: peasants and workers have all shaken off the load of disrespect and raised their head. How wonderfully easy has become man's relation with his fellows.[12]

[11]Rabindranath Tagore, 'Talks with Art Critics', Tretiakov-Gallery, Moscow, 17 September 1930, Conversations in Russia, *English Writings*, Volume III, p. 929.

[12]Rabindranath Tagore, *Letters from Russia*, Moscow, 19 September 1930, Calcutta: Visva-Bharati, 1960, pp. 7–9.

I am highly honoured at the invitation to appear in this hall and I am grateful to Dr Petrov for the kind words he has said about me. I am thankful to the people for giving me the opportunity of knowing this country and seeing the great work which the people are doing in this land. My mission in life is education. I believe that all human problems find their fundamental solution in education. And outside of my own vocation as a poet I have accepted this responsibility to educate my people as much as lies in my individual power to do so. I know that all evils, almost without exception, from which my land suffers are solely owing to the utter lack of education of the people.

Poverty, pestilence, communal fights and industrial backwardness make our path of life narrow and perilous owing to the meagreness of education. And this is the reason why, in spite of my advanced age and my weak health, I gladly accepted the invitation offered to me to see how you are working out the most important problem of education in this country. I have seen, I have admired and I have envied you in your great opportunities. You will know that our condition in India is very similar to yours. She has an agricultural population which is in need of all the help and encouragement that you have given the people in this country. You know how precarious is the living which depends exclusively upon agriculture, and so how utterly necessary it is for the cultivators to have the knowledge of up-to-date methods of producing crops in order to meet the increasing demands of life.

Our people are living on the verge of perpetual famine, and do not know how to help this because they have lost faith and confidence in their own humanity. This is the greatest misfortune of our people, three hundred million men and women burdened with profound ignorance, without any hope in life.

So I came to this land to see how you deal with this problem, you who have struggled against the incubus of ignorance, superstition, and apathy which were once prevalent in this land among the working-men and the peasantry. The little that I have seen has convinced me of the marvellous progress that has been made, the miracle that has been achieved. How the mental attitude of the people has changed in such a short time, it is difficult for us to realize, who live in the darkest shadow of ignorance and futility. It gladdens my heart to know that the people, the real people who maintain the life of the society and bear the burden of civilization, are not deprived of their own rights and that they enjoy an equal share of all the advantages of a progressive community.[13]

It is not easy to know one's true self. The single thread that unifies the various experiences of life eludes discovery. If Providence had not blessed me with a long span of life and had denied me the opportunity of reaching the ripe old age of seventy, then I would never have got the chance of forming a clear picture of my own self. I have looked upon a self split up in diverse ways; I have engaged myself in various activities, with the result that the essential 'I' is scattered into fragments. After traversing this long circular road of my life, now when the time of my leave-taking draws near I am able to survey the entire orbit. And I can now realize that I have but one introduction to the world—which is that I am a poet and nothing else. My personality as revealed from time to time to various persons through the media of diverse activities, does not express myself as a whole. I am neither a philosopher nor am I deeply versed in scriptures; I am neither a preceptor nor a leader of men.

There was a time when I said, 'I don't want to be the leader of new Bengal in the new era.' That was very true. Those who come as messengers and prophets of the Immaculate One, who cleanse the world of its sins and inspire men to perform good and blameless deeds—they are worthy of my veneration. But my seat is not by them. But when that one white radiance becomes many, when it shoots out into a multi-coloured coruscation and irradiates the world, then I become the herald of the multiform. We artists and poets are messengers of the *abih* or light which is intoxicated with this spontaneous joy of universal creation. We dance and make others dance, we laugh and make others laugh, we paint, we sing. To realize the play of this Diverse One in the depths of my heart and to give it outward expression—that is my task. I lay no claim to lead men

---

[13]Rabindranath Tagore, 'Farewell Speech in Moscow', September 1930, *English Writings*, Volume III, pp. 936-37.

to their destination, my part is to walk with the wayfarer. We are here to add our supply of joy to the wayside pleasures, to the cool shade, to the wealth of the greenery, to the beauty of flowers and foliage and to the song of birds. I have taken upon myself the task of distributing the diverse delights of the One who disports himself as many, here, there and everywhere, in melody, songs, dances, pictures, forms and colours, in the clash of joy and sorrow and in the conflict of good and evil. I have been charged with the duty of decorating the various allegories of His playroom—this is my one and only introduction. I have been described by other adjectives as well; some have called me a mystic sage, others have given me the post of a schoolmaster. But from early childhood I have given my schoolmaster the slip for the sake of playing; so tuition is not my function either.

I have no idea what I have achieved or what will survive after me. I shall not yearn after lasting results. The presiding deity of my life plays, but cares for nothing; the playroom he builds today with his own hands, he pulls down himself tomorrow. The *alpona*,[14] with which this grove of mango trees was decorated yesterday, was all washed away by the restless storm last night, and our artists had to do it all anew.

If I have been able to supply a few toys to the playroom of the great god of time, I do not expect them to be preserved for all time to come. Broken toys will be thrown into the dust-heap. It will be enough for me if during the tenure of my life I succeeded in filling an earthen cup with the drink of delight. The next day the drink will be finished and the cup will be broken to bits, but the feast will not have been in vain. On the occasion of the completion of my seventieth year, in the name of the god of joy, let me remind everybody that the flavour of the game is spoilt by the fruitless efforts to adjudge my superiority or inferiority. We must forget the wrangling of critics with their measuring rods. I have no desire to scramble for the popular prizes of cheap reputation which lie scattered in the dust. May I never be so lacking in sense as to cry myself hoarse over the wages of my labour.

---

[14]Alpona is an artistic ritual in the form of hand-painting on the floor, done usually by the women of the household on auspicious occasions.

In this ashram too, only its *expressive* activities are to be traced to me. The organization of the ashram is in the hands of the organizers. I wanted to give shape to man's innate desire of self-expression. That is why I sought a sequestered place, a *tapovana*,[15] to form a suitable setting. My ambition was to become the playmate of the budding children, not amidst the brick and mortar of cities, but under the canopy of the blue sky, in these unconfined spaces open to sunrise and sunset. My duty is to help in expressing the beneficent and beautiful form of life which has evolved in this small community of hearts in this ashram. Not that I have not initiated other activities here, but my real place is there where it has taken a form and a shape. I am to be found in the dumb anguish of the villages yearning for expression. That I have started classes for the education of children is of secondary importance. My endeavour has been to remove that which hampers the early expression of their tender life, their dawning desire to learn, the newly-sprouted seedlings of their efforts. Otherwise I would have been lost in a wilderness of rules, regulations and syllabus. They are necessary but they are not of first importance. My friends are there to look after them.[16]

---

[15]A forest hermitage.

[16]Rabindranath Tagore, 'A Poet's Testament', Address on the poet's seventieth birthday, 8 May 1931, in Bengali. English translation in the *Visva-Bharati Quarterly*, May-June 1944, pp. 1–4.

24

MORE TRAVEL, MORE POETRY, MORE DRAMA

In April 1932, Rabindranath went to Persia and Iraq. This was the first time he was travelling in an aeroplane. Tragedy followed when his only grandson Nitu died on 7 August 1932. Nitu was Mira's son and was studying printing technology in Germany. Rabindranath wrote the poem 'Mrityunjay' (Conqueror of Death) to come to terms with the loss. He continued with his activities as usual. In September 1932, he went to Poona to visit Mahatma Gandhi who had resorted to a 'fast unto death' on the issue of the Communal Award.[1] Rabindranath was deeply shaken by the sight of Gandhi's frail body lying in jail and felt anxious about the future of the untouchables without Gandhi. He published an essay titled 'Mahatmaji and the Depressed Humanity' in 1932. In 1933, he wrote *Chandalika* (The Untouchable Girl), a drama condemning the injunctions of Hindu society over caste, and followed it up with a satire called *Tasher Desh* (The Kingdom of Cards) on the deadweight of Hindu custom. During 1934–36, he toured many parts of India and Ceylon with students of Visva-Bharati who staged these dramas. In this way, he could enjoy the sight and sound of his own artistic creations and also raise funds for Visva-Bharati. In September 1937, he composed *Barsha-Mongol* to celebrate the rainy season and staged it in Calcutta. In this period, he published seven volumes of poetry, two novels, and directed five of his dance-dramas for the stage, including *Mayar Khela* (Play of Dreams) in 1939. Although he no longer travelled to the West at that time, he and the British humanist Gilbert Murray continued to correspond keenly for the promotion of international cooperation.[2]

---

[1]The Communal Award (1932) granted separate electorates not only for the Muslims of India but all other minority communities including the untouchables.

[2]Gilbert Murray (1866–1957), classicist and internationalist, became Regius Professor of Greek at the University of Oxford in 1908.

Pen-and-ink, 1939

Who am I to these Bushire crowds? In my work, thought, and everyday life, I am far out of their world. When I was in Europe, the people there knew something of me as a poet, and so could judge me on materials before them. These people also believe me to be a poet, but solely by force of imagination. To them, I am a poet, not of this or that kind, but in the abstract; so that nothing stands in the way of clothing me with their idea of what a poet should be. Persians have a passion for poetry, a genuine affection for their poets, and I have obtained a share of this affection without having to show anything for it in return.[3]

So long as our plane was passing over Bengal, it flew low. The villages, clustering around pieces overgrown with weeds, appeared like tiny islands dotted over an expanse of bare fields. From our height they looked like cosy green nooks, but our hearts could feel the thirst of the parched land suffering at the approach of summer, its inhabitants having no resource except the whimsical favours of the Rain-God.

Men, beasts and birds were all out of sight. No sound, no movement, no sign of vitality—a world seemingly deserted by life lay before us, swathed in a patch-work shroud. As we rose higher, even this remnant of form was reduced to a pattern of scratchy lines, as though some extinct country of a forgotten name had recorded its annals on a drab surface in unknown characters of undecipherable meaning . . .

Up to this time we had not felt its motion very much, but suffered from the intolerable din of its propellers—there was no possibility of communication between passengers. My ears stuffed with cotton-wool, I could only look about me. In the front row was a Dane, employed in a sugar-cane plantation in Manila, now going home. He had been busy following our route on a partly rolled-up map, occasionally helping himself to bread and cheese, or chocolates. He had brought along with him a pile of newspapers which he perused one after the other. There were also three

---

[3]Rabindranath Tagore, 'Journey to Persia', *Tagore Reader*, p. 12.

wireless operators who, taking turns, sat in their corners with the apparatus strapped to their ears, taking notes or writing their reports between intervals of eating and dozing. Together with the pilots, these comprised our little community, snatched off the earth into isolation, pursuing a course through infinite solitude.[4]

Persia's introduction came to me when I was a boy. It was that of the ideal Persia, the Persia of the poet, the Persia which sends her welcome in songs to strangers across all barriers of geography.

My father was a great scholar. He was intoxicated with Hafiz verses. When I was a boy I often used to listen to the recitation of those poems, and he translated them to me with a fervour of enjoyment that touched my heart.

The vision of Persia was invoked in my imagination by the voice of your own poets, who brought to my mind's sky the breath of your spring breeze with the enchantment of its blossoming roses and nightingales' songs. My arrival in your land today is therefore a continuation of the same enchantment and I am glad to mingle my voice with the rejoicing of life which has broken out in the air of your beautiful country fragrant with the perfume of orange blossoms.

It brings to my mind once again how my father to the end of his days derived deep consolation from your poets' songs assimilating them in his devotional life.

It is fortunate for me that I am able to come to lay my thankful thoughts to the shrines of your great poets. I wish it could have been done on this auspicious occasion in a poet's own manner. But unfortunately I feel like a specimen bird in a museum showcase where the rigid wings are unable to display their dance of a colourful life. My voice is muffled in an alien language, which cannot rhythmically respond to my muse. And therefore, the true token of my reverent gratitude I offer in unuttered words to the

---

[4]Rabindranath Tagore, from the aeroplane, 11 April 1932, Ibid., pp. 11-12.

undying memory of your poets and my salutation to the immortal spirit of Persia in which were cradled, and in which still live, the spirits of those singers.[5]

Friends, I thank you from the depths of my heart for your warm welcome. I feel that you are one with me in fellowship and share with me the belief that humanity is one; that differences of race and religion cannot stand in the way of our common pursuit of truth and love.

Friends, I have come here to this great land with that faith in man which is sorely needed in this strife-ridden tired world of today. Risking the strain of a difficult journey, in my old age, I have come here to seek new confirmation of my faith in the linked destiny of man. And I am thrilled by what I have seen and felt in this country which under a great monarch, one of the greatest men of this age, has already achieved. Iran today has not only proved the majesty of its own soul but shed the lustre of its glory far and wide, inspiring humanity with a new vision of fulfilment. Asia is awake today, she is once more now to offer her spiritual gift to the world, the message of brotherhood, of freedom, of federation in the task of establishing peace and goodwill.[6]

I heartily thank Your Majesty for the kind invitation to your kingdom and the hospitality graciously offered to me tonight.

Not being a man of any political importance, not having any significant place in the confederacy of nations that are swaying the material destiny of the present-day world, I might have considered such honour ill-fitted to a person like myself. But I am certain that it is meant for the cause I espouse and the vocation I claim to be mine own. And therefore, I must never shrink from it in false modesty but congratulate one of the modern

---

[5]Rabindranath Tagore, 'Lectures in Iran and Iraq', *English Writings*, Volume III, p. 648.
[6]Rabindranath Tagore, to the Armenians, Ibid., p. 649.

rulers and shapers of history for the recognition he has offered to a member of the fellowship of poets whose mission it is to light lamps along the unending path of human culture. I cannot, therefore, help rejoicing at the fact that in spite of an insistent preoccupation of utilitarian urgency of this machine-driven age, a man of letters finds his welcome in this distracted world for any service he may have rendered to humanity in her all but repressed desire for spiritual self-realization.

In ancient Asia, the men whose function was to make human mind fertile with living wealth of beauty and noble aspiration received their highest rewards from the monarchs not merely in a spirit of patronage but that of a high responsibility and cultured appreciation. I am sure that this individual fact of a poet belonging to a distant corner of the earth and speaking a different language finding his seat of welcome at your Majesty's table this evening is not a mere accident but has a deeper historical significance. It is a generous gesture of a renascent Asia, its expression of the intellectual hospitality to all manifestations that transcend temporal standard and indicate our path to inner perfection. Human civilization has crossed the boundaries of racial and national segregation. We are today to build the future of man on an honest understanding of our varied racial personality which gives richness to life, on tolerance and sympathy and cooperation in the great task of liberating the human mind from the dark forces of unreason and mutual distrust of homicidal pride of sect and lust of gain. I pray that Iraq may realize this great responsibility of a coming civilization.

Iraq, the land where great historical ages have mingled their glories, lying in the central zone of traffic between West and East may rightly hope to become one of the living links of a coming federation of the peoples of the world. With her vision of far-away beckoning horizons, her glittering atmosphere and the vast voice of her sky, her twin great rivers flowing down through shining centuries of splendour, let her win her right to a boundless freedom in a world of greatness and proclaim under her high-vaulted heavens the majesty of the spirit of man which is the sacred shrine of the spirit of God.

At the conclusion, let me read the verse which I have specially written for the occasion and which may be translated thus:

The night has ended.
Put out the light of the lamp
of thine own narrow dark corner
smudged with smoke,
the great Morning which is for all
appears in the East.
Let its light reveal us to each other
who walk on the same path
of pilgrimage.[7]

You must have heard I was travelling in Persia. It was nice. I was told about your bad cough on my return. Did you neglect yourself in the cold? It is good to know you are much better now. If you desire we can send your mother to stay with you for some time. We will get somebody to accompany her. Tell me what you wish.

It has been extremely hot here, but hopefully the rains will come down soon. Everything is beginning to look green. There is a huge crop of mangoes this year. With so much poverty in the country there will at least be no dearth of mangoes!

It is summer time in Europe—which is like our spring season here. I was in Persia during the months of April and May. It was not at all hot there. It was really like our winter. Persia is 4000 to 5000 feet above sea level, like our Kurseong.[8]

'Mrityunjay' (Conqueror of Death)

You seemed from afar
titanic in your mysterious majesty of
terror.

---

[7]Rabindranath Tagore, Ibid., pp. 656-57.

[8]Rabindranath to Nitu, his grandson, Santiniketan, 21 June 1932, *Chitthi Patra* IV, p. 184. Translated by UDG.

With palpitating heart I stood before your
                    presence,
Your knitted brows boded ill
and sudden came the blow with a growl and a crash.
My bones cracked,
with bowed head I waited
for the final fury to come.

It came.
And I wondered, could this be all of the
                    menace?
With your weapon held high in suspense
you looked mightily big.
To strike me you came down
to where I crouched low on the ground.
You suddenly became small
and I stood up.
From thence there was only pain for me
but no fear.
Great you are as death itself,
but your victim is greater than death.[9]

It has given me very deep delight to hear from you and to receive your
invitation to collaborate with you in exploring the possibilities of closer
intellectual and cultural cooperation between the West and the East. My
young friend Chakravarty[10] has already conveyed to me your greetings
and good wishes and told me about your conversations with him
which led to your decision that there should be, under the auspices of the
International Institute of Intellectual Cooperation, an open exchange of

---

[9]*Poems*, no. 93, pp. 138-39. Bengali original 'Mrityunjay', *Parisesh*, 1932, written on news
of his grandson's death.

[10]Reference is to the poet Amiya Chakravarty. See chapter 8, note 14.

correspondence between us on some of the vital problems of international relationship. I feel particularly happy that the letter from Europe should have come personally from yourself, and I can assure you that I shall consider its points carefully and write an answer to it as soon as I am able to do so.[11]

I must confess at once that I do not see any solution of the intricate evils of disharmonious relationship between nations, nor can I point out any path which may lead us immediately to the levels of sanity. Like yourself, I find much that is deeply distressing in modern conditions, and I am in complete agreement with you again in believing that at no other period of history has mankind as a whole, been more alive to the need of human cooperation, more conscious of the inevitable and inescapable moral links which hold together the fabric of human civilization. I cannot afford to lose my faith in this inner spirit of Man, nor in the sureness of human progress which following the upward path of struggle and travail is constantly achieving, through cyclic darkness and doubt, its ever widening ranges of fulfilment. Willingly therefore I harness myself, in my advanced age, to the arduous responsibility of creating in our Educational Colony in Santiniketan a spirit of genuine international collaboration based on a definite pursuit of knowledge which is carried on in an atmosphere of friendly community life harmonized with Nature, and offering freedom of individual self-expression. This work which I have to continue in the face of desperately adverse circumstances, has yet struck root in the soil of India, and sent out its branches to the wider arena of humanity, and it carries, I believe, a very deep affinity with the activities of the League of Intellectual Cooperation with which I am already associated.

My occasional misgivings about the modern pursuit of Science is directed not against Science, for Science itself can be neither good or evil, but against its wrong use. If I may just touch here on your reference to

---

[11]Rabindranath to Gilbert Murray, Santiniketan, 1 September 1934, Gilbert Murray Papers, Modern Manuscripts Department, Bodleian Library, University of Oxford.

machines, I would say that machines should not be allowed to mechanize human life but contribute to its well-being, which, as you rightly point out, it is constantly doing when it is man's sanity which controls the use of machinery.

I would like here to quote a passage from one of my writings published in April 1929 which I think may interest you. You will find that it is impossible for me not to accept the true spirit of Science as a pure expression of the creative soul of man.

> Personally I do not believe that Europe is occupied only with material things. She may have lost faith in religion, but not in humanity. Man, in his essential nature, is spiritual and can never remain solely material. If, however, we in the East merely realize Europe in this external aspect, we shall be seriously at fault. For in Europe the ideals of human activity are truly of the soul. They are not paralysed by shackles of scriptural injunctions. Their sanction lies in the heart of man and not in something external to him. This freedom from the changeless, irrational bondage of external regulations, is a very big asset in modern Europe. He gets this through the urge of his own innate ideals, not because some revered pandit has *ordained* it.
>
> It is this attitude of mind in Europe which is essentially spiritual. For true spirituality always brings freedom with it. The freedom that Europe has achieved today in action, in knowledge, in literature and in art, is a freedom from the rigid inanity of matter. The fetters that we forge in the name of religion, enchain the spiritual man more securely than even worldly ties. The home of freedom is in the spirit of man. That freedom refuses to recognize any limit either to action, or to knowledge. It is courageous enough to cross over the barriers of nature, and the limitations of natural instincts; it never regrets immediate loss that may, or may not, lead to gains in a far distant future.
>
> When the aeroplane goes up in the sky, we may wonder at it as the perfection of material power; but behind this lies the human spirit, strong and alive. It is this spirit of man which has refused to recognize the boundaries of nature as final. Nature has put the fear of death in man's mind to moderate his power within the limits of safety; but man in Europe has snapped his fingers at Death and torn asunder the bonds. Only then did he earn the right to fly—a right of the gods . . .

Unfortunately for us, however, the one outstanding visible relationship of Europe with Asia today is that of exploitation; in other words, its origins are commercial and material. It is physical strength that is most apparent to us in Europe's enormous dominion and commerce, illimitable in its extent and immeasurable in its appetite. Our spirit sickens at it. Everywhere we come against barriers in the way of direct human kinship. The harshness of these external contacts is galling, and therefore the feeling of unrest ever grows more oppressive. There is no people in the whole of Asia today which does not look upon Europe with fear and suspicion.

There was a time when we were fascinated by Europe. She had inspired us with a new hope. We believed that her chief mission was to preach the gospel of liberty in the world. We had come then to know only her ideal side through her literature and art. But slowly, Asia and Africa, have become the main spheres of Europe's secular activities, where her chief preoccupations have been the earning of dividends, the administration of empires, and the extension of commerce.

Europe's warehouses and business offices, her police outposts and soldiers' barracks, have been multiplied, while her human relationships have declined.

Towards those who have been exploited, there always is wont to grow up a feeling of contempt. For exploitation itself becomes easier, if we can succeed in creating a callousness towards those who are its victims. Just as whenever we go out fishing we are inclined to regard fishes as the least sensitive of all living creatures, so it becomes quite pleasant to loot the Orient, if only we can make our own moral justification easy by relegating coloured races to the lowest groupings of mankind.

Thus modern Europe, scientific and puissant, has portioned out this wide earth into two divisions. Through her filter, whatever is finest in Europe cannot pass through to reach us in the East. In our traffic with her, we have learnt, as the biggest fact of all, that she is efficient, terribly efficient. We may feel astounded by this efficiency; but if, through fear, we bring to it our homage of respect, then we ourselves need to realize that we are fast going down to the very depths of misfortune; for to do such homage is like the crude barbarity of bringing sacrificial offerings to some god which thirsts for blood. It is on account of this fact, and in order to retain her self-respect, that the whole of Asia today denies the moral superiority of Europe. At the same time, to withstand her ravages, Asia is preparing to imitate the ruthless aspect which slays, which eats raw flesh, which tries to make the swallowing process easier by putting the blame on the victim.

But this, as we realize is only one side, however real and painful, of the Western civilization as it appears to us in the East. The Western humanity, ˙when not affected by its unnatural relationship with the East, preserves its singular strength of moral conduct in the domain of its social life which has its great inspiration for all of us. It is easy enough for us, when someone reviles us for our social evils, to point at worse evils in Europe; but this is negative. The bigger thing to remember is that in Europe these evils are not stagnant. There, the spiritual force in man is ever trying to come to grips. While, for instance, we find in Europe the evil Giant's fortress of Nationalism, we also find Jack the Giant-killer. For, there is growing up the international mind. This Giant-killer, the international mind—though small in size—is real. In India, even when we are loudest in our denunciation of Europe, it is often her Giant's fortress that we long to build with awe and worship. We insult Jack with ridicule and suspicion. The chief reason for this is that in India we have ourselves become material-minded. We are wanting in faith and courage. Since in our country the gods are sleeping, therefore, when the titans come, they devour all our sacrificial offerings— there is never a hint of strife. The germs of disease are everywhere; but man can resist disease only when his vital force is active and powerful.

So, too, even when the worship of the bloodthirsty and false gods of self-seeking is rampant on all sides, man can lift up his head to the skies if his spirit is awake. Both matter and spirit are active. They alone become entirely materialistic who are only half men, who cripple the native majesty of the spirit before the blind repetition of unintelligent activities; who are niggardly in knowledge and palsied in action; who are ever insulting themselves by setting up a meaningless ritualism in the place of true worship; who have no difficulty whatever in believing that there is special sanctity inherent in particular forms and peculiar rites, even when their significance is neither known nor knowable.

I know how reluctant it makes us feel to give any credit for humanity to the Western civilization when we observe the brutalities into which this nationalism of theirs breaks out, instances of which are so numerous the world over—in the late war, in the lynching of negroes, in cowardly outrages allowed to be committed by European soldiers upon helpless Indians, in the rapacity and vandalism practised in Peking during the Boxer War[12] by the very nations who are never tired of vulgarly applying barbaric epithets to each other according to the vicissitudes of political expediency and passion. But while I have never sought to gloss over or keep out of mind any of these ugly phenomena, I still aver that in the life of the West they have a large tract where their mind is free; whence the circulation of their thought currents can surround the world. This freedom of the mind's ventilation following the constant growth of a vigorous life bears in it the promise of righting the wrong and purifying the noxious accumulation within.

To me, the mere political necessity is unimportant; it is for the sake of our humanity, for the full growth of our soul, that we must turn our mind towards the ideal of the spiritual unity of man. We must use our social strength, not to guard ourselves against the touch of others, considering it as contamination, but generously to extend hospitality to the world, taking all its risks however numerous and grave. We must manfully accept the responsibility of moral freedom, which disdains to barricade itself within dead formulae of external regulation, timidly seeking its security in utter stagnation. For, men who live in dread of the spirit of enquiry and lack courage to launch out in the adventure of truth can never achieve freedom in any department of life. Freedom is not for those who are not lovers of freedom and who only allow it standing space in the porter's vestibule for the sake of some temporary purpose, while worshipping, in the inner shrine of their life, the spirit of blind obedience.

In India, what is needed more than anything else, is the broad mind which, only because it is conscious of its own vigorous individuality, is not afraid of accepting truth from all sources. Fortunately for us we know what such a mind has meant in an individual who belongs to modern India. I speak of Ram Mohan Roy. His learning, because of its depth and comprehensiveness, did not merely furnish him with materials of

---

[12]Also known as the Third China War, 1900-01.

scholarship, but trained his mind for the free acceptance of truth. Ram Mohan Roy developed the courage and capacity to discriminate between things that are essential and those that are non-essential in the culture which was his by inheritance. This helped him to realize that truth can never be foreign, that money and material may exclusively belong to the country which produces them, but not knowledge, or ideas, or immortal forms of art.

The very magnitude of mind of such men becomes almost a grievance for smaller personalities, and Ram Mohan has been misunderstood by his own countrymen because he had in him the modern spirit of freedom and comprehensive grasp of truth. We must, however, never make the mistake that those great men who are belittled by their contemporary compatriots do not represent their countries; for, countries are not always true to themselves.

In Ram Mohan's life we find a concrete illustration of what India seeks, the true indication of her goal. Thoroughly steeped in the best culture of his country, he was capable of finding himself at home in the larger world. His culture was not for rejection of those cultures which came from foreign sources, on the contrary, it had an uncommon power of sympathy which could adjust itself to them with respectful receptiveness.

The ideal I have formed of the culture which should be universal in India, has become clear to me from the life of Ram Mohan Roy. I have come to feel that the mind, which has been matured in the atmosphere of a profound knowledge of its own country, and of the perfect thoughts that have been produced in that land, is ready to accept and assimilate the cultures that come from foreign countries. He who has no wealth of his own can only beg, and those who are compelled to follow the profession of beggary at the gate of the intellectually rich may gain occasional scraps of mental food, but they are sure to lose the strength of their intellectual character and their minds are doomed to become timid in touch and in creative endeavour.[13]

---

[13]Rabindranath to Gilbert Murray, Santiniketan, 16 September 1934, Ibid. Also see copy of letter in English Letters, File: Murray, Gilbert. (RBA.)

25

CRISIS AND HOPE:
MY LAST YEARS, 1937–41

In September 1937, Rabindranath fell critically ill and went into coma for three days. The first thing he did on recovering was to paint a landscape. He also wrote poems which expressed his feelings of being in a 'borderland' between life and death. He called this collection of poems *Prantik* (The Borderland). The last two poems there revealed his anxiety over the threat of another war in Europe. What also distressed him at this time was a letter from Yone Noguchi[1] who insisted that Japan's military action in China was necessary for Asia's liberation. Rabindranath saw little hope of bringing the world closer, or indeed of creating a moral awareness against militant nationalism. Sadly, the Second World War broke out in his lifetime.

Rabindranath did not live to see India's freedom from imperial rule. I believe this was not one of his prime regrets. He worried much more that the villages hardly changed. 'I see imperfection before me,' he wrote about his work of village reconstruction in 1938.[2] His deepest regret was that imperial rule had created an Indian elite which neglected the Indian masses. He was much more concerned about his country's social injustices than he was over political freedom. He put his absolute faith in Gandhi's leadership of the destitute millions even when he and Gandhi differed about political methods. 'Who else has felt so many men of India to be of his own flesh and blood?' he wrote about Gandhiji.[3] His address for his eightieth and last birthday ended on a message of hope for humanity despite uncertainties at home and the world. He named this essay 'Crisis in Civilisation'.

---

[1]Yone Noguchi (1875–1947), known in Japan as Yonejiro Noguchi, influential poet and writer.

[2]Rabindranath to Sukumar Chatterji, 28 Baisakh 1345 (11 May 1938), Bengali Letters, File: Chatterji, Sukumar. (RBA.) Translated by UDG. Sukumar Chatterji worked as superintendent at the Sriniketan Institute of Rural Reconstruction during 1938-39.

[3]Rabindranath Tagore, 'The Call of Truth', *Mahatma and Poet*, p. 76.

Allow me to thank you for your kind letter. You are one of those few Englishmen who maintain, often against odds, the prestige of humanity for your people and help us to cling to a hope for the future of the civilization that is menaced from all sides. I take this opportunity to let you know my genuine admiration for yourself and your works which I have always enjoyed. Incidentally I may mention that your book on the Greek Epics has helped me greatly to understand the genesis and character of the ancient epics of India.[4]

By segregating ethics to the Kingdom of Heaven and depriving the Kingdom of Earth from its use, man has up to now never seriously acknowledged the need of higher ideals in politics or in practical affairs. That is why when disagreements occur between individuals—violence is not encouraged but punished, but when the combatants are nations, barbaric methods are not only not condemned but glorified. The greatest of men like Buddha or Christ have from the dawn of human history stood for the ideal of non-violence, they have dared to love their enemies and defied tyranny by peace, but we have not yet claimed the responsibility they have offered us.

Fight is necessary in this world, combat we must and relentlessly against the evils that threaten us, for by tolerating untruth we admit their claim to exist. But war on the human plain must be what in India we call *dharma yuddha*—moral warfare. In it we must array our spiritual powers against the cowardly violence of evils. This is the great ideal which Mahatma Gandhi represents, challenging his people to fearlessly apply man's highest strength not only in our individual dealings but in the clash of nation and nation.

In the barbaric age, men's hunger did not impose any limits on its range of food which included even human flesh, but with the evolution of human society this has been banished from extreme possibility: in a like manner we await the time when nothing may supposedly justify the use of violence whatever consequences we are led to face. Because, success in a conflict

---

[4]Rabindranath to Gilbert Murray, 26 January 1937, Murray Papers, Modern Manuscripts Department, Bodleian Library, University of Oxford.

may be terrible defeat from the human point of view, and material gain is not worth the price we pay at spiritual cost. Much rather should we lose all than barter our soul for an evil victory. We honour Mahatma Gandhi because he has brought this ideal into the sphere of politics and under his lead India is proving every day how aggressive power pitifully fails when human nature in its wakeful majesty bears insult and pain without retaliating. India today, inspired by her great leader, opens the new chapter of human history which has just begun.[5]

I am profoundly surprised by the letter that you have written to me: neither its temper nor its contents harmonize with the spirit of Japan which I learnt to admire in your writings and came to love through my personal contacts with you. It is sad to think that the passion of collective militarism may on occasion helplessly overwhelm even the creative artist, that genuine intellectual power should be led to offer its dignity and truth to be sacrificed at the shrine of the dark gods of war.

You seem to agree with me in the condemnation of the massacre of Ethiopia by Fascist Italy but you would reserve the murderous attack on Chinese millions for judgement under a different category. But surely judgements are based on principle, and no amount of special pleading can change the fact that in launching a ravening war on Chinese humanity, with all the deadly methods learnt from the West, Japan is infringing every moral principle on which civilization is based. You claim that Japan's situation is unique, forgetting that military situations are always unique, and that pious warlords, convinced of peculiarly individual justification for their atrocities, have never failed to arrange for special alliances with divinity for annihilation and torture on a large scale.

Humanity, in spite of its many failures, has believed in a fundamental moral structure of society. When you speak, therefore, of 'the inevitable means, terrible it is though, for establishing a new great world in the Asiatic continent'—signifying, I suppose, the bombing of Chinese women

[5]Rabindranath Tagore, 'Moral Warfare', *Gandhi*, Calcutta: Visva-Bharati, 1963, pp. 66-67.

and children and the desecration of ancient temples and universities as a
means of saving China for Asia—you are ascribing to humanity a way of
life which is not even inevitable among the animals and would certainly
not apply to the East, in spite of her occasional aberrations. You are building
your conception of an Asia which would be raised on a tower of skulls. I
have, as you rightly point out, believed in the message of Asia, but I never
dreamt that this message could be identified with deeds which brought
exaltation to the heart of Tamerlane[6] at his terrible efficiency in manslaughter.
When I protested against 'Westernization' in my lectures in Japan, I
contrasted the rapacious imperialism which some of the *nations* of Europe
were cultivating with the ideal of perfection preached by Buddha and Christ,
with the great heritages of culture and good neighbourliness that went
into the making of Asiatic and other civilizations. I felt it to be my duty
to warn the land of bushido, of great art and traditions of noble heroism,
that this phase of scientific savagery which victimized Western humanity
and led their helpless masses to a moral cannibalism was never to be
imitated by a virile people who had entered upon a glorious renascence and
had every promise of a creative future before them. The doctrine of 'Asia
for Asia' which you enunciate in your letter, as an instrument for political
blackmail, has all the virtues of the lesser Europe which I repudiate and
nothing of the larger humanity that makes us one across the barriers of
political labels and divisions. I was amused to read the recent statement of
a Tokyo politician that the military alliance of Japan with Italy and Germany
was made for 'highly spiritual and moral reasons' and 'had no materialistic
considerations behind it'. Quite so. What is not amusing is that artists and
thinkers should echo such remarkable sentiments that translate military
swagger into spiritual bravado. In the West, even in the critical days of war
madness, there is never any dearth of great spirits who can raise their voice
above the din of battle, and defy their own warmongers in the name of
humanity. Such men have suffered, but never betrayed the conscience of
their peoples which they represented. Asia will not be Westernized if she
can learn from such men: I still believe that there are such souls in Japan

---

[6]Mongol ruler (1339–1405), also known as Timur, who conquered Persia, northern India
and Syria, and established his capital at Samarkand; ancestor of the Mughal dynasty in India.

though we do not hear of them in those newspapers that are compelled at the cost of their extinction to represent their military master's voice.

'The betrayal of intellectuals' of which the great French writer spoke after the European war,[7] is a dangerous symptom of our age. You speak of the savings of the poor people of Japan, their silent sacrifice and suffering and take pride in betraying that this pathetic sacrifice is being exploited for gun running and invasion of a neighbour's hearth and home, that human wealth of greatness is pillaged for inhuman purposes. Propaganda, I know, has been reduced to a fine art, and it is almost impossible for non-democratic countries to resist hourly doses of poison, but one had imagined that at least the men of intellect and imagination would themselves retain their gift of independent judgement. Evidently such is not always the case: behind sophisticated arguments there seems to lie a mentality of perverted nationalism which makes the 'intellectuals' of today go blustering about their 'ideologies', dragooning their own 'masses' into paths of dissolution. I have known your people and I hate to believe that they could deliberately participate in the organized drugging of Chinese men and women by opium and heroin, but they do not know; in the meanwhile, representatives of Japanese culture in China are busy practising their craft on the multitudes caught in the grip of an organization of wholesale human pollution. Proofs of such forcible drugging in Manchukuo and China have been adduced by unimpeachable authorities. But from Japan there have come no protests, not even from her poets.

Holding such opinions as many of your intellectuals do, I am not surprised that they are left 'free' by your Government to express themselves. I hope they enjoy their freedom. Retiring from such freedom into 'a snail's shell' in order to savour the bliss of meditation 'on life's hopeful future' appears to me to be an unnecessary act, even though you advise Japanese artists to do so by way of change. I cannot accept such separation between an artist's function and his moral conscience . . .

---

[7]Reference here is to Julien Benda (1867–1956), author of *La Trahison des Clercs*, 1927, translated into English as *The Treason of the Intellectuals*, 1928. The translation is also known as *The Betrayal of the Intellectuals*. Benda was a humanist and rationalist who accused his contemporary thinkers of abandoning the truth and succumbing to political passions.

I speak with utter sorrow for your people; your letter has hurt me to the depths of my being. I know that one day the disillusionment of your people will be complete, and through laborious centuries they will have to clear the debris of their civilization wrought to ruin by their own warlords run amok. They will realize that the aggressive war on China is insignificant as compared to the destruction of the inner spirit of chivalry of Japan which is proceeding with a ferocious severity. China is unconquerable, her civilization, under the dauntless leadership of Chiang Kai-shek, is displaying marvellous resources; the desperate loyalty of her peoples, united as never before, is creating a new age for that land. Caught unprepared by a gigantic machinery of war hurled upon her peoples, China is holding her own; no temporary defeats can ever crush her fully aroused spirit . . .

You do not realize that you are glorifying your neighbour at your own cost. But these are considerations on another plane: the sorrow remains that Japan, in the words of Madame Chiang Kai-shek[8] which you must have read in the *Spectator*, is creating so many ghosts. Ghosts of immemorial works of Chinese art, of irreplaceable Chinese institutions, of great peace-loving communities drugged, tortured, and destroyed. 'Who will lay the ghosts?' she asks. Japanese and Chinese people, let us hope, will join hands together, in no distant future, in wiping off memories of a bitter past. True Asian humanity will be reborn. Poets will raise their song and will be unashamed, one believes, to declare their faith again in a human destiny which cannot admit of a scientific mass production of fratricide.[9]

Today I complete eighty years of my life. As I turn back to the long stretch of years behind me and view them in clearer perspective, I am struck by the change that has taken place in my attitude and in the psychology of my countrymen, a change that is tragic.

---

[8]Madame Chiang Kai-shek (1897–2003), born Soong Mei-ling, married Chiang Kai-Shek in 1927. She is the author of a series of articles called 'What War Is Teaching China', published in the English newspaper *Spectator* in 1938, to which Rabindranath is referring.

[9]Rabindranath to Yone Noguchi, Santiniketan, 1 September 1938, English Letters, File: Noguchi, Yone. (RBA.)

Our direct contact with the wide world of humanity grew out of our link in history with the British race. They came to us with a great literary tradition in which they were truly revealed. The learning we received in those days was meagre and far from diverse; science was still beyond our reach. We leaned heavily on English literature—its appreciation became a mark of culture. We endlessly echoed Burke's eloquence and Macaulay's[10] rhetorical strains. We eagerly discussed Shakespeare and Byron and the humanistic political philosophy of the time. True, we were already resolved on gaining our national liberation; but, deep in our hearts, there was a great belief in the liberalism of the British—the vanquished were sure to be led to the path of freedom by the victors themselves. Had not England been an asylum, often, for political refugees, for men who had struggled and suffered in the cause of their country? This humanism in the British people had our sincere respect. I may add in this context that, during my first visit to Britain in my early youth, I had the chance to listen to John Bright in the House of Parliament as well as outside. His large-hearted radicalism which was far above all nationalist bias made so strong an imprint on my mind that something of it lingers still in these days of sad disillusionment.

Not that the dependence on our rulers' bounty was a matter of pride. This much was commendable, though: we did have the eyes to see intimations of human goodness in an alien race and felt no hesitation in paying it our tribute. The worthiest gifts of human heritage cannot remain the monopoly of a particular land or people; nor do they build a miser's secret hoard that must show no diminution. So it is that English literature, out of which we have gained real sustenance, evokes a response deep within us even today.

It is hard to find an apt Bengali equivalent for the English word 'civilization'. The civilization of our ancient times was called by Manu[11] *sadachar*, proper conduct. It consisted of a set of conventions which became the social code. Formalism, often unjust, often tyrannical, grew at the

---

[10]Thomas Babington Macaulay (1800–59), English Whig politician and historian.

[11]The *Laws of Manu* (c. 1500 BC), or the *Samhitas*, governed the day-to-day activities of ancient India.

expense of freedom of thought. The tenets of conduct which Manu laid down hardened into time-honoured tradition.

In my boyhood, the English-educated section of our people felt stirrings of revolt against the rigid social code—the Bengali literature of the time carries portrayals of that revolt. In place of the set code we began to accept the ideal of 'civilization' as represented by the English term and illustrated by the British character.

In my own home, this change, backed by reason, was warmly greeted and its effect was felt both in theory and practice. Born in such an atmosphere, and impelled by my natural bias towards literature, I saw the British occupying a pedestal of glory.

That early period of my life ended in an agony of disenchantment. I started to discover more and more how those who professed the highest civilized values could cast them aside with the utmost ease whenever their national interest were at stake.

The moment came when I had to pull myself away from preoccupation with literature. For, the sight of the terrible poverty of the Indian masses grew inescapable. I realized that perhaps in no other modern state was there such a complete denial of the basic needs of living: food and clothing, education and health services. And yet it was the exploited resources of this country that had been adding, year on year, to the wealth of the British race.

Lost in the glamorous aspects of British culture, I had never thought that out of it could come so cruel a distortion of long cherished values; that distortion, I knew at last, was the emblem of a civilized nation's contempt and callousness towards our vast masses.

This helpless country has been denied mastery over the machine, by means of which the British have strutted as a world power. Meanwhile, through these years, Japan has been using that mastery for a rapid expansion of her economy. I have seen with my own eyes the extent of Japan's prosperity and national uplift. I have witnessed, again, in Moscow the tireless energy with which the Russians have tried to wipe out from their country disease and illiteracy, ignorance, penury, and every outward mark of shame. Free from racial prejudice, the Soviets have projected all over their domain the power of human fellowship. The swift and surprising progress they have attained makes me at once happy and jealous!

One unusual aspect of Soviet life that impressed me in Moscow was that the tie of common interests resulted in a great joint endeavour and prevented communal differences from developing into political conflict. Today there are in the world two great Powers, the British and the Russians, who dominate a large number of nationalities. The British have trampled on the manhood of the subject races under their rule, keeping them in a moribund state. It is otherwise in Soviet Russia which has political attachments with many Muslim tribes in its territory. The Government have striven hard and unceasingly for the welfare of those peoples, trying to harmonize the interests of all.

I have also seen Iran, long squeezed between the grindstones of two European Powers, now liberated and working to fulfil her destiny. During my recent visit there I discovered to my delight that the Zoroastrians, once at the mercy of the major community, no longer suffered from repression. Iran's new life started from the time she freed herself from the entanglements of European diplomacy. With all my heart I wish Iran well.

Turning to a neighbouring state, Afghanistan, I find that, while much remains to be done in the fields of education and social development, there are real prospects of continuous progress; for, no European power has yet succeeded in bringing the land of the Afghans into its suffocating grip.

India, however, bearing the immense deadweight of British rule, lies effortless and inert. I recall the tragic history of another country with a great and ancient civilization: China. The British doped the people of China with opium and followed up with territorial aggression. The memory of these happenings had barely dimmed when another outrage came. Japan started to swallow up North China, and that act of brigandage was cynically waved aside by British statesmen as a minor incident. Later, these statesmen lent a crafty hand in wrecking the Republic of Spain.

On the contrary, I saw also how a group of brave Englishmen laid down their lives fighting for freedom in Spain. True, no such generous impulse had stirred in English hearts when an Asian country, China, faced peril; nevertheless, the heroic self-sacrifice in the cause of a European republic vindicated the true English spirit to which in earlier years I had offered homage. And the contrast struck me with renewed force, so that I have to tell this sad story of my gradual loss of faith in the civilization of the West.

Here in India, the calamity of civilized rule is apparent not only in the grievous lack of the bare necessities of life—food, clothing, educational and medical facilities—but even more deplorably in the way the nation has been split, divided against itself. To make matters worse, our social conditions alone are held in blame for the wretched state of affairs, even though this evil could not have taken shape without secret support from the topmost level in the administration.

I do not believe that we Indians are in any way inferior to the Japanese in intellectual calibre. The sharpest contrast in the destinies of the two Eastern peoples lies in the fact that, while India has been at the mercy of the British Power, Japan has never suffered from alien domination. We know, indeed, what we have been robbed of. All that the so-called civilized rule has given us is 'law and order' and the instruments of a police state. The spirit of liberty has yielded to the display of barefaced might. The withholding of the most precious elements in human relationships has altogether blocked the path of our progress.

And yet it has been my privilege to come in contact with big-hearted Englishmen of surpassing goodness, and it is on account of them that I have not lost faith in the people to whom they belonged. There was Andrews, for instance; in him I had for a very close friend an Englishman, a real Christian and a gentleman. Today, in death's perspective, his complete selflessness and brave magnanimity is all the more luminous. We in India are indebted to Andrews for many acts of love and devotion. But speaking from a personal angle, I am specially grateful to him for this reason: he helped me to regain in my old age some of that sincere respect for the British people which I had acquired in my youth under the power of their literature. The memory of Andrews perpetuates for me the nobility of the British heart. I have counted men like him as my most intimate friends and they are friends of all humanity. To have such men was for me an enrichment of my life. It is they who will save British honour from shipwreck. At any rate, if I had not seen them and known them, my disillusionment about the peoples of the West would have gone unchallenged.

Meanwhile, the spectre of a new barbarity strides over Europe, teeth bare and claws unconcealed in an orgy of terror. From one end of the Continent to the other the fumes of oppression pollute the atmosphere.

The spirit of violence dormant perhaps in the psychology of the West has roused itself and is ready to desecrate the spirit of Man.

The turning of the wheel of fortune will compel the British one day to give up their Indian empire. But what kind of India will they leave behind, what stark misery? When the stream of their two centuries' rule runs dry at last, what a waste of mud and filth will be revealed, bearing a tale of utter futility! There was a time when I used to believe that the springs of a true civilization would issue out of the heart of Europe. Today, as I am about to quit the world, that faith has gone bankrupt.

I live today in the hope that the Saviour is coming, that he will be born in our midst in this poverty-shamed hovel which is India. I shall wait to hear the message he brings with him, the supreme word of promise he speaks unto man from this Eastern horizon to give faith and strength to all who hear.

I look back on the stretch of past years and see the crumbling ruins of a proud civilization lying heaped as garbage out of history! And yet I shall not commit the grievous sin of losing faith in Man, accepting his present defeat as final. I shall look forward to a turning in history after the cataclysm is over and the sky is again unburdened and passionless.

Perhaps the new dawn will come from this horizon, from the East where the sun rises; and then, unvanquished Man will retrace his path of conquest, despite all barriers, to win back his lost heritage.

The hour is near when it will be revealed that the insolence of might is fraught with great peril; that hour will bear out in full truth of what the ancient sages have proclaimed:

> *Adharmenaishate tabat tato bhadarni pasyati*
> *Tatah sapatnan jayati samulastu binayasyati*

By unrighteousness man prospers, gains what seems desirable, defeats enemies, but perishes at the root.[12]

---

[12]Rabindranath Tagore, *Crisis in Civilisation*, 8 May 1941, Calcutta: Visva-Bharati, 1941. The full text is reproduced above.

'Bismay' (Endless Wonder)

Once again I wake up when the night has
        waned,
when the world opens all its petals once
        more,
and this is an endless wonder.
Vast islands have sunk in the abyss
        unnamed,
stars have been beggared of the last flicker
        of their light,
countless epochs have lost all their ladings.
World-conquerors have vanished into the
        shadow of a name
behind dim legends,
great nations raised their towers of triumph
as a mere offering to the unappeasable
hunger of the dust.
Among this dissolving crowd of the
        discarded
my forehead receives the consecration of
        light,
and this is an endless wonder.

I stand for another day with the
        Himalayas,
with constellations of stars.
I am here where in the surging sea-waves
the infuriate dance of the Terrible
is rhythmed with his boisterous laughter.
The centuries on which have flashed up
        and foundered
kingly crowns like bubbles

have left their signature on the bark of
        this aged tree,
where I am allowed to sit under its ancient
        shade for one more day,
and this is an endless wonder.[13]

---

[13]*Poems*, no. 92, pp. 136-37. Bengali original, 'Bismay', *Parisesh*, 1932.

PART TWO

MY THOUGHTS

26

O N   M Y S E L F

I have a relationship with the world which is deeply personal. It is not of mere knowledge and use. All our relationships with facts have an infinite medium which is Law, *satyam*; all our relationship with truth has an infinite medium which is Reason, *jnanam*; all our personal relationship has an infinite medium which is Love, *anandam.*[1]

I have felt the meeting of the East and West in my own individual life. I belong to the latter end of the Nineteenth Century. And to our remote country in Bengal, when I was a boy, there came a voice from across the sea. I listened to it. It would be difficult to imagine what it meant for me in those days. We realized the great heroic ideal which had been held in Ancient Greece and that art which gave expression to its greatness. I was deeply stirred, and felt as if I had discovered a new planet on the horizon.[2]

India has two aspects—in one she is a householder, in the other a wandering ascetic. The former refuses to budge from the home corner, the latter has no home at all. I find both these within me. I want to roam about and see all the wide world, yet I also yearn for a little sheltered nook; like a bird with its tiny nest for a dwelling, and the vast sky for flight.

I hanker after a corner because it brings calmness to my mind. My mind really wants to be busy, but in making the attempt it knocks so repeatedly against the crowd as to become utterly frenzied and to keep buffeting

---

[1] *Thoughts*, p. 19.
[2] 'Meeting of the East and the West', *English Writings*, Volume III, p. 631.

me, its cage, from within. If only it is allowed a little leisurely solitude, and can look about and think to its heart's content, it will express its feelings to its own satisfaction.

This freedom of solitude is what my mind is fretting for; it would be alone with its imaginings, as the Creator broods over His own creation.[3]

I have just received your letter requesting me to preside over the next Congress. Believe me, it is painfully difficult for me to refuse any invitation coming from you concerning our country. But one of the very few things that I know for certain about myself is that I am wholly unfit for politics. Whenever, urged by some necessity of special circumstances, I have tried to dabble in it I have injured myself, consequently injuring those works which it is my mission to perform. Also I believe in our *shastric* injunction to retire from all activities of public life after a certain period, not to be arbitrarily fixed, but whenever an individual receives inner warnings combined with sure hints from his waning physical powers. This is an excuse which I never could offer to anybody else but yourself, knowing that you will understand me and help me in keeping myself free from all responsibilities that are sure to disturb me in my final adjustment of life.[4]

I have nothing to do directly with politics. I am not a Nationalist, moderate or immoderate in my political doctrine or aspiration. But politics is not a mere abstraction, it has its personality and it *does* intrude into my life where I am human. It kills and maims individuals, it tells lies, it uses its sacred sword of justice for the purpose of massacre, it spreads misery broadcast over centuries of exploitation, and I cannot say to myself, 'Poet, you have nothing to do with these facts, for they belong to politics.' This politics assumes its fullest diabolical aspect when I find all its hideous

[3]Balia, February 1893, *Glimpses of Bengal*, pp. 93–95.

[4]Rabindranath to Annie Besant, 15 October 1918, *Select Letters*, pp. 211-12. Annie Besant (1847–1933), theosophist and founder of the Indian Home Rule League (1916).

acts of injustice find moral support from a whole nation only because it wants to enjoy in comfort and safety the golden fruits reaped from abject degradation of human races.[5]

Dearest friend, the continual enjoyment of sympathy and fellowship with which I have been surrounded since I came to the Continent makes it so difficult for me to sit down and write letters. I can hardly realize how it has become possible for me to have occupied the hearts of these people to which I could only find access through a very meagre and imperfect medium of translation. The welcome which has been accorded to me in all the countries that I have travelled in Europe has been deeply genuine and generous to the extreme. This makes it delightfully easy for me to give out the best that I have in me in an easy flow of communication. For a literary man the greatest joy is in the expression of his personality. It is a light which shines in its perfection of truth only where the atmosphere is transparent. I feel it clear that my relationship with Continental Europe is natural and unobstructed, being disinterested. In England, I have distinctly felt in my last visit, it is obscured owing, I am sure, to the politics that ever stands between our people and yours, consciously or unconsciously.[6]

Even when I was very young, my mind ever sought for all experiences in an environment of completeness. That is to say, fact indicated some truth to me, even though I did not clearly understand it. That is why my mind was constantly struck with things that in themselves were commonplace.

When I watched, from over the wall of the terrace of the inner apartments of our Jorasanko house, the coconut trees and the tank surrounded by the huts of the milk-vendors, they came before me with a more-than-themness that could not be exhausted. That faculty—though subsequently mingled with reasoning and self-analysis—has still continued in my life. It is the

---

[5]Rabindranath to William Rothenstein, Brussels, 6 October 1920, *Imperfect Encounter*, pp. 277-78.

[6]Ibid.

sense and craving for wholeness. Constantly, it has been the cause of my separation from others and also their misunderstanding of my motives.[7]

But of one thing you may be certain, that I have a natural power of resistance in me against intoxication produced by praise, and my mind at the present moment is not in a dazed state of drunkenness. I am not least oblivious of the fact that the breath of official suspiciousness can blight in a moment my cherished scheme. But I have already told you in my last letter that I try to follow the teaching of *Gita* according to which all idealism should spurn to seek their value in success, but only in truth. So long as my motive is true, my method is honest and the process of my work open to the view of all comers from all countries I shall not be ashamed of the meagreness of result, poorness of appearance, or afraid of an utter failure at the hands of a ruling power which would hesitate to allow us freedom for giving expression to our higher nature.[8]

I am humble in my estimate of my own worth and the only claim I have upon my fellow beings is the claim of love which I feel for them. My whole heart shrinks from the idea of raising a special platform for myself in order to receive homage from the people and play the part of a teacher to them who have any regard for me; and I implore you not to create a situation which will be against my nature.[9]

All along my literary career I have run against the taste of my countrymen, at least those of them who represent the vocal section of my province. It has hardly been pleasant to me, but it has had the effect of making me reconciled to my mental loneliness. In the West—for some little while in

---

[7]Rabindranath to C.F. Andrews, New York, 14 January 1921, *Letters to a Friend*, p. 315.

[8]Rabindranath to William Rothenstein, Geneva, 8 May 1921, *Imperfect Encounter*, pp. 286-87.

[9]Rabindranath to Count Hermann Keyserling, 20 May 1921, English Letters, File: Keyserling, Hermann. (RBA.) Count Hermann Alexander Keyserling (1880–1946), admirer of Rabindranath, was a hereditary count from Estonia who founded the 'School of Wisdom' in Darmstadt, Germany, in 1920.

England and lately in the continental countries of Europe—the recognition which I met with came to me as a shock of surprise.

When a poet's life's works are accepted by his fellow beings it gives him a sense of intellectual companionship with his readers which is precious. But it has a great danger of growing into a temptation—and I believe, consciously and unconsciously I have been succumbing to it with regard to my Western readers. But I have this paradox in my nature that when I begin to enjoy my success I grow weary of it in the depth of my mind. It is not through any surfeit of it, but through something in it which hurts me. Reputation is the greatest bondage for an artist. I want to emancipate my mind from its grasp not only for the sake of my art, but for the higher purposes of life, for the dignity of soul. What an immense amount of unreality there is in literary reputation, and I am longing—even while appreciating it like a buffalo the luxury of its mud bath—to come out of it as a *sanyasi*, naked and aloof. A gift has been given to me—this great world—which I can truly enjoy when I am simple and natural. I am looking back to those days of my youth when I had easy access into the heart of this universe—and I believe I shall yet again recover my place there when I am able to sever my mind from the attraction of the literary world which with its offer of rewards tries to standardize creative visions according to criterions distractingly varied and variable.[10]

I know, as a poet, my work is not for achieving immediate results in urgent human affairs. Even my idea of the International University, growing into an obsession, is hampering me in my life's work. What have I to do with establishing solid institutions, fixed and firm upon big funds and public approbation? I clearly feel that it is wasting my life setting up stone idols on costly altars; some day they will all come down with their own weight.[11]

[10]Rabindranath to Edward Thompson, Santiniketan, 20 September 1921, *Difficult Friendship*, pp. 132-33.

[11]Rabindranath to Thomas Sturge Moore, 20 October 1921, Sturge Moore Papers, Senate House Library, University of London.

It is not any particular criticism that has disturbed my mind. I have been feeling for some time that I am surrounded on all sides by words and works and things which are not truly mine and therefore which obscure the vision of the world that has been God's gift to me. I am feeling homesick for that life of mine which once had its perfect freedom of simplicity. I have gradually allowed myself to grow dependent upon other people's opinions. I suppose it naturally comes out of a certain amount of success. When you have your store of reputation to defend and augment, and are burdened with a mission, you are tempted to recruit for your allies, forgetting that very often they have to be bribed at the cost of truth. My life seems to be struggling to cut its path across all outside impositions that are barring the passage of the light which gives it life and inspires its songs. I long to end my life as I began it, to make a supreme effort to regain my Paradise.[12]

I am very hard pressed over Visva-Bharati. It is the financial burden that is making me old. I was young at heart when I turned sixty. But I have grown old at sixty-three. I had vowed not to die feeling old whatever my age. I have not been able to live up to it.[13]

I understand this conflict in his mind for I myself have a kind of civil war constantly going on in my own nature between my personality as a creative artist, who necessarily must be solitary, and that as an idealist who must realize himself through works of a complex character needing a large field of collaboration with a large body of men. My conflict is within myself between the two opposite forces in my character, and not, as in the case of Pearson,[14] between my individual temperament and the surrounding circumstance. Both of the contending forces being equally natural to me I cannot with impunity get rid of one of them in order to simplify my life's problem. I suppose a proper rhythm is possible to be

---

[12]Rabindranath to Edward Thompson, probably January 1922, *Difficult Friendship*, pp. 136-37.

[13]Rabindranath to Edward Thompson, 15 January 1924, Ibid., pp. 152-53. Original letter is in Bengali. Translated by UDG.

[14]Reference is to W.W. Pearson, see chapter 13, note 1.

attained in which both may be harmonized, and my work in the heart of the crowd may find its grace through the touch of the breath that comes from the solitude of the creative mind.[15]

I carry an infinite space of loneliness around my soul through which the voice of my personal life very often does not reach my friends—for which I suffer more than they do. I have my yearning for the personal world as much as any other mortal, or perhaps more. But my destiny seems to be careful that in my life's experience I should only have the *touch* of personality and not the *ties* of it. All the while she claims my thoughts, my dreams and my voice, and, for that, detachment of life and mind is needed. In fact, I have constantly been deprived of opportunities for intimate attachments of companionship to last long. Then again I have such an extreme delicacy of sensitiveness with regard to personal relationships that even when I acknowledge and welcome it I cannot invite it to the immediate closeness of my life. This deficiency I acknowledge with resignation knowing that it is a sacrifice claimed of me by my Providence for some purpose which he knows.[16]

It may be difficult for you to realize that I am a shy individual brought up in retirement from my young days. And yet my fate takes every opportunity to drag me into a crowded publicity. I often wish that I had belonged to that noiseless age when artists took their delight in their work and forgot to publish their names. I feel painfully stupid when I am handled by the multitude who by celebrating some particular period of my life indulge in their avidness of some sort of a crowd ritual which is mostly made of unreality.[17]

---

[15]Rabindranath to Romain Rolland, 28 February 1924, English Letters, File: Rolland, Romain. Photocopy. (RBA.)

[16]Rabindranath to Leonard Elmhirst, Shanghai, 16 June 1924, English Letters, File: Elmhirst, L.K. Photocopy. (RBA.)

[17]Rabindranath to Edward Thompson, Santiniketan, 10 April 1935, *Difficult Friendship*, pp. 185-86.

I feel relieved to know from your letter that my poem on Africa has pleased you, for it was with great diffidence I permitted the poem to be sent to the *Spectator*. I have no faith left in my English and it is seldom that I ever attempt writing in your language. It is more with my brush and paint that I while away my time and try to forget that I am a poet.[18]

I am surprised you complain of a break-up but can you not realize my condition? 76 and yet the load of a big reputation and the exhausted exchequer of a growing University. But you know 'renunciation is not for me'[19] and I shall yet stick it through.[20]

Andrews has sent a cable saying Nitu's condition is getting worse. I apprehended this from the time I came to know he has phthisis. I had hoped his health would improve in Europe. He was much better while he stayed in Mainz. I don't think he could tolerate the cold and the hard work in Leipzig. My regret is that it was I who sent him there.

I have repeatedly made mistakes with my own family. Now I have done it again. I feel mortified.

Surrounded by all the sadness in the world I feel loathe to make so much of my personal pain. Had it just been my loss I might have accepted it. But given Mira's deprivations I feel wretched to think what she will have to suffer. That is why I cannot but blame my own injudiciousness.[21]

---

[18]Rabindranath to Edward Thompson, 4 June 1937, Ibid., p. 204, 'To Africa', *Spectator*, 7 May 1937. The poem was provoked by Mussolini's invasion of Abyssinia in 1935, reiterating Rabindranath's anger against militant nationalism.

[19]Reference is to a song from *Gitanjali*, no. 73, reproduced on facing page.

[20]Rabindranath to Ernest Rhys, 31 December 1936, English Letters, File: Rhys, Ernest. Copy. (RBA.) Ernest Rhys (1859–1946), literary scholar and author of *Rabindranath Tagore: A Biographical Study* (1915). He was founder editor of the Everyman's Library for English Literature.

[21]Rabindranath to Rathindranath, 17 June 1932, Bengali Letters, File: Tagore, Rathindranath. (RBA.) Translated by UDG.

If we stay too attached to our small personal worlds we fall prey to imagining small insults and harbouring hurt feelings. I had my share of pain but I might have been more miserable if I had stuck to my personal likes and dislikes. That did happen in my literary world, causing me to hit out at my own countrymen with my grievances. My own mental health was as much to blame for this as anything else.

In this new year, I am trying to calm myself. We are all part of a large humanity with an existing history of happiness and suffering. It will be a shame if I am unable to connect with that history and mope away in my self-imposed little corner. How long will I be in the world that I can afford to shut out its 'sweetness and light' from my life? I have resolved to live at peace with myself in my remaining days.[22]

'Bairagyo Sadhoney Mukti' (Deliverance in Renunciation)

Deliverance is not for me in renunciation. I feel the embrace of freedom in a thousand bonds of delight.

Thou ever pourest for me the fresh draught of Thy wine of various colours and fragrance, filling this earthen vessel to the brim.

My light will light its hundred little lamps with Thy flame and place them before the altar of Thy temple.

No, I shall never shut the doors of my senses. The delights of sight and hearing and touch will bear Thy delight.

Yes, all my illusions will burn into illumination of joy, and all my desires ripen into fruits of love.[23]

[22]Rabindranath to Mira, Santiniketan, 1 Baisakh 1344 (14 April 1938), *Chitthi Patra* IV, pp. 161-62. Translated by UDG.

[23]Rabindranath Tagore, *Gitanjali* (*Song Offerings*), no. 73, Reprint, London: Macmillan, 1957, p. 68. Bengali original, 'Bairagyo Sadhoney Mukti', *Naibedya*, 1901.

We all have a realm, a private paradise, in our mind, where dwell deathless memories of persons who brought some divine light to our life's experience, who may not be known to others, and whose names have no place in the pages of history. Let me confess to you that this man lives as one of those immortals in the paradise of my individual life.

He came from Sweden, his name was Hammargren.[24] What was most remarkable in the event of his coming to us in Bengal was the fact that in his own country he had chanced to read some works of my great countryman, Ram Mohan Roy, and felt an immense veneration for his genius and his character. Ram Mohan Roy lived in the beginning of the last century, and it is no exaggeration when I describe him as one of the immortal personalities of modern time. This young Swede had the unusual gift of a farsighted intellect and sympathy, which enabled him even from his distance of space and time, and in spite of racial differences, to realize the greatness of Ram Mohan Roy. It moved him so deeply that he resolved to go to the country which produced this great man, and offer her his service. He was poor, and he had to wait some time in England before he could earn his passage money to India. There he came at last, and in reckless generosity of love utterly spent himself to the last breath of his life, away from home and kindred and all the inheritances of his motherland. His stay among us was too short to produce any outward result. He failed even to achieve during his life what he had in his mind, which was to found by the help of his scanty earnings a library as a memorial to Ram Mohan Roy, and thus to leave behind him a visible symbol of his devotion. But what I prize most in this European youth, who left no record of his life behind him, is not the memory of any service of goodwill, but the precious gift of respect which he offered to a people who are fallen upon evil times, and whom it is so easy to ignore or to humiliate. For the first time in the modern days this obscure individual from Sweden brought to our country the chivalrous courtesy of the West, a greeting of human fellowship.[25]

---

[24]Karl Erik Hammargren (1858–94), came from Sweden to Calcutta in 1893 where he was associated with the Brahmo Samaj.

[25]Rabindranath Tagore, 'East and West', *Creative Unity*, pp. 101-02.

27

ON RELIGION

I hope before long to bring out my book about the question of Religion and my idea of it. I have been, all through my life, from my boyhood, receiving the development of my religious ideas almost unconsciously till the cycle is complete and today I have given expression to my experience of religion in these lectures.[1] I am sure that before the year is out these papers will be published. In them you will see discussed what I consider the true spirit of religion, about my idea of all different religions, what they mean. I have never discussed this subject, it is rather difficult to say anything about it, so I ask my hearers to have patience till the book is out which will be called 'The Religion of Man'. If I have a message that message will come out in this book, the message of my life, and my thoughts I have been thinking, and the experience I have gone through, and now I have become conscious of the meaning which religion has for my soul. I have tried to make it clear, which is difficult because every experience is difficult to express and to describe, yet I have tried my best to give it some expression.[2]

I was born in a family which, at that time, was earnestly developing a monotheistic religion based upon the philosophy of the Upanishad. Somehow, my mind at first remained coldly aloof, absolutely uninfluenced by any religion whatever. It was through an idiosyncrasy of my temperament that I refused to accept any religious teaching merely because people in my surroundings believed it to be true. I could not persuade myself to

---

[1] Rabindranath gave the Hibbert Lectures at the University of Oxford in 1930. The lectures were published in 1931 as *The Religion of Man: Being the Hibbert Lectures for 1930*.

[2] Rabindranath Tagore, Ms. Accession no. 329, 'Talks in Geneva', 1930, in English. (RBA.)

imagine that I had a religion because whom I might trust believed in its value.

Thus my mind was brought up in an atmosphere of freedom—freedom from the dominance of any creed that had its sanction in the definite authority of some scripture, or in the teaching of some organized body of worshippers. And, therefore, the man who questions me has every right to distrust my vision and reject my testimony. In such a case, the authority of some particular book venerated by a large number of men may have greater weight than the assertion of an individual, therefore I never claim any right to preach.

When I look back upon those days, it seems to me that unconsciously I followed the path of my Vedic ancestors, and was inspired by the tropical sky with its suggestion of an uttermost Beyond. The wonder of the gathering clouds hanging heavy with the unshed rain, with the sudden sweep of storms arousing vehement gestures along the line of coconut trees, the fierce loneliness of the blazing summer noon, the silent sunrise behind the dewy veil of autumn morning, kept my mind with the intimacy of a pervasive companionship.

Then came my initiation ceremony of Brahminhood when the Gayatri verse of meditation was given to me, whose meaning, according to the explanation I had, runs as follows:

> Let me contemplate the adorable splendour of Him
> who created the earth, the air and the starry spheres,
> and sends the power of comprehension
> with our minds.

This produced a sense of serene exaltation in me, the daily meditation upon the infinite being which unites in one stream of creation my mind and the outer world. Though today I find no difficulty in realizing this being as an infinite personality in whom the subject and object are perfectly reconciled, at that time the idea to me was vague. Therefore the current of feeling that it aroused in my mind was indefinite, like the circulation of air—an atmosphere which needed a definite world to complete itself and satisfy me. For it is evident that my religion is a poet's religion, and neither that of an orthodox man of piety nor that of theologian. Its touch comes to me through the unseen and trackless channel as does the inspiration of my songs. My religious life has followed the same mysterious line of growth as has my poetical life. Somehow they are wedded to each other and, though their betrothal had a long period of ceremony, it was kept secret from me.[3]

I had been blessed with that sense of wonder which gives a child his right of entry into the treasure house of mystery in the depth of existence. My studies in the school I neglected, because they rudely dismembered me from the context of my world and I felt miserable, like a caged rabbit in a biological institute. This, perhaps, will explain the meaning of my religion. This world was living to me, intimately close to my life, permeated by a subtle touch of kinship which enhanced the value of my being.[4]

My religion is my life—it is growing with my growth—it has never been grafted on me from outside. I had denied God when I was younger just as the flower in its pride of blossoming youth completely ignores the fruit which is its perfection. But now that the fruit is here with the mystery of the immortal life hidden in the core of its seed I accept it simply as I accept the reality of my own person though I have no logic to explain its existence. Therefore I am not at all anxious about the godlessness of your gardener. For all growth is a rhythm and all true religion is a part of true religion—it is hopeless when it is an absolute negation, when it has no seed of life in it, when it is a sign of decay and of death.[5]

[3]*The Religion of Man*, pp. 91–93.

[4]Ibid., p. 99.

[5]Rabindranath to Robert Bridges, 8 July 1914, Bridges Papers, Modern Manuscripts Department, Bodleian Library, Oxford. For Robert Bridges, see chapter 14, note 14.

I do not subscribe to theories of religion. I say nothing when there is a discourse on *dvaitavada* or *advaitavada*, dualism or non-dualism. I have understood that the God-within-me finds expression in happiness. That happiness takes over everything—my body, my mind, my universe, my age-old past, my unending future. I don't understand this fully. I think it must be *lila*, the mystery of life. I am steeped in it. The fact that I can savour the light, the morning sky, the evening clouds, that I can enjoy the foliage and the faces of loved ones, are all the result of this overpowering sensation which plays like shadows in the joys and sorrows of my life.

This is what my Creator has done for me. He has blessed me with the realization that I am connected with Him by a bond of mutual love. I do believe it is He who provides all my pleasures, and He who embraces me in my agonies. That gives me the solid faith that nothing is lost, that it is all a part of life's total picture. Let me quote from an old letter of mine:

> I cannot claim I am able to understand and absorb religion in its general sense. But I can say with certainty that there is something that is *living* in me. It is a feeling of mystery, not a dogma, it is a distinct awareness in the mind. I can sense that my life's joys and sorrows and my faith will together give my life a certain harmony. I don't know whether the scriptures are true or false. What I do know is that they mean nothing to me. I also know that my inner realization will depend on my own thoughts and actions. Like an idea or a verse which can't be broken up by spelling every word of it, our joys and sorrows can't be separated from life's total picture. Whenever I feel the unity of the creative power within myself I also feel connected to the infinite creativity of the universe. Like the sun, the moon, and the stars, I become aware of an abiding creative power within me which is in control of my desires and my disappointments. Who can tell where all this will lead to because we have so little knowledge. We don't even know what is contained in a single speck of dust. All I have learnt is that my personal losses will find their natural place if I can connect to the vastness that exists in time and space.
>
> I have come to see myself as a part of that vastness—to understand that nothing, not even an atom, can survive without me. Therefore my sense of the beauty of an autumn morning is not unlike the

relationship I enjoy with my family. That is how the luminous space around me enters the depths of my heart. Its absolute grandeur comes to me in the cadences and colours of my songs. I feel we are in continuous dialogue day and night.

The creative power I describe in the letter above—the power that has helped me to come to terms with my life's joys and sorrows and to unite me with the universe—is the One I call *jiban debata*, Lord of my life.[6]

'Jiban Debata' (Lord of My Life)

Lord of my being, has your wish been
    fulfilled in me?
Days have passed without service and
    nights without love.
Flowers have dropped on to the dust
    and have not been gathered for
    your acceptance.
The harp string strung with your own
    hands have slackened and lost their
    notes.
I slept in the shadow of your garden
    and forgot to water your plants.
Is the time over now, my lover? Have
    we come to the end of this play?
Then let the bell ring of departure, let the
    morning come for the freshening
    of love.
Let the knot of a new life be tied for us
    in a new bridal bond.[7]

---

[6] *Atmaparichay*, pp. 14–16. Translated by UDG.
[7] *Poems*, no. 11, p. 27. Bengali original 'Jiban Debata', *Chitra*, 1896.

I believe in a spiritual world, not as anything separate from this world, but as its innermost truth. With the breath we draw, we must always feel this truth; that we are living in God. Born in this great world, full of the mystery of this infinite, we cannot accept our existence as a momentary outburst of chance, drifting on the current matter towards an eternal nowhere. We cannot look upon our lives as dreams of a dreamer who has no awakening in all time. We have a personality to which matter and force are unmeaning unless related to something infinitely personal, whose nature we have discovered, in some measure in human love, in the greatness of good, in the martyrdom of heroic souls, in the effable beauty of Nature, which can never be a mere physical fact nor anything but an expression of personality.[8]

At the outburst of an experience which is unusual, such as happened to me in the beginning of my youth, the puzzled mind seeks its explanation in some settled foundation of that which is usual, trying to adjust an unexpected inner message to an organized belief which goes by the general name of a religion. And, therefore, I naturally was glad at that time of youth to accept from my father the post of secretary to a special section of the monotheistic church of which he was the leader. I took part in its services mainly by composing hymns which unconsciously took the many-thumbed impression of the orthodox mind, a composite smudge of tradition. Urged by my sense of duty I strenuously persuaded myself to think that my mental attitude was in harmony with that of the members of our association, although I constantly stumbled upon obstacles and felt constraints that hurt me to the quick.

At last I came to discover that in my conduct I was not strictly loyal to my religion, but only to the religious institution. This latter represented an artificial average, with its standard of truth at its static minimum, jealous of any vital growth that exceeded its limits. I have my conviction that in religion, and also in the arts, that which is common to a group is

---

[8]Rabindranath Tagore, *Personality*, pp. 154-55.

not important. Indeed, very often it is a contagion of mutual imitation. After a long struggle with the feeling that I was using a mask to hide the living face of truth, I gave up my connection with our church.

About this time, one day I chanced to hear a song from a beggar belonging to the Baul[9] sect of Bengal. We have in the modern Indian religion deities of different names, forms and mythology, some Vedic and others aboriginal. They have their special sectarian idioms and associations that give emotional satisfaction to those who are accustomed to their hypnotic influences. Some of them may have their aesthetic value to me and others philosophical significance over-encumbered by exuberant distraction of legendary myths. But what struck me in this simple song was a religious expression that was neither grossly concrete, full of crude details, nor metaphysical in its rarefied transcendentalism. At the same time it was alive with an emotional sincerity. It spoke of an intense yearning of the heart for the divine which is in Man and not in the temple, or scriptures, in images and symbols. The worshipper addresses his songs to man the ideal, and says:

> Temples and mosques obstruct thy path,
> and I fail to hear thy call or to move,
> when the teachers and priests angrily crowd round me.

He does not follow any tradition of ceremony, but only believes in love. According to him:

> Love is the magic stone, that transmutes by its touch
> greed into sacrifice.

He goes on to say:

> For the sake of this love heaven longs to become earth
> and gods to become man.

---

[9] A baul is a wandering minstrel singing philosophical songs about the common ways of life.

Since then I have often tried to meet these people, and sought to understand them through their songs, which are their only form of worship. One is often surprised to find in many of these verses a striking originality of sentiment and diction; for, at their best, they are spontaneously individual in their expressions.[10]

I have already made the confession that my religion is a poet's religion. All that I feel about it is from vision and not from knowledge. Frankly, I acknowledge that I cannot satisfactorily answer any questions about evil, or about what happens after death. Nevertheless, I am sure that there have been some moments in my own experience when my soul has touched the infinite and has become intensely conscious of it through the illumination of joy. It has been said in our Upanishad that our mind and our words come away baffled from the Supreme Truth, but he who knows truth through the immediate joy of his own soul is saved from all doubts and fears.[11]

That which I value most in my religion or my aspiration, I seek to find corroborated, in its fundamental unity, in other great religions, or in the hopes expressed in the history of other peoples. Each great movement of thought and endeavour in any part of the world may have something unique in its expression, but the truth underlying any of them never has the meretricious cheapness of utter novelty about it. The great Ganga must not hesitate to declare its essential similarity to the Nile of Egypt, or to the Yangtse-Kiang of China.[12]

---

[10]*The Religion of Man*, p. 110.
[11]Ibid., pp. 107-08.
[12]*Thoughts*, p. 113.

O how may I express that secret word?
O how can I say He is not like this, and He is like that?
If I say He is within me, the universe is ashamed:
If I say that He is without me, it is falsehood.
He makes the inner and the outer worlds to be indivisible one;
The conscious and the unconscious, both are His footstools.
He is neither manifest nor hidden, He is neither revealed nor
   unrevealed:
There are no words to tell that which He is.[13]

---

[13]Poem no. IX, *One Hundred Poems of Kabir*, Translated by Rabindranath Tagore, Assisted by Evelyn Underhill, London: Macmillan, 1926, p. 9.

28

ON NATURE

From the first time that I can remember, I was passionately fond of Nature. Oh! it used to make me mad with joy when I saw the clouds come up in the sky one by one. I felt, even in those early days, that I was surrounded with a companionship very intense and very intimate, though I do not know how to name it. I had such an exceeding love for Nature, that I cannot think in what way to describe it to you; but she was a kind of loving companion, always with me, and always revealing to me some fresh beauty.[1]

From my earliest years I enjoyed a simple and intimate communion with Nature. Each one of the coconut trees in our garden had for me a distinct personality. When, on coming home from the Normal School, I saw behind the sky-line of our roof-terrace blue-grey water-laden clouds thickly banked up, the immense depth of gladness which filled me, all in a moment, I can recall clearly even now. On opening my eyes every morning, the blithely awakening world used to call me to join it like a playmate; the perfervid noonday sky, during the long silent watches of the siesta hours, would spirit me away from the workaday world into the recesses of its hermit cell; and the darkness of night would open the door to its phantom paths and take me over all the seven seas and thirteen rivers, past all possibilities and impossibilities, right into its wonderland.[2]

---

[1] Rabindranath to C.F. Andrews, in conversation, London, September 1912, *Letters to a Friend*, p. 22.

[2] *Reminiscences*, pp. 226-27.

From my infancy I had a keen sensitiveness which kept my mind tingling with consciousness of the world around me, natural and human. We had a small garden attached to our house; it was a fairyland to me, where miracles of beauty were of everyday occurrence.

Almost every morning in the early hour of the dusk, I would run out from my bed in a great hurry to greet the first pink flush of the dawn through the shivering branches of the palm trees which stood in a line along the garden boundary, while the grass glistened as the dewdrops caught the earliest tremor of the morning breeze. The sky seemed to bring to me the call of a personal companionship, and all my heart—my whole body in fact—used to drink in at a draught the overflowing light and peace of those silent hours. I was anxious never to miss a single morning, because each one was precious to me, more precious than gold to a miser. I am certain that I felt a larger meaning of my own self when the barrier vanished between me and what was beyond myself.[3]

When I became one with this universe, when the green grass grew on my very being, and the autumn light drenched me, when the pores of my youthful body were aroused by the fragrance of the mother earth all green with vegetation, when I lay under the bright sky, spreading myself over distant lands and waters . . . I can even now remember the sensation of those moments when the autumn sun cast an unspoken happiness over me and a larger-than-life creative power entered my subconscious. It is as if that consciousness passed from me into every blade of grass and into the roots of every tree, causing the mustard fields and the leaves of the coconut palm to quiver with the outburst of life's passion.[4]

The mango blossoms have appeared in our ashram. The air is full of music, heard and unheard, and I do not know why we should be callous to the call of the seasons and foolishly behave as if the Spring and the

---

[3] *The Religion of Man*, pp. 98-99.
[4] *Atmaparichay*, p. 23. Translated by UDG.

Winter are the same to human beings, with the same round of works to follow, without having the option to be occasionally useless and absurd ... I am in that mood when one forgets that he has any other obligations to meet than to be good for nothing and glad.[5]

This world has been my very own for a long time but, like one loved from time immemorial, is forever new to me ...

I can remember a time when many ages ago a young earth emerged from a bath in the sea to welcome the young sun. It was then that I too sprung out of this young earth as a tree blossoming with life ...

That is when I first drank the sunlight with all my being, like one shaken out of life's blindness and as delighted as a newborn baby to embrace mother earth and drink the milk of her breast. Awakened by the joy, I broke out into flowers and new leaves. The rain clouds came and touched me as if with the caress of familiar hands.[6]

I quote here from three of my old letters where I expressed my feelings about Nature:

The beautiful days and nights fade from my life because of my failure to receive them. The colours, the light and shadow, a sky full of silent celebration, the absolute peace and beauty of the earth, all add up to a vast festive playground of continuous activity. How can we not respond to this amazing activity? How can there be such a separation between us and Nature? If a single star has taken millions of years to light the sky, if it has travelled millions of miles in continuous darkness to enter this universe, how can it not reach our hearts ...?

We live in a strange environment where humans are busy making rules, putting up barriers, and drawing curtains lest they see Nature with their

---

[5]Rabindranath to C.F. Andrews, Santiniketan, probably February 1914, *Letters to a Friend*, p. 40.

[6]*Atmaparichay*, pp. 23-24. Translated by UDG.

eyes. Truly strange are the earth's human inhabitants. It is a wonder that they have not put caps on the flowering trees nor raised marquees to hide the moon. What is it that these self-blinded people want to see as they move about in their closeted palanquins?[7]

It is not yet five o'clock, but the light has dawned, there is a delightful breeze, and all the birds in the garden are awake and have started singing. The *koel* seems beside itself. It is difficult to understand why it should keep on cooing so untiringly. Certainly not to entertain us, nor to distract the pining lover—it must have some personal purpose of its own. But, sadly enough, that purpose never seems to get fulfilled. And yet it is not down-hearted, and its Coo-coo! Coo-coo! keeps going, with now and then an ultra-fervent trill. What can it mean?

And then in the distance there is some other bird with only a faint chuck-chuck that has no energy or enthusiasm, as if all hope were lost; none the less, from within some shady nook, it cannot resist uttering this little plaint: chuck, chuck, chuck.

How little we really know of the household affairs of these innocent winged creatures, with their soft breasts and necks and their many-coloured feathers! Why on earth do they find it necessary to sing so persistently?[8]

When I returned home from my second voyage to England, my brother Jyotirindra and sister-in-law were living in a riverside villa at Chandernagore, and there I went to stay with them.

The Ganga again! Again those ineffable days and nights, languid with joy, sad with longing, attuned to the plaintive babbling of the river beneath the shade of its wooded banks. This Bengal sky full of light, this south breeze, this flow of the river, the right royal laziness stretching from

[7]Ibid., pp. 22-23. Translated by UDG.
[8]Bolpur, 31 May 1892, *Glimpses of Bengal*, pp. 69-70.

horizon to horizon and from green earth to blue sky, all these were to me as food and drink to the hungry and the thirsty. Here it felt indeed like home, and in these I recognized the ministrations of a Mother.[9]

One day, I was out in a boat on the Ganga. It was a beautiful evening in autumn. The sun had just set; the silence of the sky was full to the brim with ineffable peace and beauty. The vast expanse of water was without a ripple, mirroring all the changing shades of the sunset glow. Miles and miles of a desolate sandbank lay like a huge amphibious reptile of some antediluvian age, with its scales glistening in shining colours. As our boat was silently gliding by the precipitous river bank, riddled with the nest-holes of a colony of birds, suddenly a big fish leapt up to the surface of the water and then disappeared, displaying on its vanishing figure all the colours of the evening sky. It drew aside for a moment the many-coloured screen behind which there was a silent world full of the joy of life. It came up from the depths of its mysterious dwelling with a beautiful dancing motion and added its own music to the silent symphony of the dying day. I felt as if I had a silent greeting from an alien world in its own language, and it touched my heart with a flash of gladness.[10]

One day late in the afternoon, I was pacing the terrace of our Jorasanko house. The afterglow of sunset combined with the wan twilight in a way which seemed to give the approaching evening a specially wonderful attractiveness for me. Even the walls of the adjoining house grew beautiful. Is this uplifting of the cover of triviality from the everyday world, I wondered, due to some magic in the evening light? Never!

I could see at once that the evening had come within me; its shades had obliterated my *self*. While the self was rampant during the glare of day, everything I perceived was mingled with and hidden by it. Now that

---

[9]*Reminiscences*, p. 208.
[10]Rabindranath Tagore, *Sadhana: The Realisation of Life*, Reprint, London: Macmillan, 1966, p. 110.

the self was put in the background, I could see the world in its own true aspect. That aspect has nothing of triviality in it, it is full of beauty and joy.[11]

Tonight the moon is at its full, and its large round face peers at me through the open window on my left, as if trying to make out whether I have anything to say against it in my letter—it suspects, maybe, that we mortals concern ourselves more with its stains than with its beams.

A bird is plaintively crying tee-tee on the sandbank. The river seems not to move. There are no boats. The motionless groves on the back cast an unquivering shadow on the waters. The haze over the sky makes the moon look like a sleepy eye kept open.

Henceforward the evenings will grow darker and darker; and when, tomorrow, I come over from the office, this moon, the favourite companion of my exile, will already have drifted a little farther from me, doubting whether she had been wise to lay her heart so completely bare last evening, and so covering it up again little by little.

Nature becomes really and truly intimate in strange and lonely places. I have been actually worrying myself for days at the thought that after the moon is past her full I shall miss the moonlight more and more; feeling further and further exiled when the beauty and peace which awaits my return to the riverside will no longer be there, and I shall have to come back through darkness.[12]

From the bank to which the boat is tied, a kind of scent rises out of the grass, and the heat of the ground, given off in gasps, actually touches my body. I feel that the warm, living earth is breathing upon me, and that she, also, must feel my breath.

The young shoots of rice are waving in the breeze, and the ducks are in turns thrusting their heads beneath the water and preening their feathers. There is no sound save the faint, mournful creaking of the

---

[11]*Reminiscences*, p. 216.
[12]Shelidah, 9 January 1892, *Glimpses of Bengal*, pp. 54–56.

gangway against the boat, as she imperceptibly swings to and fro in the current . . .

I sat wondering: Why is there always this deep shade of melancholy over the fields and river banks, the sky and sunshine of our country? I came to the conclusion that it is because with us Nature is obviously the more important thing. The sky is free, the fields limitless; and the sun merges them into one blazing whole. In the midst of this man seems so trivial . . .

The contrast between the beautiful, broad, unalloyed peace of Nature—calm, passive, silent, unfathomable—and our own everyday worries, paltry, sorrow-laden, strife-tormented, puts me beside myself as I keep staring at the hazy, distant, blue line of trees which fringe the fields across the river.

Where Nature is ever hidden, and cowers under mist and cloud, snow and darkness, there man feels himself master; he regards his desires, his works as permanent; he wants to perpetuate them, he looks towards posterity, he raises monuments, he writes biographies; he even goes the length of erecting tombstones over the dead. So busy is he that he has not the time to consider how many monuments crumble, how often names are forgotten.[13]

I have no anxiety about the world of Nature. The sun does not wait to be trimmed by me.

But from the early morning all my thoughts are occupied by this little world of myself. Its importance is owing to the fact that I have a world given to me which is mine. It is great because I have the power to make it worthy of its relationship with me; it is great because by its help I can offer my own hospitality to the God of all the world.[14]

[13]Shazadpur, June 1891, Ibid., pp. 27–30.
[14]'Thoughts from Rabindranath Tagore', *English Writings*, Volume III, p. 30.

I blew out the lamp with the idea of turning into bed. No sooner had I done so, through the open windows, the moonlight burst into the room, with a shock of surprise.

That little bit of a lamp had been sneering dryly at me, like some Mephistopheles:[15] and that tiniest sneer had screened off this infinite light of joy issuing forth from the deep love which is in all the world.

If I had gone off to bed leaving the shutters closed, and thus missed this vision, it would have stayed there all the same without any protest against the mocking lamp inside. Even if I had remained blind to it all my life—letting the lamp triumph to the end—till for the last time I went darkling to bed—even then the moon would have still been there, sweetly smiling unperturbed and unobstructive, waiting for me as she has throughout the ages.[16]

I believe that there is an ideal hovering over and permeating the earth—an ideal of that Paradise which is not the mere outcome of fancy, but the ultimate reality in which all things are and towards which all things are moving. I believe that this vision of Paradise is to be seen in the sunlight, and the green of the earth, in the flowing streams, in the gladness of springtime, the repose of a winter morning, in the beauty of a human face and the wealth of human love. Everywhere in this earth the spirit of Paradise is awake and sending forth its voice. It reaches our inner ears without our knowing it. It tunes our harp of life, urging us to send our aspiration beyond the finite, as flowers send their perfume into the air and the birds their songs.[17]

---

[15]Mephistopheles is a devil in Christian mythology whose name evolved during the Renaissance. In the German legend, Faust represented him as the personification of all evil.

[16]'Thoughts from Rabindranath Tagore', *English Writings*, Volume III, p. 58.

[17]*Thoughts*, p. 107.

29

ON MY COUNTRY

Big trees are standing in the flood water, their trunks wholly submerged, their branches and foliage bending over the waters. Boats are tied up under shady groves of mango and bo tree, and people bathe screened behind them. Here and there cottages stand out in the current, their inner quadrangles in the water.

As my boat rustles its way through standing crops it now and then comes across what was a pool and is still to be distinguished by its clusters of water-lilies and diver-birds pursuing fish.

The water has penetrated every possible place. I have never seen such complete defeat of the land. A little more and the water will be right inside the cottages, and their occupants will have to put up *machans* to live on. The cows will die if they have to remain standing like this in water up to their knees. All the snakes have been flooded out of their holes, and they, with sundry other homeless reptiles and insects, will have to chum with man and take refuge on the thatch of his roof.

The vegetation rotting in the water, refuse of all kinds floating about, naked children with shrivelled limbs and enlarged spleens splashing everywhere, the long-suffering patient housewives, exposed in their wet clothes to wind and rain, wading through their daily tasks with tucked-up skirts, and over all a thick pall of mosquitoes hovering in the noxious atmosphere—the sight is hardly pleasing!

Colds and fevers and rheumatism in every home, the malaria-stricken infants constantly crying—nothing can save them. How is it possible for men to live in such unlovely, unhealthy, squalid neglected surroundings? The fact is we are so used to bear everything, hands down—the ravages of Nature, the oppression of rulers, the pressure of our shastras to which we have not a word to say, while they keep eternally grinding us down.[1]

One need not dive deep, it seems to me, to discover the problem of India; it is so plainly evident on the surface. Our country is divided by numberless differences—physical, social, linguistic, religious; and this obvious fact must be taken into account in any course which is destined to lead us into our own place among the nations who are building up the history of man. The trite maxim 'History repeats itself' is like most other sayings but half the truth. The conditions which have prevailed in India from a remote antiquity have guided its history along a particular channel, which does not and cannot coincide with the lines of evolution taken by other countries under different sets of influences. It would be a sad misreading of the lessons of the past to apply our energies to tread too closely in the footsteps of any other nation, however successful in its own career. I feel strongly that our country has been entrusted with a message which is not a mere echo of the living voices that resound from Western shores, and to be true to her trust she must realize the divine purpose that has been manifest throughout the history; she must become conscious of the situation she has been instrumental in creating—of its meaning and possibilities.

It has never been India's lot to accept alien races as factors in her civilization. You know very well how the caste that proceeds from colour takes elsewhere a most virulent form. I need not cite modern instances of the animosity which divides white men from negroes in your own country, and excludes Asiatics from European colonies. When, however, the white-skinned Aryans on encountering the dark aboriginal races of India found themselves face to face with the same problem, the solution of which was either extermination, as has happened in America and Australia, or a modification in the social system of the superior race calculated to accommodate the inferior without the possibility of either friction or fusion, they chose the latter. Now the principle underlying this

---

[1]On the way to Dighapatiaya, 20 September 1894, *Glimpses of Bengal,* pp. 142–44.

choice obviously involves mechanical arrangement and juxtaposition, not cohesion and amalgamation. By making very careful provision for the differences, it keeps them ever alive. Unfortunately, the principle once accepted inevitably grows deeper and deeper into the constitution of the race even after the stress of the original necessity ceases to exist.

Thus, secure in her rigid system of seclusion, in the very process of inclusion, India in different periods of her history received with open arms the medley of races that poured in on her without any attempt at shutting out undesirable elements. I need not dwell at length on the evils of the resulting caste system. It cannot be denied, and this is a fact which foreign onlookers too often overlook, that it served a very useful purpose in its day and has even up to a late age been of immense protective benefit to India. It was largely attributed to the freedom from narrowness and intolerance which distinguishes the Hindu religion and has enabled races with widely different cultures and even antagonistic social and religious usages and ideals to settle down peaceably side by side—a phenomenon which cannot fail to astonish Europeans, who, with comparatively less jarring elements, have struggled for ages to establish peace and harmony among themselves. But this very absence of struggle, developing into a ready acquiescence in any position assigned by the social system, has crushed individual manhood and has accustomed us for centuries not only to submit to every form of domination, but sometimes actually to venerate the power that holds us down. The assignment of the business of government almost entirely to the military class reacted upon the whole social organism by permanently excluding the rest of the people from all political cooperation, so that now it is hardly surprising to find the almost entire absence of any feeling of common interest, any sense of national responsibility, in the general consciousness of a people of whom as a whole it has seldom been any part of their pride, their honour, their dharma, to take thought or stand up for their country. This completeness of stratification, this utter submergence of the lower by the higher, this immutable or all-pervading system, has no doubt imposed a mechanical uniformity upon the people but has at the same time kept their different sections inflexibly and unalterably separate, with the consequent loss of all power of adaptation and readjustment to new conditions and forces. The regeneration of the Indian people, to my mind, directly and perhaps solely depends upon the removal of this condition. Whenever I realize the hypnotic hold which this gigantic system of cold-blooded repression has taken on the minds of our people, whose social body it has so completely entwined in its endless coils that the free expression of manhood even under the direst necessity has become almost an impossibility, the only remedy that suggests itself to me and which even at the risk of uttering a truism I cannot but repeat, is—to educate them out of their trance.

I know I shall be told that foreign dominion is also one of the things not conducive to the free growth of manhood. But it must be remembered that with us foreign dominion is not an excrescence, the forcible extirpation of which will restore a condition of normal health and vigour. It has manifested itself as a political symptom of our social disease, and at present it has become necessary to us for effecting the dispersal of all internal obstructive agencies. For, we have now come under the domination not of a dead system, but of a living power, which, while holding us under subjection, cannot fail to impart to us some of its own life. This vivifying warmth from outside is gradually making us conscious of our own vitality and the newly awakened life is making its way slowly, but surely, even through the barriers of caste.

The mechanical incompatibility and consequent friction between the American colonies and the parent country was completely done away with by means of a forcible severance. The external force which in eighteenth-century France stood to divide class from class [could] only be overcome by *vis major* to bring emancipation to a homogeneous people. But here in India are working deep-seated social forces, complex internal reactions, for in no other country under the sun has such a juxtaposition of races, ideas and religions occurred; and the great problem which from time immemorial India has undertaken to solve is what in the absence of a better name may be called the race problem. At the sacrifice of her own political welfare, she has through long ages borne this great burden of heterogeneity, patiently working all the time to evolve out of these warring contradictions a great synthesis. Now has come the time when she must begin to build, and dead arrangement must gradually give away to living construction, organic growth. If at this stage vital help has come from the West even in the guise of an alien rule, India must submit—nay welcome it, for above all she must achieve her life's work.

She must take it as a significant fact in her history that when on the point of being overcome with a torpor that well nigh caused her to forget the purpose of what she had accomplished, a rude shock of life should have thus burst in upon her, reminding her of her mission and giving her strength to carry it on. It is now manifestly her destiny that East and West should find their meeting place in her ever-hospitable bosom. The unification of the East which has been her splendid if unconscious achievement must now be consciously realized in order that the process may be continued with equal success and England's contribution thereto utilized to full advantage.

For us, there can be no question of blind revolution, but of steady and purposeful education. If to break up the feudal system and the tyrannical conventionalism of the Latin church which had outraged the healthier instincts of humanity, Europe needed the thought impetus of the Renaissance and the fierce struggle of the Reformation, do we not in a greater degree need an overwhelming of higher social ideals before a place can be found for true political thinking? Must we not have that greater vision of humanity which will impel us to shake off the fetters that shackle our individual life before we begin to dream of national freedom?

It must be kept in mind, however, that there never has been a time when India completely lost sight of the need of such reformation. In fact, she had no other history but the history of this social education. In the earliest dawn of her civilization there appeared amidst the fiercest conflict of races, factions and creeds, the genius of Ramachandra and Krishna introducing a new epoch of unification and tolerance and allaying the endless struggle of antagonism. India has ever since accepted them as the divine will incarnate, because in their life and teachings her innermost truth has taken an immortal shape. Since then all the illustrious names of our country have been of those who came to bridge over the differences of colours and scriptures and to recognize all that is highest and best as the common heritage of humanity. Such have been our emperors Asoka and Akbar, our philosophers Shankara and Ramanuja, our spiritual masters Kabir, Nanak, Chaitanya and others not less glorious because knit closer to us in time and perspective.[2] They belong to various sects and castes, some of them of the very 'lowest', but still they occupy the ever-sacred seat of the guru, which is the greatest honour that India confers on her children. This shows that even in the darkest of her days the consciousness of her true power and purpose has never forsaken her.

The present unrest in India of which various accounts must have reached you, is to me one of the most hopeful signs of the times. Different causes are assigned and remedies proposed by those whose spheres of activity necessarily lead them to a narrow and one-sided view of the situation. From my seclusion it seems to me clear that it is not this or that measure, this or that instance of injustice or oppression, which is at the bottom. We have been on the whole comfortable with a comfort unknown for a long time, we have peace and protection and many of the opportunities for prosperity which these imply. Why then this anguish at heart? Because the contact of East and West has done its work and quickened the dormant life of our soul. We have begun to be dimly conscious of the value of the time we have allowed to slip by, of the weight of the clogging effete matter which we have allowed to accumulate, and are angry with ourselves. We have also begun vaguely to realize the failure of England to rise to the great occasion, and to miss more and more the invaluable cooperation which it was so clearly England's mission to offer. And so we are troubled with a trouble which we know not yet how to name. How England can best be made to perceive that the mere establishment of the Pax Britannica cannot either justify or make possible her continued dominion, I have no idea; but of this I am sure that the sooner we come to our senses, and

---

[2]Asoka the Great (304 BC–232 BC) was the emperor of the Mauryan Empire from 273 BC to 232 BC, his kingdom extending over most of south Asia, from present-day Afghanistan and parts of Persia in the west to Bengal and Assam in the east and to Ceylon down south; Jalaluddin Mohammad Akbar or Akbar the Great (1542–1605) is generally regarded as the greatest of the Mughal emperors; Shankara (788?–820?), philosopher and theologian, became a monistic Hindu ascetic and exponent of the Advaita Vedanta School of philosophy; Ramanuja (1017–1137), philosopher, regarded as the greatest exponent of Visishtadvaita Vedanta.

take up the broken thread of our appointed task, the earlier will come
the final consummation.[3]

India's Prayer

Thou hast given us to live.
Let us uphold this honour with all our
    strength and will;
For thy glory rests upon the glory that
    we are.
Therefore in thy name we oppose the
    power that would plant its banner
    upon our soul.
Let us know that thy light grows dim in the
    heart that bears its insult of bondage.
That the life, when it becomes feeble,
    timidly yields thy throne to untruth.
For weakness is the traitor who betrays
    our soul.
Let this be our prayer to thee—
Give us power to resist pleasure where it
    enslaves us.
To lift our sorrow up to thee as the
    summer holds its midday sun.
Make us strong that our worship may
    flower in love, and bear fruit in
    work.
Make us strong that we may not insult
    the weak and the fallen,

---

[3]Rabindranath to Myron H. Phelps, 'The Problem of India', A Letter, Santiniketan,
4 January 1909, in the *Modern Review,* August 1910, pp. 184–87. Myron Phelps (1856–1916),
American lawyer with a keen interest in India.

That we may hold our love high where
      all things around us are wooing
      the dust.
They fight and kill for self love, giving
      it thy name.
They fight for hunger that thrives on
      brother's flesh,
They fight against thine anger and die.
But let us stand firm and suffer with
      strength
for the True, for the Good, for the
      Eternal in man,
for thy Kingdom which is in the union
      of hearts,
for the Freedom which is of the Soul.[4]

I love India, not because I cultivate the idolatry of geography, not because I have had the chance to be born in her soil, but because she has saved through tumultuous ages the living words that have issued from the illuminated consciousness of her great sons—*Satyam, Jnanam, Anantam Brahma*, Brahma is truth, Brahma is wisdom, Brahma is infinite; *Santam, Sivam, Advaitam*, peace is in Brahma, goodness in Brahma, and the unity of all beings.

> *Brahma-nishtho grhasthah syat tatvajnana-prakurvita*
> *Yad yad karma prakurvita tad Brahmani samarpayet*

The householder shall have his life established in Brahma, shall pursue the deeper truth of all things and in all activities of life dedicate his works to the Eternal Being.

---

[4]*Poems*, no. 61, pp. 92-93. Written in English and read by the poet on the occasion of the Calcutta session of the Indian National Congress, 1917.

Thus we have come to know that what India truly seeks is not a peace which is in negation, or in some mechanical adjustment, but that which is in Sivam, in goodness; which is in Advaitam, in the truth of perfect union; that India does not enjoin her children to cease from karma, but to perform their karma, in the presence of the Eternal, with the pure knowledge of the spiritual meaning of existence; that this is the true prayer of Mother India.

Ya eko-varno bahudha saktiyogat varnan anekan nihitartho dadhati
Vichaiti chante visvamadau sa no buddhya subhaya samyunaktu

He who is one, who is above all colour distinctions, who dispenses the inherent needs of men of all colours, who comprehends all things from their beginning to the end, let Him unite us to one another with the wisdom which is the wisdom of goodness.[5]

Swadeshi, Swarajism, ordinarily produce intense excitement in the minds of my countrymen, because they carry in them some fervour of passion generated by the exclusiveness of their range. It cannot be said that I am untouched by this heat and movement. But somehow, by my temperament as a poet, I am incapable of accepting these objects as final. They claim from us a great deal more than is their due. After a certain point is reached, I find myself obliged to separate myself from my own people, with whom I have been working, and my soul cries out: 'The complete man must never be sacrificed to the patriotic man, or even to the merely moral man.'

To me, humanity is rich and large and many-sided. Therefore I feel deeply hurt when I find that, for some material gain, man's personality is mutilated in the Western world and he is reduced to a machine.

The same process of repression and curtailment of humanity is often advocated in our country under the name of patriotism. Such deliberate

---

[5]Rabindranath Tagore, 'Open Letters, Speeches, Tributes', in *English Writings*, Volume III, pp. 820-21.

impoverishment of our nature seems to me a crime. It is a cultivation of callousness, which is a form of sacrilege. For God's purpose is to lead man into perfection of growth, which is the attainment of a unity comprehending an immense manifoldness. But when I find man, for some purpose of his own, imposing upon his society a mutilation of mind, a niggardliness of culture, a Puritanism which is spiritual penury, it makes me inexpressibly sad.[6]

The present day world belongs to the Western world ... and really Scientific culture is the gift of the Western world to humanity. It is a great gift. We are doomed if we don't consider this gift, and the reason why we have been deprived of it so long is rather a paradox. You know how Japan in 50 years' time completely mastered the technique of the Western Science and she has made wonderful progress to such an extent that she can compete with Western nations who have had a like start ... We have already produced some scientists known to the world. I have been in touch with a very great scientist in Germany, Einstein, who came into contact with some of our students and scientists who have wonderful minds ...

You must realize this fact, as I told you, about 80% of the Indian peoples are in a chronic state of famine, only 5% is literate, that is to say, hardly educated. What is the use of our talking of culture, what infinitesimal quantity of it reaches us and what are we going to do with it. Of course it goes without saying that if we could have better opportunities to have this culture in adequate measure it would be an immense benefit, not only to us, but I feel absolutely certain to the civilization of this world. I hope that the time will come when we shall have the same advantages to educate ourselves in an adequate way, and I shall be only too grateful if the Western culture could reach my country.[7]

---

[6]Rabindranath to C.F. Andrews, 14 January 1921, *Letters to a Friend*, pp. 115-16.

[7]Rabindranath Tagore, 'Talks in Geneva', 1930, Ms. Accession no. 329, in English. (RBA.)

I would request you to include Japan in your itinerary: India will be with you in your appeal to the moral conscience of Asia which Japan cannot afford to kill in a mania of spiritual suicide. The pathway which led from India to her great neighbours in the East is now partly closed through centuries of neglect; we have to remove the weeds, and also the recent barriers erected by fratricidal politics so that once more the traffic of human interchange can continue, linking our country with Japan and China. India's great awakening had crossed deserts and mountains, the overflow of her glorious epoch of culture touched far continents and left permanent deposits in distant shores of Asia. In my visits to China and Japan, and to Siam, Java and Bali, I felt profoundly moved to find how the communion of her cultures persisted even up to our own days and I cannot help hoping that as a messenger from India's youth you would give strength to the historic forces of Asiatic unity, bringing new urge of neighbourly understanding to our Eastern peoples. India herself is passing through an eclipse when her own reality is lost to her in a haze of parochial politics, sectarianism, and domestic contention: contact with a greater world of Eastern culture will, I fervently hope, help in removing her obsessions and enliven her national existence with a new humanity.[8]

'Sarthoko Janomo Amaar'
(The Blessed Land of My Birth)

Blessed am I that I am born to this land
and that I had the luck to love her.

What care I if queenly treasure is not in
her store but precious enough is
for me the living wealth of her
love.

---

[8]Rabindranath to Jawaharlal Nehru, 17 July 1939, Nehru Papers, Nehru Memorial Museum and Library, Teen Murti, New Delhi.

The best gift of fragrance to my heart is
        from her flowers and I know
        not where else shines the moon
        that can flood my being with such
        loveliness.

The first light revealed to my eyes was
        from her own sky and let the same
        light kiss them before they are
        closed for ever.[9]

---

[9]*Poems*, no. 38, p. 60. Bengali original, 'Sarthoko Janomo Amaar', *Baul*, 1905.

30

ON BRITISH RULE IN INDIA

Though, ever since your arrival here, I have felt it my duty to communicate to you my own ideas about the mission which has brought you to this land, I have refrained from doing so, because I have no scheme to offer you. Where there are two parties in question, a scheme can only become perfect when it is based upon a perfect knowledge of the aims and motives of both. But unfortunately in India, the people and the government are very far apart; and when, as in the present circumstances, mutual understanding is essential, we find that the way has never been paved, and therefore any reasonable negotiation between both parties has become extremely difficult. We are told that at the present moment the British people are favourably inclined to listen to our claims. But in order to put these claims in a practical form, we on our side must not only know how much we are fit to receive, but more so, how much our rulers are ready to give us. That does not wholly depend upon the justice of our cause or even of our worthiness. It depends, taking human nature as it is, upon the power of the ruling race to share with us what it has entirely in its own hands. As far as we can judge, the men who represent the British people in India are extremely reluctant to concede to us any power which now they fully enjoy themselves; and it seems it deeply hurts their susceptibilities to form any relationships with us on the basis of equality. (Knowing this, and also knowing that the habit of dependence upon outside favour for the uplift of our nation is demoralizing,) I have generally kept aloof from all political movements started by my countrymen.

Morally considered, the worst of all human relationships is that of the giver and receiver—at least, it is almost as bad as that of the parasites and their victims. And therefore I have ever felt it my duty to warn my countrymen against taking to such a slippery path of moral degradation.

What I have always proposed to my countrymen is to organize ourselves to help our own people in all departments of life. Many of the activities which come within the functions of the state in a free country have to be taken up, however difficult that may be, by our people in their own social programme; because in India the state and the people are not one, and therefore service to our own country can never be truly rendered by us through the agency of Government. It is of higher importance to a people to be able to feel that they are actively serving their own country than that they are being well governed. It is not at all flattering to us, and far less to the British rule in India, that after more than a century of Western dominion we are still considered unfit to serve our country in its internal administration. The perpetual humiliation of such an unnatural condition is growing more and more irksome for us as the years pass by. We bitterly feel the hopelessness of our situation when we know that it pacifies the conscience of our rulers to be able to proclaim to the world that we have an inherent deficiency in our character and we are despised because we are despicable by nature.

Of all others in India, the Bengali people have been specially selected for vilification, till we have almost become ashamed to claim human sympathy from our rulers. The stages through which these people have passed are interesting to follow. The first thing we did was to welcome the Congress movement with joy, thinking it to be the best opportunity for us to prove that we were alive to the needs of our country and to express our aspiration for more freedom in its administration. That movement had its attraction for us in a vague belief that there was some analogy between England and India with regard to the relationship between the Government and the people, and the Congress had the character of the Opposition party in the British Parliament. It gave us a sense of pride to think that in lecturing and passing resolutions we were heroically proving our manhood. To my mind, it would have been an act of statesmanship if our Government had taken this opportunity of establishing some real relationship with this institution, making it a field where the people and the rulers could truly meet. However, it received very little encouragement from the English people, though its founder himself was an Englishman and a few other Englishman of chivalrous nature took prominent part in it. As Congress became a wholly one-sided institution, having no real connection with our Government, gradually its proceedings degenerated into playing at politics, losing all sense of proportion and responsibility.

The great expectation which this Congress movement raised in our minds died away as we found that it received more kicks than half pence from our Governors, and also when we felt to our cost that its capacity for consumption was far greater than its productive power. The eternal repetition of its begging formulae began to jar upon the nerves of the present generation of our youths, especially as the alms bowl grew more and more burdensome, not with gifts but with its own weight of futility. Just at this psychological moment came Lord Curzon, who had the peculiar autocratic temperament to be readily infected by the antipathy against the Bengali race. Rightly or wrongly, we suspected that the proposed partition of Bengal was like a knife aimed at the solidarity of the Bengali speaking race. In spite of the vociferous clamours of our political bodies we were told by the authorities meekly to take this partition as an accomplished fact. It was brought home to us with tremendous force that the deepest sentiment of the people could be disregarded by the rulers of the country. And yet we had the humiliating experience of Lord Ripon's[1] administration when the sentiment of the Anglo-Indians prevailed over the authority of the head of the Government. It brought out the insult of our position in vivid colours and our people came to realize that they had no vital connection with our ruling body and therefore the ideal of politics pursued so long by us was nothing but mendicancy, which never can lead to true wealth but only to that poorness of spirit which is the worst foundation for national welfare. This sudden great disturbance in the attitude of our mind (which had hitherto to take for granted that everything of any real value must come to us from the one fountainhead, namely the generosity of the British people) gave rise to an intellectual rebellion against the ideals of the West. In our bitterness of heart we criticized the European civilization and condemned it to an extent that was suicidal to our cause

---

[1]Lord Ripon (1828–1909), Governor General of India, 1880–84.

and led to the upholding of social customs in which lies our source of weakness. Along with this we fiercely tried to repudiate the West in all concerns of our life, and our boycott movement had something in it which was not mere spitefulness, but pride struggling to assert itself even where it was poor.

This was the time when, roughly speaking, our young men became divided into two groups—one trying to serve the country by helping the poor, teaching the ignorant, tending the sick, introducing new industries and reviving old ones without looking for help from the Government; the other attempting to gain freedom and national self-respect by undermining the British government by all kinds of secret organizations.

This has led to the repressive measures whose latest outcome is the internment policy. Our Government being, as I have said, far apart from our people cannot but entertain suspicions in times of difficulty—the suspicions that are indiscriminating. Therefore, its repressive measures become terribly destructive, stamping out life itself in order to drive away disease.

As a result of this, that spirit of service, to which our young men were beginning to open their minds, is on the point of being banished from Bengal. For where there is the least stir of movement there are attracted the black clouds of blind suspicion. This is not only costing us very dear, but creating a perpetual source of trouble to the Government. As this suspiciousness grows into a permanent habit, both on the part of the ruled and the rulers, true understanding between them becomes impossible and evil creatures taking advantage of this vicious atmosphere thrive upon treacherous lies. It is the most demoralizing state of things for the governing powers when they perforce have to employ for their purposes men who are traitors to their country, who are callous enough to victimize our youths and boys, some of whom are of the noblest character, on mere suspicion and sometimes on evidence manufactured by themselves. If I know anything of the British character I am sure it is bringing shame and disgust into the minds of those officials who have to deal with such an unclean abomination. If this inexhaustible source of mutual misunderstanding be left to perpetuate itself then the policy of wholesome repression also has to be made eternal, and one must not judge the merit of such a policy by any amount of outward success, but must rather count its cost in the loss of moral prestige.

Our young men in Bengal know that they are not trusted by their Government—they are spied upon, they are harassed, their field of employment is narrowed, they suffer for those very qualities which are encouraged in the country of their rulers. When they dedicate their lives for the welfare of their country, independent of Government help, their very success is looked upon with misgivings.

When notice is drawn to this desperate state of things we are asked to consider the exceptional difficulties of the present-day Government. But that we refuse to do, and also are unable to do, because our Government and our people are not an organic whole. We can only know our sufferings, which are all the greater because we cannot have any personal pride in our Government, or be in any way responsible for it. We are also told that in England itself during this war-time the condition is not much better—but there the people have the great compensation of knowing their Government to be their own, therefore they never can imagine it to be the interest of their legislators to strike at the root of their manhood, to crush their spirit of independence.

The only course which can be taken for removing this growing evil is to establish a natural connection between the people and the Government, so that we may feel that through the Government we have the power to serve our own country, that it is the true centre of our national life, where a great Western people is in collaboration with us in one of the noblest missions of humanity. The conflicts will be endless and repressive measures impotent to check them so long as we remain the passive recipients of favours from an alien organization, mechanical, almost devoid of human attributes. We must fully realize the hand of providence in the advent of the English in India before we can be reconciled to it, and this can only happen if its moral significance shines above all purposes of selfish gain. If such a great ideal has not been evolved out of the long British rule in India then it is a failure not only for us but also for England. And I feel sure that, in as far as this British rule represents mere power over a subject race and exploitation of a foreign country, it has been the sure cause of degeneracy to the English people whose greatest strength was love of freedom and of humanity.

I have not formulated any scheme in my letter but only let you know what I feel about that which I believe is nearest your own heart. The psychology of the question is of more importance than any particular system or method, and unless your people are fully awake to the great moral responsibility and realize the sufferings and humiliation with which the millions of India are burdened—their joyless existence dark, because bereft of all expectation of a great future—you shall never be able to give us anything in that true spirit which will bring more blessings upon yourselves than upon the people whom you help.[2]

When I was about to embark for America only a few days ago, some newspaper cuttings from Japan came to my hands containing information about a prosecution of some Hindus in San Francisco for revolutionary intrigue against the British government. I find that the prosecution counsel mentions my name implicating me in this charge of conspiracy, assuring the court that he has documentary evidence to support it. It is also stated that my last tour to America was undertaken at the instigation of some German agents to whom I gave to understand that Count Teranchi was favourable to my secret proposals and Count Okuma sympathetic.[3]

Though I feel certain that my friends in America and my readers there who have studied my writings at all carefully can never believe such an audacious piece of fabrication, yet the indignity of my name being dragged into the mire of such calumny has given me great pain. It is needless to

---

[2]Rabindranath to Edwin Montagu, Calcutta, 6 April 1918, Ms. Accession no. 350, pp. 45–59, in English. (RBA.) Edwin Samuel Montagu, (1879–1924), British Liberal politician, Secretary of State for India, 1917–22.

[3]On the advice of British Intelligence, the US government cracked down on Indian revolutionaries abroad and brought them to trial in 1917-18. At one point in the trial, a letter was produced in which an Indian in Washington DC stated that Rabindranath had enlisted support for their cause when he met the prime minister of Japan, Count Okuma. A telegram was also produced from an Indian revolutionary living in New York showing evidence of their support for Rabindranath's speeches.

tell you that I do not believe in patriotism which can ride roughshod over higher ideals of humanity, and I consider it to be an act of impiety against one's own country when my service is offered to her which is loaded with secret lies and dishonest deeds of violence. I have been outspoken enough in my utterances when my country needed them, and I have taken upon myself the risk of telling unwelcome truths to my own countrymen, as well as, to the rulers of my country. But I despise these tortuous methods adopted whether by some Government or other groups of individuals, in which the devil is taken into partnership in the name of duty. I have received great kindness from the hands of your countrymen and I entertain great admiration for yourself who are not afraid of incurring the charge of anachronism for introducing idealism in the domain of politics, and therefore I owe it to myself and to you and your people to make this avowal of my faith and to assure your countrymen that their hospitality was not bestowed upon one who was ready to accept it while wallowing in the sub-soil sewerage of treason.[4]

I do not know whom I should pity more—our people or our Government. The utter demoralization of the latter is becoming so ugly in its enormity that the very success which it may breed will be monstrous, imposing a long lasting and terrible burden upon its present power. Of one thing our authorities seem to be unconscious—it is that they have completely lost their moral prestige. I can recall the time when our people had great faith in the justice and truthfulness of the British government. But I am positive that there are few individuals in the whole of India who sincerely believe in its promises, its communiqués, avowed motives and decisions of its commissions. It was almost ludicrous to find how our masses during the late war refused to accept as true every news of success of the allies that came to them from the English source. This loss of faith in their rulers may or may not be justified, but it is a significant fact, and if our rulers

---

[4]Rabindranath to Woodrow Wilson, Calcutta, 9 May 1918, English Letters, File: Wilson, Woodrow, Typed copy. (RBA.) Woodrow Wilson (1856–1924), twenty-eighth President of the USA, 1913–21.

have any statesmanship left in them they ought seriously to consider it. They have far too much been taken up with keeping up their prestige of power which is the biggest rift in their armour. For the mere sight of power in itself is insufferable to man and God alike unless it stands upon the truth of moral law.[5]

It hurts me very deeply when I think that there is hardly a corner in the vast continent of Asia where men have come to feel any real love for Europe. The great event of the meeting of the East and the West has been desecrated by the spirit of contempt on the one side and a corresponding hatred on the other. The reason is, it was greed which brought Europe to Asia and the threat of physical power which maintains her there. This prevents our mutual relationship from becoming truly human and this makes it degrading for both parties. Parasitism, whether based upon power or upon weakness, must breed degeneracy. We who in our bind of caste deprived man of his full dues of rights and respect, are paying the penalty now, and instead of the soul current running through our society we have left to us the dry sand-bed of dead customs. And the time seems fast approaching when the soul will be sucked dry from the civilization of Europe also by growing lust for gain in her commerce and politics, unless she has the wisdom and power to change her mind and not merely her system.[6]

Stung by the insult of cruel injustice, we try to repudiate Europe, but by doing so we insult ourselves. Let us have the dignity not to quarrel or retaliate; not to pay back smallness by being small ourselves. This is the time when we should dedicate all our resources of emotion, thought and character to the service of our country in a positive direction of duty. We are suffering because of our offences against Sivam, against Advaitam. We

---

[5]Rabindranath to C.F. Andrews, 24 April 1919, Collection: C.F. Andrews. (RBA.)
[6]Rabindranath to Romain Rolland, 14 October 1919, English Letters, File: Rolland, Romain. Photocopy. (RBA.)

spend all our energy in quarrelling with the punishment and nothing of
it is left for the reparation of wrongs we have done and are doing. When
we have performed our part of the duties, we shall have the fullest right
and power and time to bring others to book for their transgressions.[7]

Recently I chanced to find a copy of Professor Lowes Dickinson's[8] report
of his travels in the East. It made me realize clearly the mentality of the
British people in their relation to India. When the author indicates in it
the utter difference of their temperament from ours, it fills me with despair
at the unnaturalness of our relationship, which is so humiliating on our
side and so demoralizing on theirs.

In the pamphlet, he quotes, with approval, a remark made to him by
an Englishman, an officer, in India, whom he describes as 'intelligent and
enlightened'. It is about the maintaining by Englishmen of an impassable
social gulf between themselves and the people of India, and it says: 'An
Englishman cannot be expected to lose his own soul for the sake of other
people's politics.'

Here the author parenthetically explains the word 'soul' by saying that
it denotes the habits and traditions of one's race.

All this means that Englishmen feel a sense of irreconcilable contradiction
between their nature and others; and therefore we are like twins, who, by
some monstrous freak of destiny, have been tied together back to back. He
concludes the summary of his report by saying: 'But my own opinion is
that India has more to gain and less to lose than any other Eastern country
by contact with the West.'

He contemptuously ignores the fact that where no communication of
sympathy is possible, gifts can be hurled but not given; that while counting
the number of gains by the receiver, we have also to consider the fracture
of his skull; and while thanking the doctor for the rest cure, we must
hasten to negotiate with the undertaker for the funeral.

---

[7]Rabindranath to C.F. Andrews, Paris, 7 September 1920, Collection: C.F. Andrews. (RBA.)
[8]Goldsworthy Lowes Dickinson (1862–1932), author.

It is the very irony of fate for us to be blamed by these people about the iniquity of our caste distinctions. And, yet, never in the blindness of our pride we can lose our souls, although we may lose our caste which is a merely conventional classification. The analogy would be perfect, if the division of railway compartments, with its inequality of privileges, was defended by the railway directors as being necessary for the salvation of the passengers' souls.

Only think in this connection of the ideal which the life of Akbar represented. The Emperor's soul was not afraid, for its own safety, of the touch of a neighbouring humanity but of the want of touch. Aurangzeb, on the other hand, who was certainly 'intelligent and enlightened' and meticulously careful about keeping intact what he considered to be his soul, represented a force, insolent and destructive. Such an enormous difference in the ideals of these two most powerful monarchs of Mughal India sprang from fundamentally different interpretations of the word 'soul'.

Lowes Dickinson has mentioned about the possibility of India being benefited by her contact with the West. Very likely he meant the contact to be like that of the root of a tree with the water in the soil. I admit the light of Europe's culture has reached us. But Europe, with its corona of culture, is a radiant idea. Its light permeates the present age, it is not shut up in a single bull's eye lantern, which is some particular people from Europe who have come to us in India, yet we are repeatedly asked to be grateful to this bull's eye lantern and prostrate ourselves before it with loyalty and reverence. But this is not possible; for it is a mere lantern, it has no soul. Not only that, but it circumscribes the light to a narrow circle of barest necessity. The full radiation of European culture has pervaded Japan because it has not come to her through an unnatural glare of a miserly lens, exaggerating the division between the small shining patch and the vast obscure.

It is our pride which seeks difference, and gloats upon it. But sympathy is a higher quality, being our spiritual organ of sight: it has the natural vision of the Advaitam. The world is an ever moving multitude with an eternal unity of movements, which must not be retarded in any of its parts by a break of cadence. The world of man is suffering because all movements in its individual parts are not in harmony with one another and therefore with the whole: because the relationship of races has not been established in a balance of truth and goodness. This balance cannot be maintained by an external regulation, as in a puppet show. It is a dance which must have music in its heart to regulate it. This great music of love is lacking in the meeting of men which has taken place in the present age; and all its movements in their discongruity are creating complexities of suffering.

I wish I could write to you simple letters giving our detailed news. But the worldwide agony of pain fills my mind with thoughts that constrict natural communications of personal life.[9]

All true ideals claim our best, and it cannot be said with regard to them that we can be content with the half, when the whole is threatened. Ideals are not like money. They are a living reality. Their wholeness is indivisible. A beggar woman may be satisfied with an eight-anna bit when sixteen annas are denied her; but a half-portion of her child she will never consent to accept!

I know there is a call for me to work towards the true union of East and West. I have been unconsciously getting ready for this mission. When I wrote my *Sadhana* lectures, I was not aware that I had been fulfilling my destiny. All through my tour I was told that my *Sadhana* had been of real help to my Western readers. The accident that made me translate *Gitanjali* and the sudden unaccountable longing which took me over to Europe at the beginning of my fiftieth year—all combined to push me over to a path whose destination I did not clearly know when I first took it. This, my last tour in Europe, has made it definitely known to me.

But, as I have said before, the claims of all great ideals have to be fully paid. Not merely the negative moral injunction of non-violence will suffice. It is a truism to say that the creative force needed for true union in human society is love. Justice is only an accompaniment to it, like the

---

[9]Rabindranath Tagore, 'On British Mentality in Relation to India', *Modern Review*, Calcutta, April 1921, pp. 753–55.

beating of a tom-tom to the song. We in the East have long been suffering humiliation in the hands of the West. It is enormously difficult for us either to cultivate or express any love for Western races—especially as it may have the appearance of snobbishness or prudence. The talk and behaviour of the Moderate Party in India fail to inspire us because of this—because their moderation springs from the colourless principle of expediency. The bond of expediency between the powerful and the weak must have some element in it which is degrading. It brings to us gifts for which we can claim no credit whatever, except, perhaps, persistency of expectation and unbaffled employment of importunity . . .

However, my point is that, as an idealist, it is immensely difficult for me to nourish any feeling of love for those people who themselves are neither eager to offer it to us nor care to claim it from us. But never let me look at that condition as an absolute one. There are screens between us which have to be removed—possibly they are due to the great inequality of circumstances and opportunities between the two parties. Let us, by every means in our power, struggle against our antipathies—all the while taking care to keep wide open channels of communication through which individuals, from both sides, may have facilities to meet in the spirit of good fellowship.[10]

---

[10]Rabindranath to C.F. Andrews, 9 July 1921, *Letters to a Friend*, pp. 153-54.

31

TO MY FRIENDS

God bless you! Your letter with your glorious news has taken me to ecstatic heights this morning. I bow down to that God who has lifted India from her shame through your work . . .

I beg of you not to return to India prematurely. You must do everything possible for your scientific endeavours—if need be, you must fight the demons and rescue Sita from her bondage. And, if I can raise some funds to build a bridge,[1] I will have hoodwinked the country into some gratitude for me!

There are 10–11 days to Bela's wedding. My joy is all the more with the news of your success. You have lighted an invisible lamp for the occasion. I was in a lot of difficulty but have forgotten all of that now. My only regret is that I cannot be present to celebrate your achievement nor shake your hand in congratulation afterwards.[2]

I am in Tripura. I am staying as the Maharaja's house guest.[3] You know how much he respects you. Therefore I feel no hesitation in coming to him for your needs. He will soon send you ten thousand rupees by the mail, and another ten thousand later in the year. He would have willingly spared all of fifty thousand rupees for your scientific work had he not already started on a few expensive building projects. He has endeared me to him even more with this offer of help—it is hard to come by such natural generosity.

---

[1] Sita is the heroine of the epic Ramayana; building a bridge is a reference to the story of Sita's rescue from Lanka for which Lord Rama had to construct a bridge over the seas.

[2] Rabindranath to Jagadish Chandra Bose, 4 June 1901, *Chitthi Patra* VI, pp. 28-29. Translated by UDG.

[3] Radha Kishore Manikya (1856–1909), Maharaja of Tripura.

You must spare yourself excessive fatigue. We will lovingly and patiently be at your side no matter how long it takes for the results of your discoveries. Be assured we aren't rushing you. We are only too willing to wait for as long as you need to complete your work. How can *we* possibly make any demands on *you*? We will be failing badly if we can't do something to compensate for your hardships. How much does my little effort mount to? Not enough to make demands on you. What I have given to you is my heart's love and that love comes with my admiration. All I expect in return is your love. You must believe this that the Maharaja has given you money not to make you indebted to him. If anything, he feels indebted to you. The One who has blessed you with talent will bless you also with the determination to succeed.[4]

On reaching London I took shelter in a hotel. It was as if I found myself in the crowded gateway of moving traffic. What transpired inside remained a mystery, nor was acquaintance possible with the inmates. I just watched the people—coming and going. All I could see was there was no end of hurry and bustle. What the business was about passed my comprehension . . .

Foreigners who come here for the first time cannot escape this first impression of the huge human machine of the god of history . . .

But one cannot keep on seeing man only as a machine. If I cannot see the man in him why did I come all this way? It is of course much easier to see him as a cog in the wheel than as he is by himself. Unless he takes you of his own accord into the inner compartments of his mind, you cannot gain admission to the essential man. It is not so simple as buying a ticket to a theatre. You cannot gain that admission for any price—simply because it is priceless.

Luckily for me I got that one rare chance. I came by a friend. There are some who are born friends. It does not lie with all of us to be so. In order to become a true friend one has to give oneself. As in the case of other charities, this gift presupposes a fund to draw upon . . . The friend I am

---

[4]Rabindranath to Jagadish Chandra Bose, October/November 1901, *Chitthi Patra* VI, p. 39. Translated by UDG.

talking about is a famous artist; his name is William Rothenstein. In India I had met him for a brief while. As a matter of fact at the time of setting out for Europe I had felt attracted by the prospect of coming closer to him. The moment I met him I felt as if in a trice I had crossed over the gateway of the hotel. Now there was nothing to stop me.[5]

My dear friend, the very first moment I received the message of the great honour conferred on me by the award of the Nobel Prize my heart turned towards you with love and gratitude. I felt certain that of all my friends none would be more glad at this news than you. Honour's crown of honour is to know that it will rejoice the hearts of those whom we hold the most dear.[6]

You know it had been the source of a rare great pleasure for me while in England to be able to admire your manly power of appreciation which was without a tinge of meanness or jealousy. I could have gladly sacrificed my Nobel Prize if I could be left to the enjoyment of this friendliness.[7]

Dear friend, Your letter has stirred my heart to its depths, it has made the morning light brighter for me and wafted the breath of peace from our Santiniketan ashram into my room in this American boarding house. It has been doubly welcome to me owing to other letters brought by the same mail complaining of the financial difficulties of our school. But God gives infinitely more than he claims and it is with a feeling of gladness I am preparing myself for more sacrifice. Your letter had largely contributed to that gladness of spirit, and I feel so thankful for it! My visit to Europe had enlarged my life in more ways than one but the best things I have

---

[5]Rabindranath Tagore, 'Bondhu' (Friend), 1912, *Bharati*, Kartik 1319 (November 1912), written about William Rothenstein. English translation in the *Visva-Bharati Quarterly*, X, Part IV, February–April 1945, pp. 157-58.

[6]Rabindranath to William Rothenstein, 18 November 1913, *Imperfect Encounter*, p. 140.

[7]Rabindranath to Thomas Sturge Moore, 17 February 1914, Sturge Moore Papers, Senate House Library, University of London.

gained there are friends whose love helps me in my life. I feel I have known you all my days and the light of our love will ever become brighter in days to come and help us to our way to God.

I am looking forward to the time when I shall meet you in India and take up the same mission of spiritual service.[8]

To W.W. Pearson

> Thy nature is to forget thyself;
> But we remember thee.
> Thou shinest in self-concealment
> revealed by our love.
>
> Thou lendest light from thine own soul
> to those who are obscure.
> Thou seekest neither love nor fame;
> Love discovers thee.[9]

You are away quite a long time, but we have not yet grown reconciled to your absence. You are not a mere part of our organization, but because you represent the life of the place we miss some vital source of joy and strength when we miss you. However, we know that the series of experiences you are going through in your travels will bring to us a new current of rich life when you return to us, will impart a fresh vigour of confidence to the experiments we are carrying on. The work which you have started in Surul is a work of creation, for in it you are not following some fixed path prescribed in books, but giving expression to your own creative personality to which even the opposition of obdurate materials ultimately brings help for shaping the structure. I only hope that this creative spirit which constantly guides the process of living adjustment between the inner ideal

---

[8]Rabindranath to W.W. Pearson, Urbana, Illinois, 15 January 1913, English Letters, File: Pearson, W.W. (RBA.)

[9]*Collected Poems and Plays of Rabindranath Tagore*, Reprint, London: Macmillan, 1985, p. 457.

and the ever changing circumstances you will leave behind when one day you will be compelled to leave us. But I feel almost certain that never in your life you will be able to desert your Surul permanently—for the only true world for a man is the world of his own making, as for God is this universe. How few men have the good fortune to find for himself the freedom, the material and the opportunity to be able to secure his place as the Colleague of his Creator.[10]

It is difficult for me fully to associate you with your new adventure in its present surroundings.[11] I have come to love the picture of you in the simple and beautiful background of Surul with all its pathetic failings and daily struggle with difficulties that are pitiful and yet of great significance. I cannot have your constantly helpful companionship in a task which needs for its fulfilment an immense wealth of energy and the optimistic courage of youthfulness. I feel extremely tired and the little surplus of inner resources that I still have left in me naturally dreams of its last ceremony of oblation in literature. However, your spirit will still work in Surul and I shall always remember you not merely as a friend but as a sharer in the intimacy of a conjoint creation.[12]

Your letter has given me great pleasure and specially reminded me of an intimate evening in the quaint little room you had then in London. Last year, while travelling in Europe I tried to find out your address and to see you once again. Ezra Pound,[13] whom I met in Paris, informed me that you were in indifferent health and staying somewhere in Italy.

---

[10]Rabindranath to Leonard K. Elmhirst, Santiniketan, 12 April 1923, English Letters, File: Elmhirst, L.K. Photocopy. (RBA.)

[11]This is a reference to Dartington Hall in Totnes, Devonshire, where Leonard Elmhirst and Dorothy Elmhirst Straight founded a college of arts and science on the Santiniketan–Sriniketan model.

[12]Rabindranath to Leonard K. Elmhirst, Vienna, 21 October 1926, English Letters, File: Elmhirst, L.K. Photocopy. (RBA.)

[13]Ezra Pound (1885–1972), American poet and critic, resident in Europe from 1908 to 1945.

I dared not seek you in that country for, as you may know, I had seriously displeased Mussolini by my criticism of his cruel policy of persecution.[14]

Your letter seems to come to me from a remote age reminding me of those days of my acquaintance with you, intense and intimate. Though I had already left behind one half of a century of my life when I visited your country, I felt that I had come to the beginning of a fresh existence young with the surprise of an experience in an atmosphere of kindly personalities. I often remember a meeting with you in that chamber of yours, quaintly unique, that seemed to me, I do not know why, resonant of an old-world silence, and though I find it difficult distinctly to recollect the subject of our talk the feeling of it lingers in my mind like the aroma of a rich and rare wine.

I know you have entered into an epoch of life which is vague to me and distant, but I shall always remember the generosity of your simple and sensitive poetic youth which exercised in my mind a profound attraction for your genius.[15]

When my mind was steeped in the gloom of the thought that the lesson of the late war had been lost and that the people were trying to perpetuate their hatred, anger and greed into the same organized menace for the world which threatened themselves with disaster, your letter came and cheered me with its message of hope . . .

It is enough for me to know that the higher conscience of Europe has been able to assert itself in the voice of one of her choicest spirits through the ugly clamours of passionate politics, and I gladly hasten to accept your

[14]Rabindranath to W.B. Yeats, Santiniketan, 4 October 1931. English Letters, File: Yeats, W.B. Copy. (RBA.)

[15]Rabindranath to W.B. Yeats, Santiniketan, 16 July 1935, English Letters, File: Yeats, W.B. Copy. (RBA.)

invitation to join the ranks of those free souls who in Europe have conceived the project of a Declaration of Independence of the Spirit.[16]

Your letter has given me great delight. I feel certain that your friendship will greatly strengthen me in my purpose and in time of difficulty and disappointment will keep up my spirit. You speak of the barrier of language. It is there no doubt—but what is most precious in us does find its way through it. The child hides the sun but cannot extinguish the day.[17]

I have received your book dealing with myself.[18] I believe it is my sensitiveness born of my egotism which makes me shrink from attending to any discussions concerning me. But I have read your book all through. I am sure you have tried to be fair in your estimate of my works. About the comparative merits of my individual productions I myself am undecided though I have my preferences with which I never expect my readers always to agree . . .

You have spared yourself no trouble in your attempt to understand me, and I am sure your book is the best one that has yet appeared about myself. I must thank you for this—at the same time I wish I could altogether lose the memory of my fame as a poet.[19]

Do not misunderstand me and never think I am angry. I am going through a period of struggle in my mind desperately seeking my path across things

---

[16]Rabindranath to Romain Rolland, Santiniketan, 24 June 1919, English Letters, File: Rolland, Romain. Photocopy. (RBA.) The 'invitation' refers to a letter from Romain Rolland to Rabindranath, 9 July 1919, enclosing a list of the signatories to the *Declaration of Independence of the Spirit* which included Benedetto Croce, Georges Duhamel, Albert Einstein, Herman Hesse, Heinrich Mann, Bertrand Russell, Jules Roman and Stefan Zweig among others. See English Letters, File: Rolland, Romain. (RBA.)

[17]Rabindranath to Romain Rolland, Santiniketan, 23 April 1921, English Letters, File: Rolland, Romain. Photocopy. (RBA.)

[18]This is a reference to Edward Thompson's *Rabindranath Tagore: His Life and Work*, Calcutta, 1921.

[19]Rabindranath to Edward Thompson, Santiniketan, 20 September 1921, *Difficult Friendship*, pp. 132-33.

that do not belong to my nature. If I have given expression to the restlessness which come over me, please do not think I am holding you responsible for this state of things. I have been expecting you for long. Please do not disappoint me if you can help it.[20]

As regards my attitude towards you, I am afraid you do me injustice if you think I ever thought of you as an enemy of my people. While not agreeing with all you have said or written on India, I have never questioned your sincerity or your love and affection for our people. It is best you mentioned the matter and I get a chance of explaining myself.[21]

Indeed, it is a great pity that the Europeans have come to us as Imperialists rather than as Christians and so have deprived our people with their true contact with the religion of Jesus Christ. A few individuals like C.F. Andrews, whom we have known as the true followers of their Teacher, have created in us a respect for Christianity which the most brutal *lathi* charges, shootings and detentions without trials of the British government in India have failed totally to dissipate.[22]

The last days have been overshadowed by the death of my dear friend and intimate companion and fellow worker Charlie Andrews, after an illness of more than two months in a Calcutta hospital. He gave himself so unstintingly in friendship and generosity that it is difficult to realize how great will be the blank left by his passing; for us it is an unspeakable loss. His life was an unfailing inspiration, he was a more than dear friend.[23]

---

[20]Rabindranath to Edward Thompson, Santiniketan, 2 October 1921, Ibid., p. 136.
[21]Rabindranath to Edward Thompson, Santiniketan, 6 February 1934, Ibid., p. 169.
[22]Rabindranath to Edward Thompson, Santiniketan, 27 October 1937, Ibid., p. 198.
[23]Rabindranath to Romain Rolland, Santiniketan, 10 April 1940, English Letters, File: Rolland, Romain. Photocopy. (RBA.)

You must have received the shocking news of the death of Charlie Andrews. It has been a great personal loss to me—for, as you know, he was one of my closest friends and associates. Sorrows like these are the penalty of a long life and I believe I cannot complain.[24]

---

[24]Rabindranath to Edward Thompson, Santiniketan, 11 April 1940, *Difficult Friendship*, p. 217.

32

FROM MY POEMS AND SONGS

To My Wife

I

'SMARAN' (IN REMEMBRANCE)
7 Agrahayan 1309 (23 November 1902)

Love, thou hast made great my life with
      death's magnificence, and hast
      tinted all my thoughts and dreams
      with radiant hues of thy farewell
      rays.

The tear-washed limpid light reveals at
      life's last sunset-point the hints
      of Paradise, where descending flame
      of Kiss from starry sphere of love
      lights the sorrows of our earth to
      splendour of their end, in one
      blazing ecstasy of uttermost
      extinction.

Love, thou hast made one vast wonder
      Life and Death for me.[1]

---

[1] *Poems*, no. 31, p. 52. Bengali original in *Smaran*, no. 13, 1902. The dedication in *Smaran* was '7 Agrahayan 1309' (23 November 1902), the date of Mrinalini's death.

II

As the tender twilight covers in its fold of
        dusk-veil marks of hurt and wastage
        from the dusty day's prostration,
        even so let my great sorrow for thy
        loss, Beloved, spread one perfect
        golden-tinted silence of its sadness
        o'er my life.

Let all its jagged fractures and distortions,
        all unmeaning scattered scraps and
        wrecks and random ruins, merge in
        vastness of some evening stilled with
        thy remembrance, filled with endless
        harmony of pain and peace united.[2]

On the Swadeshi Movement in Bengal

'Ebar Tor Mara Gange Baan Esechhe'
(Boatman, Pull Up Your Oars)

The flood, at last, has come upon
your dry river-bed.
Cry for the boatman,
cut the cordage,
launch the boat.

Take your oars, my comrades,
your debt has grown heavy,
for you have spent idle days at the
        landing,
hesitating to buy and sell.

---

[2]Ibid., no. 32, p. 53. Bengali original in *Smaran*, no. 24, 3 January 1903.

Pull up the anchor,
set the sails,
let happen what may.[3]

'BIDHIR BADHAN KATBE TUMI' (FATE-FORGED BOND)

Shalt *thou* cut asunder this Fate-forged bond?
Art thou indeed so mighty?
Art thou so mighty?
To break us and build, shall thy hand avail?
Art thou indeed so haughty?
Art thou so haughty?
Shalt thou forever chain us back?
Shalt thou forever hold us down?
Nay, so much strength you have not!
Nay, that chain shall not hold!
Howsoever your edicts bind,
Even in the weak, is power.
Howsoever your greatness swells,
God overrules.
When you have struck down our strength,
You too shall surely die—
Grown heavy and overladen, your boat shall sink.[4]

'BANGLAR MATI, BANGLAR JAL' (BENGAL, OUR LAND)

Let the earth and the water, the air and
        the fruits of my country be sweet,
        my God.

---

[3]Ibid., no. 39, p. 61. Bengali original, 'Ebar Tor Mara Gange Baan Esechhe', *Gitabitan*, 1905.
[4]*Visva-Bharati Quarterly*, Vol. XI, Part II, p. 86. Bengali original, 'Bidhir Badhan Katbe Tumi', *Rakhi Sangit*, 1905. This song was originally composed in 1905 in the heat of the anti-partition agitation in Bengal. Rabindranath sang it through the streets of Calcutta, heading a huge procession.

Let the homes and marts, the forests
  and fields of my country be full,
  my God.
Let the promises and hopes, the deeds
  and words of my country be true,
  my God.
Let the lives and hearts of the sons and
  daughters of my country be one,
  my God.[5]

From *Gitanjali* (*Song Offerings*)

'Jethay Thakey Sabar Adhom' (Poorest, Lowliest and Lost)

Here is thy footstool and there rest
thy feet where live the poorest, and
lowliest, and lost.

When I try to bow to thee, my
obeisance cannot reach down to the
depth where thy feet rest among the
poorest, and lowliest, and lost.

Pride can never approach to where
thou walkest in the clothes of the
humble among the poorest, and lowliest,
and lost.

My heart can never find its way to
where thou keepest company with the
companionless among the poorest, the
lowliest, and the lost.[6]

---

[5]*Poems*, no. 43, p. 65. Bengali original, 'Banglar Mati, Banglar Jal', *Gan*, 1908.
[6]*Gitanjali* (*Song Offerings*), Reprint, London: Macmillan, 1957, poem no. 10, p. 8. Bengali original 'Jethay Thakey Sabar Adhom', poem no. 107, *Gitanjali*, 1910.

'BHAJAN PUJON SADHON ARADHANA' (DELIVERANCE)

Leave this chanting and singing and
telling of beads! Whom dost thou
worship in this lonely dark corner of a
temple with doors all shut? Open
thine eyes and see thy God is not before
thee!

Here is where the tiller is tilling
the hard ground and where the path-
maker is breaking stones. He is with
them in sun and in shower, and his
garment is covered with dust. Put off
thy holy mantle and even like him come
down on the dusty soil!

Deliverance? Where is this deliverance
to be found? Our master himself
has joyfully taken upon him the bonds
of creation; he is bound with us all for
ever.

Come out of thy meditations and
leave aside thy flowers and incense!
What harm is there if thy clothes
become tattered and stained? Meet
him and stand by him in toil and
sweat of thy brow.[7]

[7]Ibid., poem no. 11, pp. 8-9. Bengali original 'Bhajan Pujon Sadhon Aradhana', poem no. 119, *Gitanjali*, 1910.

While in Europe

'CHHUTIR BANSI BAJLO' (A HOLIDAY MELODY)
Munich, 1926

The flute-sound of a holiday music
floats in the air.
It is not the time for me to sit and brood
     alone.
The *shiuli* branches shiver
with the thrill of an impending flower-
     time,
the touch of the dew is over the woodland.

On the fairy web in the forest path
the light and shadow feel each other.
The tall grass sends waves of laughter to
     the sky in its flowers,
and I gaze upon the horizon, seeking
     for my song.[8]

'SAKAL BAELAR ALOY BAJE' (TAKE UP YOUR FLUTE, POET)
Nuremberg, 1926

The morning-light aches
with the pain of parting.
Poet, take up thy flute!
Let be, if thou must depart, and go,
leaving thy song to the flowers
in this dew-dripping autumn.
Such a morning will come again
at the gold-tinted border of the East
with *kunda* flowers in her locks.

---

[8]*Poems*, no. 76, p. 113. Bengali original, 'Chhutir Bansi Bajlo', 1926, *Gitabitan*.

In the shady garden path, plaintive with
      dove's cooing,
tender with the caressing enchantment of
      the green,
will rise again the vision of this light,
her steps tinkling with the anklet of thine
      own songs,
Let be, if thou must depart.[9]

To Lord Buddha

'HINGSHAY UNMATTA PRITHIVI' (OH WORLD FULL OF HATRED)

The world today is wild with the
      delirium of hatred,
the conflicts are cruel and unceasing in
      anguish,
crooked are its paths, tangled its bonds
      of greed.
All creatures are crying for a new birth
      of thine,
Oh Thou of boundless life,
save them, rouse thine eternal voice of
      hope,
Let Love's lotus with its inexhaustible
      treasure of honey
open its petals in thy light.

O Serene, O Free,
in thine immeasurable mercy and goodness
wipe away all dark stains from the heart
      of this earth.

---

[9] Ibid., no. 79, p. 116. Bengali original, 'Sakal Baelar Aloy Baje', 1926, *Gitabitan*.

Thou giver of immortal gifts
Give us the power of renunciation
and claim from us our pride.
In the splendour of a new sunrise of
        wisdom
let the blind gain their sight
and let life come to the souls that are
        dead.

O Serene, O Free,
in thine immeasurable mercy and goodness
wipe away all dark stains from the heart
        of this earth.

Man's heart is anguished with the fever
        of unrest,
with the poison of self-seeking,
with a thirst that knows no end.
Countries far and wide flaunt on their
        foreheads
the blood-red mark of hatred.

Touch them with thy right hand,
make them one in spirit,
bring harmony into their life,
bring rhythm of beauty.

O Serene, O Free,
in thine immeasurable mercy and goodness
wipe away all dark stains from the heart
        of this earth.[10]

---

[10]Ibid., no. 88, pp. 129–31. Bengali original, 'Hingshay Unmatta Prithivi', 1927, *Natir Puja*, 1932.

To Nandalal Bose

You maker of pictures,
a ceaseless traveller among men and
       things,
rounding them up in your net of vision
and bringing them out in lines
far above their social value and market
       price.

Yonder colony of the outcaste,
its crowd of rustic roofs,
and an empty field in the background
scorched by the angry April sun
are hurriedly passed by and never missed,
till your wayfaring lines spoke out;
they are there,
and we started up and said, indeed they
       are.

Those nameless tramps fading away
       every moment into shadows
were rescued from their nothingness
and compelled us to acknowledge
a greater appeal of the real in them
than is possessed by the rajahs
who lavish money on their portraits of
       dubious worth
for fools to gape at in wonder.

You ignored the mythological steed of
       paradise
when your eyes were caught by a goat
who is only noticed with your expostulation

when straying on our brinjal plot.
You brought out its own majesty of
        goatliness in your lines
and our mind woke up into a surprise.
The poor goat-seller remains ignorant
        of the fact
that the picture does not represent the
        commonplace beast that is his own,
but it is a discovery.[11]

On the Munich Pact

'PRAYASCHITTO' (ATONEMENT)

In the upper sky, lamped by science,
the night forgets itself,
while in the underground gloom
lean hunger and bloated voracity
crash against each other
till the earth begins to tremble
and the pillars of triumph
are perilously cracked,
swaying on the brink of gaping gulfs.

Do not howl in fear
or angrily judge God,
let the swelling evil burst itself in pain
and vomit out its accumulated filth.

When the victims of carnivorous rage
are dragged by the competition of
        ravenous fangs,

---

[11]Ibid., no. 105, pp. 172-73. Bengali original, 'Chhobi Ankiye', 1937. This poem is addressed to the painter Nandalal Bose (1882–1966) who had sent Rabindranath a sketch of a goat.

let the hideousness of the blood-soaked
       blasphemy
arouse divine anger heralding a heroic
       peace
out of an awful retribution.

They throng in the church
in a primitive frenzy of faith made keen
       by fear
which hopes to flatter their God
into a complacent mood
into a feebleness of leniency.
They feel half sure that peace will be
       brought down
into this demented earth
by the mere volume of their wailing
       uttered in sacred text.

They have confidence in their indulgent
       God
who may send them timely wisdom
to divert all sacrifices needed for the
       worship
towards the less strong,
leaving their own soiled hoardings
       undivided.

But let us hope,
for the sake of the dignity of moral justice
       in this world,
that God will never suffer to be cheated
       of His due
by the miserly manipulation of a
       diplomatic piety

carefully avoiding all cost to itself,
that a terrible penance may have to be
      passed through
to its ultimate end,
leaving no remnant of poison
in a treacherously healing star.[12]

To Christ, Son of Man

'Aek Din Jara Merechhilo' (Kill, Kill, They Shout)

Those who struck Him once
In the name of their rulers,
are born again in this present age.

They gather in their prayer-halls
      in a pious garb,
they call their soldiers,
'Kill, Kill', they shout;
in their roaring mingles the music of
      their hymns,
while the Son of Man in His agony
      prays, 'O God,
fling, fling far away this cup filled with
the bitterest of poisons.'[13]

---

[12]Ibid., no. 110, pp. 187–89. Bengali original, 'Prayaschitto', 1938, *Nabajatak*, 1940. This poem reflects the poet's reaction to the Munich Pact and was sent to Professor Vincenc Lesny (1882–1953) of Charles University, Prague, who had been visiting professor at Visva-Bharati in 1923 and 1928. The Munich Pact (1938) shook the confidence of the Eastern European countries in the goodwill of the Western democracies.

[13]Ibid., no. 112, p. 192. Bengali original, 'Aek Din Jara Merechhilo', Christmas Day, 1939, *Punascha*, 1940.

To My Country

'CHITTO JETHA BHOY SHUNYO' (WHERE THE MIND IS WITHOUT FEAR)

Where the mind is without fear and the head is held high
                    Where knowledge is free;
                    Where the world has not been broken
up into fragments by narrow domestic
                    walls;
                    Where the words come out from the
                            depth of truth;
                    Where tireless striving stretches its arms
                            towards perfection:
                    Where the clear stream of reason has
                    not lost its way into the dreary desert
                            sand of dead habit;
                    Where the mind is led forward by
thee into ever-widening thought and
                    action—
                    Into that heaven of freedom, my
                    Father, let my country awake.[14]

To Mahatma Gandhi

'GANDHI MAHARAJ-ER SISHYA' (WE WHO FOLLOW
MAHATMA GANDHI)

We who follow Gandhi Maharaja's lead
have one thing in common among us:
we never fill our purses with spoils from the poor
nor bend our knees to the rich.

---

[14]*Gitanjali (Song Offerings)*, poem no. 34, pp. 27-28. Bengali original, 'Chitto Jetha Bhoy Shunyo', *Naibedya*, 1901.

When they come bullying us
with raised fist and menacing stick,
we smile to them, and say:
your reddening eye may startle babies out of sleep
but how frighten those who refuse to fear?

Our speeches are straight and simple,
no diplomatic turns to twist their meaning;
confounding penal code
they guide with perfect ease the pilgrims
to the border of jail.

And when these crowd the path to the prison gate
their stains of insult are washed clean,
their age-long shackles drop to the dust,
and on their forehead are stamped
Gandhiji's blessings.[15]

Santiniketan School Song

'AMADER SANTINIKETAN' (OUR OWN SANTINIKETAN)

She is our own, the darling of our hearts, Santiniketan.
        Our dreams are rocked in her arms.
Her face is a fresh wonder of love every time we see her,
        for she is our own, the darling of our hearts.

In the shadows of her trees we meet,
        in the freedom of her open sky.
Her mornings come and her evenings

---

[15]Rabindranath Tagore, *Mahatma Gandhi*, Calcutta: Visva-Bharati, 1963, p. 58. English translation by the poet, 1940, published in *Visva-Bharati Quarterly*, February 1941. Bengali original, 'Gandhi Maharaj-er Sishya', 1938.

bringing down heavens' kisses,
making us feel anew that she is our own, the darling
of our hearts.

The stillness of her shades is stirred by the woodland
whisper;
her *amlaki* groves are aquiver with the rapture of
leaves.
She dwells in us and around us, however far we may
wander.

She weaves our hearts in a song, making us one in music,
tuning our strings of love with her own fingers;
and we ever remember that she is our own,
the darling of our hearts.[16]

---

[16]*Collected Poems and Plays of Rabindranath Tagore*, Reprint, London: Macmillan, 1985, pp. 457-58.

SELECT BIBLIOGRAPHY

UNPUBLISHED ARCHIVAL SOURCES

At Rabindra Bhavana, Visva-Bharati University, Santiniketan:

Collection of Rabindranath's Correspondence: Bengali Letters and English Letters
Collection of Rabindranath's Literary Manuscripts
Collection of C.F. Andrews Papers
Collection of Prasanta Chandra and Rani Mahalanobis Papers
Collection of Tagore Estate Papers

At Nehru Memorial Museum and Library, Teen Murti, New Delhi:
Nehru Papers—Pre-1947

At Bodleian Library, University of Oxford, England:
Collection of Edward Thompson Papers
Collection of Gilbert Murray Papers
Collection of Robert Bridges Papers

At the University of London, England:
Senate House Library's Collection of Thomas Sturge Moore Papers.

BOOKS

(Rabindranath's works listed refer to the editions used)

Bhattacharya, S., ed., *The Mahatma and the Poet: Letters and Debates between Gandhi and Tagore 1915–1941*, New Delhi: National Book Trust, 1997

Chakrabarty, Ajit Kumar, *Brahmavidyalay*, in Bengali, Calcutta: Visva-Bharati, 1358 (1952)

Chakravarty, Amiya, ed., *A Tagore Reader*, Boston: Beacon Books, 1966

Chakravarty, Bikash, ed., *Poets to a Poet 1912–40: Letters from Robert Bridges, Ernest Rhys, W.B. Yeats, Thomas Sturge Moore, R.C. Trevelyan to Rabindranath Tagore*, Calcutta: Visva-Bharati, 1998

Das, Sisir Kumar, ed., *The English Writings of Rabindranath Tagore*, Volume I, Poems, New Delhi: Sahitya Akademi, 1994

———, *The English Writings of Rabindranath Tagore*, Volume II, Plays-Stories-Essays, New Delhi: Sahitya Akademi, 1996

———, *The English Writings of Rabindranath Tagore*, Volume III, A Miscellany, New Delhi: Sahitya Akademi, 1996

Das Gupta, Uma, *Santiniketan and Sriniketan: A Historical Introduction*, 'Visva-Bharati Quarterly Booklet', Santiniketan: Visva-Bharati, 1977

———, 'Rabindranath Tagore on Rural Reconstruction: The Sriniketan Experiment, 1921–41', *The Indian Historical Review*, New Delhi, 1977, IV, no. 2

———, 'Santiniketan and Sriniketan', *Introduction to Tagore*, Calcutta: Visva-Bharati, 1983

———, 'Santiniketan: The School of a Poet' in Mushirul Hasan, ed., *Knowledge, Power and Politics: Educational Institutions in India*, New Delhi: Roli Books, 1998

———, 'Tagore's Educational Experiments in Santiniketan and Sriniketan, 1901–41' in S. Bhattacharya, ed., *The Contested Terrain: Perspectives on Education in India*, New Delhi: Orient Longman, 1998

———, ed., *A Difficult Friendship: Letters of Edward Thompson and Rabindranath Tagore*, New Delhi: Oxford University Press, 2003

———, *Rabindranath Tagore: A Biography*, New Delhi: Oxford University Press, 2004

Datta, Krishna and Andrew Robinson, *Rabindranath Tagore: The Myriad Minded Man*, London: Bloomsbury, 1995

———, eds, *Selected Letters of Rabindranath Tagore*, Cambridge: Cambridge University Press, 1997

Deb, Chitra, *Thakur-barir Andarmahal*, in Bengali, Revised edition, Calcutta: Ananda Publishers, 2003

Dyson, Ketaki Kushari, ed., *In Your Blossoming Flower-Garden: Rabindranath Tagore and Victoria Ocampo*, New Delhi: Sahitya Akademi, Reprint, 1996

Elmhirst, Leonard, ed., *Poet and Plowman*, Calcutta: Visva-Bharati, 1975

Hay, Stephen N., *Asian Ideas of East and West: Tagore and His Critics in Japan, China and India*, Cambridge: Harvard, 1970

Kripalani, Krishna, *Rabindranath Tagore: A Biography*, Second revised edition, Calcutta: Visva-Bharati, 1980

———, *Dwarkanath Tagore, A Forgotten Pioneer: A Life*, New Delhi: National Book Trust, 1980

Lago, Mary, ed., *Imperfect Encounter: Letters of William Rothenstein and Rabindranath Tagore 1911–1941*, Cambridge: Harvard, 1972

Majumdar, Swapan, ed., *Rabindra-Granthasuchi*, in Bengali, Calcutta: The National Library, 1395 (1988)

Kalidas Nag, ed., *Tagore and China*, Calcutta: 1945

Paul, Prasanta Kumar, *Rabijibani*, an ongoing biography in Bengali, volumes I–IX, Calcutta: Ananda Publishers, 1982–2003

Pearson, W.W., *Shantiniketan: The Bolpur School of Rabindranath Tagore*, London: Macmillan, 1917

Rhys, Ernest, *Rabindranath Tagore: A Biographical Study*, New York: Macmillan, 1915

Roy, Kshitis, 'A Chronicle of Eighty Years', *Rabindranath Tagore: A Centenary Volume*, New Delhi: Sahitya Akademi, 1961

Tagore, Rabindranath, *Gitanjali (Song Offerings)*, London: Macmillan, 1913

———, *The Crescent Moon*, London: Macmillan, 1913

———, *Sadhana: The Realisation of Life*, Originally written in English, London: Macmillan, 1913

———, *The Hungry Stones and Other Stories*, Translated by several writers, London: Macmillan, 1916

———, 'The Message of the Forest', *The Modern Review*, volume xxv, no. 5, May 1919, pp. 453-54

———, *Nationalism*, Originally written in English, Reprint, London: Macmillan, 1920

———, 'On Constructive Work—A Letter', *The Modern Review*, Calcutta, March 1921

———, *Glimpses of Bengal*, London: Macmillan, 1921

———, *Lover's Gift and Crossing*, London: Macmillan, 1923

———, *Talks in China*, Originally written in English, Calcutta: Visva-Bharati, 1925

———, *One Hundred Poems of Kabir*, Translated by Rabindranath Tagore, Assisted by Evelyn Underhill, London: Macmillan, 1926

———, *An Eastern University*, Santiniketan: Visva-Bharati, 1927

———, *The Growth of Visva-Bharati 1901–1921*, Santiniketan: Visva-Bharati, 1928

———, *City and Village*, Santiniketan: Visva-Bharati, 1928

———, *Sriniketan: The Institute of Rural Reconstruction*, Santiniketan: Visva-Bharati, 1928

———, *Thoughts from Rabindranath Tagore*, Revised edition of *Thought Relics* (1921), contains translations from the Bengali and partly written originally in English, London: Macmillan, 1929

———, *Letters to a Friend*, Revised edition of *Letters from Abroad* (1924), George Allen and Unwin, Edited with Two Introductory Essays by C.F. Andrews, Reprint, New York: Macmillan, 1929

———, *The Religion of Man, Being the Hibbert Lectures for 1930*, Originally written in English, London: George Allen and Unwin, 1931

———, *Mahatmaji and the Depressed Humanity*, Calcutta: Visva-Bharati, 1932

———, *My Reminiscences*, Translated by Surendranath Tagore (1917), London: Macmillan, 1933

———, *Pashchatyo Bhromon*, in Bengali, Calcutta: Visva-Bharati, 1343 (1936)

———, *Crisis in Civilisation*, Calcutta: Visva-Bharati, 1941

———, *Buddhadeva*, in Bengali, Calcutta: Visva-Bharati, 1363 (1956)

———, *Santiniketan Brahmacharyasram*, in Bengali, Calcutta: Visva-Bharati, 1958

———, *Personality*, Originally written in English, Reprint, London: Macmillan, 1959

———, *Letters from Russia*, Translated by Sasadhar Sinha (1934), Calcutta: Visva-Bharati, 1960

———, *My Boyhood Days*, Translated by Marjorie Sykes (1940), Reprint, Calcutta: Visva-Bharati, 1961

———, *Towards Universal Man*, ed., Bhabani Bhattacharya, Translated by various writers, Introduction by Humayun Kabir, Bombay: Asia Publishing House, 1961

———, *Europe Jatrir Diary*, in Bengali, Calcutta: Visva-Bharati, 1368 (1961)

———, *Europe Prabasir Patra*, in Bengali, Calcutta: Visva-Bharati, 1368 (1961)

———, *Creative Unity*, Originally written in English, Reprint, London: Macmillan, 1962

———, *The Diary of a Westward Journey*, Translated by Indu Dutt, Connecticut: Greenwood, 1962

———, *Palli Prakriti*, in Bengali, Calcutta: Visva-Bharati, 1368 (1962)

———, *Mahatma Gandhi*, Calcutta: Visva-Bharati, 1963

———, *Asram-er rup o bikash*, in Bengali, Calcutta: Visva-Bharati, 1967

———, *Gitabitan*, in Bengali, volumes I–III, Calcutta: Visva-Bharati, 1373–75 (1966–68)

———, *Bankim Chandra*, in Bengali, Calcutta: Visva-Bharati, 1977

———, *Collected Poems and Plays of Rabindranath Tagore*, Reprint, London: Macmillan, 1985

———, *Visva-Bharati*, in Bengali, Calcutta: Visva-Bharati, 1989

———, *Shiksha*, in Bengali, Revised edition, Calcutta: Visva-Bharati, 1397 (1990)

———, *Atmaparichay*, in Bengali, Reprint, Calcutta: Visva-Bharati, 1400 (1993)

_____, *Rabindra-Rachanabali* (Collected Works), volumes I–XXVIII, Calcutta: Visva-Bharati, volumes I–XXVII, 1346–72 (1939–65), volume XXVIII, 1402 (1995)

_____, *Prachin Sahitya*, in Bengali, Reprint, Calcutta: Visva-Bharati, 1407 (2000)

_____, *Santiniketan Vidyalaya 1901–2000*, Calcutta: Visva-Bharati, 2000

_____, *Poems*, Collection includes translations done by Rabindranath Tagore and translations authorized by him, Reprint, Calcutta: Visva-Bharati, 2002

_____, *Chitthi Patra* (Collected Letters), in Bengali, volumes I–XIX, Calcutta: Visva-Bharati, 1942–2004

Tagore, Rathindranath, *On the Edges of Time*, Second edition, Calcutta: Visva-Bharati, 1981

Thompson, Edward J., *Rabindranath Tagore: His Life and Work*, Calcutta: YMCA, 1921

_____, *Rabindranath Tagore: Poet and Dramatist*, Reprint, New Delhi: Oxford University Press, 1991

Tinker, Hugh, *The Ordeal of Love: C.F. Andrews and India*, New Delhi: Oxford University Press, 1979

INDEX